# THE JOHN A. MACDONALD ALBUM

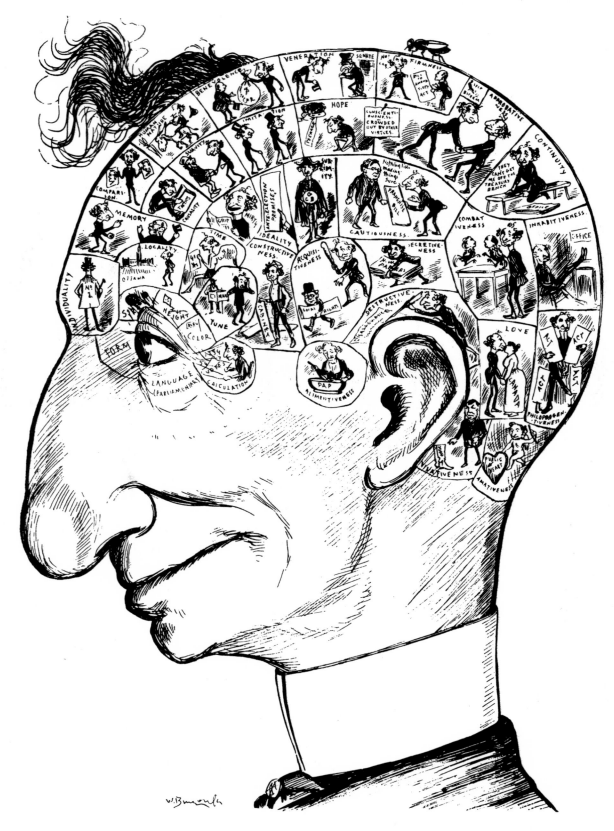

# Phrenological Chart of the Head of the Country.

This gentleman [Sir John A.] has a remarkably sharp and active organization. The mental temperament predominates, which gives him quickness, clearness, and intensity of mind. He has also a full degree of the motive temperament which gives a wiry toughness and strength of organization, elasticity of action, and a good degree of endurance, which sustains him in the mental labours induced by his highly wrought nervous temperament.

There is a great prominence of the lower portion of the forehead, indicating large perceptive organs which give a quick, ready, and clear perception of facts, things, business, and whatever comes within the range of practical life and effort. This is essentially an intelligent forehead. He is strongly endowed with order which renders him methodical and systematic in whatever he does. His language, which is indicated by the fullness and prominence of the eye, indicates uncommon power of speech, ability to talk with ease, clearness, and copiousness, and also to remember everything he reads. His locality would enable him to remember the place on a page where a fact was recorded. His large eventuality renders him capable of retaining the history and the incidents which form a part of his experience or of that which he gathers from reading.

The upper part of his forehead is not as large. He is not so much a philosopher as he is a practical man. He has to do with facts and their bearing on common life. He is fond of wit and amusement, must be excellent in conversation, and at home in the social circle. He has respect for whatever is venerable. The organs which give firmness, pride, ambition, energy are strongly developed but not distinctly seen.

Such persons need an abundance of sleep, temperate habits, much exercise in the open air, and relaxation of mind and cultivation of bodily vigour, otherwise they break down early because they overdo and exhaust their vitality prematurely.

*The American Phrenological Journal, 1887*

# THE JOHN A. MACDONALD ALBUM

## LENA NEWMAN

Tundra Books

Published simultaneously in Canada by
Tundra Books of Montreal, Montreal, Quebec H3G 1S9
and in the United States of America by
Tundra Books of Northern New York, Plattsburgh, N.Y. 12901


Library of Congress Card no. 74-83070
ISBN 0-912766-12-3


Legal Deposit, Third Quarter
Quebec National Library
ISBN 0-88776-051-1

The tartan on the cover is The Macdonald, which may or may not be the one that John A. wore.
The Macdonalds, a large clan, wear many tartans: the old colours, dress colours and hunting colours,
not to mention the tartans worn by branches of the family such as Macdonald of the Isles and
Macdonnell of Glengarry. A picture of John A. in Highland costume is not known to exist, though
we know that he owned a kilt. The cartoon on the cover (and many cartoons throughout the
book) is the work of J. W. Bengough, perhaps the only artist to capture the real John A. — his humour,
his roguishness, his frailties, his humanity.

Typeset by Typographic Service, Montreal, in 10 on 11 Baskerville with Garamond headings.
Printed by offset in the United States by Froelich/Greene Inc. Hand-bound by A. Horowitz & Son.


Designed by Max Newton


Special editing: Carolin Wilson, Wayne Fulks
Production: Ed Greenwood and Warren Burles


Tundra Books Inc. has applied funds from its Canada Council block grant for 1974 to the
editing of this book.


The author also wishes to acknowledge the assistance of the Canada Council. The completion of
this project was made possible by a grant under the Canadian Horizons Programme.

The life of Sir John A. Macdonald is the history of Canada.

*Sir Wilfrid Laurier*

*To my daughter Elaine and her husband Vijay*

*To my son David and his wife Phyllis*

*To my grandchildren Harold and Susan*

Lady Elizabeth Longford, author of *Welling-ton – The Years of the Sword* and *Wellington – Pillar of State,* has written, "It is now accepted that the private lives of the great men are relevant, and that even the greatest has his human weaknesses. In Wellington's case, many private letters and journals have appeared throwing light on his marriage and alleged love affairs. My aim has been to use every available document, military, political and personal, which illuminates Wellington the man."

In an essay on books, Michel de Montaigne wrote, "I love historians who are very simple . . . who bring to the task only the care and diligence of collecting all that comes to their knowledge and of faithfully recording all things without choice and selection, leave our judgement intact for discerning the truth . . . He presents to us even the variety of rumours that were circulating and the different reports that were made to him. It is the naked, and unformed manner of history; everyone may make his profit of it according to his understanding."

*Also by Lena Newman*

*An Historical Almanac of Canada*

# Contents

Although John A. was known for his exceptional sense of humour, photographs which show him smiling or laughing are almost nonexistent. Because of the limitations of the camera and the fashion of the time, most nineteenth-century photographs tend to be serious, stuffy and posed.

*RB*

8

*PAC*

# *Meet the man behind the statesman*

# John A. is warm, generous, loving family man

## *He liked ties, liquor, children, jokes, intrigue and getaway doors*

John A. bought his ties by the dozen paying $3.00 for each lot. He liked English peppermints, paid ten cents for a shave and used Bay Rum, French Pomade and hair restorative. He was frugal and practiced many small economies. He had his umbrella repaired for one shilling. He had his shoes mended and paid his tailor twenty-five cents to renew his vest; this same tailor took pains to please him by putting new sleeves into a coat for $2.00. Hoping to relieve his aching feet, John A. asked his bootmaker to elasticize three pairs of boots, at sixty cents a pair. The Prime Minister suffered from corns and used corn plasters. He could not afford to keep a carriage or sleigh, hired a cab for $1.00 and often rode the public horse-drawn cars.

Chemist bills disclose a tendency towards beef, iron and wine tonic, Vichy water, barley sugar, lavender water, violet powder and Pear's Soap. The bill from John Musson, Chemist, Druggist and Apothecary, dated October 7, 1861, is itemized as follows:

| | | £ | s | d |
|---|---|---|---|---|
| Feby 10 | 1 Box Toilet Vinegar 15/ | | | |
| | 1 Bot Jockey club 5/ | 1 | | |
| | 1 Bot Frangipanni 5/ | | | |
| | 1 Bot Lubins Erlantine 3/6 | | 8 | 6 |
| | 1 Bot Ess. Boquet 3/6 | | | |
| | 1 Bot Wicker Cologne 5/ | | 8 | 6 |
| | 1 Bot P. C. oil 3/ | | | |
| 14th | 2 Boxes Pastilles 2/ | | | 5 |

| | | | | |
|---|---|---|---|---|
| April 14 | Blue Pills 1/   May 30 | | | |
| | 2 Frangipanni Sachets 5/ | | | 6 |
| May 30 | 1 Pkg Court Plaster 1/3 | | | |
| | July 18 1 Bot P. C. oil 2/6 | | 3 | 9 |
| Sept 25 | 1 Bot P. C. oil 26/ Oct. 9 | | | |
| | 1 Bot Hair Restorative 5/ | | 7 | 6 |
| Oct 9 | 1 Bot Electric oil 1/3 | | | |
| | 1 Bot Pomade in wood | | | |
| | case 8/9 | | 10 | |
| | 1 Bot Hair oil in Wood | | | |
| | case | | 7 | 6 |

*PAC*

While a widower, John A. bought hair restorative, perfume and pomade.

| | | | | |
|---|---|---|---|---|
| 13 | 1 Bot Pain Killer 1/3 1 doz | | | |
| | Assorted Perfumes 42/ | 2 | 3 | 3 |
| Jan 25 | 2 bot do 2/6 | | 2 | 6 |
| March 16 | 1 lge Box Toilet Vinegar | | 18 | |
| | 1 Sponge 20/ 1 Box | | | |
| | P.C. oil 2/6 | 1 | 2 | 6 |
| April 22 | 2 Toothbrushes 2/6 | | | |
| | 26th 2 Nailbrushes 4/6 4/ | | 11 | |
| 26 | 1 Pkt Court Plaster 1/3 | | | |
| | 2 Bots P.C. oil 5/ | | 6 | 3 |
| June 8 | 1 Perfume Lamp 30/ 1 gold | | | |
| | topped bottle 37/6 | 3 | 7 | 6 |
| | 1 Sachet 2/6 1 Drink 4/ | | | |
| | 1 Bot Perfume 3/ | | 5 | 10 |
| | 1 Sponge 17/6 | | | |
| | 1 Toilet Bottle 31/ | 2 | 8 | 6 |
| | | £15 | 2 | 1 |

## Neurotic about Health

John A. was preoccupied, even neurotic, about his health and tried many remedies of one kind or another. At various times it was given out by his friends and colleagues that he was afflicted with catarrh of the stomach, agonizing gallstone attacks, frequent colds, chills, bronchitis, sciatica, cholera and cancer. His opponents were apt to suggest that these were euphemisms for an overindulgence in drink. Certainly John A. overtired and "groaning for rest," looked forward to the sea voyages to Great Britain as beneficial to his health — and perhaps to his insobrieties.

In the midst of bills indicating thrift, we are

*(continued)*

happy to note that in 1879 Lady Macdonald ordered from London a silk tea gown for £6/6/– and a pair of corsets for £1/8/6.

Scraps of paper and old account books list food purchases and a set of recipes in Lady Macdonald's handwriting. An expenditure of $1.00 for oatmeal emphasized the Scottish heritage of the master of the house. Twelve pounds of corned beef cost sixty cents; three and a half pounds of steak was thirty-three cents; four cents bought kidneys and threepence blotting paper. Lamp glasses and coal oil were bought frequently.

There is a sad little memo for "$1.25 for toy animals" — probably for the Macdonalds' sick little girl. There are several notations of a sum for the collection plate at church.

At no time is there any feeling of high living or extravagance. According to an old bank account that covered household expenses (Bank of Montreal 1878 - 1881) there was never more than just enough to cover what needed to be paid. John A., a success in public life, once lamented that he did not have "a shilling to jingle on a tombstone"; he was unable to amass a competence for himself and his family. He bought land rapidly, even rashly, but there is little to show that he ever profited very much from his property dealings – or anything else. There is a story (probably true) that concerned friends once "sneaked" some money into Lady Macdonald's account. Ever punctilious where his family was concerned, he wrote his sister in 1876: "I am sending you $8.00 [in payment for a $7.50 item]. Please give the fifty cents to the maid. I forgot to tip her."

Through a vast number of letters, for he was an inveterate letter writer, through the diary kept by his second wife, through legendary anecdotes attributed to him, through old newspapers, through the marvelous and often biting cartoons of the period, through the comments of his colleagues and members of the Opposition — John A. is revealed as a warm, loving man with deep qualities of understanding and loyalty. Faults? Indeed for he was human after all! Perhaps his very failings endeared him to those about him.

### Wife Writes Diary

John A.'s second wife started her diary about four months after their marriage. With insight and wit she gives us a warm and sensitive picture of the two worlds — private and political — of the Macdonalds.

*In theory I regard my husband with much awe, in practice tease the life out of him . . . As for Sir John, the doctor tells me he is working himself to death, and to my anxious wifely heart, it hurts me terribly . . . Sir John wore his Star for the first time tonight. I was so proud of him and of it and he looked so well. Surely he deserves it for he has faithfully served both Queen and Country . . . What a bustling day! All the servants important and in a hurry, and I, in my best black velveteen gown receiving New Year visitors. The house was thronged from noon till dinnertime. Some 130 in all wished me and mine all happiness for the New Year between mouthfuls of hot oyster soup and sips of sherry. Sir John spoiled everything by having ordered a Council. I had set my heart on having him with me and lo! he went away before one single caller had rung the bell . . . A sad scene today. It is extremely painful being asked to beg John to interfere in getting places for my friends. He is so just that I know it is distressing to him to be asked for what he does not think it right to give.*

If we do not define letters in a narrow sense but include in our estimate telegrams and administrative memoranda, we find that Macdonald wrote and signed at least 30,000 pieces of correspondence. From such a wealth of written material, the man emerges. Many facets of his character — his likes and dislikes — are made known to the student and historian. His love of politics and parliamentary life is particularly clear.

The papers that have come to light are probably only a small portion of his voluminous output. We will never know how many letters he wrote. Relatively few have survived which do not relate either to political or to family affairs. There are scarcely any for the years, between 1873 and 1878 when he was not in office, but nevertheless very much in the limelight as a prominent politician and lawyer.

Carefully catalogued Macdonald memorabilia are available to the general public in archives, museums, universities, libraries and public institutions, some of which have been designated as national shrines. Archivists are searching out items that are still scattered about the country. The most outstanding collection is at the Public Archives of Canada, Ottawa, where there is a steadily growing assortment of manuscripts and pictures. The Queen's University Archives, Kingston, is also an excellent source. The little Notre Dame College, of Wilcox, Saskatchewan, has a veritable gem – the original Confederation papers, with the signatures of John A. Macdonald and George Etienne Cartier. Other Confederation documents are in the Lawrence Lande Foundation for Canadian Historical Research at McGill University.

The examination of files in archives can be a very tedious difficult chore for the researcher who must often decipher almost illegible handwriting. In the case of John A.'s correspondence this does not hold true. His calligraphy was like his mind — clear and logical. (Young John A.'s teacher, according to E. B. Biggar, an early biographer, "frequently exhibited the clean kept books of young Macdonald to some careless student for emulation, and often selected specimens of the neat penmanship of the boy to put to shame some of the slovenly writers of the class.")

Even when burdened with wearisome campaigns, he wrote regularly to his mother, his sisters, his wife's sister, his colleagues – although he has been quoted as saying "A person should never write, if he can speak to the person instead." He wrote quick little notes, enlivened by some witty account of his doings and showing his interest in the recipient's welfare. He wrote anywhere and everywhere, travelling on steamers ("I can scarcely write from the tremours."), while listening to soporific debates in the House, as well as while nursing his invalid first wife. Through letters he wooed the unaffiliated voters — "loose fish" as he called them. He was in constant touch with loyal friends. His letters are a key to his nature: he really cared for those around him.

PAC

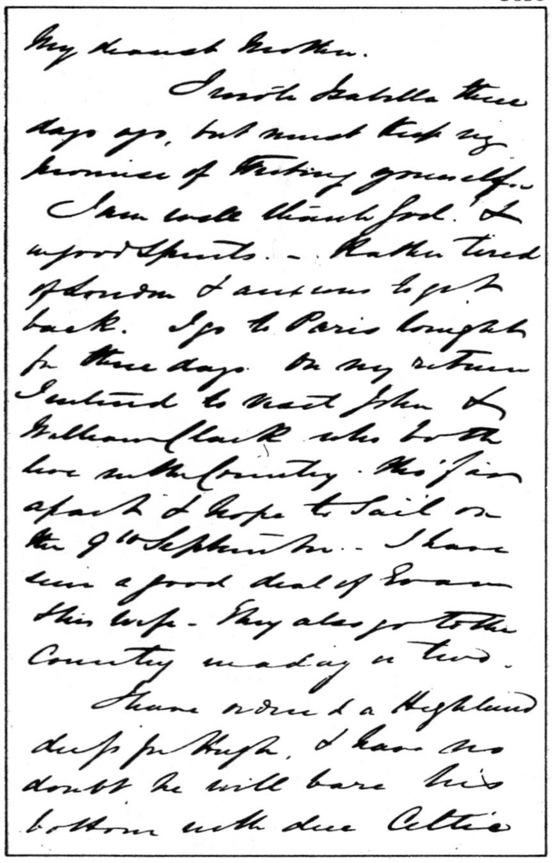
My dearest Mother.
I wrote Isabella three days ago, but must keep my promise of writing yourself. — I am quite well thank God & in good spirits. — Rather tired of London & anxious to get back. I go to Paris tonight for three days. On my return I intend to visit John & William Clark who both live in the Country. [illegible] apart & hope to sail on the 9th September. — I have seen a good deal of Evan this trip. — They also go to the Country in a day or two.
I have ordered a Highland dress for Hugh, & have no doubt he will bare his bottom with due Celtic

John A. wrote this letter to his mother during one of his many trips to Britain. A devoted family man, he wrote often to his mother, sisters, wife and children.

CIN

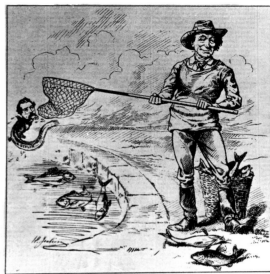

The wily old fisherman catching the "loose fish" as he called undecided voters.

### Bored by Verbosity

He did not speak often in the House, and seldom at great length. He considered a twenty-minute speech to be about right. He spent so many hours in the parliamentary library and with his books at home that he was usually well prepared and developed his ideas lucidly and speedily, well within his own time limit. But, and this is inherent in his character, though rallying from a severe illness (or a prolonged drinking spree) he could still speak carefully, impressively and at length when he felt it was warranted. His famous five-hour speech at the time of the Pacific Scandal is a case in point.

However his exasperation with long-winded speeches is plainly indicated in letters which were often scribbled from his seat in the House. "The House is very impatient, but the Opposition will talk." "Our Opposition has no idea of the proposition and dwells as long on trifles as on matters of importance." "I write to you while a M.P. with a voice like an ophicleide [wind instrument] is roaring against the CPR." "We hope to close by Tuesday or Wednesday but the Opposition by their loquacity and obstruction may keep us still longer."

Sometimes to escape "boring eloquence" he communicated with his second wife in the gallery, by using the sign language for the deaf, which they had both learned for that purpose, or by sending her "little scribbles." His impatience and his devious nature were shown in other ways. He had a "getaway" door through a secret staircase to avoid the importunate and the tedious,

*(continued)*

#### A Story with a Sting

Unable to resist the sly quip, no matter how corny, Sir John A. had a story for every occasion. Canada's mosquitoes were then so thick that a man could hardly open his mouth without having it filled with the pesky insects. Sir John A. told of a man sleeping under a mosquito net when one side of it was accidentally raised. So many mosquitoes swarmed in that they pushed him out of bed!

Although he was not handsome, John A. could look quite dashing. He dressed elegantly, always in fashion. He liked red ties and British tailoring.

An early photograph of Queen's University, which John A. helped to found and in which he always retained an interest.     *Queen's*

and he had an astonishing way of vanishing in order to escape a confrontation.

### Damnedest Liar in Canada

He could always be counted on for a swift rejoinder. Once he was stopped on King Street in Toronto by a leading citizen who said, "Sir John, a friend says you are the damnedest liar in all Canada." Very quietly and seriously John A. replied, "I daresay it's true enough."

On another occasion John A. was attacked in the House concerning his party's proposals for training young Canadian seamen. "I trust," said his opponent, "the Honourable Gentleman informed other governments that his intentions are strictly pacific." "No," replied John A. "Our intentions are confined solely to the Atlantic."

In all walks of life, in his family circle, in his legal duties and in his political career, one characteristic stood out – he had a wonderful way of soothing ruffled feelings, of softening antagonisms among friends and adversaries. (Once during a particularly hot debate, John A. made peace by saying, "Let us not have anything hostile between these two gentlemen. We will not have a duel system.")

In her diary his wife wrote: "I tell him that his good heart and his amiable temper are the great secrets of his success."

Lord Carnarvon, Secretary of State for the Colonies from February 1874 until January 1878, sent his hopes for Macdonald's success in the opening of the new session: "My only regret is that I cannot have the pleasure of watching you 'handle the ribbons.' Everybody seems to agree that your management of the House is as neat a specimen of coaching as anyone need wish to witness."

### Closely Knit Clan

John A. comes through as a very lovable man of great charisma with personal magnetism

### Drinking Cabinet

A member once came to Sir John A. and said, "There are many complaints about the disgraceful drinking habits of Thomas D'Arcy McGee. You must speak to him."

After putting it off as long as possible, Sir John A. admonished McGee in these words: "Look here, this Government can't afford two drunkards, so you've got to stop!"

to a high degree. He had a deep need to give of himself. The Macdonalds were a closely knit clan. The habit of family responsibility was instilled in him as a youngster and never left him. The problems of his kinsmen were his problems. As soon as he began to earn, he contributed to the family budget.

When his father died he shouldered the obligation of his widowed mother and two unmarried sisters, in addition to the care of his son and his invalid wife. Nor was this all. With a cousin he accepted the moral liability to care for other members of the family – two widows and their children. He used his scant free time to give them guidance. When John A. married for the second time, he accepted his wife's family as his own; her mother and her brother moved in with the Macdonalds.

Perhaps one of the reasons that John A. was so beloved is that he laughed easily and often. As a youth he was known as a prankster. He kept the habit of extravagant monkey tricks and hid behind them when life became dark. If there is laughter in this book, if we see his absurdities, he would probably not mind too much. He was reputed to like a risqué story, to be a master of the double entendre. A bit of an actor, he had excellent timing with a ribald remark. Those were coarse, earthy times. A gregarious worldly man, he loved people about him. He sought to lose himself in their merrymaking.

Above all, he was a full-time politician. Other interests were put behind him. He was a romantic with a touch of the cloak-and-dagger spirit about him. He took his politics as an adventure replete with grandiose situations, intrigues, plots, speculations, hazards and chances. There was no end to his imaginative even notorious ploys. He risked much for a coup.

His male companions – and much of his time was spent with them – gave him strong, deep devotion. Women of all ages found him fascinating. He loved children and got along well with them – his easy way drew them to him. He had special riddles, games, jokes and stories for the young ones around him. In Kingston, he was often seen in his tall silk hat at marbles with little boys, and teasing and chatting with little girls. He sent this conundrum to a small niece, Jane Greene: "Why is mixing wine or adulterating sugar a more heinous crime than murder? Because murder is a gross offence but adulterating is a grocer offence."

It was with children that he experienced the great tragedies of his life. Of his three children the first, John Alexander, died in infancy. His

daughter Mary was afflicted by hydrocephalus (water on the brain) and was an invalid all her life. His middle child, Hugh John, was brought up by his grandmother and aunts after the death of the boy's mother.

John A. was always a controversial figure. No one was indifferent to him. He inspired deep devotion in many – and just as great distrust in others.

### "Disregards Truth"

In 1858 the *Toronto Colonist*, then a leading paper of John A.'s own party, wrote in an editorial about him: " . . . a man whose political and personal treachery we are in a position to demonstrate at any moment — whose utter want of principle, of common decency, can be established without much trouble, whose disregard of truth has become a byword amongst all those who know him, whose mean malignity and habit of foul slander are known to all who have the misfortune of being connected with him in private life."

### "Demoralizes Youth"

In 1882 a Presbyterian clergyman wrote to the *Galt Reformer*: "No man in this Dominion, in my opinion, has done so much as he to demoralize the youth of the country by enthroning trickery and fraud, thus impressing them with the thought that the best way to gain positions of honour and emolument is by trickery, fraud, lying and deception. It can't be otherwise than have a ruinous influence on the morals of his followers."

### "Wins the Hearts of Men"

And yet Sir Wilfrid Laurier, a political opponent but a great admirer of Sir John A., said of him that he was "endowed with this inner, subtle, undefinable characteristic of soul that wins and keeps the hearts of men . . . his actions displayed unbounded fertility of resource, a high level of intellectual conception, and, above all, a far-reaching vision beyond the event of the day, and still higher, permeating the whole, a broad patriotism, a devotion to Canada's welfare, Canada's advancement, and Canada's glory."

Our first Prime Minister has been described as a political conniver, an alcoholic, a near rogue, a lonely man, a gifted parliamentarian, a wit, an idealist. What was the man *really* like?

*Lena Newman*

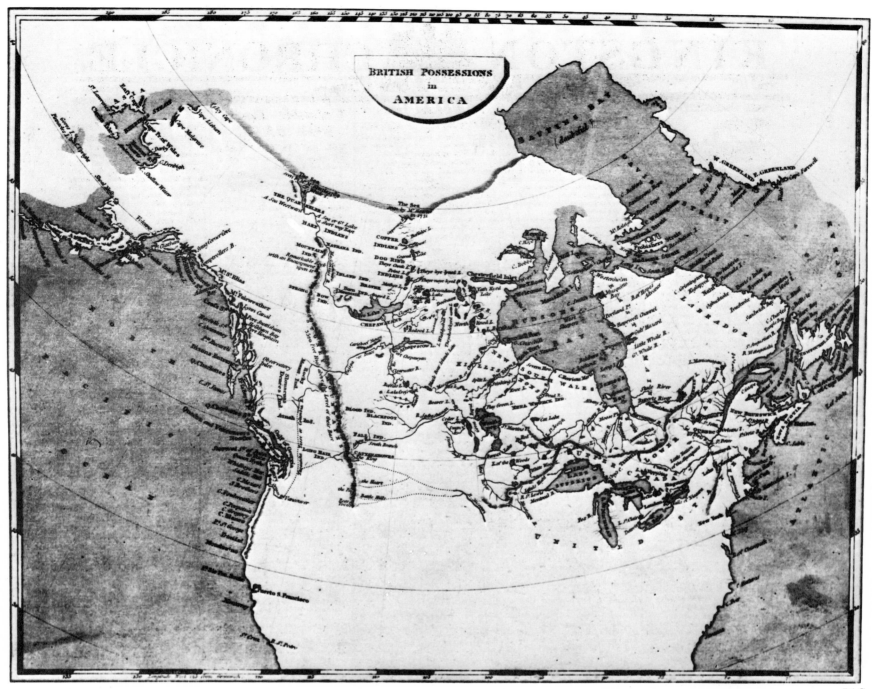

These two maps, drawn in 1802 and 1898, show how Canada changed in John A.'s lifetime. More than any other individual, he helped to effect that change.

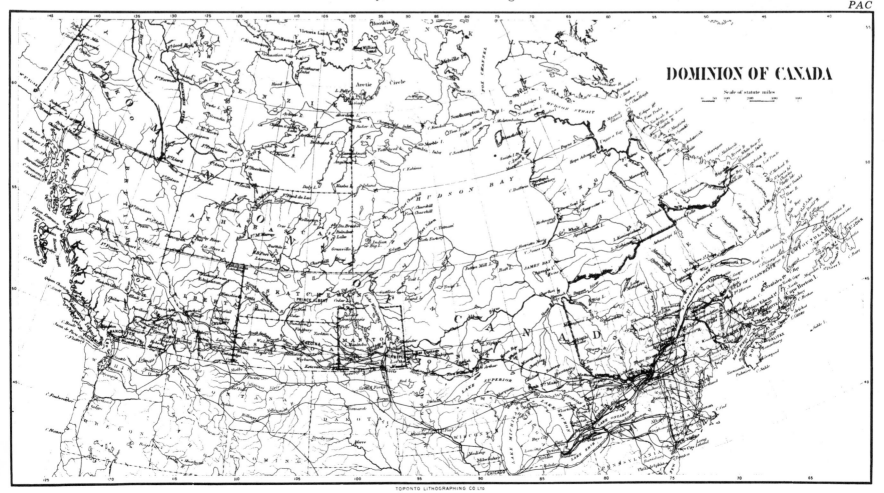

# KINGSTON  CHRONICLE.

**VOL. II.]**     FRIDAY, (AFTERNOON) JULY 21, 1820.     **[No. 61.**

---

## THE FRONTENAC

Steam Vessel will start from Kingston for York, and Niagara on the 1st, 11th, and 21st days of the present month, and from Niagara for Kingston on the 5th, 15th, and 25th days of each month with as much punctuality as the nature of the Lake Navigation will admit of.

*Kingston, May 19th, 1820.*   19

THE Subscriber having rented that commodious Stone House, the property of Peter Grant, Esq. and lately occupied by Mr. Daniel Brown, proposes keeping a house of

### Entertainment, (Sign of the Black Horse)

for the accommodation of Strangers, and others who may have the goodness to favour him, and to each of whom every attention will be paid in the cleanest and comfortable manner of exertion, and the smallest favour thankfully acknowledged by the Public's

Humble Servant,
**SAMUEL MERRILL.**
*Kingston, 5th May, 1820.*   709

## TO LET.

A STONE HOUSE, upon the Hill above the Methodist Chapel, a story and a half high, with Kitchen and Cellar under, with two fifths of an acre, well enclosed; at present occupied by Mr. Dodsfell.—Possession will be given on the 1st of May.

For terms apply to —— Corbett, or William Mitch. — Kingston.

*Kingston, 7th April, 1820.*

---

### F. B. SPILSBURY,

**Surgeon, R. N.**
*Late Surgeon of H.M.S. Prince Regent, on Lake Ontario,*

Intends practising in the various branches of his Profession, at his residence, next door to John McLean, Esq. Store.

*Kingston, Oct. 6th, 1819.*   41

THE Subscriber begs leave respectfully to inform his friends and the public in general, that he has established a

### PAINT SHOP

a few rods south of Mrs. Patrick's Tavern, where will be kept constantly all kinds of PAINTS, prepared ready for the brush.

House, Sign, Waggon, Sleigh, and Ornamental Painting,

done at the shortest notice, together with raw and boiled Oil, which will be disposed of as cheap as can be procured in this town, for Cash only.

**THEODORE BROCKETT.**

N. B. Two good workmen at journeyman Painting, will find employ, by applying to the subscriber.

*Kingston, 6th April, 1820.*

THE Subscribers being duly nominated Executors to the late Will and Testament of the late Lawrence Herchmer, Kingston Merchant, request all persons indebted to his estate to make immediate payment, and those having demands against the said estate to bring them forward without delay.

**JOHN KIRBY.**
**GEO. H. MARKLAND.**
*Kingston, 9th Nov. 1819.*   46

## NOTICE.

Books of Subscription for the

## Bank of Kingston

will be opened at the Director's Room in the Bank of Upper Canada, on the 24th August next, and kept open each day from the hour of ten till three o'clock, until further notice.

*Kingston, 27th July, 1819.*   31

---

### Kingston Branch of the Montreal Bank.

ANY sum required may be obtained at the Office for good Bills, on Montreal, Quebec, Bills of Exchange on London —— for these.—Notes also will be discounted at thirty, sixty, and ninety days.

**THOMAS MARKLAND.**
*Agent*

*Kingston, 9th Nov. 1818.*   11

## FOR SALE.

A FARM in the front Concession of the Township of Augusta, three and a half miles below Brockville, containing 150 acres, about 75 of which is under improvement. There is a large barn store house on the premises, built of stone. Sober and honest, a creek runs, &c. The farm is very eligible —— that the extensive situation —— a country residence. It could be sold on liberal terms, and possession given immediately. For terms apply to

R. & W. MORRIS.
*Brockville, 16th May, 1820.*

---

## Notice.

THE Land Board, for the Midland District for the ensuing six months, will meet on Wednesday in each week, at the Court House in the Town of Kingston, at the hour of 12 o'clock at noon, for the purpose of receiving applications for lands, from the undermentioned description of persons, viz.

Emigrants, and others coming to the Province and bringing due Certificates of being British born subjects.

All old settlers that have resided in the District previous to the late war, and produce Certificates of having done their duty in its defence.

The terms of the grants are the performance of the settling duties within Eighteen Months from the date of the location; and the payment of the following fees, authorised by an order in Council of 14th December, 1819.

On Grants of 100 acres    incipient Emigrants settlers,
On Grants of 100 acres, £30
On Grants of 200 do.   30

Payable in three equal instalments, viz.

The first on the receipt of the Location Ticket, the second on Certificate of the settlement; the third on the receipt of the Fiat for the patent.

No certificate can be entertained unless accompanied by a written character, or a satisfactory reason shewn for such not being produced.

By order of the Board,
**JAMES NICKALLS, Junr.**
*Clerk.*

*Kingston, Feb. 14th, 1820.*   8

N. B. To prevent disappointments to persons applying for lands; it is necessary to state that the Board has no power to grant Lands to the Children of U. E. Loyalists; Militia men who served in the Flank companies during the war; Naval or Military claimants, all such must make application to York.

TO BE SOLD, and immediate possession given, the following Lots of Land, in the 6th Concession of the Township of Elmsley, viz. 17, 20, 22, 24, 29, 30, most eligibly situated on the North side of the Rideau Lake, which forms their southern boundary; the great road to the Perth Settlement, leading through one of the Lots. They abound in excellent Timber, which from its being contiguous to water communication may be rafted to Montreal at a trifling expence. The quality of the soil and other advantages are such as to render this a desirable purchase to Farmers or persons engaged in the Lumber Trade. For terms of payment and other particulars apply to William Marshall, Esq. Perth Settlement, John Kirby, Esq. Kingston, or the subscriber, in Woodhouse, London District.

**ROBERT NICHOL.**
*Rawdon 18, 1819.*   47tf

JOHN KINCAID, BEGS leave to inform his friends and the public generally, that he has opened a House of Public Entertainment near W. F. Peake's Wharf, in the Village of Brockville, under the Sign of the

### Brockville Hotel;

Where he hopes, by a strict attention to those who may favour him with a call, to merit a share of the public patronage. He will always have on hand all kinds of Liquor, of the best quality.

*Brockville, Jan. 1820.*   22w8

N. B. Good Stabling for Horses.

---

## To Clothiers.

For sale, a quantity of TEAZLES,
Tho. S. Whitaker, &c.
*August 19, 1819.*   34

For sale at this Office.

A FEW copies of a SERMON, preached at Quebec, on the 12th of September, after the death of His Excellency the Duke of Richmond, by the Rev. and G. J. Mountain, A. B. Bishop's Official in Lower Canada, and Rector of Quebec.   41

## BANK NOTICE.

A General Meeting of the Stockholders of the Bank of Upper Canada, will be held at the Bank on Monday the 17th of July next, at 12 o'clock, for the purpose of electing and amending some of the articles of association.

S. BARTLET, *Cashier.*
*Kingston, June —*   21

## Window Glass.

THE subscribers have on hand a consignment of WINDOW GLASS, of 7 by 9 —— by 9 by 10, to be —— of excellent quality, and warranted to —— in good order for sale at very low prices for cash or —— approved credit.

THOS. WHITAKER & Co.
*May 17.*   20

## MONTREAL ALMANACKS For 1820.

For sale at this Office.

---

### ALEXANDER ASHEN,

## Merchant Taylor,

HAS received from Montreal a most choice and excellent assortment of the best Wool of England superfine

Cloths and Cassimeres,

with Trimmings, and every thing complete.

A. Ashen informs his friends and the public that he is now working up those Cloths, &c. at his old stand, where orders will be thankfully received, and executed on the shortest notice, and on the lowest terms for Cash, or short approved credit.

*Kingston, Sept. 10, 1819.*

## BANK CALL.

THE Stockholders of the Bank of Upper Canada are hereby required to pay in addition twenty-five dollars on each share, on or before the 11th of August next. Any Stockholder failing to make the said payment will forfeit his shares, agreeable to the 21st article of the incorporation of the Bank; which is as follows:—If there shall be a failure in payment of any part of the sum or shares subscribed by any person or persons, on paying such public or more severally the party so failing, or paying the first instalment of ten per centum hereunder, the amount of eight per centum before required to be made, shall satisfactorily forfeit the said deposit to and for the use of the said Company, and the stock shall be held at public sale for the behoof of the company—and in case of any delay or failure in the payment of the subscribed instalments, after the said and second instalments, any Stockholder so neglecting to pay the amount of his instalments, that shall for the first ten days of such neglect forfeit to the use and benefit of the remaining stockholders five per centum upon the whole amount of his stock previously paid in, and for the second and third ten days, five per centum on equal four of his payment, making together a forfeiture of fifteen per centum for thirty days, and if at the expiration of sixty days after such instalment shall have become due, it shall be unpaid, then the whole amount of stock, together with the whole amount paid on the same, shall be forfeited to the use and benefit of the remaining stockholders aforesaid, and the stock to be at the disposal of the directors, for the benefit of the said company.

S. BARTLET, *Cashier.*
*Kingston, June 7, 1820*

## NOTICE.

ALL persons indebted either by Note or Book Account, to the estate of the late Richard R. Bilton, Esq. deceased, are requested to pay the same without delay, and those to whom the estate is indebted will present their accounts duly authenticated for adjustment, to Alan MacLean Esquire, one of the Executors to said estate.

*Kingston, June 5, 1820.*   24tf

## SURGEON BOYD,

HAVING heard that it has been reported that he does not attend Patients in the country, begs leave to contradict it, and to assure the public that he will be at all times willing to attend his friends in the Country as well as in the Town, on moderate terms.

*Kingston, June 12, 1820.*   24tf

## NOTICE.

ALL persons indebted to the late Co-partnership of Richard Robison and David Secord, are requested to make immediate payment to the surviving partner, David Secord, and those to whom the said Co-partnership may be indebted, are requested to send in their accounts for adjustment and payment.

*Kingston, 27th May, 1820.*   21tf

## TO LET.

A COMMODIOUS HOUSE, near Doctor Keating's, two stories high, with seven rooms, a Kitchen, and a Cellar under the whole, a good yard and stable; also a very good Spring near the house. For further particulars apply to

**JAMES ROBINS.**
*Kingston, 4th June, 1819.*   23

## NOTICE.

THE Board for Militia Pensions, will meet on the last Monday in February, and continue to sit the same day in each Month, until the business of this District, as regards the same is finished.

**JOHN P. FERGUSON.**
*Kingston, Feb. 18, 1819.*   6

## NOTICE

ROBERT TURNBULL, from Markham, on the southern border of Scarboro', who is now supposed to be residing a long part of Upper Canada, is requested to send his address to the Office of the Kingston Chronicle, for the information of a relative, who feels interested in his welfare, and is desirous of corresponding with him.   16

## BLANKS.

For the Courts of Request, and various other kinds, for sale at this Office.

---

### Valuable Lands FOR SALE.

IN the Midland District, County of Prince Edward, & Township of Amelisasburgh.

Lot 23, in the front Concession, on Lake Ontario, lying to the eastward of Nicholson's Island.

Lots 21, and 24, in the second Concession of said Township; the whole containing six hundred acres.

For particulars inquire at the Office of the Kingston Chronicle, or of the Hon. JAMES BABY, York.

N. B. All persons are cautioned against cutting or destroying the timber on the above lands, as they will certainly be prosecuted.

*Kingston, March 7, 1820.*   10 tf

## NOTICE.

A Assignment having been made to the subscriber of all the Lands, Goods, and debts, belonging to the late firm of James Ranken & Co. of Ernest Town, Merchants, as well as those belonging to James Ranken individually, for the benefit of creditors. Notice is hereby given to all persons having claims against he said firm, or James Ranken, to present them forthwith, duly authenticated; and such as stand indebted are desired to pay their respective amounts to Chas. A. Hagerman, Esq. of Kingston, on or before the first day of December next.

**JOHN KIRBY.**
*Kingston, 1st September, 1819.*   36

## A HORSE Suspected to have been Stolen.

A Person calling himself John Rees, or Reele, understood to go about 5 ft. dark complexion, thin nose, and rather a downcast look, arrived here on Sunday last with a very fine Horse, which he offered for sale for very low. that it excited the suspicions above mentioned. He was recognized, and supposed to have stolen a horse from Bernard Polly, of Yonge, in 1814, and selling him to a Mr. Yoke, of Holdwell; he has been taken on Mr. Polly's complaint, and committed to the cells for further examination.

The Horse is bay and well made, with four rather light bay, dark mane and tail, a little white on the left hind foot, a large white spot (I think an artificial one) on his forehead, and said to be 5 or 6 years old.

I purchased the Horse from the person who was taking into custody, for £25 or £30, and shall endeavour to keep him for the rightful owner; any further information on the subject will be given by writing to the subscriber.

**H. SPAFFORD.**
*Brockville, June 27th, 1820.*

## Schola Medicine.

Established in Montreal, November 1st, 1819.
By William Wood of the Bush.
M. R. C. B. L. &c. &c.

THE second course in the above establishment will commence the first Monday in September.

The Lectures during the first month will be gratis to the public.—The private course will commence the first of October, and continue till the month of May.

The course will comprise Lectures on Anatomy, Physiology, Pathology, Surgery and the Practice of Physic.

Lectures (during the Private Course) on Anatomy, Wednesdays and Fridays, at the o'clock in the evening.

P. S. Dr. W. will take a few Medical Gentlemen to reside with himself; other arrangement shall be made to render the course of considerable advantage, such Gentlemen who purpose studying in this establishment are requested to give early information.

Anatomical Theatre,
18, St. Paul Street,
*June 22, 1820.*

## Hibernian Society.

IRISH Emigrants who wish to keep their Children placed at school in Kingston, may apply to any of the members of the Society, or to the President, James Ferguson, Esq.—Further particulars will be made known to them by their apply-ing to Mr. W. McConnell, Treasurer.

*Kingston, June 16, 1820.*   24

## NOTICE.

LETTERS of Administration having been granted to me on the Estate of the late Roderick Matheson, Esquire, it is requested that all persons whatsoever that have any claim against that Estate will present them for payment; and that all who are indebted to it will pay the amount due, without delay to

**JAMES RANKEN.**
*Administrator.*
*Bath, 18th June, 1820.*

---

### A REWARD OF Two Hundred and Fifty Pounds

WILL be paid by the subscriber to any person who shall discover the person or persons who, on the night of June last, did break open the Branch of the Montreal Bank of five dollars each, eighteen amount of two thousand pounds.

By direction of the Directors of the Montreal Bank.

**THOMAS MARKLAND.**

*Kingston, 23rd Nov. 1819.*   47

## LETTER II.

TO WILLIAM WELLS, ESQ.

Sir,

I have received at the first number of——

---

*The Macdonald family arrived in Kingston on July 17, 1820.*

# PART ONE   1815-1842

*Macdonald was an immigrant who made good and who made Canada in the process.* T. C. Douglas

This serene Glasgow Street of the early 1800s gives little indication of the miseries that afflicted the poor of that city from 1816 to 1820 and forced many Scots, including the Macdonalds, to emigrate. John A. was born in 1815, the year Napoleon was defeated at Waterloo. In 1816 and 1817, the stagnation of trade caused mass unemployment. In 1818 typhus fever struck. In 1819 thousands paraded in the streets demanding employment or bread.

In the early 1800s Glasgow children loved to play a game called "Charlie ower the water" (a reference to Bonnie Prince Charlie). The object was to run across the street without being "tigged."

A favourite game of children in Glasgow when John A. was a lad was marbles, known as "bools." A "pock" — i.e. a sack or bag — of these was standard equipment for boys.

*Glasgow*

The Glasgow riverbanks in the early nineteenth century could be used for elegant diversion for the rich of the city.

# Glasgow in John A.'s boyhood — City of fun and poverty

John A. Macdonald was born at Brunswick Place, across the Clyde River from Glasgow, Scotland, in January 1815. He was the eldest son of Hugh Macdonald and Helen Shaw. The General Registry Office, Edinburgh, gives the tenth as his birthdate, but his father entered it in a memo book as the eleventh, and that is the day that Canada honours as his anniversary.

### Glaswegians Described

In *A Popular Sketch of the History of Glasgow* (1882) Andrew Wallace describes the Glaswegians of the early 1800s: "A prominent feature of the Glasgow citizen was what may be called his public spiritedness — his patriotism and deep interest in the affairs of the nation at large.... Still another feature may be stated — viz., their high animal spirits, their buoyant and somewhat rude humour and joviality. The heartiness and thoroughness which characterized them in their business and commercial pursuits were carried into their social relationships and hours of relaxation.... When the ladies retired upstairs to enjoy their dish of tea and scandal, the lords of creation remembered these fair ones no more that night, but lingered over the flowing bowl till far in the morning, and indeed till they lost all memory whatever.... The lower classes of the community, however, were much more frugal in their habits of life than they are at the present time. The bill of fare at their various meals was by no means so costly as that of our working men nowadays. Their breakfast consisted almost exclusively of the 'halesome parritch,' with a little milk or small beer to accompany it, and it was only on Sundays they were able to indulge in the luxury of tea. The almost invariable dinner consisted of broth and beef, varied occasionally with a sheep's head and trotters, or a salt herring and potatoes, while their frugal supper was but a repetition of their morning repast. Practical joking and coarse wit... was a feature of Glasgow social life, and sometimes it was carried to absurd and dangerous lengths."

*The New Statistical Account of Scotland* describes the poverty, recession and epidemics following the end of the Napoleonic War that forced many Scots — including the Macdonalds — to emigrate: "In the latter end of 1816, and beginning of 1817, the stagnation of trade was such, that the working classes in the city and suburbs could not find employment. The distress of the workers was so great, that it was found necessary to raise money for their relief by voluntary subscriptions.... In 1818, the lower classes of this city and suburbs were severely afflicted with typhus fever.... During the period of the disease, upwards of 5,000 apartments in the city and suburbs were fumigated, 600 lodging houses were examined, infected bedding was burned, and the owners supplied with new bedding. In 1819, the working classes were again thrown into great distress from want of employment.... At this alarming crisis, when thousands of workers paraded the streets demanding employment or bread, upwards of 600 persons were almost instantly employed at spade work, or breaking stones for the roads.... The distress and dissatisfaction continued during the greater part of 1820 when large distributions of clothing, meal, and coals were given to such persons as could not find employment."

### Brings Down House

John A.'s political career started in Glasgow — according to E. B. Biggar, who wrote an early biography of him — when at the age of four he "mounted a table and began a speech. What he lacked in language he made up in gesticulation. But in the midst of a peroration, he whirled off the table and struck his forehead on a chair, bringing down the house."

Old Glasgow newspapers describe the games that John A. might have played as a child: "In the game of 'shinty' the performers were divided into two sections, and were armed with long sticks called shinties, perhaps because of

---

### The Scottish Clan Macdonald

*Motto*  Per mare per terras (by sea and by land).

*Gaelic name*  MacDhòmhnuill.

*Origin of name*  Dhohnull (Gaelic for "world ruler").

*War cry*  Fraoch Eilean.

*Pipe music*  March of the Macdonalds.

---

their aptness to occasion injuries to the shin bones or heel steps of the performers. A ball was thrown between the contending forces, and was hit and driven hither and thither until finally it was driven beyond the bourne on either side, and whoever reached that goal claimed the victory. In summer time large parties were assembled on the Green or on any vacant ground to play this very boisterous game.... There were also the favourite 'marbles' or as more familiarly known 'bools.' A plentiful store of these in a pock formed a portion of the equipment of youth."

Another writer reminisced about the juvenile games of early nineteenth century Glasgow: "Before we can play at any game it is necessary to 'coont' for who will be 'het' and as the 'coonting' varies, I will just begin by citing the two most popular, firstly —

> *As eenty teenty vigity veg,*
> *Ell dell draw my leg,*
> *Urkey burkey taury rope,*
> *Ann pan pease Jock.*

And again —

> *Mrs. M'Clusky's very good whisky,*
> *No. 9 Bell's Wynd,*
> *Up a stair — down another,*
> *Next door to Punch's mother.*

"*Charlie ower the water* was played by running across the street without being 'tigged.' ... *Hit a'* was an amusing and highly recreative game, played with an old hat, old boot, sheep's bladder, ball or anything soft. It kept every player in a continual good humour. The game was played by simply lifting the missile and throwing it at anyone near enough to get a good crack. But the more rapid it was played the more fun evolved."

THE EMIGRANTS WELCOME TO CANADA.

# MACDONALDS IMMIGRATE

## 42 days to Quebec, 12 more to Kingston

### "Unseaworthy" ship later abandoned at sea; 100 acres and hardships await settlers

When John A. was five, the family immigrated to Canada on the *Earl of Buckinghamshire,* a full-rigged sailing ship that had been built six years before — in 1814 — at Montreal, then an active shipbuilding centre.

#### Ship Utterly Unseaworthy

In his biography of Macdonald, E. B. Biggar writes that the ship was "utterly unseaworthy; and the following year, while bringing out to Canada a cargo of 600 immigrants, she went down with all on board and was never heard of more." However, Lloyd's of London's records show that the ship was abandoned at sea on October 14, 1822, while on a voyage from Quebec to Greenock. On November 5, the ship drifted onto shore at Galway Bay and went to pieces. The crew, except for two men who were washed overboard, arrived at Cork on October 19 in the *Mary.* No mention is made of how the passengers fared — or if there were any.

Young John A. — a bright-eyed lively child —

probably enjoyed the long sea voyage, unaware of the discomforts experienced by his parents and other steerage passengers.

#### Advice to New Settlers

Books such as Stuart's *The Emigrant's Guide to Upper Canada* contained all kinds of advice for the new settlers. "Emigrants are received as subjects, and are required, before they receive lands, to take the oath of allegiance. They should not expect pecuniary assistance of any kind; neither provisions nor utensils. The magnitude of the national debt, and of the public burthens, forbid their being furnished with any.... The government can only supply them with land. The usual quantity lately given has been one hundred acres to each man arrived at the age of twenty-one, or upwards.

"A condition attends every grant. It is, that a certain portion of the land shall be cleared and cultivated, and a small log house of certain dimensions built, within a certain time...."

"The original settlers are extremely hospitable and kind. They are as willing to yield as to receive assistance; and an industrious, sober, and good-tempered stranger, may, under mercy, depend upon the most friendly furtherance from them in his efforts after independence....

"The first object to emigrants lately arrived, is to avoid every excess of every kind; to be temperate in all things; and to provide, as far as possible, against exposure to the inclemencies of the weather, particularly of the night air.

"For this purpose, an ample supply, particularly of blankets, should be laid in at Quebec, or at Montreal....

"Where clear, good spring or river water cannot be had, the water for drinking should

---

In 1832, twelve years after the Macdonalds arrived, J. Dunbar Moodie immigrated to Canada and wrote these lines about his new country. Perhaps the Macdonalds felt the same way!

*Oh, the cold of Canada nobody knows,*
*The fire burns our shoes without warming our toes*
*Oh dear! What shall we do?*
*Our blankets are thin — and our noses are blue.*
*Our noses are blue and our blankets are thin,*
*It's at zero without, and we're freezing within!*
*Oh dear, what shall we do?*

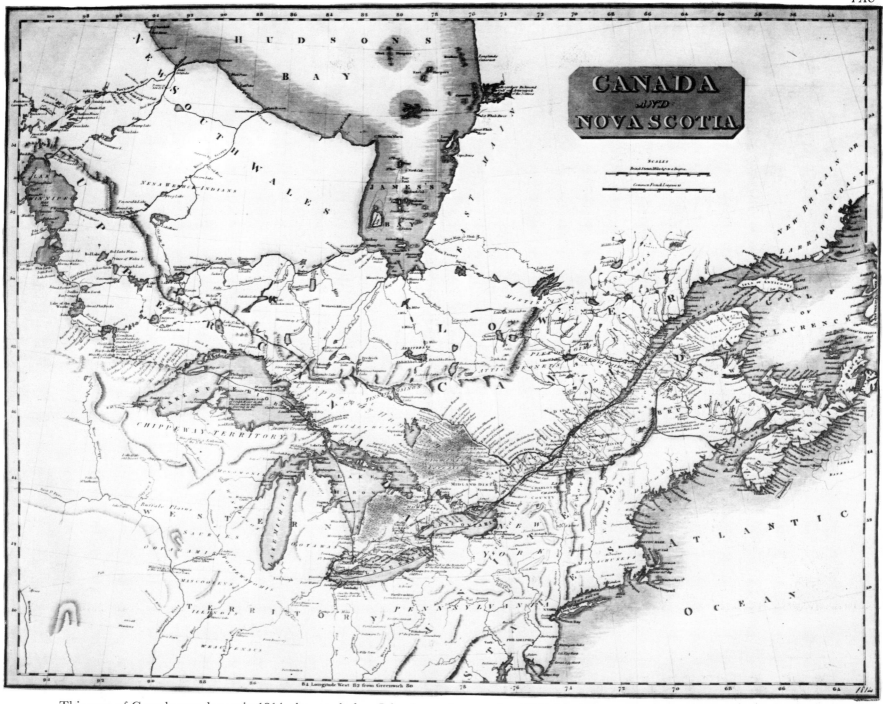

This map of Canada was drawn in 1814, the year before John A. was born, and published in 1821, the year after the Macdonalds arrived.

Lord Ashburton to John Quincy Adams, US Ambassador, London, 1818: "I wish the British Government would give you Canada at once. It is fit for nothing but to breed quarrels."

### NOTICE TO EMIGRANTS.

RESOLVED at the last monthly meeting of the *Quebec Emigrants' Society,* that a list of applications be kept by them of all Strangers desirous to find out the residence of their relatives; and also of those settled in this country, wishing to communicate to their friends the place of their abode, for which purpose there will be a list of names kept in the following form, viz :—

| Persons desirous to communicate to their friends the place of their residence in Canada— | Persons desirous to find out the residence of their friends in Canada— |

The first application is—Richard Semings Combe, No. 87, Saint Paul street, Montreal, expects his wife & two children from England.

Which list will be read on board of ships arriving with settlers; and it is not doubted but that all Editors of Newspapers in this country will insert the same in their papers free of charge.

None but applications post paid will be attended to. Emigrants' Society, Quebec, 7th June, 1820.

### TO LET,

The Macdonalds arrived in Quebec on June 24, 1820. This notice had appeared in *The Quebec Mercury* a few days before.

always be boiled, and suffered to cool, before it is used.

"In damp situations, which are exposed to agues, I esteem a moderate use of liquor to be healthful; but it would be better never to use it, than to use it with the smallest degree of intemperance."

A very conservative family, the Macdonalds took root naturally in the Midland District of Upper Canada which was originally peopled by United Empire Loyalists. The mother, especially, was proud of the many members of their family who had served in the wars of the Empire.

A servant girl, who accompanied a family of immigrants to Upper Canada in 1832, wrote home to Ireland. "I am now growing plump and fat and well to look at as John tells me . . . . What flogged all that I have ever seen was making sugar out of a tree. Not a word of a lie do I tell you. You make a hole in the tree (the Maypole they call it) and out comes the sugar, like sweet water, thick like and you boil it. But where's the use of telling you, as you have no sugar trees at home.

"And then there's the bumpkin pie, which they give to workmen; but that's aisy enough. The master doesn't like it. You takes and slices it like apples, and gives it plenty of the maypole, and a pinch or two of cloves and a glass of whisky, which is like ditchwater here, and it's mighty good eating.

Your affectionate schoolfellow, Bridget"

### Coffee, Tea or Dandelion?

The Canadian has always loved his tea and coffee. What substitutes our early settlers developed! They made teas from the leaves and roots of maidenhair fern, cherry bark, sage, thyme, chocolate root, marsh rosemary and mountain sweet — all of which were healthful and (we hope) good. From the Indians they learned to make Oswego Tea from the Purple Bergamot, which grows in Alberta. This drink was prized as a conditioner and a cure all. Coffees were brewed from dried potatoes, rye, wheat, toasted bread, beans, peas, barley, corn, acorns and dandelions. In *Roughing It in the Bush* Susanna Moodie tells how she made "excellent" coffee from dandelion roots. (This was in the fall of 1835.) "I washed the roots . . . without depriving them of the fine brown skin, which contains the aromatic flavour so like coffee while roasting. I cut them the size of a kidney bean, and roasted them on a pan in the stove oven, until brown and crisp as coffee. I ground and transferred a cupful of the powder to the coffee pot, pouring upon it scalding water and boiling it briskly for a few minutes. The result was beyond my expectations — far superior to the common coffee procured at the stores."

Like their relatives, the Macdonalds settled near Kingston to carve out a new way of life in this new land.

### Kingston's Unpaved Streets

In *The Advantages of Emigration to Canada* (published in 1831) William Cattermole describes Kingston: "It is perhaps the finest-built town in the Province, and is well situated on the north side of the Saint Lawrence, it was founded in 1783, and now presents a front of nearly ¾ of a mile; in 1828, by census, its population appeared 3,528, but has greatly increased since it was taken, this did not include the troops of the garrison; the streets are regular, but not paved, and like most towns in America, running at right angles. The houses are well built, and chiefly of stone, and present an idea of more comfort than any town in the Upper Province, with little taste as to architectural design or beauty. The public buildings are a government house, courthouse, a Protestant and Catholic church, a gaol and hospital, besides the garrison, block houses, &c. This town has risen considerably in mercantile importance within a few years, strong hopes being entertained, and endeavours having recently been made to induce the Imperial Parliament to remove the seat of Government from York to Kingston, an idea which now appears totally abandoned. The first

**THE EMIGRANT's GUIDE**
TO
*UPPER-CANADA,*
Or Sketches of the present state of that Province, collected from a Residence therein during the years 1817, 1818 and 1819, interspersed with reflections.
*By C. STUART, Esq.*
*Published in London, 1820.*
A few copies of the above useful Work may be had at the Subscribers' Book Store, FREE-MASONS' HALL.
*THOs. CARY, Jr. & Co.*

*The Quebec Mercury* carried this advertisement for *The Emigrant's Guide.*

week in April, Kingston is all bustle for the spring trade, which continues till late in Autumn, during which period vast numbers of schooners from 80 to 150 tons, which navigate the lakes, frequent this port, the steam-boats also add much to its animation. . . .

"The land about Kingston is very inferior, full of stones and rocks, but good land may be found a few miles from it, particularly about the Bay of Quinte. . . . The bulk of the inhabitants are Irish, Scotch, and American."

### Church of Scotland

The Macdonalds were Church of Scotland worshippers. In his book *Emigrants; In a Series of Letters From Upper Canada,* the Reverend William Bell describes the Churches of Scotland in Kingston: "In *Kingston* there are two Presbyterian congregations, and neither of them of long standing. The first was formed in 1817, and they sent to Scotland for a minister soon after. . . . They had, in the preceding year, commenced building a handsome stone church, which is now finished in a very elegant manner. The congregation, which consists chiefly of Scotch emigrants, is numerous and respectable, and seems to be in a prosperous condition. The second congregation of Presbyterians in *Kingston,* consists chiefly of persons from the United States."

The Reverend Bell also lists average prices of provisions, livestock, wages, etc. of 1823 comparing them to the higher prices in 1817 (note that the prices are given either in dollars or in pounds, shillings and pence):

|  | In 1817 | In 1823 |
|---|---|---|
| A barrel of flour | 14 dollars | 4 dollars |
| A bushel of potatoes | 2 do. | 1 shilling |
| A bushel of Indian corn | 2 do. | 2 do. |
| A bushel of wheat | 4 do. | 4 do. |
| Beef or mutton | 9d. | 3d. |
| Pork | 10d. | 3d. |
| Butter | 1s. 8d. | 8d. |
| Cheese | 1s. | 6d. |
| Loaf sugar | 2s. | 1s. |
| Maple sugar | 1s. 3d. | 4d. |
| A man servant | 16 dollars a month | 6 dollars |

THE

# YOUNG EMIGRANTS;

OR,

PICTURES OF CANADA.

CALCULATED TO

AMUSE AND INSTRUCT THE MINDS OF

YOUTH.

BY THE AUTHOR OF

"*Prejudice Reproved,*" "*The Tell-tale,*" &c.

London:

PRINTED FOR HARVEY AND DARTON, GRACECHURCH-STREET.

1826.

An 1826 children's book of romantic engravings and sentiments "calculated to amuse and instruct" gave selective information about life among settlers.

| | |
|---|---|
| A woman 6 do. | 3 do. |
| A good horse 100 do. | 60 do. |
| A good cow 30 do. | 20 do. |
| A sheep 5 do. | 2 do. |

## Hardships of Settlers

*The Emigrant's Guide* warns that life was often hard for settlers in the new country: "When lately passing through Montreal (in October, 1819), an elderly man entered a shop where I stood, and asked the shopkeeper for some assistance for his family, which he declared to be large, and to be in a deplorable condition. I learnt that he was a recently arrived emigrant, and accompanied him to his lodgings. There I found his wife, a decent woman, of middle age, extended in a confined room, extremely reduced by a dangerous fever, and surrounded by seven poor little children, three of whom were sick, and all of whom were helpless.... The poor man... had reached Montreal, just before the beginning of the long and rude winter of that place; to see his family pining in sickness and in want amongst strangers, while the indispensable attendance which they needed forbade him to engage in work which would necessarily have separated him from them, and at the same time, sent him, an often rejected beggar, to the cold and foreign hand of charity."

Enduring hardships and the severity of the winters, the Macdonalds patterned their lives on what they had known in Scotland. Young John A. and his siblings seem to have had a happy childhood. Their easygoing and cheerful father tried his hand at various times as a shopkeeper, manufacturer and miller, but with little success.

Young John A. was growing tall and spindly with strange fuzzy hair that curled in a dark mass. His lanky figure and long lumpy nose caused the girls to mock him as "Ugly John Macdonald" but his intelligent face was pleasing, and he was already showing that he had a natural way with people. All ages were drawn to him.

> Did any of the settlers from the old country wish to return? Said one in Upper Canada in the 1800s: "I have never been home again, although I have often wished to see the place, and I don't think my sons and other Canadians appreciate it half enough; but I have never heard of any emigrant wanting to go back to *live*. If you have thriven here, you are too high to have aught to do with them you have left; and those above you, no matter how you have thriven, are too high to have aught to do with you."

## "Our Red Brethren"

Passages from *The Emigrant's Guide* show the thoughts of the author towards the Indians. Presumably these attitudes were shared even by educated settlers, perhaps out of fear, certainly out of ignorance. The greatest failure of John A.'s career was his inability to understand Louis Riel. Did it result from such early conditioning?

"Here I proceed to complete the sketch of this interesting and unhappy people.... They are orderly, I believe, and somewhat industrious; blessings which they owe, under Providence, to the zeal of the Roman Catholic Church, the

A view of the edges of Kingston, seen through a group of trees, by artist J.P. Cockburn, July 29, 1829.

### For Posterity

When the cornerstone of the Kingston County Courthouse and Jail was laid on May 17, 1824, by Sir Peregrine Maitland, the Lieutenant-Governor, the following items were placed in the compartment for posterity: parchment with inscription; *St. Ursula's Convent, or the Nun of Canada*, the first novel printed in Upper Canada; *Upper Canada Herald* of May 11; *Kingston Chronicle* of May 14; the November 1823 issue of *Christian Register*; the *Upper Canada Almanac* for 1824; report of the Bible Society for 1824; report of the Female Benevolent Society, 1824; a York Bank bill; a sovereign, George IV; several silver and copper coins.

general character of which I deplore....

"They depart imperfectly from their native habits. Their total number is small. With some exceptions, they derive but little benefit from the liberal reserves of the best lands, which the parental wisdom of the Government has secured for them....

"In their natural state, the most ferocious cruelty is equally congenial to them with the most attentive kindness.

"Nor are their manners, notwithstanding this melancholy sketch of them, devoid of interesting particulars. They are still hardy.... Towards each other, they display the most spontaneous and kindly spirit of equity. When they receive a bit of bread or meat, or a little flour, or milk, &c., it is carefully and attentively divided into proportionate shares before it is attempted to be used....

"But still they are a degraded race, and seem rapidly sinking to extinction. In the course of another half century, no genuine trace of them probably will remain in our borders."

The following estimate of the distance from Quebec to Kingston, the time the journey would take and the cost is taken from *The Emigrant's Guide to Upper Canada*.

| Miles | | £ | s. | d. | Time. Days. |
|---|---|---|---|---|---|
| | **BY STEAM-BOATS.** | | | | |
| 180 | From Quebec to Montreal | 3 | 0 | 0 | 2 or 3 |
| | **BY LAND.** | | | | |
| 9 | From Montreal to La Chine          Stage ... | 0 | 5 | 0 | 1 or less |
| | A cart ... | 0 | 12 | 6 | |
| | **BY BOATS.** | | | | |
| 111 | From La Chine to Prescot. Price according to the terms made on the spot. The hire of a whole boat of from two to three tons burthen, completely equipped for the passage, is about £20: say an individual place ........ | 1 | 0 | 0 | 6 or 8, or 10 |
| | Eight days provisions from Montreal to Prescot, say (This is supposing the provisions to be carried with you, and used in the boat); and this is independent of lodging, (unless you choose to lodge in the boat, which would be extremely uncomfortable); and of the transport of baggage. | 1 | 0 | 0 | |
| | **BY STEAM-BOAT.** | | | | |
| 60 | From Prescot to Kingston | 1 | 0 | 0 | 1 |
| **360 miles** | | | **£6/17/6** | | **12 days** |

> ——Ship Earl of Buckinghamshire, Thomas Johnson, 42 days from Greenock, to Mr. Burnett, ballast, 200 settlers——has been on shore in the Traverse.

*The Quebec Mercury* reported the arrival of the ship that brought the Macdonalds.   *PAC*

The Macdonalds had been in Upper Canada only two years when they experienced the first of what would be many personal tragedies in John A.'s life. His younger brother, James, aged five and a half, was struck brutally by a babysitter and died. Shortly afterwards the Macdonalds moved from Kingston to nearby Hay Bay, Adolphustown, Bay of Quinte. The house they lived in is shown above. (The picture was drawn from memory in 1891, the house having burned down some years before.)

RB

# Little brother killed by servant

## *All of parents' hopes now centre on John A.*

The Macdonald family suffered tragedy in 1822, shortly before moving from Kingston to Hay Bay. On a pleasant evening in May, Mr. and Mrs. Macdonald decided to go for a walk. John A.'s little brother, James, ran after them, begging to be taken along. They decided against it, and left him at home in the care of a servant man. When little James would not stop crying, the unsympathetic servant either pushed or struck him, and the boy fell with such force that he was killed. The *Kingston Chronicle* recorded the death:

### Died

On Monday the 22d ult. James, second son of Mr. Hugh McDonald, Merchant of this town, aged five years and six months.

John A.'s other brother, William, had died in infancy, before the family left Scotland. Now John A. was his mother's only surviving son, and on him she pinned all her hopes.

It is said that the reason that Scottish immigrants played such an important role in early Canadian life was because they could read and write. Certainly they placed a high value on education. John A.'s mother kept him in school, convinced of his ability.

### John A. Goes to School

The schoolhouses of the area were all pretty much the same: there was a long rude board that ran round three sides and served as desks for the pupils. The teacher's desk in front was no finer. There was a pail of water in one corner. Usually the schoolmaster was a Scotsman, who handed out rebukes and birchings generously. One of John A.'s teachers — "Old

Hughes" — had perfected a method of taking a boy by the collar and giving him a lift off his feet and a resounding whack at the same time. The skill with which he did this was very interesting to all the boys — except the victim. And Johnny must have enjoyed the exhibition, though he had no love for the chief performer, upon whom he played more than one sly trick.

His father hoped that John A. would become a lawyer, and said of his pranks, "No matter! There goes the Star of Canada!" and "Nae, nae, ye'll hear something from Johnny yet!" His mother always said that "John will make more than an ordinary man." Scottish dominie Pringle, of the Royal Grammar School, said, "Johnny Macdonald has a heid on him like a mon."

John A. walked three miles to school from

the family's home at Hay Bay, Adolphustown, Bay of Quinte. Later, when business vicissitudes caused his father to move, John A. was left with friendly Scottish landladies and relatives so that he could attend the best schools in Upper Canada — the Midland District Grammar School and the Maxwell Academy. There is no doubt that the fees were a heavy drain on the family funds, but his mother particularly felt that he must have his chance.

### Better Lawyer than Clergyman

He had such a clever way of talking himself out of scrapes that one teacher predicted, "You'll make a better lawyer than a clergyman." (A few years later, when John A. was singing in a church choir, the minister remarked that he'd make a better politician than a singer!) As popular with his companions as he was later

*Osborne*

# SCENES IN AMERICA,

FOR THE

AMUSEMENT AND INSTRUCTION

OF LITTLE

TARRY-AT-HOME TRAVELLERS.

BY THE REV. ISAAC TAYLOR.

LONDON:

PRINTED FOR HARRIS AND SON,

CORNER OF ST. PAUL'S CHURCH YARD.

1821.

Title page on one of the most charming children's books on early explorations in Canada, which may have delighted John A.

to be with his associates, John A.'s boyhood passed agreeably. He did not care for athletics, but did love to run in his bare feet, carefree and merry.

Probably John A. used such early schoolbooks as: *A Concise Introduction to Practical Arithmetic*, compiled by the Reverend John Strachan and printed by Nahum Mower of Montreal (the first textbook written especially for the children of Upper Canada, 1809): *Mavor's Spelling Book*, 1828; *The Grammar of the English Language*, English exercises and English reader by Lindley Murray.

John A. was fond of verses. When he was

The Bay of Quinte where John A. passed his childhood summers, when he was not at school in Kingston, may not have looked so romantic as W. H. Bartlett drew it for the above engraving in the late 1830s, but it was beautiful.

thirteen he sent these lines to his cousin, Maria Clark:

*The laughter-loving goddess Mirth,*
*Whom lovely Venus, at a birth*
*With two sister Graces more,*
*To ivy-crowned Bacchus bore,*
*To Scotia Inverness once flew*
*To sip the honey'd mountain dew;*
*She there met Love, that wanton boy,*
*Who does the hearts of youth annoy,*
*And there resolved to form a mind*
*With wit and loveliness combined.*
*For this they got some white, clear clay,*
*And then, before the dawn of day,*
*They picked the wild flowers of the mount,*
*And bathed their bosoms in a fount;*
*With these they formed a beauteous frame,*
*Well known for wit and mirth by fame;*
*Mirth then found a lovely smile,*
*And Cupid added a wanton wile;*
*To these, the sigh which Pity wears,*
*And Phaeton's pining sister's tears,*
*All these, with clay our earthly part,*
*Formed a feeling, laughing heart,*
*To these were placed the ethereal spark,*
*And from this rose Maria Clark.*

### "I Had No Boyhood"

Although his headmaster Cruikshank regarded him as a most promising student, John A. left school in 1830, at the age of fifteen. Later in life he often deplored his lack of higher education. "If I had had a university education," he once confided to his secretary, Joseph Pope, "I should probably have entered upon the path of literature and acquired distinction therein." His letters were always interesting and entertaining. As his speeches in the years ahead were to show, he had spent time, with profit, on the study of Latin, French and mathematics. Above all, he had already developed a profound love of books.

John A.'s formal education over, he began to look about him for an occupation. "I had no boyhood," he said. "From fifteen I began to earn my own living." That same year he paid the £10 fee, and the Law Society Common Roll, No. 210 of Osgoode Hall, the Law Society of Upper Canada, indicated that: "John Alexander McDonald [note the misspelling] was admitted as a student in Hilary Term, 10th year of George IV's reign, 1829-30."

*(continued)*

# Kingston a good place for a bookworm

Upper Canada was the most active centre of bookselling and publishing in British North America. The *Kingston Gazette* was established in 1810, ten years before the Macdonalds came to the area.

What was being published? Some schoolbooks, political pamphlets, religious tracts and the like. There were few children's books as we know them. Instead a variety of small tracts were deemed to be useful and entertaining for young people. What books there were for juniors came from England and the United States.

In the early 1800s Stephen Miles, printer, ran a small bookstore and lending library in Kingston. His earliest competitor, Hugh C. Thomson, founded the *Kingston Herald* in 1819 and was most energetic in the publishing field. He issued two early volumes of verse in 1824 and a two-volume novel *St. Ursula's Convent, or The Nun of Canada*, the first piece of fiction by a native Canadian, Julia Beckwith Hart, wife of a Canadian bookbinder. It appeared anonymously. *St. Ursula's Convent* was very much the soap

opera of its time offering plot and counterplot with something for everyone: romance, adventure, shipwreck, incest, religion, war and even silver mining. Actually there were enough plots for several novels! Although 165 copies were printed, only three and a half sets are known to still exist. One set is owned by the Toronto Public Library, one by the Library of Congress in Washington and one by the Library of the University of New Brunswick. The half set is the second volume and it is privately owned. Although these books are priceless today the Toronto Library picked up its prize about seventy-five years ago for eight dollars.

An earlier book, *The History of Emily Montague*, printed in London in 1769, is often erroneously cited as the first Canadian novel. Its author, Frances Brooke, was the wife of the first clergyman of the Church of England in Quebec City. She wrote on the manners and life of that area. In the book she says, "I would rather live at Quebec, take it all in all, than in any town in England, except London; the manner of living here is uncommonly agreeable."

# Birch rod kept handy in schools of Scottish settlers

*march of Intellect*

*School in Adelaide
visited Dec 1845
Teacher Mr St Leger
Sketched at the time*

Typical of schools attended by the children of Scottish immigrants in Upper Canada was this one in Adelaide. The Scottish schoolmaster, an authoritarian figure who believed in corporal punishment as an incentive to learning, was known as a *dominie,* and John A. liked to assert his independence by playing tricks on one of his dominies called "Old Hughes," who was noted for his style of birching.

## An Accident Averted

John A.'s nephew reported that "little Johnnie was very fond of playing soldier. He was always captain and his two sisters were the company. One day Louisa would not march properly, but went skipping about the room to his great indignation; so he picked up an old gun, and, pointing it at her, called out in wrathful tones, 'Louie, if you don't be quiet, I'll shoot you!' She still kept playing about and he repeated the threat. His sister, Margaret, got very frightened and cried out, 'Oh! Johnnie, Johnnie, put that gun down,' which he did, most providentially, for it was afterwards ascertained to have been loaded."

## Remedies

Dip a penny in vinegar and rub over fever blisters till they disappear.

Eat a large slice of bread spread with fresh skunk oil morning and evening to cure rheumatism.

Pitch of pine trees will cure sores and boils.

Cayenne pepper and soda will prevent nightmares.

Castor oil will end warts. Apply the oil when the moon is full. As the moon wanes the warts disappear and won't come again.

## Sir John A.'s Fishy Reply

*Allen Ross Davis tells this story in* Bay of Quinte Landmarks:

When Sir John A. Macdonald was addressing a political meeting in Adolphustown Town Hall, the chairman called upon Gilbert "Guy" Casey, an old resident, to address the packed audience. He said: "As you all know, my farm nearly adjoins the farm on Hay Bay, where the Macdonald family lived. The morning after they moved in, while I was fishing in Hay Bay at the front of our home, I noticed this lad, John A., coming along the shore where I was catching some very good fish — perch, bass and pickerel. As he came up I flung out a pretty big one, and throwing it from my line up on the bank, I spoke to this big-nosed Scotch kid, about eight years old, while I was putting another worm on my hook. He told me his name, and where he lived, with his two sisters, and father and mother, as he examined the fish, flopping about on the bank. He was greatly excited, and rushed down to the water as I pulled them out, and then up the bank as I threw them to safety. This went on for some time when, as I turned to throw up another fish, I saw the rascal legging it for home as fast as he could go, with my biggest and choicest black bass. I yelled at him, but he only ran the faster, and never let up till he reached home. Now, Mr. Chairman, before this large audience of electors of Adolphustown, I charge this candidate of that deliberate theft, many years ago, and, sir, if he will not acknowledge it here and now, and ask my pardon, I shall vote and use my influence against him in the election."

Sir John was as solemn, when he arose from his seat on the platform, as was the speaker who had just sat down, and the grave faces of the audience displayed their fear that Casey had been nursing an old grudge all these years, the telling of which, and the demand for asking his pardon might have given offence.

"Mr. Chairman, and yeomen of Adolphustown," began Sir John, slowly, and in a low tone. "What my old neighbour has told you about my theft of his beautiful fish is absolutely true; and I can recall as though it were but yesterday how frightened I was at that unearthly yell of our good friend, which almost caused me to drop the fish so as to make better speed; but I managed to hold on to it when I saw he was not chasing me. I was clean out of breath when I burst into the house and fell headlong with it on the floor, and gasped for breath as I told my father where I found it, and that there were lots more where this came from. I humbly beg your pardon, Guy, and my only regret is that I can't steal another one like it here tonight, and have it for breakfast in the morning. Mother said it was the best black bass she ever cooked."

Everyone laughed heartily. Sir John carried that meeting, and in the end won the election.

# At 15 John A. is law student

## Learns to be popular

### Opens office, starts practice; Not yet called to Bar

In Upper Canada there was as yet no formal education in law. An ambitious youth who wished to become a lawyer qualified by attaching himself to a legal firm, where he made himself useful all day and read law by night. At the beginning and end of his legal training, the apprentice faced examinations by the Law Society of Upper Canada.

Fifteen-year-old John A. followed in this tradition and was articled as a student to George Mackenzie, a prominent lawyer of Kingston, himself only thirty-five. Since John A. boarded with the Mackenzies, his tutelage continued till all hours. Mackenzie, clever, hardworking and ambitious, began to be involved in large financial and corporation matters; it was excellent experience for a beginner of John A.'s temperament.

In 1832, when Mackenzie opened a branch office at the tiny pioneer·village of Napanee, with John A. as manager, the apprentice felt that he was nearly "on his own." There he learned from his senior the well-known maxim:

*Say nothing on business without receiving a fee in advance.*

Already, a bookworm, John A. read widely in every field — novels, poetry, history, biography, philosophy, economics and politics. He seemed never to forget anything, as his colleagues were to learn. This love of books stayed with him all his life. He made friends of those who had books, and read through their collections.

### Be Free and Lively

Because John A. was considered by some to be stand-offish, Mackenzie wrote to his young law clerk: "I do not think you are so free and lively with people as a young man eager for their good should be. A dead-and-alive way with them never goes." This admonition changed John A., and he became known for his repertoire of anecdotes, for playing the fool and for his nice sense of comedy. His manner, no longer studious and reserved, brought him friends easily and he was much sought after. He had total recall of everything that he had heard or read so that he was a fascinating conversationalist and companion; he went to parties and dances, sang in the choir, and spent the occasional evening out "with the boys."

When his lawyer cousin, Luther Macpherson of Hallowell, Prince Edward County, became ill, John A., loyal to the needs of the family, took over the business. He had a good deal of responsibility with a large general practice. The way the eighteen year old handled practical matters so impressed the important citizens of Picton and Hallowell that they offered him one hundred pounds if he would remain there.

### "Hit Him Again"

According to Wallace, it was in Picton that John A. conducted his first case in court, an occasion that became famous. As Wallace tells it in his biography of Macdonald: "He had a hot Highland temper; and while arguing the case in court, he fell foul of the opposing counsel. To the scandal of the judge, the two disputants closed in physical combat in open court. The court crier was immediately

instructed to enforce order, and circling about the combatants, he proceeded to cry loudly, 'Order in the court, order in the court.' But, being a staunch friend of Macdonald's, he took the opportunity, when Macdonald came near him, to whisper loudly, 'Hit him again, John, hit him again.'"

Showing an interest in the communities of Hallowell and Picton, he became the first secretary of the Hallowell Young Men's Society and secretary of the Prince Edward District School Board.

In 1834, Kingston was hit hard by an epidemic of Asiatic cholera. Among the victims was John A.'s former employer, George Mackenzie. In these sad circumstances, John A. fell into Mackenzie's practice, which was considered one of the best in Kingston.

By 1835 clients were telling one another that "he is quick as a flash" and "we must send him to the House." They chuckled over news of his latest antics — for he had played many a joke on those about him and he was becoming known for his parts in amateur theatricals, serio-comic burlesque and the like.

Between the ages of sixteen and twenty he passed all the examinations which qualified him to become a barrister and he was fully

Hallowell as it looked to William Bartlett a few years after John A. — then eighteen — took over his cousin's law practice. Young Macdonald was so successful that the townspeople offered him a £100 retainer if he would remain with them.

prepared for his profession before he could legally practice it, not yet having reached his majority. Although he was not eligible for admission to the bar, his professional card appeared in the *Kingston Chronicle & Gazette* on August 24, 1835.

---

JOHN A. MACDONALD,
ATTORNEY, &c.
Has opened his office, in the brick building belonging to Mr. Collar, opposite the Shop of D. Prestion, Esq., Quarry Street, where he will attend to all the duties of the profession.
Kingston, 24th August, 1835       17ew

---

When he became twenty-one, in 1836, he graduated as a lawyer. The Law Society's Barrister's Roll made the announcement:

---

From the Upper Canada Gazette
OSGOODE HALL
*Hilary Term, 6th William 4.*

On Saturday the sixth day of February, in this said term of Hilary —
Mr. John Alexander McDonald was called to the degree of Barrister at Law.

---

John A. lost several of his early cases, which prompted a friend to remark, "John, we'll have to make you our Attorney-General — you're so successful at getting convictions."

### Pigs Vs. Dogs

In *Three Years in Canada* Preston describes the town where John A. practiced: " Kingston in 1837 had between 4,000 and 5,000 inhabitants.... It resembles an English village but somewhat stragglingly built.... Among the minor characteristics of Kingston, I must not omit to mention the endless outdoor squabbles of its pigs and dogs, which infest the streets in shoals. A ruthless war is waged by the canine upon the swinish multitude; and as these have a peculiar way of acknowledging such courtesies, the effect of the din of voices in discordant eloquence may readily be conceived."

John A. now had an articled clerk, sixteen-year-old Oliver Mowat, who later became Liberal Premier of Ontario and one of John A.'s main political rivals.

---

### Cure for a Sleepyhead

According to his nephew, young John A. hated to get up in the morning. He was cured of this when he was fifteen years old and living with the Mackenzies. As Macpherson tells it in his biography of his uncle: "Mrs. Mackenzie was a kind-hearted soul, but was much worried by the difficulty of getting John out of bed in the morning, he was such a sleepyhead. So one day, finding she couldn't rouse him, she darkened his room so that not a ray of light could enter. After a time he woke up, but found all darkness. After vainly trying to go to sleep again, he got up, drew the curtains, and looked out of the window, when, to his astonishment, he saw the men returning from their work. He was so ashamed that a similar difficulty never recurred."

---

# Cholera ravages Canadian cities

## 1200 die in Kingston, 2000 in Montreal

Dreadful cholera epidemics raged through Canada in 1832, 1834, 1849 and 1854.

### Cholera Hits Kingston

Burleigh gives an account of the cholera in Kingston in *Forgotten Leaves of Local History*. "The Asiatic Cholera first came to notice in Bengal in 1817. By 1823 it had reached Asia Minor and Russia. By 1830 it had spread across North and Central Europe. In October, 1831, it appeared in England, reaching London in January. Before Spring had merged into Summer, cases of cholera appeared in North and Central America.

"Having been forewarned of the impending epidemic of Asiatic Cholera, the Port Authorities in Quebec prepared for the worst. Arriving vessels were quarantined, and a careful inspection of boat and passengers was completed. The passengers were then detained for observation. Any illnesses were hospitalized until diagnosis could be made. Cholera cases were then isolated in a specially prepared section of the hospital.

"The symptoms of cholera were easily recognized — nausea and vomiting, purging, dizziness, cramps of hands and feet and abdomen, rapid loss of flesh, with a bluish tint of the skin. . . .

"The fear of the approaching scourge caused alarm in all quarters of the town of Kingston. The Board of Health planned as best they could. May 16 was observed as a Public Fast Day. It was a day of humility and prayer to ask the Deity to avert 'the impending pestilence and rescue them from the destruction that wasteth at noon-day.' A sincere attempt was made to reduce the number of illicit taverns, in the hope of reducing the consumption of strong drink. Groups of men were hired to remove the filth which littered the streets and environs. The primitive hospital operated by the Female Benevolent Society was alerted: army tents and ramshackle sheds were set up along the water front in preparation for the isolation of the immigrants and the treatment of the sick among them.

"These attempts proved futile, when, on May 20, ten days after the arrival of the first case of cholera in Quebec, the first case arrived in Kingston harbour on the Steamer *Carrick*.

"More than 1,200 persons [including John A.'s first employer, George Mackenzie] died of cholera in Kingston and neighbouring communities in 1832. Two years later, in 1834, it is reported that 300, out of a population of 5,000, succumbed to the cholera."

### "Have You Any Dead?"

Montreal was hit hard by the cholera epidemic of 1832. Almost 2,000 people died in a city of less than 30,000. Men drove carts with yellow flags in front through the streets; the drivers cried out, "Have you any dead?" Susanna Moodie was in Montreal in the summer of 1832 and recorded her impressions: "The sullen toll of the death-bell, the exposure of ready-made coffins in the undertakers' windows and the oft-recurring notice placarded on the walls, of funerals furnished at such and such a place, at cheapest rate and shortest notice, painfully reminded us, at every turning of the street, that death was everywhere — perhaps lurking in our path."

There were many cures — all unsuccessful — for cholera in the mid-1800s. One of them was to "burn a few corks to charcoal until they can be bruised as fine as lampblack. Mix two large teaspoonsful with one-half tea cup of equal parts milk and water. Take a dessert spoonful night and morning, more often if violent. A teaspoon twice a day is enough for a child."

Rumours told of Stephen Ayres — "the cholera doctor who came from nowhere" in 1832 to save many lives. First he would rub the patient with an ointment of lard, maple sugar and ashes from the maple tree; he would then give a hot draught of maple sugar and lye, causing violent

*Toronto*

---

# CHOLERA BULLETIN.

#### Printed at the Wesleyan Office.

## TO the President of the Board of Health of the Gore District:

Sir----I have this morning received a communication from Doct. GILPIN of Brantford, stating he was called to visit Three cases, which he considers exhibited characters of Spasmodic Cholera. One case, a man by the name of *Young*, proved fatal in 8 hours. The other two were convalescent when Doctor Gilpin writes.

The following is a report I submit to the Board of Health, on the above cases:

## Cases of CHOLERA in the Gore District, from June 23, to June 25, inclusive----

### Brantford, Cases THREE, Deaths 1, Convalescent 2.

(Signed)           SLADE ROBINSON,
Pres't Medical Board.

*Hamilton, June 27, 1832.*

'Cholera swept across Canada in waves between 1832 and 1854, killing thousands and striking panic everywhere. Typical of the almost daily bulletins issued is this one in Hamilton. Among the worst hit cities was Kingston, where John A.'s employer, George Mackenzie, succumbed to the disease.

perspiration. In an hour the patient's cramps subsided, he slept and woke up restored to health. It was said that the doctor cured an entire Indian village of the pestilence.

### People Drop in Streets

Mary McLean survived the cholera of 1832. Burleigh recorded her story: "On the tenth of May, 1832, my parents, with their eight children, sailed from Ireland for America and . . . landed in Quebec on the tenth of June. Imagine our feelings at finding ourselves in a plague-stricken city, where men, women and children, smitten by cholera, dropped in the streets to die in agony. Where business was paralyzed and naught prevailed but sorrow mingled with dread and gloom.

"The most skillful physicians were baffled by the scourge and were not unanimous in accounting for even its presence. Some asserting it came over in ships; others that the wind carried it; and, to prove this latter theory, hoisted a long pole, to the end of which was tied a leg of lamb, into the upper air; and certain it is that the side of the leg on which the wind blew turned putrid.

"People passed us, each holding between the teeth a piece of stick or cane about the length of a hand, and as thick as the stem of a clay tobacco pipe, on the end of which was stuck

*Lande*

---

## A FORM

OF

## PRAYER

WITH

## THANKSGIVING,

TO

## ALMIGHTY GOD:

TO BE USED UPON SATURDAY, THE 1st DAY OF NOVEMBER, 1834; BEING THE DAY APPOINTED BY PROCLAMATION FOR A GENERAL THANKSGIVING TO ALMIGHTY GOD:

To acknowledge His great Goodness and Mercy in removing from us that grievous Disease, with which several places in these Provinces have been lately visited.

### By Authority

KINGSTON, U.C.

PRINTED BY JAMES MACFARLANE AND COMPANY.

1834.

---

a piece of smoking tar. We learned this was used as a preventative.

"During the night, I became ill, and the following morning was advised to walk slowly on the wharf, which I did, and was passing a heap of coal there when suddenly, blinded and speechless but conscious, I fell against it. The captain of our ship, who was standing near, ran forward and raising my head, told his friend to bring from the ship, as quickly as possible, a tumblerful of brandy with a teaspoonful of red pepper stirred through it. This the captain poured down my throat, as if it were water. To me it was tasteless. . . . He and his friend raised and carried me to a conveyance called a sick cart. . . . We were driven to an hospital on the outskirts of the city. And soon I found myself on one of the camp beds which were placed in rows in the wards, in such a way as to accommodate as large a number of patients as possible. And off of which many a one rolled (and grovelled on the floor) while suffering indescribable torments from the deadly cramps of Asiatic Cholera which now had me in its grasp. . . .

### Coffins Made Non-Stop

"I was now in a veritable house of torture where the most appalling shrieks, groans, prayers and curses filled the air continually and, as if in answer to all this, day and night, from the sheds outside came the tap, tap, tap of the workmen's hammers; as they drove the nails into

the rough coffins which could not be put together hastily enough (for the many) whose shrieks subsided into moans which gradually died away into that silence not to be broken. And whose poor bodies were then carried to the dead house in the hospital yard, coffined, piled on the dead cart — a substitute for hearses and hurried off to what was called the Cholera Burying Ground, where so great was the Mortality at the time corpses were buried five and six deep with layers of lime between, in one grave.

"All the medical men's efforts to save were futile until I fell into their hands. And as I slowly but surely recovered, such interest was centred in my case, that four doctors at a time would stand bending over me noting anxiously each symptom of returning health. . . .

"Six weeks from the time of entering the hospital, I was sent to the recovery sheds adjoining, where, sad to say, some who were cured of cholera, contracted small pox and returned to the hospital and died. While in the recovery sheds, we were allowed daily the juice of six lemons and a handful of peppermints. My father brought me a fresh supply of both each morning. And at the end of a week was told that he might take me away."

### Dread Disease Returns

An advertisement appeared in the *Kingston Chronicle & Gazette* of August 2, 1834, for:

ANTI-CHOLERA PILLS

Surgeon Adamson, H.P. of the Bengal

---

Army, has for sale at his residence north end of the town, *Anti-Cholera Pills,* such as were used in India, and prescribed by him while military surgeon, under the command of the Marquis of Hastings, Governor General and Commander in Chief.

The same issue of the newspaper stated that there were several cases of "Asiatic or Spasmodic Cholera" in Kingston. An editorial condemned the press of Lower Canada for refusing to acknowledge that cholera had struck there. "If the papers of Lower Canada are to be believed, there has been but little or no Cholera. What is the truth? Why, that the destroying angel has cut down hundreds of victims, and this being the truth (Oh, shame!) the people of one city are absolutely *congratulated* on its favourable state of health. Are the feelings of friends and relatives at a distance thus to be trifled with? Is the unwary stranger to be entrapped into an infected atmosphere, to serve the purpose of trade? Are people to have the pestilence come upon them, like a thief in the night, without a moment's friendly warning? The silence of some of our contemporaries is criminal and shameful."

### Stock of Medicines for a Family, Upper Canada, 1832

The following ingredients (used alone or in combination) were thought to be sufficient to cure any disease:

1 oz. of the emetic herb (lobelia)
2 ozs. cayenne
½ lb. bayberry root bark in powder
1 lb. poplar bark
1 lb. ginger
1 pt. rheumatic drops (high wines, brandy, gum myrrh and cayenne)

# John A. carries musket in '37

*As a young lawyer, he eyes politics but waits*

## Kingston is capital of new "Canada"

The year 1837 saw rebellion in Upper and Lower Canada. The rebellion in Upper Canada ended quickly, and its leader fled to the United States. The rebellion in Lower Canada was more serious, complicated by bitter feelings between the French and English. After some fighting, the rebels were defeated and the leader Papineau and his followers fled to the United States. (Among those who followed Papineau in the Rebellion of 1837 were George Etienne Cartier, who would become one of the Fathers of Confederation; Hippolyte Lafontaine who was Prime Minister of Canada from 1848 to 1851; and Augustin Morin, who was an important political figure in the Hincks-Morin and McNab-Morin administrations.)

### Troops Eat Raw Sauerkraut

In *Humours of '37* Robina and Kathleen M. Lizars quote troops who fought against the rebels: "After eating, we joined the Orangemen in the next room, drinking grog and singing. That was our tenth day out, and that supper was my third meal. Generally our meals consisted of sucking a corner of a blanket; we kept our mouths moist that way, and averted faintness and reeling.... As we marched into Hamilton we had to pass by my door, so I marched . . . into it. Of my three meals in two weeks, only one was at the expense of the Government.... A private from Hamilton nearly perished after eating . . . raw frozen sauerkraut. We had no rest and little to eat; no salt at all, and our rations only frozen bread. We would gnaw and then . . . rest our jaws."

Like all able-bodied men of those days, John A. was a member of the Sedentary Militia. He said: "I carried my musket in '37.... The day was hot. My feet were blistered. I was but a weary boy and I thought I should have dropped under the weight of the old flint musket which galled my shoulder, but I managed to

> Duke of Wellington to the Colonial Office, 1837: "If you lose Upper Canada, you will lose all your colonies, and if you lose them you may as well lose London."

keep up with my companion, a grim old soldier, who seemed impervious to fatigue." However, John A. did not see combat on this or any other occasion.

### Canada Invaded!

In 1838 an armed force invaded Upper Canada from the United States. The intention was to "liberate" the Canadians. After a battle at Windmill Point, near Prescott, the whole band was either killed or captured. One of the leaders was a Pole, General Nils von Schoultz, a romantic and tragic figure. Von Schoultz had fought against the tyranny of the Russians in Poland where he had lost his entire family. An idealist, he apparently believed sincerely that the Canadians were suffering under the British yoke, and would rush to join him to fight against their oppressors.

Von Schoultz and the other leaders were put on trial, and John A. became famous for defending him — a defense which, in fact, never existed! As Biggar says, "There was no speech made by John A. Macdonald at the trial, and the stories of the great forensic effort which helped to make the young lawyer famous are baseless unless the drawing up of Von Schoultz's will could be considered a ground. Almost every biographical sketch written about Sir John speaks of this remarkable speech, which was never made.... Sir John himself, not long ago, replying to the writer on this point, wrote, 'I never delivered any speech in favour of Von Schoultz, in 1838, or at any other time.' Now, how did the impression get abroad and become fixed in the public eye as one of the romantic incidents that formed a turning point in Sir John's career? That is a mystery."

In fact Von Schoultz pleaded guilty, and so there was no defense. Macpherson suggests that "the brilliant defense with which history has credited" John A. may have been that of Daniel George, paymaster to the rebels. Brilliant though John A.'s defense was, George was convicted and hanged as was Von Schoultz.

### Von Schoultz Hangs

A seven-year-old boy witnessed the hanging of Von Schoultz on December 8, 1838. His account is recorded by Burleigh: "The morning Von Schoultz was to be hanged, I was ordered to keep at home, but I got out, attracted by the soldiers. They were about the jail. Von Schoultz came out attended by two priests, one on each side of him. He was placed in a cart and the company proceeded to the fort. Boylike I followed and was soon trudging along with the soldiers across the bridge and up the fort hill. When the gallows was reached . . . an upright post with an arm and a rope . . . the cart drove under the arm, the rope was adjusted, the prayers said, and then the cart drove ahead, leaving the man dangling from the rope. I hur-

Von Schoultz, the romantic rebel leader who wanted to "free" Canada from the British yoke, was imprisoned in Fort Henry near Kingston following his capture in 1838. John A. was often credited with defending him, but actually only drew up his will, in which he left £400 to the widows and children of the men who had been killed fighting against him.

*RB*

At the time of the Rebellion of 1837 John A. was a young lawyer of twenty-two still living with his parents in this house on Rideau Street, Kingston. He busied himself with local affairs, helping to found Queen's University and the St. Andrew's Society, while he waited for the right moment to enter politics.

ried home after the sight only to be whipped for my disobedience. Von Schoultz's remains were turned over to a Kingstonian who had them buried in the cemetery at the head of Clergy Street. He reared a stone to the memory of his countryman. Quite a few years ago the body was transferred to St. Mary's Cemetery along with many others."

It was reported that Von Schoultz left £400 to the widows and children of the Canadians who had been killed fighting against him.

With the continued expansion of business, John A. acquired another articled clerk, seventeen-year-old Alexander Campbell, who was to remain his associate for years.

In 1839 John A. became solicitor to the Old Commercial Bank and to the Trust and Loan Company, both strong corporations, and began to support his parents and sisters. He con-

---

*This letter shows John A.'s interest in righting an unfair situation:*
Kingston, December 14, 1839
My dear Sir,

Several applications have been made to me during the summer (& one, half an hour ago) by sailors who had shipped on board of American vessels, and been turned ashore without getting their wages. They are without redress as their accounts are generally under ten pounds and the Masters of the vessels are therefore free from arrest, and redress from the Court of Requests is useless. Might not the English Statutes allowing a Justice of the Peace to try claims for wages by Seamen, summarily, and empowering them to attach the vessel or her tackle be introduced into this country with advantage?

During the summer abandonment of sailors by Yankee captains is an everyday occurrence and some redress should be afforded them . . . I am

My dear Sir
Very truly yours
John A. Macdonald

---

tinued all his life as the counsellor, guardian and final arbiter of his branch of the Macdonald clan, his sense of family responsibility always strong.

---

"Canada will never cost English ministers another thought or care if they will but leave her entirely alone, to govern herself as she thinks fit." *(Humours of '37)*

---

### University Founded

An event of far-reaching significance — the creation of Queen's University — caught his imagination. In December 1839, the congregation of St. Andrew's Church met to establish a new Presbyterian college in Kingston. Young John A. seconded the resolution, regretting the limited means available to the youth of the country for the acquisition of a liberal education. Fifty years later, at the Queen's University Jubilee, Macdonald was heard to remark: "I was a young man, just commencing to practice and being a Presbyterian and a Kingstonian, I was extremely anxious that my native city should have the honour of being a University City. When I arose to move the resolution . . . I was in mortal fright and did not say a single word. *'Obstupui, steteruntque comae, vox faucibus haesit.* I was so dumbfounded my hair stood on end, and my voice stuck in my throat.' . . . I just placed the resolution in the chairman's hands and sat down. My silence was golden and I was cheered more than if I had delivered the eloquent creation I had prepared."

### Kingston Capital — For a Time

During 1840-1841 there was a stir of expectancy in Kingston. The Imperial Act of Union turned Upper and Lower Canada into the new tremendously important Province of Canada. Which city would be chosen as its capital? Former capital cities Quebec and Toronto vied with Bytown (Ottawa), Montreal and Kingston for the honour. When on February 6, 1841, Kingston was named as the capital, the 5,000 inhabitants of the town went wild with joy. John A. measured all the political excitement

---

very carefully in his mind. He was certainly in the right place at the right time.

However matters were not to remain as the Kingstonians so dearly wished. When one crisis followed another, the capital was transferred to Montreal. There the first sessions met late in November 1844, in the new Parliament House at St. Ann's Market, in what is now Place d'Youville, at the bottom of McGill Street. But after some years, the capital was moved once again — this time to Quebec. Macdonald, accepting this as inevitable, wrote to his family: "The French will, I think, be too strong for us, and we must submit going to Lower Canada."

### The St. Andrew's Society

As John A.'s success in community undertakings continued, he involved himself in organizing the St. Andrew's Society of Kingston. Much of his esprit came from his mother — tall, energetic, kind, hospitable, a genuine specimen of a Highland woman — ever his strength and guiding genius. It is said that on the night of his first election to the St. Andrew's Society "the pipers of the lodge, the brethren in kilts with John A. at their head, also in Highland costume, proceeded up Princess Street to his residence at the corner of Barrie and Princess Streets. They were met at the door by his

ILN

mother, who, when the piper stood before her, descended the steps and snapping her fingers, gave the time for an eight-hand Scotch reel, which was indulged in there and then." According to Biggar, John A. played the bagpipes.

Busy as he was, John A. made the time to serve as president of the St. Andrew's Society. About this time John A. said to friends, "If I were only prepared now, I should try for the legislature . . . but it does no harm to wait." While he waited, during the next years, he steeped himself in legal matters, and in all branches of constitutional, political and parliamentary history.

### Father Dies

The Macdonald family experienced a bereavement in 1841, with the death of the father, Hugh Macdonald, for whom John A. would name his second son. From his father, John A. inherited an easygoing understanding and tolerance. Perhaps it was these qualities — in addition to his strict honesty and his generosity — that caused Hugh Macdonald's many business failures. His Glasgow business failed, according to a nephew, "owing to the knavery of his partner. However, his own integrity was unimpeached, and he was permitted by his creditors to retain his library, silver and household effects. This library was afterwards of great use in forming the minds of the children." Hugh Macdonald failed in business enterprises in Kingston, Hay Bay and at a place called The Stone Mills. When the family returned to Kingston in 1836 he took a job in a bank, which he held until his death. The cause of his death is not recorded, but Biggar says, "It could not be wondered at that a man of hospitable disposition like Hugh Macdonald should become so addicted to it [whisky] that his days were probably shortened by it."

# John A. tours the British Isles

*In England he buys books, goes to bachelor's ball*

## In Scotland he falls in love and buys a kilt

What with grief at his father's death and constant overwork due to the expansion of his practice, John A. — who was never robust — became quite ill in 1842. Since nothing seemed to renew his energy and strength, a friend suggested that he take a trip to Great Britain, urging that the sea voyage would be beneficial.

This visit to his mother country, his first since his arrival in Canada as a child in 1820, greatly influenced John A.'s future. He loved England and Scotland, and this affection was to grow with the years and strongly influence his political actions. It also was to set the course of his family life — his first wife was a Scots lass whom he met on that very journey. (Years later he proposed to his second wife in London and was married there.)

John A. gloried in the sights and traditions of London, Oxford and Cambridge. He was ever on the go and enjoyed being entertained. As an eligible and witty young bachelor he was invited everywhere.

Loving books as he did, he added to his library with purchases to the amount of £160 from a bookstore in Chancery Lane. He may have used the winnings from a card game for this indulgence. We are told that he played *one hundred* with four friends for three nights, winning steadily. He never again played cards for money.

Back home in Canada, the Macdonalds were reassured about his health when they learned of his huge appetite. On March 3, 1842, he wrote to them from London: "You would be surprised at the breakfast I eat. Roll after roll disappear — and eggs — and bacon. My dinners are equally satisfactory to myself and expensive to my chopman. Now fancy a fried sole with shrimp sauce, a large steak, bread and cheese, a quart of London stout. . . . I find it necessary to support myself against the tremendous exercise I take every day."

John A. felt very much at home in the beautiful and romantic city of Edinburgh, where he shopped for a kilt and full Highland gear.

By the same post he wrote to his mother: "At Manchester I am going to purchase . . . damask, an iron railing for the house, and a kitchen range. Paper hangings and some chimney ornaments I shall buy and send out by Quebec. I am going to a Bachelor's Ball at Manchester, on the 30th."

### Falls in Love

In spite of the Manchester belles at the bachelor's ball and his many social invitations in London, John A. tore himself away to renew family ties with relatives in Scotland. There, he fell in love with his cousin Isabella, the daughter of Captain William Clark of Dalnavert, although she was thirty-three to his twenty-seven years. When they parted it was not for long, as a year later she came to Kingston to visit her sister, Mrs. Maria Macpherson.

Romance set the tone for John A.'s sojourn in Scotland, where he was delighted with his ancestors and felt much in harmony with their way of life. This rapport probably moved him to order for himself a full Highland costume as "worn by Gentlemen." Enclosed with the bill for the gear was a letter from his tailor in Edinburgh who included complete instructions for wearing the impressive regalia, even to the proper placing of the *Skein Dhu,* or black knife.

## Both Queen Victoria and young John A. visited this Edinburgh in 1842

EDINBURGH CASTLE FROM THE GRASSMARKET.

EDINBURGH FROM THE CALTON HILL.

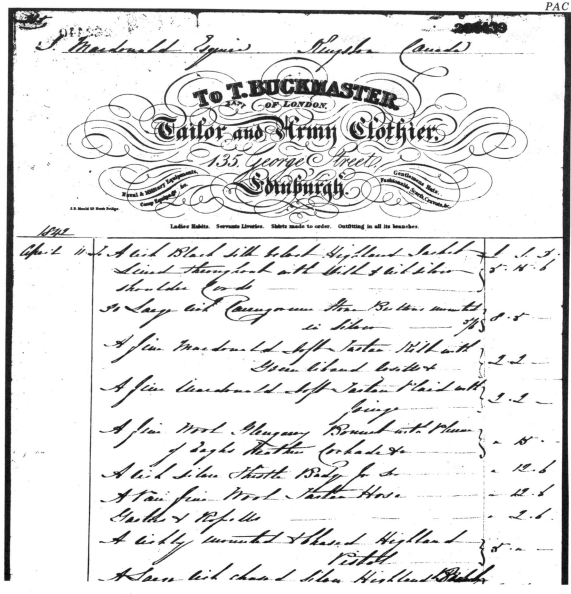

### How To Put On A Kilt
*Memorandum for Dressing*

| | |
|---|---|
| Kilt | is put on with galluses behind and to hang about an inch above the cap of the knee. Pins are used and green ribands tied in bows at right side. |
| Hose | kept up with India Rubber garters with scarlet bows, on side of leg, turning top of hose down over garters, so as the garters may not be observed. |
| Shoes | generally made of patent leather, to which is attached the silver buckles. |
| Purse | buckled over haunches to hang well down in front. |
| Belt | for waist, put on so as silver plate to be right in centre, previous to fastening, which you will please attach to the small belt by side of waist. |
| Dirk | which hangs on the right side. |
| Jacket | hook and eyed up front. |
| Scarf | hang over left shoulder and under right arm, to be tight across chest fastened with |
| Brooch | top of shoulder if anything inclining to front. |
| Shoulder belt | over right shoulder keeping the ends of the scarf clear both back and front. |
| Horn | hung over left shoulder so as to hang a little under right arm. |
| Pistol | hooked in belt left side inclining towards front. |
| Skein Dhu | or small dagger stuck into stocking outside right leg inclining towards front up to the kilt (sometimes spelled Skeann Dhu, this means the Black Knife). |

## "We have furnished you with a silk velvet Highland jacket…"

Dear Sir,

We beg very respectfully to advise having forwarded today by railway to Glasgow to sail by tomorrow's steamer from Glasgow to Liverpool, to your address in care of Mr. John Elliott, shipping agents, Box, containing the full Highland appointments which we trust will be received safe and on examination, in every respect, give satisfaction. It has been our endeavour to furnish that which in the hopes of this meeting with your entire approbation.... We have furnished you with a Silk Velvet Highland Jacket, instead of tartan as mentioned by you, as we found on our Travellers return from the North that they are more generally worn by Gentlemen as strictly in character and, of course, much richer. We endeavoured however notwithstanding to keep within the price mentioned by you. We have also thought it advisable to send you an airtight coat case. This perhaps you will not object to, as it will at all times prevent damp or dust getting to them. In case you may have an opportunity of letting any of your friends who may wish such a case supplied the price, we have taken the liberty of enclosing particulars and should we have the pleasure of receiving through your recommendations any commands, it will be at all times our constant endeavour in every respect to give entire satisfaction. For your guidance in passing on the info. we have given a few particulars on the other side in the order. You will find it most convenient.... Trusting everything will be received safe and in good order, we remain, sir, respectfully yours, T. Buckmaster, Tailor and Army Clothier, London and Edinburgh.

VIEW OF THE CUSTOM-HOUSE OF LONDON AND THE THAMES.

VIEW OF MANCHESTER.

*The Illustrated London News* published these pictures of London and Manchester in 1842, the year that John A. visited those cities.

# John A. Macdonald would always call Kingston his home

The Macdonald family attended the United Empire Loyalist Church in Kingston.

STORE FIRST OCCUPIED BY HUGH MACDONALD IN KINGSTON.

# PART TWO 1842-1860

*He was a skilled practitioner of the art of politics. I wish I had some of his skill.* Lester B. Pearson

# John A. at 29 enters Parliament

## Blood, whisky, payoffs

*Soldiers prevent massacre at polls;
Triumphant MP carried through city*

Developing his acute and discerning interest in politics, John A. offered himself successfully for municipal honours in February 1843.
To the Free and Independent Electors of Ward No. 4 in the Town of Kingston.
Gentlemen.
Permit me to lay my name before you as a candidate for your suffrages at the election in your ward — as alderman.

I can only assure you, that should I be honoured by your choice my humble exertions shall not be spared in the performance of the duties thereby imposed upon me. I have the honour to be, gentlemen,
Your most obedient servant,
John A. Macdonald

J. E. Collins in his biography of Macdonald reports that a friend of John A. was an eye-witness to that fierce election contest and said, "At every tavern found crowds drunk and fighting. Capt. Jackson, the candidate against Macdonald, had all the noisy and drunken Irishmen in town on his side. . . . I heard a ruffian named Sullivan plotting to prevent Macdonald from speaking . . . and go through his supporters. They knew me well, and I told them I had my eye on them. This prevented a great row. I found our side fairly orderly, for Macdonald had a wonderful way of casting oil on troubled waters. Jackson was overwhelmingly beaten."

### Sudden Downfall

After the votes had been counted, John A.'s supporters were carrying him through the streets in triumph, when they lost their balance and dropped him in a pile of slush. He got up and, brushing off his clothes, said, "Isn't it strange I should have a downfall so soon?"

This was the year that John A. formed a fortunate and enduring partnership with his former apprentice Alexander Campbell. The new shingle stated:

### Macdonald and Campbell
### Princess Street
### Kingston

In 1844, not yet in his thirties, John A. entered the Parliament of Upper Canada representing the Kingston Conservatives in the Legislative Assembly of Canada. The vote stood 275 for him and 42 for his opponent. About the time of the election, John A. was already showing an interest in transportation problems. He said, "In a young country like Canada, I am of the opinion that it is of more consequence to endeavour to develop its resources and to improve its physical advantages than to waste the time of the legislature and the money of the people in fruitless discussion on abstract and theoretical questions of government. One great object of my exertion . . . will be to direct the attention of the legislature to the settlement of the back township district, hitherto so utterly neglected, and to press for the construction of the long-projected plank road to Perth and Ottawa."

### Fever of Agitation

There was a fever of agitation in the air. Everybody was keenly interested in politics —

*PAC*

the cheapest and most easily available form of entertainment. Since the secret ballot did not come until 1874, there was a pretty good check on the voters who were paid off in many ways — with a drink or two, a whole bottle or a fiver. The powerful and successful "pork barrel politics" was based on the large hogsheads of meat, strategically placed, so that a "right" voter could help himself to a large dripping slab.

### Inflamed with Whisky

Of the election of 1844, Collins wrote: "The fury was not alone the property of the hustings during this campaign but it blew a hurricane through the prints as well. Every editor dipped his pen in gall; every column reeked with libel. Those who had no newspapers issued handbills that might have fired the fences on which they were posted. . . . The contest came in November, in a very hurricane of tumult. At more than one hustings blood was shed, and mutual massacre on a general scale only prevented by bodies of soldiers and special constables.

"The worst fiend known to man was loose in those days during elections — the demon of whisky. Near every booth were open houses where the excited mobs drank intoxicants fur-

nished by the candidates till they became mad. For days before polling, ill-favoured-looking persons poured into Montreal, some carrying

---

John A. on Parliament: "Parliament is a grand inquest which has the right to inquire into anything and everything."

---

dirks and slingshots and others pistols . . . and in the riots gave many a bloody account of themselves.

"These were turbulent times in many parts of Upper and Lower Canada. . . . Of a similar character were the crowds that gathered in Kingston. . . . Macdonald addressed several meetings composed of riotous men inflamed with whisky and the worst passions of party. . . . 'Never,' says an eyewitness, 'did he lose temper, but good-naturedly waited till there was a lull in the disturbance. When silence was restored, he said he knew many of the electors and they were all manly fellows — too manly, indeed, to refuse another fair play.' . . . Here was something more than soothing speech; here was the genius of Mark Antony.... Macdonald was carried through the city on a chair, the victor by an overwhelming majority."

### John A. Wears The Silk

Upon being named a Queen's Counsel in 1846, John A. shared the good news of his appointment with his wife's sister, writing that he had "The Mighty right of wearing a silk gown instead of a stuff one."

*The Globe* of Toronto described him as a "man of perfect respectability — industrious and successful in his profession — but far from possessing such talent as would warrant his being made Queen's Counsel. He is however a Presbyterian Tory; of that species of loose fish — who are guided more by personal feeling than by principle, and are prepared to take office under any administration, at the slightest possible notice."

Collins described the young politician: "In his early political life Macdonald often wore baggy trousers, a long-tailed coat and a loose necktie. There was a touch of the theatrical in his appearance — his gestures, even his walk had drama, and he had a way of taking his seat much like a bird alighting from flight. This mannerism was accompanied by a quick glance which seemed to take in everything and everybody in a moment."

However, no doubt influenced by his trip to Great Britain and his recent marriage, John A. was becoming quite elegant and distinguished, even foppish in his odd way, with a tall black hat that made him appear yet taller and thinner, a rich black neckcloth, a full-skirted high-waisted coat and checked or pale grey trousers.

Other changes too were remarked. He had turned away from the harsh whisky that men

---

### No Pay to Rebels

Tory slogan of denunciation of the Rebellion Losses Bill (1849).

---

about him consumed, for he had cultivated a taste for very dry French claret, which he found lighter than Spanish sherry and port. Champagne and brandy were also very much to his liking.

John A.'s first tenure of office was for a period of ten months in 1847 and 1848 when he was appointed Receiver-General. *The Globe,* always ready to attack him, said of the appointment: "He is a third-class lawyer, a harmless man."

Lord Elgin, Governor-General of British North America, was of a different opinion. He wrote: "The prospects of the administration are brighter — a certain Mr. Macdonald, a person of consideration among the moderate Conservative anti-Compact Party, has consented to accept the office of Receiver-General."

---

### For He Was Scotch and So Was She

*They were a couple well content*
*With what they earned and what they spent,*
*Cared not a whit for style's decree —*
*For he was Scotch, and so was she.*

*And O, they loved to talk of Burns —*
*Dear blithesome, tender Bobby Burns!*
*They never wearied of his song,*
*He never sang a note too strong,*
*One little fault could neither see —*
*For he was Scotch and so was she . . .*

*I would not have you think this pair*
*Went on in weather always fair,*
*For well you know in married life*
*Will come, sometimes, the jar and strife;*
*They couldn't always just agree —*
*For he was Scotch, and so was she.*

Jean Blewett

---

# BRITONS! AWAKE!

## "England expects every man to do his Duty."

## To His Worship the Mayor
### OF THE CITY OF KINGSTON.

We, the undersigned, request that you will convene a

# MEETING

### OF THE INHABITANTS OF THIS CITY

# ON MONDAY NEXT,

at 2 o'clock, P. M., at the CITY HALL, for the purpose of taking into consideration the propriety of transmitting to Her Majesty *without a moment's delay* a Petition praying Her to exercise Her Royal Prerogative by disallowing the Bill for rewarding Rebellion, which has been sanctioned in despite of the Remonstrances of her *Loyal Canadian Subjects,* by Her Representative. and also to recall such Representative from a Government which he can no longer administer with safety to the Province or with honor to the Crown.

Kingston, 28th April, 1849.

| | | | |
|---|---|---|---|
| John R. Forsyth, | C. Miller, | A. Foster, | William Kennedy, |
| F. A. Harper, | George Cliff sr. | Peter McDonald, | Archibald Smyth, |
| James A. Henderson, | Henry Sadleir, | James Linton, | James Bibby, |
| William Holditch, | John Macpherson, | Wm. Bowen, | James Chestnut, |
| J. Counter, | William Wilson, | George Andrews, | D. Christie, |
| John Fraser, | Samuel Muckleston, | William Breden, | John Oliphant, |
| Arch. John Macdonell, | Charles Brent, | James Gardiner, | John McQuaid, |
| John Mowat, | Thomas Deykes, | William Graham, | J. J. Burrowes, |
| James Williamson, | A. Campbell, | John Hopkins, | S. Scobell, |
| John Breakenridge, | Charles W. Jenkins, | Alexander Rose, | Richard Scobell, |
| William Wade, | E. H. Hardy, | John Besford, | Samuel Rowlands, |
| R. Allen, | George L. Mowat, | John Flanigan, | C. J. Campbell, |
| Joseph Bruce, | Thomas Penney, | J. Richardson, | Thomas Glassup, |
| D. Prentiss, | B. Meadows, | Samuel Young, | H. Yates, |
| M. Drummond, | Samuel Morley, | John Quiggin, | William Ferguson, |
| John Breden, | M. W. Strange, | D. T. Wotherspoon, | William F. Harper, |
| W. J. Goodeve, | W. A. Geddes, | George Baxter, | Lewis Cameron, |
| Thomas Maxwell, | Francis Henderson, | Thomas Thompson, | J. Wiley, |
| W. Coverdale, | James G. Fortier, | George Spangenberg, | Henry Bartliff, |
| Thomas Overend, | Robert McCormick, | James Glass, | John G. McKay, |
| Henry Andrews, | John Jenkins, | George Kennedy, | Abraham Foster, |

In compliance with the above Requisition, I hereby call a PUBLIC MEETING at the CITY HALL, on MONDAY next, the 30th of April inst., at 2 o'clock, P. M.

## FRANCIS M. HILL,
### Mayor.

This bill, which concerned indemnity to anyone — including Rebels — who had suffered losses in the Rebellion, caused much uproar. The protests resulted in riots in Montreal and in the burning of the Parliamentary buildings.

The Citadel of Kingston, as Bartlett saw it.

John A. as he looked when he married for the first time. He was twenty-eight and Isabella six years older when they wed in 1843. He had met her the year before during his trip to Scotland.

# A marriage of suffering

## For nearly 14 years Isabella is wretchedly ill

## Their first-born dies in infancy

John A. was beginning to dominate the local political scene and it was obvious to all that he was an ambitious man of good judgement. Yet he was capable of following his heart. In a day when "good marriages" were "arranged," this struggling young barrister fell passionately in love with his cousin Isabella Clark, whom he met on his trip to Scotland in 1842.

In 1843 Isabella came to Canada to visit her married sister in Kingston. Her sister's son, James Pennington Macpherson, later wrote a biography of John A. The preface begins: "I can recollect Sir John A. Macdonald as long as I can recollect anything. The first incident that I am able to recall, in connection with him, is

in the year 1843 when I was a little fellow of about four years of age. One of my mother's sisters had, shortly before, arrived from Scotland on a visit to my home in Kingston, and, by her sweet gentleness of manner and tender sympathetic nature, had completely won my baby heart. Sir John, who was always a frequent caller at the house, he being first cousin to both my parents, became more assiduous than ever in his visits, and, one day, it was explained to me that my pretty young aunt and playmate, whom I had learned to love only next to my mother, was to leave us and go away with 'Cousin John,' and would, no longer, be available to tell me fascinating fairy tales or to soothe my sorrows with

her warm caresses. The news seemed to convey the sense of a terrible impending calamity, and I gave utterance to my feelings in bitter sobs. These, in turn, were chased away by bright visions of wonderful things to happen as soon as they returned from the wedding tour and took possession of their own home to which, it was promised, I should be permitted to go as often as I liked."

John A. Macdonald and Isabella Clark were married on September 1, 1843, in St. Andrew's Presbyterian Church in Kingston. Their four-year-old nephew James Macpherson did indeed become one of their most frequent callers. "This house," he wrote later, "was situated on Brock

The only picture of Isabella Clark known to exist. Within a year of their marriage she became ill and remained mostly bedridden for the rest of her life. John A. was frequently called home by distressed friends and relatives who believed that she was on the point of death.

Street, was large and commodious and contained all the comforts and conveniences then known to Canadian civilization. There was also a fine carriage and a pair of horses, 'Mohawk' and 'Charlie.' Here I spent some of the happiest days of my life, being allowed the honour of sitting beside the coachman if the carriage was taken out, or at other times, the almost equally enjoyable privilege of being my uncle's companion in his library. We seldom talked: he was deep in his books, while I had a corner to myself where were gathered together, for my special delectation, numerous illustrated books and such captivating tales as 'King Arthur and his knights of the round table,' 'The Arabian nights

entertainment,' etc., etc. I have no doubt but that I was often troublesome, but I cannot re-collect ever receiving from him one unkind word. On the contrary, I was always made happy by a warm greeting, a pleasant smile, an encouraging word, or an affectionate pat on the head. Often I used to meet him on the street, when going to or from school, and then it was his delight to indulge in the pleasant fiction that he was my debtor to an unknown amount, and proceed to liquidate this debt to the extent of the half-pence he might have in his pocket. These sums seemed to me to represent fabulous wealth, and I grew to regard him, not only as the richest but as the most generous man I had

ever known."

### What Was Her Wretched Illness?

Almost from the beginning John A.'s marriage was clouded, for Isabella was wretchedly ill for thirteen of the fourteen years of their life together. In excruciating pain, she often used opium as an anodyne. What was her dreadful complaint? Did she suffer from tuberculosis? Cancer? Uterine neuralgia? Drug addiction brought on by the dosages she took to relieve her pain? According to Biggar, "she had been a healthy girl, but shortly after they were married she caught cold through sleeping in wet blankets on a steamer, and consumption followed. She was

*(continued)*

Bellevue House, Kingston, or — as John A. called it — The Pekoe Pagoda. When he purchased the fifteen-room Italian-style villa in 1848, he was looking forward to a happy family life with Isabella and his baby son who, John A. said, "sits by the hour now with his mother, as contentedly as possible, all smiles, and crows away from one end of the day to the other." But within the year the little lad died and, to escape the bitter memories, John A. and Isabella moved out of Bellevue House.

sent to health resorts and treated by doctors, but gradually declined."

By the time he was thirty, in 1845, John A.'s legal work and political career were going exceedingly well, but his private life was greatly troubled by the maladies of the two most important women in his life, his wife and his aged mother.

Despite her painful and serious illness, Isabella maintained a bright spirit as evidenced by this letter she wrote her sister: "Kingston, June 11, 1845 John started for Toronto last evening.... Mama has bought a London cap to send you ... just received ... pounced on it ... I am so mad about the bonnet.... I don't think I will be satisfied till I get a red petticoat for you to wear with the yellow stockings.... I bought a beautiful Rutland straw with a wreath of flowers for little Joanna."

At critical periods during his wife's indisposition, John A. literally stole time to write, sometimes daily, to her sister Mrs. Margaret Greene to keep her informed, gently and sympathetically. Two letters follow, written on successive days, just two years after his marriage. Although John A. prepares his sister-in-law for bad news, the invalid wife lived another twelve and a half years and bore him two sons.

Kingston, July 11, 1845
My dear sister,

On this day last year, we left Kingston for New York, but I fear it will be some time before we can hope to do so this year. Isabella has been ill — very ill — with one of her severest attacks. She is now just recovering and I hope has thrown off for the time her terrible disease. Still this is not certain and at all events it has left

her in the usual state of prostration that follows every attack. It may be days — nay weeks — before she has rallied sufficiently to attempt any journey. What to say or do, I know not — the summer is wearing away, and may have nearly terminated before the invalid can be moved. We shall leave the moment she can safely become a traveller and must be guided by circumstances as to the period of our stay in New Haven. I should think it likely that Dr. Knight would send her further South during the winter, and this must be done, tho' I know that Isabella would be much opposed to a separation for all winter.

### Preachy or Peachy

John A. took Isabella to Savannah, hoping that the mild weather would be beneficial to her health. While there he attended a political meeting. He was not impressed with the speaker. He wrote, "He is evidently an able man, with great fluency and force of expression, but he has the great fault of American speakers (with, I believe, the single exception of Webster) of being too theatrical in manner and style." John A. preferred English to Yankee oratory — but he did admit that night that the Americans could concoct a most acceptable peach brandy! He returned to Canada in February and wrote that he was "once more among the frosts and snows of Canada, sucking my paws like any other bear."

All the rest of our Household are well, as are Maria, the little ones, etc. etc. etc. Pray give my love and a kiss to Jane, and
       Believe me ever
         Yours most affectionately,
         John A. Macdonald
I write in the greatest hurry.

Kingston, July 12, 1845
My dearest sister,

When I wrote you yesterday, I expressed my belief that the crisis of the present attack was past. It is so, indeed, my dearest sister, in one sense, her pain has in a great measure left her, but her ability is in the greatest possible degree alarming. She is weaker than she has ever yet been, and there are symptoms, such as an apparent numbness of one limb, and an irregularity in the action of the heart, which made me send for Dr. Sampson, altho' against Isabella's wish.

### In a Most Precarious State

He saw her this morning and says he cannot relieve her and I ought not, my beloved sister, to disguise from you that he thinks her in a most precarious state. I would not write thus plainly to you did I not know your strength of mind, and the impropriety of concealing anything from you. I do not hesitate to tell you that unless God in his infinite mercy works an immediate change for the better, it is impossible for her to remain in her exhausted state for many days.
        Believe me,
         Yours affectionately,
         John A. Macdonald

Searching constantly for a climate that would be beneficial to his wife, he wrote soon after from Oswego: "The exhaustion produced by carrying Isabella down to the boat was dreadful.... We thought she would die on the deck." The following letter was written from the United States later that same year.

Columbia House, Philadelphia
October 31, 1845
My dearest sister,

After our parting on Tuesday evening, we got safely over to the American House in Jersey City. The stairs were narrow and Isphal suffered a good deal before she got to her couch. The perfect quiet of the hotel and streets was very refreshing to her after the noise of the City Hotel, and she soon rallied and was as comfortable as could be expected . . . and yesterday started for the Quaker City. Her fatigues were very great and she was obliged to subdue pain by opium . . . but kept up her spirits. . . . Only think what a journey she had. First to be carried down a narrow stair at Jersey to the cars. Second. A journey in the cars for about seventy miles to Bristol. Third. To be carried in a chair from the cars to the steamboat. Fourth. A voyage of twenty-seven miles to this city and lastly and worst of all, a quarter of a mile's drive in a hack over the rough streets here. It was enough to fatigue a convalescent. I was fearful for a confirmed invalid. I am delighted to see her bear it so well, for she, from fatigue and opium combined, slept from 10 o'clock last night until the morning and is now easy and in good spirits. She never speaks of it, but I am conscious how much she suffers from being away from you, and without the aid of your untiring and judicious attentions, which were always at hand, by night and day when needed.

However Annie and I do our d . . dest (as the Methodists say) to make her comfortable. . . . As the people of this House are civil and attentive, we shall remain until Monday morning, when, God Willing, we will leave for Baltimore by the cars. . . . As you see, we think ourselves pretty strong . . . for so great a strain on our strength.

Isa sends bushels of love to you and Jane and is anxious to know . . . how you bore your journey, how Janie's cold is, and how Uncle and Aunt Maxwell are, how Janie behaved to Mr. Kennys, when they parted in New York, etc. etc. etc. . . . We shall expect to find all sorts of correspondence awaiting us at Savannah. . . . With all sorts of love,

Most affectionately,
John A. Macdonald
Fragment of an old ballad found in the Reticule of a Lady — the Lady unknown, but the handkf, was marked J.G.C.

*How I love dear William Kennys*
*I will press him to my heart,*
*And by and bye, I'll hem his*
*Dickeys all so smart.*

Kingston, as Bartlett drew the view from the Citadel around 1840.

John A. was a tease and probably made up the verse at the end of the letter to josh his niece about her beau, Mr. Kennys.

### Purchased Dearly

About three years after their marriage Isabella became pregnant. Their nephew wrote: "Mrs. Macdonald, having become delicate, started with her husband for the Southern States in order to escape the severity of the Canadian winter. The means of travelling were then of so tedious and trying a nature that before New York was reached she had become so ill that it was impossible to proceed. My mother was sent for and remained many months nursing her sister with all the love and devotion of her warm Highland nature and, when she came back, bore in her arms a dear little baby boy to whom his father's name had been given. He remained with us for some time and became the pet and delight of the whole house."

The Macdonalds were ecstatically happy and, in spite of Isabella's weakened condition, cheerful and optimistic. She wrote her sister, "My soul is bound up in him. God pardon me, if I sin in this. But did I not purchase him dearly?"

### The Pekoe Pagoda

To make his cherished ailing wife and infant son more comfortable, John A. bought Bellevue House, Kingston — a romantic Tuscan villa. With his inimitable sense of raillery, the new proprietor poked fun at its architecture, calling it "The Pekoe Pagoda," "The Most Fantastic Concern Imaginable," "The Tea Cozy Castle," "The Tea Caddy Château," "The Eyetalian Wilar," "Molasses Hall" and "The Muscavado Cottage." About this time the proud young father told friends, "There was never a child who got through his first year with less trouble. . . . God grant it continue so. . . . The boy sits by the hour now with his mother, as contentedly as possible, all smiles, and crows away from one end of the day to the other."

### Sorrowful Farewell

But it did not continue. John A.'s nephew wrote of the death on September 21, 1848, of young John Alexander — "when at, perhaps, the most endearing age, just able to toddle about and to prattle a few words in his sweet infantile language. My mother came home one day and, in tearful words, told us of convulsions and approaching death. A day or two later we were taken to see and to bid a last sorrowful farewell to the little white-robed figure, lying so still and quiet in its tiny cot in a darkened room." No definite medical diagnosis was given out. Some said he died of a "seizure," others that he had fallen. The newspapers reported simply, "the death of the infant son of the Hon. John A. Macdonald."

Neither parent thought they would ever have another child. Isabella's condition did not improve. John A. continued to report to her sister.

My dearest Sister,

I returned last week from Toronto, my dearest sister, where I had been for the fortnight previous attending the sittings of the Court of Queen's Bench. Left poor dear Isabella in her usual state, suffering . . . only able to move from the bed to the sofa, but still patient, resigned and uncomplaining as ever. On my return I found her stronger and better. She had been practising sitting up for a few minutes daily . . . to surprise me by coming to dinner which she effected. We had our little table brought to her bedroom and there we dined in state. For the last three days she has not been so well. The 'tic' has been troubling her much and yesterday she had it severely in her head and has been obliged to take large doses of opium. . . . I am in hopes that the attack is over . . . and that she will be able to resume her habits of exercise. Her time passes very monotonously out here, but not I think unpleasantly.

I leave the house every morning at nine o'clock and then she is alone, unless occasionally visited by one of the family, or Dr. Hayward, when he is in town. But her time does not hang heavily on her hands. She has as much as she is able to, in directing the household affairs, managing her servants, etc. and I can assure you that such is her attention and method that confined to her room though she be, she makes a Capital Housekeeper. Everything is nice and tidy about the House, and my dinner, the great event of each day, about which poor Isa takes the greatest pains, is served up as well as one could wish it. And all this too, with the most laudable attention to economy, and horror of waste.

I usually return home about six . . . and after dinner I read to her while she knits, etc. till teatime, and so passes the day. . . . I make it a point to write every Sunday or Monday morning

(continued)

In spite of the terrible experiences concerning his wife's illness which he has just recounted in this letter to her sister, John A. manages to add a light-hearted postscript, teasing his niece about her current beau.

# A second son, Hugh John, is born and lives

in time for the mail. . . .

Among the Macdonald papers is a bill dated 1851 from Dr. Hayward listing almost daily house calls at five shillings, making a total of £35/15/6.

## Invisible Lady

In spite of her disabilities, Isabella tried to minister to her husband's needs and to keep their home comfortable. In a letter to his sister-in-law, John A. compared his wife to the "invisible lady" of the circus: "The invisible lady's voice, orders, and behests are heard and obeyed all over the house, and are carried out as to cupboards which she never sees, and pots and pans that have no acquaintance with her. Not a glass is broken, or a set of dishes diminished, but she knows of, and calls the criminal to account for. In fact she carries on the whole machinery as well, to appearance, as if she were bustling from but to ben in person."

He, on his part, made great personal sacrifices to help her. He took her to health resorts, sitting with her through days and sleepless nights. He neglected pressing business matters, although their debts were increasing rapidly.

With Quebec City and Toronto the seats of Government, the young husband had to be away from home for long periods. He also made long voyages to Britain. On the rare occasions when his infirm wife was strong enough, she accompanied him to Toronto to live in secluded rented rooms. The trip to Quebec was too much for her. By nature, John A. was a pleasant extrovert, and he put a good face on his troubles to hide the worry and misgivings he felt. It was essential that he be in the midst of things and to do this he had to live a "bachelor" life where men in public life congregated — in lounges, clubs and smoking rooms. With no home in which to entertain his colleagues, it is more than likely that he drank too much, with his associates or alone, to get through the many fretting frustrating hours.

He always needed money and worked hard. But as he became a leader in Government he gave less time than was required to his own affairs. He told a friend, "Debts and troubles disappear like summer flies, and new ones come." Had he continued on his growing practice he might have become a wealthy man. But politics was his love.

Those who questioned John A.'s ethics and opportunism might have done well to notice that he had never feathered his own nest, that he was a poor man all his life, with irking financial harassments. "His poverty was proof of his honour." Once when his second wife wanted to buy some property with a little sum of money she had, John A. prevented her, saying, "You had better not. Should the land become valuable, it might lead to criticism."

## Isabella Pregnant Again

To their joy, but not without misgivings, the Macdonalds found they were to have another child. John A. sent this letter to his wife's sister about ten weeks before the second son was born. They did not, as planned, name him after his brother.

My dearest Sister,

Isabella has been in great pain for some three or four days, but I am happy to say she is better tonight. . . . Her sufferings are not from her "tic" but from her situation. She was in the same way in New York and they betoken an approaching accouchement. She is not at all nervous at the anticipation, and seems to have no anxiety or apprehension. . . . All arrangements have been long made and now she waits with patience and fortitude. She has given me many directions about herself and her offspring, which any evil happen; and having done all that she could, is now content. It is her wish, as it is mine, that in case the child should be a girl, you should name it. Should it be a male, Isabella says she will accept it as the return of the firstborn and will give it the same name.

We hope to receive the expression of your wishes in this matter, my dear sister, in answer to this, as the infant may be an independent existence before this reaches you. Dr. Mair, whom Isa likes very much, attends her. He is on the Medical Staff here and is one of the best of men. As he has not made Midwifery a matter of practice, he will act as Consulting Physician and . . . call in Dr. Dickson . . . in whom he expresses great confidence and who is a very respectable medical practitioner here.

A very nice woman, a Mrs. Sutherland, has been retained as nurse, and so we are all prepared. Isa is in God's hands, and there we must leave her. . . .

The Macdonalds' second son was born on March 13, 1850, and named Hugh John, after John A.'s father. The elated and relieved John A. announced: "We have got Johnnie back again

---

Between 1824 and 1872 more than 5000 patents were granted. Some of them were:

A gauge to ascertain the tonnage of goods shipped on canal boats.

A new and useful invention to prepare lamps for producing light similar to gas.

A machine to extract stumps from new lands.

A new machine, hung with nets, for taking eels.

A plan for turning four-wheel carriages in a short space.

A limited horse swing.

A new shape of bar iron for horseshoes.

New yokes for oxen.

A useful process to manufacture leather from the skin of the whale or porpoise.

A metallic burial case.

An invention to propel boats against the wind, in all directions with the same wind.

---

One of the rooms on the first floor of Bellevue House was converted to a sickroom for Isabella. The house is now a museum and the bedroom is reconstructed as seen here. The precise nature of John A.'s first wife's illness is unclear; it was marked by fainting spells, hysteria, tics, pain and fatigue. She was probably addicted to the opium she took to relieve her condition.

## WAKING FROM THE N. P. OPIUM DREAM!

In the nineteenth century, opium was a readily available drug, an ingredient in so many patent medicines that inadvertent addiction was easy. Allusions to opium and to addiction were common, as in this Bengough cartoon which suggests that John A. — shown here in a Chinese opium den — has drugged farmers, workers and businessmen with his National Policy.

— almost his image. I don't think he is as pretty but he is not so delicate." (Like his father, Hugh John was to become a lawyer and a politician; he was eventually elected Prime Minister of Manitoba.)

### A Terror of Apprehension

Isabella never regained her health. Alarms were frequent. John A. often rushed home to Kingston, expecting the worst. Creighton gives an account of his last such hurried trip home. "The election had not yet finished when the holiday came. He had not intended to go home for Christmas; and he was still in Toronto, carrying on the battle for the last constituencies, when the message arrived from Kingston. There had been such messages before, and he had obeyed them instantly, hurrying home in a terror of apprehension.... In one sense his whole married life, ever since the terrible summer of 1845, had been one long frightened expectation of the tragic message which, in the end, must infallibly come. By Christmas night he was in Kingston, by Isabella's bedside, watching hopefully as he had watched so often before. This

time, as he must have seen immediately, there were no alternatives ahead. For three days more she dragged her broken existence along; and then on December 28, in the last exhaustion from which there was no recovery, she died. It was the expected, inevitable end for what had been for almost a dozen years a grey, unrelieved tragedy."

On Tuesday, December 29, 1857, the following announcement appeared on the front page of the *Kingston Daily News*:

### Died

On Monday, the 28th inst. of December, Isabella, wife of the Hon. John A. Macdonald in the 48th year of her age. Friends and acquaintances are requested to attend the funeral without further notice, from his mother's residence, Johnson Street, to the cemetery on Wednesday the 30th inst. at three o'clock.

It was said that she died of tuberculosis.

### Opium in the 1800s

"Opium, like many other poisons, produces after a time less effect if frequently administered as a medicine, so that the dose has to be constantly increased to produce the same result on those who take it habitually. When it is used to relieve pain or diarrhea, if the dose be not taken at the usual time, the symptoms of the disease recur with such violence that the remedy is speedily resorted to as the only means of relief, and thus the habit is exceedingly difficult to break off." (*Encyclopaedia Britannica*, Cambridge, 1911)

"The Morphia Habit arises from the constant use of morphia — taken at first, as a rule, for the purpose of allaying pain.... The habit is particularly prevalent among women and physicians.... The acquisition of the habit as a pure luxury is rare.... In women the symptoms may be associated with those of pronounced hysteria or neurasthenia." (*The Principles and Practice of Medicine, designed for the Use of Practicioners and Students of Medicine* by William Osler, M.D., 1892)

"Addicts experienced no difficulty in obtaining their drugs.... Not only did the drugstores sell the supplies cheaply and openly but all kinds of opiate-containing patent medicines were advertised. Thus the addict of the nineteenth century had unlimited sources of supply. He could buy paregoric, laudanum, tincture of opium, morphine, Winslow's Soothing Syrup, Godfrey's Cordial, McMunn's Elixir of Opium, or many other preparations. For a few cents a day he could keep himself loaded." (*Addiction and Opiates*, Alfred R. Lindesmith)

The recipe book of John A.'s second wife contains an opium-based distemper cure for puppies.

*In 1884* Grip *published this warning to wives:*

"Ah! ha!" exclaimed Mrs. Kloopity, as she rummaged the pockets of her husband's other coat. "Ah! ha! So he eats opium does he?" as she drew forth to the light a handful of No. 22 calibre revolver cartridges. "I've noticed that he looks very sleepy and drowsy about the eyes since he's been electioneering, and this *is* opium I know, for those Chinese always put it up in copper capsules and cork it up with lead. *I* know opium when I see it. But Kloopity isn't going to poison himself if *I* can help it, so I'll just throw these nasty things into the stove."

She did so.

A waving willow above an iron-rail-enclosed grave marks the spot where she sleeps.

Women should not meddle with their husband's pockets.

An advertisement that appeared in *Grip* in 1886 promised to "send a valuable TREATISE FREE to any person desiring the same that has been the means of curing many cases of Drunkenness, Opium, Morphine, Chloral and kindred habits. The medicine may be given in tea or coffee without the knowledge of the person taking it, if so desired. BOOK, giving full particulars, SENT FREE. Sealed and secure from observation."

# Forms Progressive Conservative Party

## John A. moves up quickly, defeats George Brown

## Becomes Attorney-General, then Prime Minister

### Talks of retiring: "I find the work and annoyance too much for me"

The Law Society's Benchers' Roll of Osgoode Hall, No. 76, indicates that John Alexander Macdonald became a Bencher of the Law Society in 1849.

In 1850 he sailed for Britain once again, this time to represent the Trust and Loan Company of Upper Canada on corporation matters. Better times had improved his own financial position. With the Commercial Bank as another important client, he could afford to remain in politics and at the same time provide for his family.

As the third Parliament of which John A. was a member held its sessions in 1852, how much he had grown in stature as a politician was apparent to all. Enjoying some degree of financial security, he was developing his great skills in the House. In the power struggle that was going on, he was pushing to the fore.

### Don't Meddle with Constitution

John A. was instrumental in forming the coalition which resulted in the creation of the Progressive Conservative Party in 1854. In a letter he wrote, "Our aim should be to enlarge the bounds of our Party, so as to embrace every person desirous of being counted a Progressive Conservative." Another statement of his was frequently repeated: "If there is one thing to be

---

**The Fathers of Responsible Government**

Term applied to Robert Baldwin and Louis Lafontaine about 1851.

---

avoided, it is meddling with the constitution of the country, which should not be altered until it is evident that the people are suffering from the effects of that constitution."

Only ten years after entering public life, he was named Attorney-General of Upper Canada in the McNab-Morin Government. The excitement of the election had been strenuous, but he had defeated his long-time adversary, George Brown. Financially too matters were improved. His salary was now £1250.

About this time a bill was introduced to change the name of Bytown to Ottawa. John A. was against it — he thought it absurd to name a town after the river that ran by it. "What if Paris were called *Seine*?" he asked. "Or London *Thames*?" As the place was named for Colonel By, Byzantium and Bycopolis were suggested as alternates. However, the majority preferred Ottawa.

John A.'s duties were increasingly pressing and onerous, and he was away from his Kingston

---

In 1856 John Langton wrote to his brother: "John A. Macdonald is now the recognized leader, but he is anything but strong in reality."

---

home a great deal, as he was required to live much of the time in the capital. In spite of the many burdens that he carried — or perhaps because of them — he did not seem to change his carefree ways. Perhaps he could not control his weaknesses. He was often late for important assemblies, and just as often absent altogether — sometimes for long periods. John Langton, the new Auditor-General, said: "His instincts are all good, but he takes the world too easily to be much depended on.... His integrity is very high.... He can get through more work in a given time than anybody I ever saw — and do it well."

### Dunned Again

John A. was never entirely free of debt, and dunning letters came from time to time. One, for a brooch, silver plate, engraving and crest, was submitted — with his name misspelled — on April 4, 1856, after being on the books for some months:

Mr. J. A. McDonald
Respected Sir,
You will pardon my presenting my account at this early date. The fact is that I have heavy acceptances to make next week and shall feel obliged for the above. If not convenient in cash, please send me your acceptance at 60 days, payable, at your bankers, and oblige,
*C.G. Joseph*

In 1857 John A. became Prime Minister in the Macdonald-Cartier ministry, but the Government was defeated the next year.

It was no secret that John A. loved Great

---

In the Consolidated Statutes of Canada (1859) death by hanging was the penalty for murder, treason, rape, administering poison or wounding with intent to commit murder, unlawfully abusing a girl under ten, buggery with man or beast, robbery with wounding, burglary with assault, arson, setting fire to or casting away a ship, exhibiting a false signal endangering a ship. (Endangering a railway train called for a prison term of three to seven years.) In 1864 Sarah N. was sent to gaol for three months at hard labour for attempting suicide.

---

---

Britain and the ways of the British, both political and social. When affairs of state or his legal business required his presence abroad, he went as eagerly as his responsibilities at home would allow. He felt that the long sea voyages offered him respite from his labours. So it was in a cheery frame of mind that he sailed in 1857 on the *Anglo-Saxon* bound for Liverpool. He wrote his mother from London:

York Hotel, London, August 21, 1857
My dearest mother,
I wrote Isabella three days ago, but must keep my promise of writing yourself.
I am well, thank God and in good spirits. Rather tired of London and anxious to get back. I go to Paris tonight for three days. On my return, I intend to visit John and William Clark, who both live in the country.
I hope to sail on the 9th of September. I have seen a good deal of Evan and his wife. They

---

### John A. on Schools

John A. delivered a speech at London, Canada West, in 1860 that gave his stand on the separate school issue. He said, in part: "As far as my own opinions are concerned, I am decidedly in favour of the continuance of the separate school clause, and I will tell you the reason. As a Protestant I should not like it if I ever lived in Lower Canada to be obliged to send my child to a school of which the teacher was a Roman Catholic clergyman. (Hear! Hear!) It is the duty of a religious teacher, if he believes anything to be true, to try to enforce it on the beliefs of his pupils. It is the duty of a sincere Protestant clergyman to try to proselytize every Roman Catholic. It is the duty of every sincere Roman Catholic to try to impress on others what he believes to be right. As an ardent Protestant who conscientiously believes that Protestantism and truth are one, I would not willingly subject my son to the chance of being turned by teachers into what I consider wrong. (Applause) And I appreciate the like feeling among my Roman Catholic brethren. (Renewed applause) Why the Catholics and the Protestants do not even read history alike. We look at the reigns of Henry VIII, Mary and Elizabeth from one point of view — they from quite a different one."

## A True Friend

James Pennington Macpherson, Macdonald's nephew, tells this story in his biography of Sir John A.: "When the author was a student in Macdonald's office, in 1858-9, there was attached to it an old gentleman of the name of McIntosh, who was most regular and punctual in his attendance, but had nothing to do. He had passed the allotted period of life, being over eighty years of age, was feeble of limb, and worn out mentally, yet, every day saw him occupying his seat and gazing about the office with an air of proprietorship. He apparently had no relatives or connections, and, with most men, would have been turned adrift when his usefulness was gone, or, at best, granted a sufficient sum to meet his modest wants, but he had been Sir John's, friend, and either course would have crushed his proud Scotch heart.

"One day the poor old fellow remarked, that he was not of much use and was ashamed to draw pay, but Sir John replied: 'Why, McIntosh, if you left me I would have to close the office. You have an eye on the students and keep them to their work and keep everything straight in the office. Oh! I could not part with you.'

"So he was soothed, and led to believe that his presence was essential, and thus he lived on until death called him away, happy in the sense of responsibility, and provided for up to the very last."

also go to the country in a day or so.

I have ordered a Highland suit for Hugh. I have no doubt he will bare his bottom with due Celtic dignity.

I must reserve my adventures until my return. Give all sorts of love to Moll and the parson.

Kiss Hugh for me.

Always your affectionate son,
John A.

## Double Shuffle

The year 1858 was a time of great difficulty for John A. He was to experience political setbacks at the same time as deep personal grief. Defeated in the Government, after four days he resumed office in the Cartier-Macdonald administration, first as Postmaster-General, then as Attorney-General for Upper Canada. This change of portfolios was the root of the often discussed "double shuffle"; this manoeuvre allowed all the old members of the Macdonald-Cartier administration to keep their seats while the Brown-Dorion ex-ministers lost their places and power in Parliament.

On the personal side, his life was darkened by the death of his wife. His small son, Hugh John, was taken care of by John A.'s spinster sister, Louisa; another sister, Margaret, then newly married; and John A.'s aged mother.

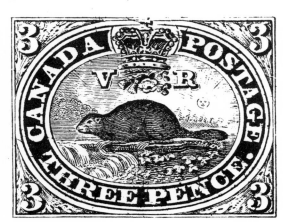

The first Canadian stamp was issued in 1853.

In Kingston the City Hall overlooked a liquor store.

With no home of his own, John A. threw himself even more energetically into politics.

The seat of Government had at various times been in Kingston, Montreal, Toronto and Quebec. Not without resentment on the part of those cities, Queen Victoria on December 31, 1857, chose Ottawa to be the new capital. This meant more and constant travel for John A. In spite of how much he seemed to enjoy the battles as well as the triumphs of politics, he was constantly talking of retiring into private life. He wrote to his sister Margaret: "We are having a hard fight in the House, and shall beat them in the votes, but it will, I think, end in my retiring as soon as I can with honour. I find the work and annoyance too much for me."

John A. took every possible opportunity to return to Kingston to visit his mother and son. He wrote to her:

My dearest mother,

I hope this letter will find you as usual. I had hoped to get down for a day, but have hitherto been prevented. I trust that ere long, I may be able to gratify my cherished desire to pay you a visit. To show you that the whole world is not ungrateful, I send you two notes, one from the Hon. Mr. Chaveau, Chief Superintendent of Education in Lower Canada, and the other from an old soldier for whom I got a company in the 100th. With all sorts of love to Hugh and the household,

Your affectionate son,
John A. Macdonald

The letter drew this comment from a biographer: "The spectacle of this busy man of middle age, in the midst of an unusually stormy session with defeat ever imminent, finding time to inform his aged mother of his 'cherished desire' to pay her a visit must be a revelation *(continued)*

### The Cabinet Maker Becomes a Mason

John A. Macdonald was forty-three years old when he became a member of the Ancient Free and Accepted Masons of Canada joining the St. John's Lodge No. 3 of Kingston, Ontario.

Masonic records show that "The thirteenth Annual Communication was held at London in 1868. This meeting was honoured by the presence of Canada's foremost statesman, Right Worshipful Brother Sir John A. Macdonald who presented his appointments as the Representative of the United Grand Lodge of England. He was received with Grand Honours and the rank of Past Grand Senior Warden was conferred upon him." The Prime Minister became an honourary member of Civil Service Lodge No. 148 in Ottawa in 1869 and of Dalhousie Lodge No. 52 in Ottawa on June 24, 1870. He became a Commuted Life Member of Zetland Lodge No. 326 in Toronto on July 23, 1875.

Although he was not extravagant, Sir John A. enjoyed goods of quality — whether for his own use or for gifts. In 1857 he bought of William Callaghan, 23 New Bond Street, London:

*A double field glass, bodies
covered with leather, fitted with
sunshades by Voigtlander, Vienna* £13/-/-
*Leather sliding case for ditto* 12/-
*Engraving name on ditto* 2/-
_____
£13/14/-

# July 1, 1859: John A. narrowly escapes drowning

## Prefers races, balls, drinking parties to law practice

to those persons who have been accustomed to form their estimate of his character upon data furnished by *The Globe*."

A letter written a few months later shows his constant concern and great love for his family.

Toronto   June 17, 1858
My dearest mother,

You must give Louisa a good scolding for me, for not writing me how you are and how you have been for the past week. Margaret used to correspond with me once a week. So tell Loo to be sure to send me a line. We are getting on very slowly in the House and it is very tiresome.

I hope we will get through the session early in July & then I will be able to go down to see you all. I long to hear of Margaret and her party. Not one word have I had of any of you. Goodbye my dear Mother. I have just made one speech & am about to make another. Love to Loo. Always my dearest mother,

yr affectionate son,
John

Now a lonely widower, John A. was considered very much of a "catch." Yet to those who sought to persuade him to marry again, he replied, "I am so accustomed to living alone, it frets me to have a person always in the house with me."

### Shipwreck!

John A. Macdonald was not likely to forget July 1. Confederation was to be ushered in

### Rep. by Pop.

An abbreviation of "Representation by Population" — a Tory Party plank about 1849-1853, later supported by the Clear Grits (Liberals) and Brown Reformers in Upper Canada.

This editorial appeared in a Kingston newspaper, *The Daily British Whig*, in December 1857: "To-morrow the Hon. John A. Macdonald will be re-elected member for Kingston, without opposition. So far as Kingston is concerned, this will be as it ought to be; for not only has he done everything in his power to benefit the city he has represented, but his position, as Prime Minister of Canada is such that his power to do the city further good is illimitable. To oppose such a member would be a suicidable measure, of which no Kingston man can presume to be guilty. But it is not at Kingston that Macdonald is standing his election — it is all over the Province. For although his seat for Kingston may be secured by acclamation, yet the same unanimity does not prevail everywhere in Canada. That the late Administration, of which he was a prominent member, was deservedly popular, we admit; that the acts of that Administration merited its popularity we also admit; but that Canada has a wayward, bigoted population must also be admitted. What the electors may do when they go to the polls is more than the far-sighted men among us can say. Our own opinion is that Mr. Macdonald will be maintained in both Upper and Lower Canada . . . and that this ministry will be most triumphant."

The following song was sung to the tune of "Oh Susanna" by the many black people who fled from the United States to Canada.

*I heard the Queen Victoria say*
*If we would all forsake*
*Our native land of slavery*
*And come across the Lake,*
*That she was standing on the shore*
*With arms extended wide*
*To give us all a peaceful home*
*Beyond the rolling tide.*
*Farewell old Mas'er,*
*That is enough for me,*
*I'm going straight to Canada*
*Where coloured men are free!*

eight years later on that date, but in 1859 on that day, he and a party of friends narrowly escaped death in a shipwreck while on an excursion on Lake Huron. The *Toronto Leader* gives an account of the accident.

### Disaster on Lake Huron

*Extraordinary Escape from Shipwreck*

"On Friday last a party of ladies and gentlemen left this city on a projected excursion to Sault Ste. Marie. Shortly before the arrival of the vessel at Lonely Island, in Georgian Bay, a part of the machinery, the cross-heads, snapped in half, and it became absolutely necessary, in consequence, for the safety of the ship, to shut off the steam. The *Ploughboy* being, like most or all of the steamers on Lake Huron, unprovided with masts, she was thus necessarily left to the mercy of the winds and waves, which drifted her at their pleasure. The danger of such a position being apparent, some of the crew volunteered to proceed in an open boat to Owen Sound, to secure the aid of the steamer *Cana-*

*dian*. But long before the assistance thus sent for could be obtained, the *Ploughboy* had been slowly but inevitably and helplessly drifting to that dangerous portion of the coast lying west of Chabot Point, and a little before the dawn of Sunday morning found the unfortunate vessel within fifty yards of a precipitous rock-bound shore, with a heavy swell of the sea setting in toward it, and a gale blowing her directly upon the breakers. Immediate death stared all the passengers in the face, it being too evident that if the vessel struck — as seemed inevitable — in a few minutes not a soul would be left to tell the tale. Husbands and wives, brothers and sisters, and all friends therefore took a last farewell, commended themselves to Providence, and prepared to meet their doom, when they were miraculously saved when just in the very jaws of death. At a distance of only forty-five yards from land, on a lee shore, and in one hundred and eighty feet of water, the anchors which had been dragging for some twelve miles, in the simple hope of postponing the fate of the ship till daylight, caught bottom and held fast the vessel."

John A. wrote to his sister about the incident:
My dear Sister,

You will see by the papers what a narrow escape we had. None of the party will again be nearer to their graves until they are placed in them. The people behaved well, the women heroically.

I am none the worse of the trip. The Governor-General will be here tonight and I hope then in a few days to get away to Washington.

Love to Mama, Hughey and Sis, not forgetting the Parson,

Yours always,
John A.

### Rule or Ruin

Phrase used by the Reformers in criticizing Sir Francis Hincks when he joined John A. in the first coalition government, known as the McNab-Morin Government.

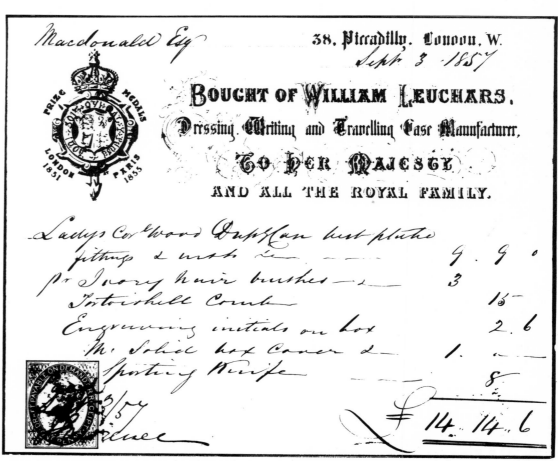

John A. enjoyed his trips to Britain. Among the Macdonald Papers in the Public Archives are many receipts from British shops, where John A. bought books and clothing for himself and gifts for his family and friends.

Montreal as John A. saw it. This photograph was taken around 1852 in the Beaver Hall Hill area. PAC

I send you specimens of the letters of congratulations I got.

*From a Mr. Geddes:*

What a narrow and providential escape *you* and your friends have made on your pleasure trip as stated in the *Leader* of yesterday.... It was an awful situation to be placed in and nothing short of the interposition of Almighty God could have saved you. It was a dreadful situation to be placed in even when the *Anchor held*. It affords me sincere and heartfelt joy to find that you are still in the Land of the living.... I hope you will never meet with such another Excursion ... placed in such an Awful Situation with Death Staring you in the face! You know Mrs. Geddes takes care to have the first read of the Newspapers when they come from the Post. She came in the Office to me with the *Leader* in her hand and could hardly tell me what it was that she wanted — Said just read that — pointing to the paragraph. It almost makes the Blood run cold to think of your Situation when you were drifting towards the Rocks!! Mrs. Geddes unites with me in kind and most sincere regards to you.

In August 1854, the *Halifax Citizen,* announcing the arrival of Canadian delegates, said, "Everybody talks *Canada* today. It is not at all surprising to see fellow-citizens trying to carry a French dictionary and a Canadian directory in one hand, and welcome their guests with the other."

*From a Mr. Greer:*

Mrs. Greer and myself were grieved to the heart to learn that you had been fated to the dreadful Calamity which thanks to an allwise providence you have escaped. You have no friends on earth who felt more grateful than ourselves for your safe deliverance from a Watery Grave. And as we know but little of OUR-SELVES let us benefit by every warning sent to us by the all wise one to live more and more unto him who is able to preserve us through life, and at last bring us to his Heavenly Kingdom. God bless and preserve you is the fervent prayer of my wife and self.

John A. was now at the head of the prosperous Kingston firm of lawyers:

**Macdonald
Macdonnell
Draper
and
Wilkinson**

One must note that John A. changed his law partners with astonishing frequency, offending the old tradition that lawyers should be constant and steady. There were obvious reasons. To be free for political life, he depended on his partners to keep the office going, to attend to the legal drudgery and time consuming duties. There is no doubt that his connections attracted a great deal of business to his office, but the results were not satisfactory and the changes continued. In his book *Kingston — The King's Town* James A. Roy tells us: "Between 1843

and 1872, Macdonald had no fewer than six partners.... Macdonald needed money to stay in Parliament and the only way he could make money was by the law and for him the law meant a partnership on a fifty-fifty basis. But he was away half the time.... Consequently there were everlasting disagreements, and changing partners. It was not only his partners who objected to his absenteeism. The time came when his constituents complained that he was devoting far too little attention to their interests and it took all of his skill to convince them to the contrary.

"Macdonald enjoyed horse races, balls, dinners and drinking parties, and slipped into Fallon's Tavern or along to his friend Metcalfe's to see how the birds were shaping for the next cocking.

"Naturally, many found themselves unable to approve either of some of his ways or of certain of his friends, but that was of small concern to John A. whose manner of living was his own responsibility."

### Representation by Population

Representation by Population: Justice for Upper Canada! While Upper Canada has a larger population by one hundred and fifty thousand than Lower Canada, and contributes more than double the amount of taxation to the general revenue, Lower Canada has an equal number of representatives in Parliament. (A statement of policy from the Toronto *Globe*, October 1, 1853)

A ball at the Music Hall of the St. Louis Hotel, Quebec City.

# John A. hosts a ball and has one

## Fountains, flowers, statues make ballroom a spectacle of wonder

The Citadel in Quebec City as it looked to William Bartlett when he visited Canada in the late 1830s.

In 1860, to honour his personal and political friends, John A., now a most important leader in Government, was pleased to entertain 800 guests at a truly magnificent Valentine Ball on February 14 in the Music Hall of the St. Louis Hotel, Quebec City. The room, described as the most beautiful in British America, became a "spectacle of wonder."

### A Fountain of Eau de Cologne

Amidst garlands of roses, a bust of Her Majesty, the Plumes of the Prince of Wales, flags and a statue of Cupid, a fountain of eau de cologne played, spraying gallons of perfumed water. Crimson draperies, new luxurious carpeting, an especially installed brilliant chandelier, Canova's famous figure of "The Dancing Girl" and another of "The Three Graces" added to the enchantment.

John A. himself, a merry host, gallantly presented valentines with "pretty little remarks" to the ladies. Later, at the supper hour, he delighted and diverted his guests still further with an extremely large pie, out of which flew four and twenty birds.

Conversation buzzed with compliments on the elegant toilettes and coiffures. There were ballgowns of silk "stiff enough to stand" that sold at $8.00, $10.00 and $12.00 a yard. Lace, for trimming, was even costlier. Many women wore tournures (bustles), mitts of Chantilly lace and fronts "en diadème."

In a speech in Kingston in 1860 John A. said, "In this country it is unfortunately true that all men who enter the public service act foolishly in doing so. If a man desires peace and domestic happiness he will find neither in performing the thankless task of a public officer."

Treasured heirloom pieces of jewelry were in evidence. Gold chains, up to sixty inches in length, and broad wedding rings had sentimental mottoes engraved on them. Jet, which took carving beautifully, was worn by those in mourning. (Even at a ball, it was customary for the bereaved to wear black onyx or black enamel mourning rings, brooches or lockets showing, under glass, a lock of hair of the departed. A widower frequently wore a watch chain made of his deceased wife's hair, fashioned with elaborate tips and clasps of engraved gold.)

One thousand ball tickets had been sent out at $1.00 each. Gentlemen in full regalia, ablaze with every possible uniform and decoration, courted the ladies and danced attendance on them into the early hours of the morning. Card tables were set up, new mirrors placed, floral centrepieces arranged and sitting out places contrived. The hall had been practically rebuilt for the occasion. For four days prior to the ball, there was tremendous activity as many workmen redecorated the apartments. Furniture was moved and replaced. Heating was inspected and new equipment installed. To add to the magnificence, the Sisters of Charity fashioned twelve large and thirty small garlands and prepared 702 flowers by hand to festoon the walls with artificial wreaths. There was a hurrying and a scurrying in both Upper and Lower Town among musicians, hairdressers, furriers, shoe stores, carters, plumbers, candlemakers, wine stewards, bartenders, waiters, carpenters, modistes, chefs, pastry cooks, florists, tailors, engravers, printers, gas-fitters, launderers, jewellers and sleigh drivers. Everybody knew that John A. was hosting a ball!

### Elaborate Preparations

A bill from Thos. Andrews, Plumber and Gas-Fitter, Tin-plate, Sheet Iron, and Copper Worker, gives an idea of some of the elaborate preparations for the ball. It is itemized as follows:

|  | £ | s | d |
|---|---|---|---|
| 3 men's time putting up scaffolding, ½ day each |  | 9 | 9 |
| cartage of scaffolding, 2 loads |  | 2 |  |
| 1 gas-fitter's time, ½ day |  | 5 |  |
| 3 feet, 8 inch 1½ inch iron pipe, to lengthen rod of lamp ⅔ day |  | 8 | 3 |
| 1 ⅝ inch brass coupling, ⅓ cutting screw and bolt of pipe line |  | 8 |  |
| Gas-fitter's time putting up lamp, one day |  | 10 |  |
| 1 man's time, do, one day |  | 5 |  |
| rent of one three-light chandelier |  | 5 |  |
| 6 bat burners, 3 jet burners, screws, one gas-fitter's time 1 day, 1 man's time, 1 day |  | 15 |  |
| carpenters taking down scaffolding |  | 4 | 6 |
| gas-fitters time lighting up hall |  | 3 |  |
| 1 ⅝ inch coupling, 4 burners, making up gas brackets, 2 cut globes, gallery and socket, 1 gas-fitters time |  | 27 | 9 |
| gas-fitters time taking down fittings etc |  | 7 | 6 |
|  | £5 | 14 | 8 |

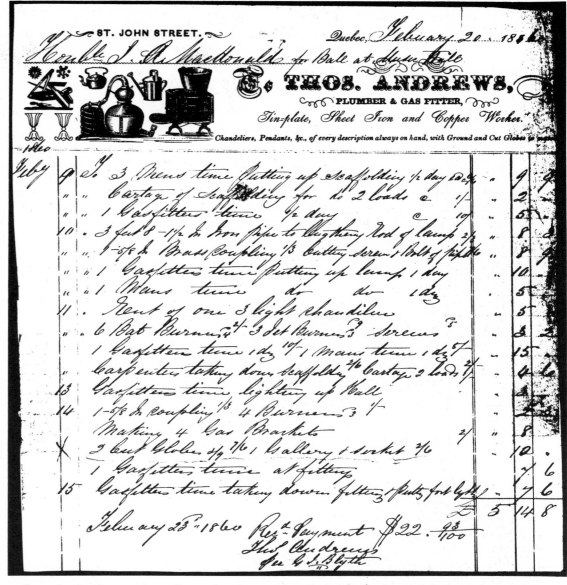

It took plumbers and gas-fitters five days to install the gaslit chandeliers for John A.'s ball, as this bill shows.

The liquor ordered for the occasion was as follows:

| | £ | s |
|---|---|---|
| 20 dozen Champagne | 75 | |
| 5 dozen Sparkling Moselle | 18 | 15 |
| 5 dozen Sherry | 12 | |
| 3 dozen Best Port | 9 | |
| 8 dozen Allsops Ale | 5 | 10 |
| 4 dozen Porter | 2 | 10 |

However that account was reduced, for the following were returned:

8 9/12 dozen Champagne
2 9/12 dozen Sparkling Moselle
1 8/12 dozen Best Port
1 1/12 dozen Sherry
1 5/12 dozen Allsops Ale
3 10/12 dozen Porter

The total cost of the liquor was £67/13/1. Supper, for the wide selection of delicacies served, came to $520. The full bill for the gala was $1606.70.

### Temper of the Times

When Sir John A. lost his temper, it was because of personal affront rather than political principle. In 1849 he came close to fighting a duel when he challenged Edward Blake. But Blake ignored the challenge, and two days later both men bound themselves to keep the peace.

In 1861 John A. was goaded into fury by Oliver Mowat, his former student and law partner and now his political antagonist. He raged across the floor and shouted at Mowat, "You damned pup, I'll slap your chops!" However John Sandfield Macdonald separated them, and John A. did not carry out his threat.

In 1876 *Hansard* reported that Sir John A. called Donald Smith (later Lord Strathcona and High Commissioner of Canada to London) "the biggest liar I ever met." What *Hansard* did not report was that Sir John A. strode belligerently towards Smith shouting, "I can lick you quicker than hell can scorch a feather!" Again, colleagues interceded before Sir John A. could carry out his threat.

In those days Members of Parliament were hardly polite in debate: they shouted, screamed and cursed at each other.

A conundrum from *The Life Boat* — a juvenile temperance magazine published in Montreal in 1853: "Why is a locomotive engine like an habitual drunkard? Because it is continually over the line, often wets its whistle and is accustomed to draughts."

"The desire of the Government is good, their motives good . . . If the Government has erred, it was an error of the head, and not of the heart or of the intention." (John A. Macdonald, Kingston, 1860)

## ODE ON THE DEPARTURE OF THE PRINCE OF WALES.

*(If the Laureate won't do his work, Punch must.)*

USPICIOUS blow, ye
    gales,
And swell the Royal
    sails
That waft the PRINCE
    OF WALES
In a vessel of the line,
Away to Canada
Across the ocean
    brine;
As the son of his
    Mamma,
His weather should
    be fine.

What transports the
    Canadians will
    evince
When they behold our
    youthful Prince!
Not ours alone, but
    also theirs,
Each colony with
    England shares
In Protestant So-
    PHIA'S heirs.
How all the bells will
    ring, the cannons
    roar!

And they who never saw a Prince before,
Oh, won't they feast him and caress him!
    Waylay him, and address him,
    His Royal Highness—bless him!—
Their demonstrations possibly may bore.

They'll make, no doubt, a greater fuss
Than what is usually made by us
    In some of our remoter parts,
    Where country Corporations see,

For the first time, HER MAJESTY—
    (May she be destined long to reign!)
When by her Parliament set free,
    She travels by a stopping train,
    BRITANNIA'S trump, the QUEEN OF HEARTS.
But still more pressing ceremony waits
The Prince in the United States;
What mobs will his hotel beset
A sight of him in hopes to get!

    What multitudes demand
    To shake him by the hand!
Hosts of reporters will his footsteps dog,
(As BARON RENFREW though he goes *incog.*)
    Take down his every word,
    Describe his mouth and nose,
    And eyes, and hair, and clothes,
With a minuteness quite absurd.

Ye free and easy citizens, be not rude,
    Disturb not our young Prince's rest;
Upon his morning toilet don't intrude:
    Wait till he's drest.
    Oh! will that Yankee not be blest
To whom the son of England's QUEEN shall say
        "Out of the way?"

    And, oh—to touch a tender theme—
    How will the fair around him throng,
    And try, forgetting all their shyness,
    To salute his Royal Highness,
    The realisation of a happy dream!
    The force of loveliness is strong.
A spark's a spark, and tinder tinder,
    And certain things in Heaven are written:
And is there any cause to hinder
    The PRINCE OF WALES from being smitten?
Transcendent charms drive even monarchs frantic.
    A German Princess must he marry?
    And who can say he may not carry
    One of Columbia's fascinating daughters
        O'er the Atlantic?
Truth many a one might force to own,
Hopes that to her the kerchief may be flung,
To the ultimate exaltation of a young
    American lady to the British throne.

# Prince of Wales visits Canada

## *John A. prominent at biggest social event of 1860*

ILN

The forty-five-year-old Macdonald was prominent at another brilliant function in 1860, for he welcomed Queen Victoria's son, Edward, Prince of Wales, on his first official royal visit to Canada. Government leaders were greatly concerned with protocol, and the Toronto *Globe*, never missing a chance to take a swipe at John A., wrote: "A great deal of time has been wasted by John A. in learning to walk, for the sword suspended to his waist has an awkward knack of getting between his legs, especially after dinner."

This poetic screed was written about the visit of the Prince of Wales to Canada at that time:

*They have dined him and wined him in manner most royal,*
*Addressed and harangued him to prove they were loyal.*
*They have bored him in parks, and they've bored him in halls,*
*Danced him almost to death in no end of balls.*
*They have bored him in colleges, bored him in schools,*
*And convinced him that Orange fanatics are fools.*

The book *Journal of H.R.H. The Prince of Wales Visit to America* (1861) gives an account of the Prince's visit to Kingston: "At

The Illustrated London News published this picture of the official residence in Quebec of the Prince of Wales during his 1860 visit.

In preparation for the visit of Prince Edward, Queen Victoria's son, to Canada, this collection of Canadian melodies "selected and arranged by Herr Schmuck of the Imperial Conservatoire of Vienna" was published in London and sold in Quebec, Montreal and Kingston.

More music to commemorate the royal visit. Orangemen used the occasion of the visit for "a grand display of so-called religious zeal" even though they had been warned that the Prince and his company would not countenance such demonstrations.

11:30 we were under weigh for Kingston, and soon reached the Lake of the 'Thousand Islands.' The scenery is pretty, but its praises are, I think, much exaggerated. . . . Kingston, the Indian *Cataraqui,* was reached at 4 p.m., and here occurred the first check to the full flow of our hitherto successful course. The Orangemen thought the occasion of the Prince's visit a good opportunity for a grand display of so-called religious zeal. Their chiefs, for the manufacture of political capital. They were determined to receive the Son of their Queen in their own way or not at all, and had prepared a gaudy display of their own peculiar symbols and habiliments, significant at least of defiance to their Roman Catholic fellow-subjects. It is impossible to enter into details which would occupy much space; suffice it to say that the Orange party, both here and elsewhere, had been distinctly warned, on the Prince first entering Canada, that any special display would be distasteful and embarrassing. Mayors promised, and performed not; Orange chiefs vapoured and paraded their bands, and flaunted their flags in the Prince's eyes as the *Kingston* lay off the pier of their town.

"The Prince, having condescended to wait thus long, determined to receive the local addresses on board the steamer, and then to proceed at once to Belleville. . . . At 1:30 p.m. we were again under weigh, leaving all the preparations for levee, dinner, and ball to the natives. The flags were still flying, drums beating, and Orangemen more confident than ever that their 'no surrender' would compass the surrender of the Prince, when we steamed away for the Bay of Quinte. Our only regret was that the more sensible, and we will hope the greater, part of the community should be disappointed of the Prince's visit, owing to the fantasies of a few enthusiasts. The ladies were, of course, the objects of our profound sympathy, for they lost their ball."

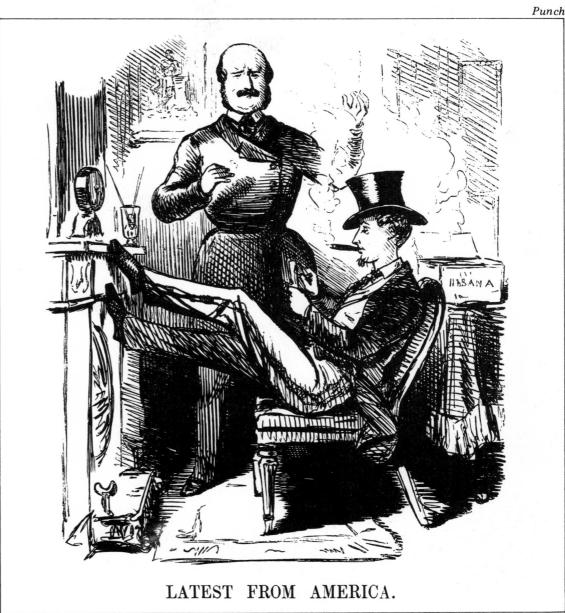

### LATEST FROM AMERICA.

The newly returned Prince of Wales relates his experiences in North America.

"John A. had the devotion of women in remarkable degree," wrote biographer John Willison. "It is rarely indeed that a political leader touches the hearts of women and only those do it who have that strange quality of attraction which we call magnetism." **PAC**

# John A. as ladies' man

## As a widower he is considered a "good catch"

*He was never handsome but he made up for it with charm and fun*

John A. was never a handsome man, for his large lumpy nose and spindly body made him a caricature rather than a model. Nevertheless, women were attracted to him.

During his school days, the girls seemed to like him. One, who later became Mrs. Thomas Wilson of Kingston, was his classmate and confessed that "John was my first love."

Biographer Sir John Willison explains: "Sir John Macdonald had . . . the devotion of women in remarkable degree. In households all over the land, they were passionate guardians of his reputation and the jealous champions of his achievements. It is rarely indeed that a political leader touches the hearts of women and only those do it who have that strange quality of attraction which we call magnetism and which God gives to so few of his creatures. A French writer has said that 'no power is equal to personal charm.' There was the secret of Sir John Macdonald's influence and ascendancy."

That John A. was a gallant beau is shown by a bill for a lady's riding whip, purchased in London for seven pounds fifteen shillings. There is no record of who was given such an expensive riding accessory.

### Charmed by Yankee Women

Two years after his first marriage he wrote to the sister of his wife confirming the gossip of the time that he liked the company of a pretty woman. The letter was sent from Philadelphia where the Macdonalds had gone for the health of John A.'s invalid wife.

My dearest Sister,

I was much gratified by the feast of Reason, but I say it with shame and confusion of face that my supper of Terrapin and Champagne lingers more pleasantly on my recollection than all the "Wise Saws and Modern Instances" that were uttered by the Savants. My spirit was willing but my flesh was weak and required those creature comforts.

It rained so tremendously yesterday that I was prevented from going to church, and as they say in Galway "I made mee Soul" at home.

Today after a saunter through this city of marble steps . . . and scrubbing brushes, I called on Mrs. Biddle, whom I found at home. I liked her self-possessed English manners very much. She is a ladylike and intelligent person, and I regret having had so small an opportunity of knowing her. . . . I forgot to tell you that Mrs. Robinson, a very pretty woman, called on Saturday, and I went to find her today, but the Directory was vague and I was stupid and

so I did not see her again, much to Isabella's delight, who says she does not like me talking so much to your lady friends. By the way, sister, there is a Latin proverb "Noscitina Sociis" which may be translated for the Country Members "Birds of a Feather Flock Together." I always considered you a Charming Woman, but I did not calculate for all your friends being so. From those I have seen, I have only to say that you will confer a great favour on me by sitting down and writing me letters of credence to *every* one of your Yankee lady friends and it will go hard but I deliver most of them. . . .

Tell Aunt Maxwell I am resolved to take her by storm some day or other. I am resolved, too, that she *shall* like me and be good to me and give me some of that gingerbread that I only got a taste of. Just enough to make me like Oliver Twist, "ask for more." With love to Jane, I remain dear sister,

Yours most truly,
John A. Macdonald

### John A. — A "Good Catch"

John A. had always been a charming companion. As he now rose to prominence as a politician, the ladies had even more reason to dream of him as a "good catch." One in particular certainly showed her feelings in a letter dated two years after the death of his first wife. From Mrs. E.M. Hall, the widow of John A.'s friend Judge Hall, came the following (love?) letter:

My loved John,

I hope I shall have a letter from you today, my darling, as if not I shall not be able to hear for another week as intending to leave here for Buckhorn tomorrow. D.V. [*Deo Volente* — God willing] Mr. Boucher went to town yesterday. . . . He is holding court today, so no hope until I return from the backwoods where I only intend to stay a week. So you will have

no letter for that time. If that is a privation to you, what must I feel — a fortnight without hearing from you. I cannot bear to think of it.

Mrs. Boucher and I spent yesterday evening with the Kirkpatricks. A lady who was there made a set at me to find out if I was to be married in the spring. I told her my mother advised me when setting out in life to "believe nothing I heard, and only half what I see" and I wished my friends would do the same. She then tried Mrs. Boucher, who told her she would not believe it till told by the parties themselves . . . that she had been asked the question at least fifty times since I came up, and when saying that I knew nothing about it, she was met by the question "What! Have you not asked her?" "Certainly not!" was her reply. The horses are ready. I must stop. . . .

Goodbye my own darling,
Love your loving Lizzie

John A.'s name was linked romantically with women wherever he travelled. Many were ambitious mothers who contrived social entertainments that he might meet their attractive, and not unwilling, daughters. While the first Confederation Conference was sitting in Charlottetown it was rumoured that he was to marry Miss Haviland, a sister of Thomas Heath Haviland who had been the Lieutenant-Governor of Prince Edward Island.

---

### Fascinations of the Turkey

In his biography of his uncle, James Pennington Macpherson describes the young John A.: "As a youth he was quiet in manner, but full of fun and mischief, quick at repartee and unable to resist a joke. One evening, at a large party, he forgot an engagement to dance a quadrille immediately after supper, and appeared to claim his partner when it was too late. She was very indignant she had lost her dance, and would not forgive. He tried to appease her in every way, but finding it of no avail, to her horror and dismay flung himself at her feet, and with eyes twinkling with merriment, but in the most heartbroken tones cried out, 'Remember! oh, remember! the fascinations of the turkey.' This was too much, and the ridiculousness of the situation, together with the laughter of the bystanders, brought about a speedy reconciliation."

---

### A Conservative Chicken

An eighty-year-old fifth generation Canadian, long time resident of Ottawa, whose ancestors came to Quebec with the army, tells this story: "I remember election time before women had the vote. Grandfather was Liberal and grandmother was Conservative. If the Liberals won, grandmother was silent. If the Conservatives won, grandmother made no comment — but she cooked a chicken."

Who was the lady for whom John A. purchased this riding whip? At the exorbitant price of £7/15/0 in 1857, it must have been quite elegant.

Eliza Grimason in middle age. No photograph of her as a young woman exists, and her name has nearly disappeared from twentieth-century biographies of John A. They met when she was about sixteen years old, and fifty-five years later when he lay dying in Ottawa she got out of her own sickbed to kneel in prayer for his recovery. He, in turn, kept her picture in his study. In 1856 John A. sold her husband the property that became Grimason House and, when she became widowed, did not press her for the balance of the payments. She turned the hotel into his campaign headquarters and presided at the victory parties held in its tavern, the only woman present. In the 1880s she visited Earnscliffe and described Lady Macdonald as "a very plain woman" who "takes good care o' Him." She outlived John A. by twenty-five years, dying in 1916 at the age of ninety-five. Her grave is contiguous to his, their tombstones almost duplicates in design.

52

Eliza Grimason in 1901 at the age of eighty with her daughter, granddaughter and great-grandson, W.A. Newlands, now a retired doctor living in New York, who provided us with these photographs from the family album.

# Who was Mrs. Grimason?

## They were friends for over 50 years; her inn was his headquarters

In June 1890, the year before his death, John A. laid the cornerstone for the new dry dock at Kingston. He was greeted by thousands of men and, although the terrain was rough, a particularly large number of women. Author E. B. Biggar describes the scene: "When Sir John had concluded a speech in which the audience pathetically protested against his statement that he was very near the end of his career, the bag-pipes struck up. While they were playing, a woman in a plain dress, but with a kind face, gently worked her way upon the platform and moved towards Sir John. As the Premier saw her he sprang to his feet, and with a 'Hello, old woman!' grasped her in his arms and gave her a hearty kiss. It was Mrs. Grimason.

" 'Who is Mrs. Grimason?' was a question asked by many a reader of the newspaper reports in which mention was made of the incident. Mrs. Grimason was a native of North of Ireland, who, with her husband, had settled in Kingston."

What else do we know of Mrs. Grimason and John A.'s relationship with her? She was the successful innkeeper of The Grimason House, 344 Princess Street, in midtown Kingston. Grimason House was known to all Tories as the unofficial political headquarters of John A. It was near his law office and many problems

were settled in its comfortable rooms.

### First Client

John A. was a young lawyer when — according to family tradition — Mrs. Grimason, at about sixteen, became his first client. John A. bought a building in 1851 which was purchased — but not entirely paid for — by Henry Grimason in 1856. When Henry Grimason died in 1867, John A. acted as adviser to Mrs. Eliza Grimason. Since she had been left with two daughters and a son, he did not press her for the balance of the payments on the property.

When he started in the practice of law, John A.'s legal mentors had encouraged him to make friends of people in all walks of life. Within the hospitable, noisy, lively rooms of The Grimason House it was easy for him to air his cheery persuasive type of banter and impress his political opinions on every type of individual. He joined his jovial companions at meals and local cockfights.

Records in Queen's University Archives state that "another favourite place for farmers during the 1800s was The Grimason House on Princess Street . . . always crowded to capacity. Apart from the country trade, this public house had a particular clientele of its own, mostly

Tory admirers of 'John A.' and his political opinions. Here on election nights 'open house' was kept for all the faithful, as the landlady was one of Sir John's most ardent supporters." (E.E. Horsey, 1942)

In *Kingston — the King's Town,* James Roy tells us that "Grimason House became in time the shrine of John A.'s worshippers with Mrs. Grimason as high priestess. . . . Mowat's Grits made one last effort to injure their opponent, they broke up a meeting at Grimason House. . . . [On special nights] Mrs. Grimason, John A.'s friend and staunch supporter, lit up Grimason House and stood free drinks to her clients."

### "I Hate Them Damn Grits!"

Donald Swainson writes: "One of the most devoted followers was Mrs. Grimason, whose Kingston tavern was for years Macdonald's local election headquarters. She was thrilled when John A. invited her to visit Ottawa. While in the Parliament Buildings, they encountered William Mulock, a distinguished Toronto Liberal. Macdonald introduced Mulock to Mrs. Grimason who immediately lectured him for his political sins. After warming up, she startled the dignified gentleman with the remark, 'I hate them damn Grits!' "

*(continued)*

Mrs. Eliza Grimason, an elegant and authoritative figure, riding out in her cutter in Kingston. Her success as an innkeeper was attested by her fortune, which was estimated at $50,000.00.

# A widow at 46, and a good businesswoman

What kind of woman was Mrs. Grimason? Photographs of her in middle age show a handsome, well-dressed woman, radiating confidence — as well she might. Events attest that she was energetic, spirited, healthy and stimulating. She was probably well endowed with charm, for she drew people to her brightly lit hotel which was always filled to capacity.

Henry Grimason had been innkeeper for only eleven years when he died. The forty-six-year-old widow then ran the business so efficiently and capably that she became independently wealthy. Her properties were estimated at $50,000.00 — a tidy sum in those days.

Inevitably there was gossip that John A. spent too much time at Grimason House. He was supposed to have kept two rooms in the hotel section for his own personal use, and it is said of a large brass bed that "John A. slept here."

Busybodies repeated rumours that he spent more nights at Grimason House than at his own residence and that Mrs. Grimason awakened him early on Sunday mornings so that he would not be late for church.

*Writing in 1891, Biggar tells us more about Mrs. Grimason.*

Her influence became no small element in an election, and it was said she could control a hundred votes. To whom these votes went need not be asked. She became so absorbed in that one personality that . . . she would be drawn to his meetings when often she would be the only female present. More than once on election night, when the returns were brought in, she would appear at Sir John's committee room, and walk up among the men to the head of the table and, giving Sir John a kiss, retire without a remark to anyone. When a political picnic was held near Kingston, Mrs. Grimason's van was always at the disposal of Sir John and his party, and in former days she always made one of the party.

She often longed to go to the Capital and see her deity on the throne of his glory or, as she expressed it, to see Sir John "take his seat" and at last, some years ago at the opening of Parliament, she made the venture. It was the event of her life, and it is no exaggeration to say that both Sir John and Lady Macdonald were proud and glad to see her.

### Visit to Earnscliffe

Lady Macdonald took her down to Earnscliffe and she never tired of telling of the kindness that was shown her. In her good rich brogue she would describe her visit: "They have a lovely place all their own, down there by the Rye-do; the house has a lovely slate roof like they have in England, and beautiful grounds, and everything in style, an' a man to wait on the dure. Lady Macdonald kapes

her own cow, and hins, and they make their own butter. They have two fine cows and six servants. Lady Macdonald showed me over the house, and in the fine big library there was my picture up beside o' His, just where He sits.

### Finds Lady Macdonald "Plain"

"After showin' me through the house, she says: 'There now, haven't I made him very comfortable?' She's a very plain woman is Lady Macdonald — not good lookin' — but oh, she's the fine eddication, and that's where she gets the best of thim. Why, I heard her talkin' Frinch to the carpenter workin' about the house. It's her fine eddication that makes her so nice, and she takes such good care o' Him. And if I went back there today she would make as much of me as if I was the richest woman in the country. His library is beautiful, and it's covered over with books to the tip top of the wall. While I was there, the man brought in his letters from the mail — as thrue as I tell ye there was the full of that of thim" (holding out her apron).

As for her sentiments concerning Sir John, words were too weak to express her worship. "There's not a man like him in the livin' earth," was her sincere and simple estimate. . . . "If he said it was so-and-so, I'd take my oath that it was so, whether I knew anything about it or not." She had nearly every photograph ever taken of Sir John, and these she prized above all things, especially the one taken in his Privy Councillor's uniform, which she described as the one "taken in his regimintals for the Queen."

When Sir John returned to power in 1878, it almost broke her heart to know that he had been personally defeated in Kingston. "I went around the next day," she said, "Cryin' till I hadn't an eye in me head. 'Never mind,' sez Sir John to me. 'They're all below me yet.' And sure he was for they elected him away out in British Columby. 'And now,' sez I to Sir John, when I knew he was in, 'take the best position you can get in the hull country, and tell them all to go to the divil.' 'Is that what you would do?' sez he. 'Yes,' sez I. He roared and laughed, and then said the country would go to the dogs if he did that.

"I hope the Lord will spare him for many a year, if it is His holy and blessed will," she would say with a sincere and reverent face, "for what will become of the country without him?" When Sir John lay sick at the time of the last election, she too lay ill. To her clergyman who called upon her, she said her own illness concerned her not, but that daily she went down upon her knees to pray that Sir John might be spared and be elected. "Usually," she added, "I don't trouble the Lord with my wordly affairs, but in a case like this you know I think it is different." Could humility to God and unselfish devotion to man be better expressed

in one sentence? It used to be her desire that when she died she should rest near him and some years ago she was fortunately able to purchase a large plot immediately adjoining the Macdonald plot in the Cataraqui Cemetery where the remains of her husband were moved.

Mrs. Grimason outlived John A. by twenty-five years. Their two graves are contiguous, the largest in the cemetery. Each has a railing around its perimeter and even the tombstones are somewhat similar, tall and slender on a broad base. The memorial spire of the Grimason family towers a little above that of the Macdonalds. The obelisk of Sir John A. is of polished granite in a buff tone; that of the Grimasons is a mottled rose. The inscription on the Grimason column reads:

---

*Henry Grimason*
*Died*
*in Kingston, Ont.*
*November 23, 1867*
*aged 56 years*
*also his wife*
*Eliza Grimason*
*Died*
*March 30, 1916*
*aged 95 years*

---

So much for the old days. Just a few years ago — in 1968 — an important Macdonald antique was presented to the nation — a ma-

hogany cradle which John A. had given to Mrs. Grimason. It is in excellent condition, quite large and sturdily built. A swing model, it is fitted with a little hood and the body is completely lined with dark red felt. Tradition has it that the cradle was brought from Scotland by John A.'s parents. The Macdonald Cradle, now in the nursery at Bellevue House, Kingston, bears a card which reads. ". . . The cradle was apparently given to Mrs. Grimason by John A. Macdonald as a keepsake. It was in the family for years and from Mrs. Grimason, it was given to Mrs. Reid who was the mother of Mrs. Theresa A. (Etta) Newlands. Mrs. Theresa A. Newlands died in about 1963-4 and the cradle became part of the estate which passed on to her son, Dr. W. A. Newlands. . . .

"The cradle was presented to the Kingston Historical Society by Dr. W. A. Newlands, Tarrytown, New York." (Dated October 22, 1968, and signed by Dr. L. J. Flynn, president of the Kingston Historical Society from 1962 until 1972.)

In 1974, Queen's University received the gift of floor plans of The Grimason House and the residences of the late Mrs. Eliza Grimason on Union Street and on Princess Street. This collection, known as the William Newlands Architectural Drawings, was donated by the Kingston architect A. J. Connidis, the Royal Bank of Canada and the Newlands family. The drawings had been found in the attic of the Royal Bank Building. *(continued)*

Among Mrs. Grimason's descendants, this was always known as "the John A. Macdonald cradle," because John A. had given it to her. According to family tradition, John A.'s parents had brought it from Scotland. Dr. Newlands gave it to the Kingston Historical Society in 1968, and it is now in Bellevue House.

"Grimason House became in time the shrine of John A.'s worshippers with Mrs. Grimason as high priestess." This is how it was believed to have looked around 1880 (although it was not called the Royal Hotel until 1933). The oil painting by F.A. Pratt shows the driveway leading to the stable yard in the rear and Princess Street, lit by gaslight and paved with granite blocks. Dr. Newlands says that as a child he saw his great-grandmother rarely because "I was not allowed to go near a hotel."

### Grimason House Today

Grimason House became The Farmer's Royal Exchange Inn around 1900 and The Royal Hotel around 1933. The property was bought by Mrs. Enid Lavin in 1956 — a century after Henry Grimason purchased it from John A. The building, now painted a dark red, is called The Royal Tavern. Still on the premises is an eighteen-foot-wide mirror and a very grand, highly ornamented cookstove — *The Superb Favourite,* made by the Doherty Mfg. Co. of Sarnia, Ontario. Finished in shiny nickel, this boasts huge ovens, hot water tanks and swinging warming plates. The stove was probably used to cook the famous twenty-five cent suppers that Mrs. Grimason served at political meetings. Against one wall is a carved sideboard, from which drinks were no doubt dispensed.

The present owner has a number of historically important documents, which trace the ownership from the time when John A. bought the property on June 13, 1851, from Matthew Rourk. (It was thought to have belonged to the Roman Catholic Church around 1840.)

The former Grimason House as it looks today. Inside, a mirror, a huge stove and a sideboard date from the time Mrs. Grimason cooked twenty-five cent suppers and dispensed free drinks to celebrate John A.'s election victories. The driveway to the stable yard has been closed in.

# PART THREE  1860-1867

*John A. Macdonald stated that his public mission in England was in favour of union and that as a conscientious man he felt bound to carry out his own theory.* Montreal Gazette

# *The mother he adored dies at 84*

## He looked like her, had her humour, memory, intelligence and endurance

A few years after the death of his wife another lonely gap opened in the life of John A. His eighty-four-year-old mother died. They had been very close. She never wavered in her belief that he was destined for great things. They were alike in many ways — both were loyal to the Crown and the Church of Scotland. Both were proud of the family participation in the wars of the Empire. Both liked a joke (although his were more inclined to be rough). Hospitable and ambitious, with a liveliness of spirit, they made friends easily, enjoying the stimulation of people around them. They didn't take themselves too seriously and were able to shrug off their troubles.

According to Biggar, John A.'s mother was "a grand old lady, and from her Sir John undoubtedly inherited most of those qualities which have made his name a word to conjure by. She was a little above the medium height, large limbed, and capable of much endurance. Her face was remarkable.... Her features were large, and, as some considered, coarse; but there beamed through her dark eye a depth of apprehension mingled with such graciousness and good-will as commanded the reverence of a passer-by. But most remarkable of anything about her were the strange lines with which her features were scored as she advanced in years, lines which were reproduced in her son in a still more striking way.... Mrs. Macdonald was a woman of deep piety as well as kindness of heart.... She had a broad Scotch accent and a pronounced sense of humour. She appreciated a droll situation or a droll saying. Those who knew her best say she had a great mind and a great memory; and had she possessed the advantages of a high education, and the opportunities some get in life, she would have been a noted woman."

Occupied as he always was with the pressures of government, John A. made it a point to write his mother regularly and to return to Kingston to visit her. He knew that she tended to his room herself, keeping it ready for his next visit. She had asked that when the time came, he would lie beside her in the Kingston Cemetery at Cataraqui — a promise that was kept.

### The Ugliest Woman
Sir John A.'s spinster sister, Louisa, was once complimented on her wit and was assured that she was the very image of her famous brother. "What a curious remark!" she exclaimed. "Everybody knows that John is the ugliest man in Canada!"

*RB*

LOUISA          MARGARET

Of the five Macdonald children, John A. was the only male to survive. His younger sister Louisa remained unmarried and was said to resemble her famous brother. Margaret, whom he called "Moll," was a year and a half older than John A. She married James Williamson, professor of mathematics and natural philosophy at Queen's University. John A.'s sisters and mother brought up his son Hugh because of the severe illness and eventual death of Isabella, the boy's mother.

*Queen's*

Professor James Williamson married John A.'s sister Margaret in 1852. He was a Presbyterian minister and — according to *Heritage Kingston* — probably the most beloved professor in the early history of Queen's. He was John A.'s good friend and made his last public speech at his brother-in-law's funeral. He continued to befriend John A.'s widow, and Baroness Macdonald wrote to him: "My good friend, ever kind and true to me, one who when *he* was gone did not fail me as did others."

58

HELEN SHAW MACDONALD

It was from his mother that John A. was said to have inherited all the qualities that made him so remarkable. She has been described as a large woman with massive, masculine features, the possessor of great will power and strong opinions, which she expressed quietly and with exceptional humour. Her intelligence and vitality impressed all who knew her. At the age of seventy-two she suffered a severe stroke, but she rallied and lived through twelve additional strokes in the next thirteen years. As he grew older, John A. came to resemble her more and more.

## THE CURSE OF CANADA.

IS THERE NO ARM TO SAVE?

# Liquor common as water

## 60 taverns in 1828 Toronto; 500 by 1870

### Saskatoon founded in 1882 as temperance colony

When John A. was young, whisky was twenty-five to fifty cents a gallon. It was kept as water in a pail with a cup beside it — the beverage of rich and poor alike. Doctors were few. Almost every medicine was made with whisky or home brew, and taken liberally. On June 12, 1828, the *Colonial Advocate,* a leading York (Toronto) paper, lamented:

#### *Taverns Corrupt Youth*

Although the official return of the population of York is under 2000 souls, there are about sixty stores, houses of entertainment or taverns, in some of which strong beer or spiritous liquors are either sold or permitted to be drank at all hours of day and night, and on all days and nights of the week. Many of these stores and taverns are creditably kept by respectable persons, but there are other houses, either of ill-fame, or the resort of the idle, the dissipated, the worthless or the profligate, which are known to the magistrates, and in some cases owned by them, but which they permit to exist and to multiply as hot beds of vice and infamy, and allurements to draw youth along the swift road that leadeth to destruction.

Many were crying out against the habitual drunken state of the early pioneers, in the smaller as well as the larger settlements. The *Colonial*

*Advocate* of May 31, 1832, reprinted an article from a London newspaper, which told of the advantages of temperance.

#### *Advantages of Temperance*

Two glasses of gin every day, at three half-pence a glass, cost four pounds eleven shillings and threepence in a year; which would pay for:

| | £ | s | d |
|---|---|---|---|
| A man's hat 6s; neckerchief 1s 4d | 0 | 7 | 4 |
| Pair men's stockings 1s 9d; pair men's shoes 8s 6d | 0 | 10 | 3 |
| Pair women's stockings 1s 7d; pair women's shoes 4s | 0 | 5 | 6 |
| Shift and muslin cap 3s 8d; flannel petticoat 2s 6d | 0 | 6 | 2 |
| Printed cotton gown 5s 6d; coarse cloth cloak 7s | 0 | 12 | 6 |
| Full sized man's cotton shirt 4s; quilting waistcoat 4s | 0 | 8 | 0 |
| Full sized fustian coat 16s; fustian trowsers lined 7s 6d | 1 | 3 | 6 |
| Pair large blankets 12s; pair cotton sheets 6s | 0 | 18 | 0 |
| | £4 | 11 | 3 |

The liquor situation became progressively worse in Canada as the century advanced. By 1870 in Toronto (York) there were 500 saloons, selling whisky at two cents a shot. Half the arrests were due to liquor. Unhappy about this way of life, a vanguard of Ontario citizens left for the west and founded the City of Saskatoon as a Temperance Colony in 1882. The following bond which the Temperance Colonists at Saskatoon were asked to sign when filing their applications for entry shows clearly that the colony was intended to be a temperance community in fact as well as name: "In con-

sideration of my acceptance by the Temperance Colonization Society (Limited) as an applicant for land covered by their agreement with the Government of this Dominion of Canada, I hereby, for myself, my heirs, executors, administrators and assigns, covenant and agree with the said society, their successors and assigns, that I, my heirs, executors, administrators and assigns will not: sell or exchange any wines, beer, ale, spirits, intoxicating liquors, or intoxicants of any kind whatever on or upon any of the lands covered by the agreement aforesaid, and further hereby agree to the insertion in any deed of any conveyance to me, my Heirs or assigns, of such portion of said lands as may be allotted to me, of such clause, as may be necessary to give full effect to the above restriction, on the penalty of forfeiting the same in case of non-observance."

Considering the social mores of the times —

*(continued)*

HOW LONG IS THIS SPREE GOING TO LAST?

Prof. Vernoy, *Electro Therapeutic { Vernoy's Improved Family Battery, manufactured and for sale Institution.} by the Electric Battery Co., 56 King St. West, Toronto.* 197 Jarvis St.

GRIP

CHINA HALL
GLOVER HARRISON IMPORTER
49 KING ST. E., TORONTO.

CHINA HALL
GLOVER HARRISON IMPORTER
49 KING ST. E., TORONTO.

VOLUME XXIV.}
No. 23.

TORONTO, SATURDAY, JUNE 6TH, 1885.

{ $2 PER ANNUM.
5 CENTS EACH.

THE WAR ON WOMEN AND CHILDREN.

*Liquor Traffic.*—With these weapons I'm as deadly as ever, and I'll show you no mercy!

VOLUME XXV. }
No. 15.

TORONTO, SATURDAY, OCT. 10TH, 1885.

{ $2 Pr
{ 5 CE

PROHIBITED FRUIT.

THE OLD, OLD ARGUMENT.

John W. Bengough, cartoonist and editor of *Grip*, was an ardent prohibitionist and often featured temperance cartoons in his magazine. All the drawings in this section are his.

### Water on the Breath

A man once approached Sir John A. and said, "I'm a member of the Temperance Society." Sir John A. replied, "Move over. Your breath is positively awful; it smells of water."

In 1881 Winnipeg had sixty-four hotels, most with saloons attached. There were five breweries and twenty-four stores where wine or liquor could be bought. The next year there were eighty-six hotels, almost all with a bar, and sixty-four stores which sold whisky by the bottle.

At one time, Sir John A. had a government with a majority of two. "Why," he said, "it's not even a drinking majority."

### Good Health

One night after taking Sir John A. home, his cabdriver, Patrick Buckley, was stopped by some parliamentarians and asked to answer honestly, "Was Sir John A. tight when you drove him home?" Patrick, in loyalty, answered, "I have driven him all these years, and I nivir seen him in better health in me life thin today."

### A Sick Joke

Sir John A. always seemed to have a quick way of saving a bad situation. During a particularly strenuous campaign, he faced a Liberal opponent at a time when he was exhausted from electioneering demands and had sought relief in drink. As he rose to make an address, Sir John A., to everyone's dismay, vomitted on the platform. In a composed manner, he said to the crowd, "Ladies and gentlemen, you must forgive me but I cannot help myself. That man," pointing to his Liberal opponent, "just makes me sick."

and the wish to seem older than his years to impress the business and political figures with whom he came in contact — it is not surprising that John A., like so many youths, developed into a heavy drinker. This weakness plagued him all his life, with debilitating and sometimes disastrous results.

### Learns from Father

John A. was not the only Macdonald who liked his drink. His father, Hugh, was also known as a heavy drinker. Biggar quotes a man named Porter, who knew father and son: "I never went to Kingston ... but what old Hugh and me had a jollification. Hugh was as fond of a good drop as John A. and me. And whenever I saw John A. on the street, why, bless you, he wouldn't wait for me to come and speak but he would duck his head in that peculiar way of his, and come right across the street to shake hands. 'Damn it, Porter,' he would say, 'are you alive yet?' Everybody drank in them days, and they had their match in me; but, dear me, whisky carried off a good many, and some of them our best men, too. And I am the only one left here of the boys of that time."

### John A. Macdonald — Son of Temperance

John A. actually took the temperance pledge in 1862 according to *The Montreal Star* of July 23: "The special meeting of Mechanic's Division, Kingston, [of the Temperance Society] on Friday evening last, called for the initiation of John A. Macdonald, was very well attended by members of the order. The Temperance Hall was thronged by both Sons and Daughters of Temperance.... On his initiation, the Hon. Gentleman delivered a brief address ... explaining the reasons which had induced him to become a Son of Temperance ... that for some time past he had been fully convinced of the evils of the drinking customs of society, and had come to a determination to renounce them on his part.... We hear that Mr. Macdonald made a very modest speech, saying that he had no political object in view by taking the present course. The officers who officiated were members of twelve or thirteen years standing."

As events were to show, John A. never became a member in good standing.

As he grew older, Sir John A. seems to have graduated from the bucket-and-cup-whisky of

his childhood to more sophisticated imported liquors, if one judges from the order he placed before the Christmas and New Year's festivities, in November 1881. His wine merchant was Quetton, St. George and Co., 16 King Street West, Toronto.

3 dozen 1 qt. Manzanilla at $9
2 dozen Porto at $13
2 dozen Porto Fino at $18
2 dozen Madeira at $20
3 dozen Medoc at $8
2 dozen St. Estephe at $16

Meanwhile Canada's self-appointed poet laureate James Gay advocated:

### Throw All Our Grog Bottles Away, Like J. Gay

*Your poet is a great advocate for good. All our duty as far as we can,*
*Is to love and respect our fellow-man;*
*Rush to do him good, that's if we can;*
*Whether Greek, Gentile, or a Jew,*
*We are in duty bound to help him through.*
*It's not the church of any kind*
*Can destroy the peace of your poet's mind;*
*He's a true believer every day,*
*Lives as happy as the flowers in May.*
*Anything for good that we can see*
*We should turn out and help like that busy bee;*
*Those are a guide for our fellow-man,*
*Doing good is their every day's plan;*
*All through the day all do their best,*
*When night comes on they take their rest.*
*All insects have their cunning ways;*
*All those are of one mind*
*To make their homes so neat and fine.*
*Oh, if man could only see,*
*And live as happy as that bee;*
*Cast off bad thoughts of any kind,*
*The world very soon would be of one mind.*
*Live on this earth in love and peace,*
*And not to act as brutes and beasts.*
*Let temperance be our guide while on this earth we stay;*
*With good of all kinds*
*Be on our minds,*
*And throw all our grog bottles away,*
*Like J. Gay.*

## Cocky Comment

At formal receptions, the Cabinet Ministers often wore their Windsor uniforms. Before one such meeting a minister who was not known for his temperate habits was trying on his hat. Sir John A. observed that it was not a very good fit. He commented, "I think a cocktail suits you better than a cocked hat!"

1 dozen Château Leoville
2 dozen Sauterne Supreme at $14
2 dozen Port C at $15
3 dozen Vin d'Eté at $15
2 dozen Vin des Princes at $22
2 dozen Sparkling Moselle at $18
1 dozen Cognac VV
½ dozen Orange Curacao
¼ dozen Maraschino
¼ dozen Chartreuse
The total bill was $467.75.

There are innumerable anecdotes about Sir John A.'s drinking habits and behaviour when drunk. Sir John A. made no secret of the fact that he liked his drink. Once, in an immigration debate, Mr. Bowell criticized Mr. Mackenzie for announcing a temperance lecture and then discussing immigration. Said Sir John A.: "That will certainly throw cold water on immigration."

Among early biographies of Sir John A. was one by J.E. Collins. Sir Richard Cartwright said of it: "There is in it something of the 'eternal fitness of things' that a gentleman who in his life has done justice to so many Collinses should at last find a Collins to do justice to him." Sir John A. laughed as heartily as anyone in the House.

## Temperance Social

The members of Burlington Lodge No. 470 had a social . . . which proved a success in every particular. The hall was comfortably filled with an intelligent audience whose countenances indicated that the wine cup was not necessary to the enjoyment of life. Ample refreshments were served. . . . Some excellent pieces were sung by the Misses Thompson, Frazer, Macdonald and Ross; also by Mr. R. Stevens, who was loudly encored. Addresses were delivered by Revd.'s Mr. Gilray and Sutherland and Dr. Fergusson. . . . Mr. Wm. Hastings recited in excellent style "The Drunkard's Child." At an early hour the audience separated, all seeming well pleased with the evening's entertainment.
*The Hamilton Evening Times,*
June 25, 1867

## Needs Support

Another story often told about Sir John A. concerns the aftermath of a dinner, where he drank too much. Obviously unsteady, he spoke to another dinner guest, a personal friend but an ardent Liberal, "I have known you for twenty-five years and you're never given me a vote yet," and he took his friend's arm and continued, "but you've got to support me now."

Once when Sir John A. was very ill, and had been semi-conscious for some time, Lady Macdonald took a flask of whisky and rubbed some of it over his face and chest. "Oh, do that again," he whispered. "It seems to do me good!"

A bill dated December 30, 1886, shows that

## WCTU — Women Continually Torment Us

PROHIBITION DOES PROHIBIT!

John A. is pictured as a worshipper of the Demon Rum. Because of his notorious drinking habits, he was regarded as the main foe of prohibition. The quote from Gladstone on the wall — "The liquor traffic is more destructive than war, famine and pestilence combined" — was a typical nineteenth-century comment. Drinking was regarded as the number one social problem and the main cause of crime, violence and broken homes.

Sir John A. ordered the following from Frederick Kingston, 25 Hospital Street, Montreal:

| | |
|---|---|
| 3 dozen bottles Vino de Porto | $21.60 |
| 3 dozen bottles Molino | 30.00 |
| 1 dozen bottles Amontillado | 13.20 |
| 3 cases Verzenan | 42.00 |
| 2 cases Carte Rosa | 36.00 |
| 4 dozen St. Estephe | 28.00 |
| 1 dozen Château Larose | 18.00 |
| 2 dozen Leoville | 24.00 |
| ½ dozen VNO Brandy | 6.60 |
| The total | $219.40 |

A bill dated May 17, 1887, shows the purchase of one case of Verzenan Champagne pints at $6.50. In February 1873 there was a bill for $125.25 for "1 Octave Sherry (17½ gals.), 2 cases Kupferberg's Moselle, 2 cases Chamoines Champagne B."

Once, after being attacked for drunkenness by George Brown, Sir John A. replied, "I know enough . . . to know that you would rather have Sir John A. drunk than George Brown sober."

## Prohibiting Prohibition

When a prohibition bill was introduced a Member of Parliament said to Sir John A., "I hope you don't intend to let that go through. It would kill us at home."

"Yes," replied the Prime Minister. "It would kill me at home too."

In 1967, ninety-one-year-old Hugh Angus Macdonald, a nephew of Sir John A., said, "I and my brother were sent into town every two weeks with an empty five-gallon 'jimmy-john' in the wagon and came back with a full one. It cost forty-five cents a gallon, and I don't know what it was."

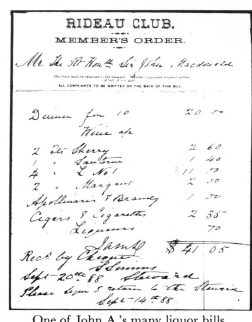

One of John A.'s many liquor bills.

## YES! THEY'D BETTER ATTEMPT A RESCUE!

While public opinion says to curb the liquor traffic, brewers march to Ottawa with a sign saying "Our craft is in danger."

# Out, in, out of office — and then "Great Coalition"

## *Macdonald and enemy George Brown unite to solve Constitution problems*

Every possible political stratagem to keep the Cartier-Macdonald coalition in office was employed, but nevertheless their administration was defeated. Now, in 1862, John A. was a Member of the Opposition.

Worn out from prolonged overwork and heavy drinking, he wrote to his sister Margaret: "I am out of office — at last free, thank God! and can now feel as a free man. I have longed for this hour and only a sense of honour has kept me chained to my post.... I have now fulfilled my duty to my party and can begin to think of myself.... I have been very ill, but am crawing about."

At this time, two significant appointive posts became available to John A. — Chief Justice and Chancellor of Canada West. He could have chosen either. But in spite of his fervent wish to return to a more or less private life, he could not bring himself to leave politics.

In 1864 John A. was back in power, but only briefly. The Taché-Macdonald administration merely lasted from March until June when the two leaders had to face the defeat in the House — by a few votes. Sectional differences and struggles incapacitated them. The crisis that followed resulted in the "Great Coalition" in which George Brown and other reformers of Canada West united with John A. and the Conservatives in order to solve the constitutional problems of the day.

Professor Paul G. Cornell, the historian, has written: "At first glance, the Great Coalition might appear to be but a uniquely brilliant move in a, till then, uninspiring game of political chess. Political opponents at that time, and unsympathetic later commentators, have suggested that political expediency was the principal motive. But they were wrong. The principals who entered the coalition did so at some considerable risk to their careers. The policy proclaimed by the coalition government pointed the way to fulfillment of major long-term goals that had been pursued by the several political parties over the course of many years."

RB

TACTICS
CAUSALITY

### The Great Coalition
On June 30, 1864, John A. joined with Reform Liberals George Brown, Oliver Mowat and William McDougall to form a ministry.

*The Globe* of Toronto, Canada West, reported in January 1864: Canada has had in the past year, an emigration from the United Kingdom of nearly 15,000 — English, 4830; Scotch, 3949; and Irish, 5580. Nine-tenths of the English and Scotch remained in Canada with friends already settled. Four-fifths of the Irish went to the U.S. The callings of the British steerings male adults were — labourers, 2726; mechanics, 1830; farmers, 1476; clerks and traders, 188; domestic service, 22; and professional men, 8.

*The Gazette,* Montreal, January 2, 1862, reported that "The Hon. John A. Macdonald has been officially gazetted 'Minister of Militia Affairs.' Mr. Macdonald has de facto acted in such capacity for some time past, and the vigour and promptness of his proceedings, the moment the word came from the Imperial Government, have commended themselves to the approval of the whole country . . . Let the present Militia Movement be the same kind of shield to Canada that the Voluntary Rifle Movement has proved to Britain."

John A. on flattery: "Almost anybody will take any amount of it."

### No Looking to Washington!
Conservative Party slogan, July 1861.

### It Makes Census
*The Gazette,* Montreal, January 24, 1862, reported the returns of the census of the British North American Provinces as follows:

| | |
|---|---|
| Canada | 2,506,755 |
| New Brunswick | 250,000 (over) |
| Nova Scotia | 330,000 |
| Prince Edward Island | 80,857 |
| Newfoundland | 122,638 |

In 1861 John A. said to the Legislative Assembly, "I trust that for ages, for ever, Canada may remain united with the mother country. But we are fast ceasing to be a dependency and are assuming the position of an ally of Great Britain. England will be the centre, surrounded and sustained by an alliance not only with Canada, but Australia, and all her other possessions; and there will thus be formed an immense confederation of freedom, the greatest confederacy of civilized and intelligent men that has ever had an existence on the face of the globe."

In Charlottetown, Prince Edward Island, on September 1, 1864, the first of three conferences that would make Confederation a reality opened. In the photograph above, John A. is at centre stage — a position he would occupy at all three conferences. Standing beside him is George Etienne Cartier and behind them is Thomas D'Arcy McGee — the two men Macdonald depended on to carry Quebec into the new union.

# John A. Macdonald — the architect of Confederation

## *"It is an opportunity that may never recur"*

## Fear of U.S. expansion northward spurs Conferences

Although John A. did not originate the idea of the British North American Union, his leading part in the conferences caused him to be known as the "Chief Architect of Confederation." Years of discussion, but no real blueprint of planning, preceded the three important meetings that made Confederation a reality. As far back as 1858, Alexander Tilloch Galt had thought of confederation. Now the time was right.

### Birthplace of Canada

It was on a fine day, September 1, 1864, that Canada East and Canada West delegates sailed into Charlottetown (since called "The Birthplace of Canada") for the opening debates on Confederation. The Canada West party arrived on the government steamer *Queen Victoria;* the Nova Scotians were on the *Heather Belle* and the New Brunswick delegation on the *Prince of Wales.*

In October, the representatives met again in Quebec City. At both of these conferences,

John A. stood out among his colleagues. It is said that he authored fifty of the seventy-two resolutions. Confederation was on its way, although the final drafting of the British North America Act did not take place for two more years.

### The Confederation Experiment

On October 11, 1864, at the Quebec Conference, John A. made an important speech: "In framing the constitution, care should be taken to avoid the mistakes and weaknesses of the United States system, the primary error of which was the reservation to the different states of all powers not delegated to the general

George Brown told his wife Anne that Confederation "will be a tremendous thing if we accomplish it. I don't believe any of us appreciate the immensity of the work we are engaged in."

government. We must reverse this process. . . . A strong central government is indispensable to the success of the experiment we are trying." (Note that he spoke of Confederation as an "experiment.")

John A.'s mind wasn't *always* on politics. In 1864 he wrote to his sister Margaret: " I have just got 'What to do with the Cold Mutton' which I will mail to you. Will you look for a little book 'Cavendish on Whist' and send it to me?" At about the same time he wrote to his other sister, Louisa: "I am pretty well just now, barring an occasional colic, which sticks to me with wonderful pertinacity." It was fortunate that his health was good, for ahead lay days of decision.

### British or Yankee

In 1865 the American Civil War was drawing to a close. What would the Americans do with their trained, armed, experienced soldiers? The rebellion in the South put down, would the Yankees look north to Canada? The Cana-

Alexander Tilloch Galt talked of Confederation as far back as 1858. He was one of the ablest men in Canadian politics but was impatient and oversensitive as well as being intelligent and imaginative. John A. said that, of the delegates to the Confederation Conferences, Galt was the only one besides himself who had "any idea of constitution making."

Samuel Leonard Tilley, a druggist, brought about prohibition in his native New Brunswick in 1855 and became so unpopular that he was voted out of office for two years. His temperance beliefs did not stop him from supporting John A. as chairman of the London Conference. He lacked Galt's imagination but his reliability and concern for details made him a valuable ally.

### Almost Fired

John A. read constantly. This habit was almost his undoing. One night during the London Conference, he retired to his bed in the Westminster Palace Hotel with a paper to read before sleeping. He fell asleep over the paper, and his lamp set the bed curtains on fire. Though scorched by the flames, fortunately he woke up before any serious damage was done, either to him or to the hotel.

dian ministers felt that the situation was grave enough to warrant a conference with the Imperial government.

Brown Chamberlin, of *The Gazette*, Montreal, wrote: "I pray you go to England. There are many true hearts who will not rest satisfied unless you do. If the wit of men can help it, there must be no failure to come to an agreement with the Mother Country.... The greatest interests, the very birthright of Britons in Canada are in your keeping.... Five years hence we shall be more truly British or altogether Yankee. Whose will be the fault if the latter should be our fate?"

### Kissing Hands

It was decided to send a delegation consisting of Macdonald, Cartier, Brown and Galt to discuss matters with the British cabinet. While in London the party resided at the Westminster Palace Hotel. The following are excerpts from a letter which Galt wrote to his wife from London on May 17, 1865: "The great event of Monday was our reception at Court. The morning was spent partly in arranging our uniforms. I had sent mine to the tailor's to put it completely en règle, as you know the gold lace was not the correct width, and I had also to get knee breeches, etc.... At a Court only those attend who are invited, and it is

"Reasons for Confederation are as thick as blackberries." — Thomas D'Arcy McGee

therefore a great distinction. Before the general reception began, the Queen ordered that we should be presented by Mr. Cardwell, as belonging to the Diplomatic Circle, and that we should have the honour of kissing hands. We were ushered in, in the order of our seniority, Macdonald, Cartier, Brown and myself.... The Queen looked very well, but little changed. She was dressed in black [the Prince-Consort had died in 1861] with a long white veil attached to the back of her head. No ornaments except a heavy pearl necklace.... The Prince looked very well and has improved greatly since he was in Canada.... We all felt that we had been treated with great distinction. Indeed our whole reception in England proves how important our mission is considered. We are treated quite as if we were ambassadors and not as mere Colonials as we have always been called. We open our formal official communications on Friday, and hope a few days will settle things."

*The Illustrated London News* of May 20, 1865, gives a slightly different account of Queen Victoria's dress at the meeting: "The Queen held her fifth Court, on Monday, at Buckingham Palace.... The Queen, accompanied by the Prince of Wales, Princess Helena, Princess Louisa, and Princess Mary, entered the Throne-room at three o'clock.... The Queen wore a black silk dress, with train trimmed with crape and jet; a Mary Queen of Scots cap, with long veil, the cap ornamented with large pearls. Her Majesty wore four rows of large pearls round

Hector Langevin on the Fathers of Confederation: "John A. Macdonald is a sharp fox . . . very well informed, ingratiating, clever, very popular. He is *the* man of the conference. Mr. Tupper of Nova Scotia is capable but too incisive; he makes many bitter enemies for himself; he is ambitious and a gambler. Samuel Leonard Tilley of New Brunswick is a deft trimmer, clever and adroit . . . one of the most distinguished men of the Maritimes."

On occasion men who were in the habit of supporting John A. broke away on particular issues. When Senator Dickey of Nova Scotia opposed Confederation John A. said, "Why did you kick up your heels? Have you gone over to the other side?"

"No," said Senator Dickey. "I am still a Conservative. I shall support you whenever I think you right."

John A. twinkled, "Anybody may support me when I am right. What I want is a man who will support me when I am wrong."

the neck, and pearl brooches, the ribbon and star of the Order of the Garter, the Victoria and Albert order, and the order of Louise of Prussia. A number of distinguished persons had the honour of receiving invitations to attend the Court. Previously to the reception the Right Hon. Edward Cardwell presented the Hon. J. A. Macdonald, the Hon. G. E. Cartier, the Hon. George Brown, and the Hon. Alexander Galt, who had the honour of kissing her Majesty's hand.... After the reception her Majesty left the palace at a quarter-past six o'clock for Windsor Castle. The Queen drove through Hyde Park to the Paddington Station of the Great Western Railway in an open carriage and four, attended by the Equerries on horseback."

### Oxford Honours John A.

After the meeting, John A. remained in England, where he felt so at home, for another week. He moved in smart and sophisticated circles, accepting many invitations to country estates. At Oxford University he received an honourary degree. *The Illustrated London News* gives this account in its "Universities and Public Schools" report for June 24, 1865: "At Oxford the annual procession of racing-boats took place
*(continued)*

John A. to anti-Confederationists: "Gentlemen, you are mad!"

Anti-Confederationist Joseph Howe was a poet, journalist and publisher. He called Confederation the "botheration scheme" and threatened to "drive a coach and pair" through the Act. It took the combined diplomacy and persuasive efforts of John A. and Charles Tupper (a fellow Nova Scotian) to win him over. He joined the Conservative Cabinet in 1869.

Charles Tupper was Premier of Nova Scotia during the Confederation Conferences, where he was an enthusiastic supporter of Macdonald. Later he held several Cabinet posts in John A.'s Government and became Prime Minister of Canada briefly in 1896. He was a tenacious fighter, often referred to as the Cumberland Warhorse (for the constituency that he represented).

on the Isis, on Monday evening, and was witnessed by some thousands of spectators. The festivities of the day concluded with a grand masonic ball in the Corn Exchange, given by the Apollo University Lodge of Freemasons. All the élite of the University, county, and the principal visitors staying in Oxford were present.... The honourary degree of Doctor in Civil Law was conferred on Lord Lyons, Lieutenant-General Sir Hugh H. Rose, Count Melchior de Vogüé, the Hon. John Alexander Macdonald, Henry James Summer Maine, Robert Christison, M.D., and William Stokes, M.D. The usual speeches and recitations followed the ceremony of conferring degrees."

To his sister Louisa, John A. reported: "The greatest honour ... much sought after by the first men.... I was only too happy." A few months later, on board the steamer *Victoria,* he wrote to the same sister: "My dear Louisa, I am on my way back from Ottawa to Montreal. I have taken a house there, where Bernard [Hewitt Bernard, his secretary and friend] and I intend living. I want to know what you have got in the way of furniture that you can spare me. There is some bed and table linen I suppose. Send me a list to Quebec on receipt of this.... The Ottawa people gave me a great luncheon yesterday. I can scarcely write for the tremour of the table. So you can scarcely read this."

### John A. Appeals to the Queen

During the Parliamentary Debates on the subject of Confederation of the British North American Provinces, 1865, Attorney-General John A. Macdonald moved "that a humble Address be presented to Her Majesty, praying that she may be graciously pleased to cause a

John A. Macdonald on the proposed Senate (1865): "The rights of the minority must be protected, and the rich are always fewer in number than the poor."

measure to be submitted to the Imperial Parliament for the purpose of uniting the colonies of Canada, Nova Scotia, New Brunswick, Newfoundland and Prince Edward Island in one Government.... When this union takes place we will be at the outset no inconsiderable people.... I am satisfied that under this union, our population will increase in a still greater ratio — with increased credit — with a higher

The Confederation scheme inspired many lively debates and caused some strange political behaviour. Some Members of Parliament even went so far as to take the temperance pledge, according to a letter written by a politician in 1865: "I will make it my business to see J.A. [Macdonald] altho it is not a very easy matter, considering in what plight the Ministry is at present, since their pet scheme of Confederation has received such a sudden check by the overwhelming overthrow of its supporters in New Brunswick. This has caused much ululation and lamentation and some defection in the ministerial camp here. This has compelled them since the last sad news have arrived to keep to the temperance pledge. They are all, without exception, continually in their place in the House, and none more so than our friend J.A. who the night before last made a most unmerciful onslaught on Sandfield who bore the attack with all the meekness and patience of a true Christian! Cartier fights like a Bantam cock and McGee is not slow in aiming a thrust with his double-edged weapon. The other evening Sandfield was boasting of his religious liberality, or rather indifference. Yes, said McGee, you are like the blank page that is found in the Bible, between the Old and New Testament, without belonging to either."

position in the eyes of Europe — with the increased security we can offer to immigrants who would naturally prefer to seek a new home in what is known to them as a great country than in any one little colony or another — with all this I am satisfied that, great as has been our increase in the last twenty-five years since the Union of Upper and Lower Canada, our future progress, during the next quarter of a century, will be vastly greater. (cheers) ... In conclusion, I would again implore the House not to let this opportunity to pass. It is an opportunity that may never recur.... If we do not take advantage of the time, if we show ourselves unequal to the occasion, it may never return, and we shall hereafter bitterly and unavailingly regret having failed to embrace the happy opportunity now offered of founding a great nation under the care of Great Britain and our Sovereign Lady, Queen Victoria" (loud cheers amidst which the honourable gentleman resumed his seat).

During these same debates on Confederation, a member feared that confederated Canada, as a result of greater strength, might withdraw from the Mother Country. To this John A. replied, "I believe it will have the contrary effect. I believe that as we grow stronger, that, as it is felt in England, we have become a people, able from our union, our strength, our population, and the development of our resources to take our position among the nations of the world, she will be less willing to part

On July 27, 1866, the *Acadian Reporter* said, "We don't know each other. We have no trade with each other. We have no facilities, no resources, or incentives to mingle with each other. We are shut off from each other by a wilderness geographically, commercially, politically and socially."

At the Quebec Conference in October 1864, Macdonald is said to have authored fifty of seventy-two resolutions forming the basis of Confederation. Canadian history reveals few personal and political enmities as intense and enduring as that between Macdonald and his Liberal opponent George Brown, but on one great issue they were united — Confederation. Here they are seen side by side; Brown is seated third from the left with John A. flamboyant in light-coloured trousers slouching beside him.

with us than she should be now.... The colonies are now in a transition state. Gradually a different colonial system is being developed — and it will become, year by year, less a case of dependence on our part, and of overruling protection on the part of the Mother Country, and more a case of a healthy and cordial alliance.... England will have in us a friendly nation — a subordinate, but still a powerful people — to stand by her in North America in peace or in war."

### Politicians Confer in London

When the London Conference opened in 1866 there were five Nova Scotians, five New Brunswickers and six Canadians present at the Westminster Palace Hotel. John A. was named chairman on the first day, and as in Charlottetown and Quebec, he took a particularly prominent part in the discussions. There were delaying tactics, and much exacting and concentrated attention to detail before the British North America Act was finally passed on March 28, 1867.

Lord Carnarvon, the Colonial Secretary, voiced the feelings of the Imperial Parliament and the new Dominion of Canada when he said, "We rejoice that we have shown neither indifference to their wishes nor jealousy of their aspirations but that we honestly and sincerely, to the utmost of our power and knowledge, fostered their growth."

Before Confederation, the New York *World* wrote that five or six million dollars "judiciously expended" could arrange the annexation of Canada to the United States.

Quebec City as the Fathers of Confederation saw it when they met there to set up "the experiment" of Confederation, as John A. called it. This photograph was taken in 1865 — a year after the Conference — by Canada's great pioneer photographer, William Notman.

John A. was twenty-one years older than his bride. He was fifty-two and she thirty-one when they married. These pictures were taken in 1868, a year after their wedding.

# John A. marries Susan Agnes Bernard

## Nine years of widowerhood end in London just before Confederation

### *Macdonald is asked to be first Canadian Premier*

The loyalty, strength and persistence that John A. had shown throughout the long turbulent years preceding Confederation were recognized and honoured when he was selected as the first Prime Minister of Canada. With achievement, political success and honours, John A. was to know personal happiness as well. *The Times* of London carried this announcement on Wednesday, February 21, 1867: "On Saturday, the 16th last, at St. George's Church, Hanover-square, by the Right Rev. the Lord Bishop of Montreal, Metropolitan of Canada, assisted by the Rev. G. Dickson, of St. James's Pimlico, the Hon. John Alexander Macdonald, Her Majesty's Attorney-General for Upper Canada, to Susan Agnes, daughter of the late Hon. T. J. Bernard, Member of Her Majesty's Privy Council of the Island of Jamaica."

John A. and his bride had a great deal in common. She had been brought up in an administrator's and a lawmaker's atmosphere. She shared with John A. a love of Great Britain and of British ways. Yet she too had lived in pioneer settlements similar to those in which he had been raised. Her mother was Theodora Folks Hewitt who, after her husband's death in 1864, left

Jamaica to settle in Barrie, Simcoe County, in the heart of the United Empire Loyalist area.

The bride's tall, handsome brother, Colonel Hewitt Bernard, was a distinguished civil servant and the secretary to the Confederation Conference in Quebec City in 1864 and in London in 1866. He was John A.'s secretary and, although ten years younger, his close friend. While John A. was a widower, he and Hewitt shared living quarters in Ottawa, in a house

> Lady Macdonald seldom spoke in public. When she was given a writing desk by the workingmen of Brantford, she made this brief acceptance speech, "I think, Mr. President, it is very hard of Mr. Hawkins to say that I must make a speech. I need not tell you I cannot make a speech. I leave speechmaking to my husband, who, I am proud to think, can make very good ones. I am proud of my welcome to Brantford, but almost for the first time in public I raise my voice to say how much obliged I am, how flattered and how very much pleased."

they dubbed "The Quadrilateral." Thus John A. had known Agnes Bernard, a slender girl with burnished copper hair, for some years. Through her brother, Hewitt, it is more than likely that John A.'s faults, as well as his many virtues, were known to Miss Bernard.

John A. was attracted to her for Miss Bernard had the very qualities that he wanted in a wife. She was known for her sparkling conversation, intelligence and literary taste, and was ambitious to emulate her cousin, Lady Barker, a clever magazine writer who became the wife of Sir F. Napier Broome, a Governor of one of the Australian colonies. She did succeed in her hopes and later became a fairly regular contributor to several London periodicals.

#### Refused

According to Biggar, John A. had proposed to Agnes in Canada, but she had refused him. "One can well understand that no matter how much she may have loved him in return, or how much she may have admired his great talents, there was the danger that her happiness might be destroyed by linking her life to one who, at times, plunged so deeply into dissipation." Biggar continues, "As time went on, the great

St. George's Church, Hanover Square, as it looked when John A. and Agnes were married there on February 16, 1867. The wedding was attended by a large number of Canadians who were in London to ensure the passage of the Confederation Bill through the British Parliament. The wedding breakfast was enlivened by John A's witty remarks about believing in "union" — both political *and* personal.

ing of the British North America Bill in the House of Lords, and John A. had to be back for the second and third readings which were due to occur soon after.

Shortly after the honeymoon John A. wrote to his sister:

March 21, 1867
48 Dover St., London
My dear Louisa,

Thanks for congrats.... I have now been married one month and five days and feel quite as if it had been this day year. I have no photographs of Agnes taken here, but enclose you a very indifferent one taken in Toronto. It gives but an indication of her appearance.

You will have seen by the papers that she and I were at court and kissed hands. Now you must understand that this was not a general Levee or Drawing Room where everyone goes, but a special Court at which only those specially commanded appear. This took place at three. In the morning at half-past twelve, I and four others as a special honour had private audiences of Her Majesty. We went in separately. I went in first as head of the Conference. There were only in the room, the Queen, Princess Louise, and Lord Carnarvon, the Colonial Secretary. On entering, the Queen put out her hand, on which I knelt and kissed it. On rising, she said, "I am very happy to see you on this occasion." I bowed. "I hope all things are going well with you." I said that I was "happy to inform Her Majesty that all things had been prosperous with us; and by the aid of Lord Carnarvon, our mission had made great progress and there had been no delays."

Her Majesty said, "It is a very important measure, and you have all exhibited so much loyalty." I replied, "We have desired on this occasion to declare in the most solemn and emphatic manner our resolve to be under the sovereignty of Your Majesty and your family forever." And so ended the audience. She had kind words for all who followed — Mr. Cartier, Galt, Tupper and Tilley. Lord Monck is to return to Canada as Governor-General, and has, but this is *entre nous*, charged me with the formation of the first government as Premier.

We have been quite Lions here. My wife likes it for its novelty to her, but it is rather boring to me as I have seen it all before.

Affectionately yours,
John A.

## Accomplished and Popular

With her upbringing and personality, Susan Agnes Bernard Macdonald was the perfect politician's wife. She was intelligent and well read. She was regal and dignified in appearance. She enjoyed entertaining and was a good hostess. She was held in very high esteem by all Canadians. A biography of Sir John A. written in 1883 describes her: "The crown to Sir John's social success is given by the place his very accomplished and popular wife Lady Macdonald fills at the capital. Of the society circle there, is she voted pre-eminently, the queen; where in every project of social enterprise she is the first and the last, and no less the favourite of the elderly and the demure, than of the young folk. To go to Ottawa and mention the name of Lady Macdonald to any of the young people there, is at once to bring forth a paean in her praise. Everything, they tell you that is to be 'got up,' Lady Macdonald has a hand in, not indeed that she seeks to take this place or even cares for it; but so kindly is her nature that she is prodigal both of her time and energy to make everything agreeable; while it is a fact that nothing seems to go on so harmoniously or successfully when she is not at its head and front. Verily, then she seems to be in the social, what her husband is in the public, sphere. In political questions

question of Confederation began to absorb his mind and lead him to higher efforts of statesmanship, while the hope of still winning the woman he had set his heart upon inspired him with renewed efforts to conquer an appetite which was now fighting to conquer him. There were also handwritings on the wall, warning him of broken health and an ignoble ending to a brilliant life." So John A. cut down on his drinking, and when he again proposed to Agnes, in London, he was accepted.

### A Chance Meeting

According to other sources, Agnes and her mother were living in London at the time of Confederation. Quite by chance she and John A. happened to meet one day on Bond Street and — according to the Montreal *Gazette* — "acquaintanceships were destroyed. A few days before Christmas Sir John proposed."

Canadian newspapers reprinted accounts of the nuptials from London journals: "On February 16, 1867, at the wedding of Miss Susan Agnes Bernard to the Honourable John A. Macdonald, the bride wore white satin, Brussels lace and orange blossoms. The four bridesmaids were attired in blue and pink with pink crepe bonnets and long tulle veils, after the fashion of the day. They included Miss Emma Tupper, daughter of Sir Charles Tupper; Miss Jessie McDougall, daughter of the Honourable William McDougall; and Miss Joan Archibald, daughter of Sir

Adams Archibald, all delegates who had gone to London to see the Confederation Bill through the Imperial Parliament. The ceremony was performed at St. George's Church, Hanover Square, London, by His Lordship, the Bishop of Montreal and Metropolitan, by special dispensation of the Archbishop of Canterbury. The bride was given away by her brother, Col. Hewitt Bernard, and the groomsman was D. Bruce Gardyne, Esq. The bride's mother and several relatives in England were present. After the wedding ceremony the party partook of breakfast at the Westminster Palace Hotel. This, we are told, was very brilliant. The health of the bride and bridegroom, the only toast drunk, was proposed by Lt.-Governor and Hon. Francis Hincks, C.B., in a neat and appropriate speech. The Hon. John A. Macdonald responded in his most felicitous manner. He stated that his public mission in England was in favour of UNION and that as a conscientious man he felt bound to carry out his own theory, at which there was much merriment. The breakfast party broke up about two o'clock, and the happy couple left by the three o'clock train for Oxford, where it was their intention to stay for a few days. The bride received very valuable and elegant presents as well from her English connections as the Colonists in London." The Canadian delegates presented her with a beautiful carbuncle.

The honeymoon had to be brief, for the wedding took place four days after the first read-

*(continued)*

LADY AGNES MACDONALD, 1881

"Either in England or the United States, such a personality as hers would have found a more interesting environment and wider appreciation. Here (in Ottawa) her superiority in knowledge of public affairs and general intellectuality over every other woman whose husband is in Parliament is so marked that comparison is out of the question."

*Lady Macdonald wrote this letter to Judge James Robert Gowan of Barrie:*

My Dear Judge,

I am sorry to say that there is no present prospect of my going to Barrie. We shall remain here till Saturday noon then go on to Picton, and later, I shall perhaps be able to go up for a day or two, but I can form no plan yet.

I assure you it is a great disappointment. Shut up here in a *very* noisy hotel, canvassing quietly for some time, and all our friends begged that Sir John would remain until after the polling day Thursday next.

I do not like to leave him, for he has not been well, and the Election work tells upon him.

I dare say you saw that he (Sir John) had given Mr. Caruthers a well deserved Box on the ear! When he came back from the Nomination & I asked him how he could do such a wicked, rude action, Sir J. said in the meekest tones "What *can* one do, my dear, but that when a man tells you in public that you have told a *fib?*" (using however a word that as a lady I can't spell!!)

He is working very hard pulling the wires on all hands. I hope D'Alton Mc-Carthy will get in — so much depends on personal popularity.

Sir John joins me in kindest regards. I still hope to get a peep at you all before going east.

I remain,

Yrs very truly,
Agnes Macdonald

British American Hotel
Kingston,
Saturday

*(Courtesy of William P. Wolfe)*

---

*This paragraph about Lady Macdonald appeared in* The Dominion Illustrated *of December 8, 1888. It seems to have been reprinted from a Washington newspaper, but no credit was given.*

Apart from the Queen's representatives, the "first lady" in Canada is the wife of the Premier. Lady Macdonald will be remembered by many in Washington, whither she accompanied Sir John at the time of the last commission to settle the fishery question. In appearance she has altered very little since then, except that her dark hair has turned a snowy white; and this, rolled back from her forehead, gives a look of softness and gentleness to a face more expressive of purely intellectual qualities.

Lady Macdonald is a remarkable woman, even in this age of remarkable women. Her mind has the masculine qualities of breadth and grasp and accuracy and logic, yet she is capable of the tenderest expression of womanly sympathy, the finest tact and the keenest feminine appreciation. But for the service she has rendered the country in being the stay and support, the intelligent and capable companion of her husband through so many critical years of his public life, Lady Macdonald would have had no province in Canada. Either in England or the United States such a personality as hers would have found a more interesting environment and wider appreciation. Here her superiority in knowledge of public affairs and general intellectuality over every other woman whose husband is in Parliament is so marked that comparison is out of the question.

### LADY AGNES MACDONALD IN 1885
The pressures of maintaining dignity and courage while coping with the needs of her handicapped daughter and John A.'s turbulent political career — and his private lapses into intemperance — are finally taking their toll in white hair.

too this gifted lady takes no little interest, and her judgement is said to be scarce less sound than that of Sir John, who, it is whispered, is in the habit of consulting her when he is about to take some important political step.... She is no less warmly admired by ladies whose husbands are politically opposed to Sir John than by those of his own friends. In domestic life, Lady Macdonald is a model woman... keeping a household that might well be the envy of any circle; attending to Sir John at late sittings of the house, and as Mrs. Disraeli used to do, and as Mrs. Gladstone does, wrapping up her husband after he has made a speech, and zealously guarding his health at home or

while travelling. And to quote the young people again, who will insist on telling their gratitude, she is ready at five minutes warning, no matter how fatigued she may be, to have lunch for a tired toboggan or snowshoe party, or to accompany gatherings of young folks as chaperon. Add to this her genial and kindly manner, her charity to the scores who will press their wants upon a lady in high station, and especially when they find her heart tender and her purse open. Altogether Lady Macdonald is a worthy mate for her thrice worthy and distinguished husband." (J. E. Collins)

When Sir John A. died in 1891 his widow was made Baroness Macdonald of Earnscliffe, in recognition of his services to Canada and the Empire. After his death, she lived in Europe until her own death in 1920. She was buried at Ocklynge Cemetery, in Eastbourne, on the south coast of England. The memorial tombstone — a six-foot granite cross and kerb — was marked with the following inscription:

*In loving memory of*
*Susan Agnes*
*Baroness Macdonald*
*Widow of Sir John*
*Macdonald*
*Late Prime Minister of Canada*
*Died at Eastbourne*
*5th September 1920 aged 84*
*Jesu Lover of My Soul*
*Let Me to Thy Bosom Fly*

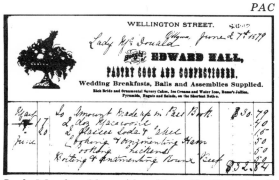

Lady Macdonald considered herself a "laborious" and "awkward" housekeeper, but she enjoyed entertaining Sir John A.'s political friends as long as he was present because "his pleasant easy manners make all go on well."

# CANADA IS BORN
# JULY 1, 1867

## *"The new Dominion came noisily into existence"*

## "It has been a hot gusty day, but these are gusty times" — Lady Macdonald

Lady Macdonald, a bride of only a few months, made the first entry in her new diary about Confederation Day. "It has been a hot gusty day," she wrote. "But these are gusty times. This new Dominion of ours came noisily into existence on the first and the very newspapers look hot and tired with the weight of Cabinet lists.... In theory I regard my husband with much awe, in practice tease the life out of him.... Today, he rebelled, poor man, and ordered me out of the room... but he relented, the good old boy, and after he called me back, he got the worst of it."

### Salute of 101 Guns

Confederation Day was ushered in at Ottawa with a salute of 101 guns, the peal of church bells, fireworks, speeches and parades. There were similar demonstrations in other parts of Canada. Inscriptions proclaimed "Good Luck to the Confederacy" and "Bienvenue à la Nouvelle Puissance."

Of course, Confederation was front-page news in papers all over Canada. *The Globe* of Toronto gave a detailed and lucid picture of Confederation in a ten-column article which appeared on July 1. The editor and owner of *The Globe* was George Brown, who enjoyed, as Goldwin Smith said, " a long reign of literary terror." However in 1864 Brown had proved himself to be a real statesman when he formed a coalition with John A. Macdonald and George Etienne Cartier to plan a federal union. Brown had stayed up all night to write the 9,000 word article on Confederation.

### Ox Roasted in Toronto

In the city news, the same issue of *The Globe* reported: "On Saturday night, the Post Office

### Naming the Baby

*The Gazette,* Montreal, February 4, 1867: "The selection of the name for the confederated provinces is to be left to Her Majesty the Queen, but we understand that the favourite amongst the delegates during their conference was that of Canada or Canadia."

*The Gazette,* February 26, 1867: "We learn from a correspondent in London that the name of the Confederation will likely be *The Dominion of Canada.*"

*The Gazette,* March 1, 1867: "The title of the Confederation is to be *Canada* — not the Kingdom of Canada. The statuary description will not be any longer Province or Colony, but Dominion... Her Majesty's Government, to whom the choice was left, have preferred the word Dominion."

*The Gazette,* March 8, 1867: "Let us speak out! We are assisting at the birth of history."

## *John A. knighted, becomes Sir John A.*

illuminations were tried, and looked very fine. Surmounting the whole is a Crown, with the letters V. R. on each side; underneath are the Prince of Wales' feathers, in the centre, and two stars, one on each side, with the motto 'Dominion of Canada.'

"On the roofs of houses and elsewhere, in all directions, flag-poles were being hoisted into the air to do their part in the celebration of Confederation Day. A programme of celebration arranged by the Government included a Grand Review of Her Majesty's Troops, regulars and volunteers, on the Bathurst Street Commons at ten a.m. At three o'clock there was a grand Balloon Ascension from Queen's Park. In the evening there were concerts given by the bands of the Tenth Royal Regiment and the Grand Trunk Brigade in the form of a Grand Promenade at Queen's Park accompanied by the

most magnificent display of fireworks ever exhibited in Canada.

"Another grand celebration took place on the evening of the same day at the Horticultural Gardens.... The gardens were brilliantly lighted, and a large tent set up for refreshments of strawberries, ice cream, etc. The concert was at eight p.m. and dancing commenced at ten-thirty. Tickets were twenty-five cents, children's tickets ten cents. The bands of the Thirteenth Hussars and the Seventeenth Regiment played, among other selections, pieces by Donizetti, Kappe, Burchart, Rossini and Benedict."

*The Globe* also announced that "At six a.m. an immense ox will be roasted.... The roasting will occupy a large portion of the day and the meat will afterwards be distributed among the poor of the city."

# BY THE QUEEN.
# A PROCLAMATION
## For Uniting the Provinces of Canada, Nova Scotia, and New Brunswick into One Dominion under the Name of CANADA.

**VICTORIA R.**

**W**HEREAS by an Act of Parliament passed on the Twenty-ninth Day of March One thousand eight hundred and sixty-seven, in the Thirtieth Year of Our Reign, intituled " An Act for the Union of Canada, Nova Scotia, and New Brunswick, and the " Government thereof, and for Purposes connected therewith," after divers Recitals, it is enacted, that " it shall be lawful for the Queen, by and with the Advice of Her Majesty's most Honorable " Privy Council, to declare by Proclamation that on and after a Day therein appointed, not being " more than Six Months after the passing of this Act, the Provinces of Canada, Nova Scotia, and " New Brunswick shall form and be One Dominion under the Name of Canada, and on and after " that Day those Three Provinces shall form and be One Dominion under that Name accordingly:" And it is thereby further enacted, that " such Persons shall be first summoned to the Senate as " the Queen, by Warrant under Her Majesty's Royal Sign Manual, thinks fit to approve, and " their Names shall be inserted in the Queen's Proclamation of Union:" We therefore, by and with the Advice of Our Privy Council, have thought fit to issue this Our Royal Proclamation, and We do Ordain, Declare, and Command, that on and after the First Day of July One thousand eight hundred and sixty-seven the Provinces of Canada, Nova Scotia, and New Brunswick shall form and be One Dominion under the Name of Canada. And We do further Ordain and Declare, that the Persons whose Names are herein inserted and set forth are the Persons of whom We have, by Warrant under Our Royal Sign Manual, thought fit to approve as the Persons who shall be first summoned to the Senate of Canada.

| FOR THE PROVINCE OF ONTARIO. | FOR THE PROVINCE OF QUEBEC. | FOR THE PROVINCE OF NOVA SCOTIA. | FOR THE PROVINCE OF NEW BRUNSWICK. |
| --- | --- | --- | --- |
| JOHN HAMILTON, | JAMES LESLIE, | EDWARD KENNY, | AMOS EDWIN BOTSFORD, |
| RODERICK MATHESON, | ASA BELKNAP FOSTER, | JONATHAN M'CULLY, | EDWARD BARRON CHANDLER, |
| JOHN ROSS, | JOSEPH NOËL BOSSÉ, | THOMAS D. ARCHIBALD, | JOHN ROBERTSON, |
| SAMUEL MILLS, | LOUIS A. OLIVIER, | ROBERT B. DICKEY, | ROBERT LEONARD HAZEN, |
| BENJAMIN SEYMOUR, | JACQUE OLIVIER BUREAU, | JOHN H. ANDERSON, | WILLIAM HUNTER ODELL, |
| WALTER HAMILTON DICKSON, | CHARLES MALHIOT, | JOHN HOLMES, | DAVID WARK, |
| JAMES SHAW, | LOUIS RENAUD, | JOHN W. RITCHIE, | WILLIAM HENRY STEEVES, |
| ADAM JOHNSTON FERGUSON BLAIR, | LUC LETELLIER DE ST. JUST, | BENJAMIN WIER, | WILLIAM TODD, |
| ALEXANDER CAMPBELL, | ULRIC JOSEPH TESSIER, | JOHN LOCKE, | JOHN FERGUSON, |
| DAVID CHRISTIE, | JOHN HAMILTON, | CALEB R. BILL, | ROBERT DUNCAN WILMOT, |
| JAMES COX AIKINS, | CHARLES CORMIER, | JOHN BOURINOT, | ABNER REID M'CLELAN, |
| DAVID REESOR, | ANTOINE JUCHEREAU DUCHESNAY, | WILLIAM MILLER. | PETER MITCHELL. |
| ELIJAH LEONARD, | DAVID EDWARD PRICE, | | |
| WILLIAM MACMASTER, | ELZEAR H. J. DUCHESNAY, | | |
| ASA ALLWORTH BURNHAM, | LEANDRE DUMOUCHEL, | | |
| JOHN SIMPSON, | LOUIS LACOSTE, | | |
| JAMES SKEAD, | JOSEPH F. ARMAND, | | |
| DAVID LEWIS MACPHERSON, | CHARLES WILSON, | | |
| GEORGE CRAWFORD, | WILLIAM HENRY CHAFFERS, | | |
| DONALD MACDONALD, | JEAN BAPTISTE GUÉVREMONT, | | |
| OLIVER BLAKE, | JAMES FERRIER, | | |
| BILLA FLINT, | Sir NARCISSE FORTUNAT BELLEAU, Knight, | | |
| WALTER M'CREA, | THOMAS RYAN, | | |
| GEORGE WILLIAM ALLAN. | JOHN SEWELL SANBORN. | | |

**Given at Our Court at Windsor Castle, this Twenty-second Day of May, in the Year of our Lord One thousand eight hundred and sixty-seven, and in the Thirtieth Year of Our Reign.**

## God save the Queen.

LONDON : Printed by GEORGE EDWARD EYRE and WILLIAM SPOTTISWOODE, Printers to the Queen's most Excellent Majesty. 1867.

# "La Confédération la seule voie pour arriver à l'indépendance politique" — La Minerve

### Bells and Bagpipes in Hamilton

The June 29th issue of *The Evening Times* of Hamilton described the celebrations that were to take place in that city: "The arrangements seem to be complete, and every indication promises one of the most enthusiastic and imposing demonstrations to mark the dawning era of the new Dominion... ever witnessed in Hamilton.... The earlier moments of the new Dominion will be attended with a roar of artillery and the ringing of the bells of the city, which will commence at twelve midnight on the morning of the memorable first. The salute and chime of bells will be repeated at six a.m. continuing for half an hour." The same issue also carried a notice for the local Scots:

*Clann Nau Gaeil*
*Agus Ceol Nau Feann*

"All Highlanders are requested to assemble in front of the City Hall, on Monday July 1 at nine a.m. to join in the Confederate Procession, headed by the Pipers." The paper also announced that: "The Steamer *Princess of Wales* will on Monday July 1 leave her wharf, Hamilton, at nine a.m. for the Beach, touching at Oaklands. Returning... at six o'clock, affording ample time to see the fireworks and other amusements. Fare to Oaklands and back fifteen cents. Fare to Beach and back — twenty-five cents."

### Speculation in Victoria

The following editorial appeared in *The Daily British Colonist and Victoria Chronicle* on Confederation Day. It was entitled "Birth of a Nation" and the subtitle was "Our Prospects As a Member": "This will be a memorable day for British North America. The Dominion of Canada, which is destined eventually to play an important part in the world's history, will be inaugurated by the formation of a ministry composed of some of the best and greatest minds on the continent.... When a paper representing the interests of Confederacy in an important city of Canada tells its readers that 'the entire stretch of British territory from the Atlantic to the Pacific must form one chain of United Colonies'; that the 'duty of the Canadians is to facilitate as rapidly as possible the admission of British Columbia into the Confederacy'; that 'temporary obstacles, owing to the vast distance, must be overlooked'; and that 'the expense of a railway to the Pacific, soon to be undertaken, must be looked steadily in the face'; we say unhesitatingly that the moment has almost arrived when great and beneficial change will take place in our political affairs, and when emerging from the cloud of political misery that has so long shrouded our prospects, we shall soon be standing in the sunshine of Liberty and Constitutional Goverment.

"Let us always bear in mind... that when we go into the Confederacy it must be on FAIR and EQUITABLE TERMS, such as we have confidence in the Canadians to believe they will only offer."

### Reaction of the French

French-language newspapers also carried stories and articles on Confederation:

From *Le Courrier du Canada,* Québec, 28 juin 1867: "Malgré nous, nous sommes forcés de reconnaître dans ce concours inouï de circonstances exceptionellement heureuses le doigt de la providence. Tout, dans la transformation

---

politique par laquelle nous venons de passer, semble avoir un caractère providentiel, depuis la première phrase jusqu'à la dernière. Voyons plutôt."

From *La Minerve,* Montréal, vendredi matin, 28 juin: "Il circule une foule de rumeurs sur la conduite que va tenir l'opposition Bas-Canadienne, dans le prochain parlement fédéral. Naturellement, nos adversaires acceptent la Confédération. Comment pourraient-ils faire autrement? La Confédération est aujourd'hui un fait accompli. On ne nie pas un fait.

"Mais la Confédération n'est pas seulement un but; c'est un moyen. Pour nous, c'est la planche de salut qui nous préservera de l'annexation, c'est la seule voie qui nous soit offerte pour arriver à l'indépendance politique, commerciale et industrielle....

"La Confédération... est un outil; à nous de nous en servir, et d'en faire un bon usage. Nous assistons, aujourd'hui à l'inauguration d'un nouveau système politique qui doit nous remplir d'un légitime orgueil pour notre influence dans le passé, et d'une grande confiance dans l'avenir. Le Canada est maintenant une Puissance."

From *L'Ordre, Union Catholique,* Montréal, lundi, 1er juillet 1867: "Nous entrons aujourd'hui dans une des phases les plus importantes de notre histoire: une constitution est remplacée par une autre constitution qui s'étend maintenant sur quatre provinces au lieu de deux, avec la perspective d'embrasser plus tard toutes les possessions anglaises de l'Amérique du Nord. Comme celui auquel il succède, le nouveau régime a été littéralement imposé au Bas-Canada pour satisfaire l'ambition d'hommes

---

### Unfriendly Neighbours

"The Confederation scheme is highly disagreeable to the United States Government which considers that the plan will be a deathblow to the hopes of annexation. That Government has now in this country an agent in the person of a leading North American colonist (Hon. Joseph Howe) who was formerly the ablest advocate of Confederation, but ever since its recent visit to Washington has been its most bitter opponent. It is a little singular that the only London papers which oppose Confederation are the three which have always sided with the United States when any question has arisen between that Government and our own. Opposition from them is, of course, a very strong indirect argument in favour of the project. It is precisely the same thing here. The Opposition to the project of Confederation comes from the papers which have 'sided' with the United States." (*The Gazette,* Montreal, January 16, 1867)

---

politiques: sera-t-il plus heureux que le premier?

"L'avenir le dira.

"En attendant, nous entrons dans la Confédération avec crainte, mais avec le ferme espoir de détourner à temps de notre race les dangers que nous avons tant raison d'appréhender."

From *Le Pays,* Montréal, 2 juillet: "Présent de trois canonnières. Les journaux ministériels n'ont pas en ce moment d'assez grands mots pour témoigner leur reconnaissance au gouvernement anglais, pour le présent qu'il vient de nous faire de trois canonnières actuellement sur les lacs. Voici en quoi consiste ce cadeau. Le gouvernement anglais entretenait à ses frais les équipages de ces trois vaisseaux, pour la protection de ses possessions en Amérique; maintenant ce sera le peuple canadien qui paiera ces frais, toujours pour le même objet. C'était pour des présents de ce genre que le poète latin s'écriait: 'Times Danaos et Dona Ferentes'."

From *Le Courrier du Canada,* Québec, 3 juillet: "Lundi, Québec a célébré, sinon avec pompe du moins avec enthousiasme, l'inauguration de la nouvelle constitution. Dès le matin, les rues étaient sillonnées par des milliers de curieux; en certains endroits des drapeaux flottaient gaiement au vent. Partout les affaires étaient suspendues, les magasins fermés.... Les démonstrations ont été favorisées toute la journée par un temps splendide."

### Right Man in Right Place

*The Ottawa Citizen* of July 5, 1867, commented upon the new administration: "The distribution of officers in the Administration, has, we think... been admirably made. Sir John A. Macdonald as Premier and Minister of Justice, is eminently 'the right man in the right place.' As the most prominent statesman in the Dominion and a constitutional lawyer of acknowledged great ability, it is no more than fitting that he should be the head of the first Privy Council and entrusted with the duty of setting the machinery of Confederation to work. As to the appointment of Mr. Cartier as Minister of Militia and his fitness to be entrusted with matters of military detail, there may be some differences of opinion; but as he possesses an indomitable will, great energy and a remarkable combativeness of disposition we see no reason why he should not turn out to be the most efficient Minister of Militia the country ever had.... The appointment of Mr. Galt as Minister of Finance must meet the approval of the great majority of our people, for he is, undoubtedly, the first financier in the Dominion and his ability is universally conceded."

*The Patriot,* a semi-weekly of Charlottetown, Prince Edward Island, said on July 6, 1867: "The New Dominion ship of state was launched on Monday last, amid the rejoicings of Confederates all over the Provinces. In Halifax, Saint John, and all the other principal cities of CANADA, an effort was made to keep high holiday. Among the celebrations on the occasion, that at Halifax seems to have been one of the most imposing. Salutes, prayer meetings, *(continued)*

# La Minerve,

## JOURNAL POLITIQUE, COMMERCIAL, LITTÉRAIRE, AGRICOLE ET D'ANNONCES.

**VOL. XXXIX.**    ÉDITION QUOTIDIENNE. MONTREAL, 1er JUILLET 1867.    **No. 271.**

Comme Canadiens-Français, la position qui nous est faite dans la Confédération est excellente. Nos droits ont été reconnus dans leur signification la plus large.

Lord Carnarvor, en présentant le projet de Confédération à la Chambre des Lords, a pris la peine de citer les traités consentis entre la France et l'Angleterre, lors de la cession du Canada, il y a un siècle. Il a reconnu, de la manière la plus formelle, que nos droits continuaient d'être garantis par la nouvelle constitution, et que si notre position était modifiée, elle l'était à notre avantage.

Telle est, d'ailleurs, la signification que l'on doit attacher à cette constitution. On y voit la reconnaissance de la nationalité canadienne-française. Comme nationalité distincte et séparée, nous formons un état dans l'état, avec la pleine jouissance de nos droits, la reconnaissance formelle de notre indépendance nationale.

Nos institutions religieuses sont laissées au gouvernement du Bas-Canada; nos richesses les plus vastes, les questions d'éducation qui sont pour nous l'avenir de notre pays, en un mot ce que nous avons de plus cher et de plus précieux est laissé à notre administration particulière. A nous d'en tirer profit.

Nous entrons dans la confédération avec toutes les garanties que nous pouvions désirer. Nous avons pour nous la liberté, la justice, la loi.

L'avenir est à nous, si nous voulons nous en emparer; serions-nous donc trop faibles, trop ignorants ou trop lâches pour ne plus défendre notre nationalité? Allons-nous renoncer à notre histoire, à nos traditions, à nos droits, à notre mission, parcequ'il y a des obstacles sur la route, parceque les résultats ne sont qu'en proportion du travail? Les nations indolentes n'ont jamais eu longue vie; et l'avenir est aux peuples qui personnifient le courage, la constance et l'énergie.

# "Perhaps by and by some of us will rise to the level of national statesmen" — John A.

orations, processions, reviews, sports and illuminations made up the programme of the day."

### Fastings and Humiliation

*The Ottawa Citizen* of July 12, 1867, described the feelings of some anti-Confederates: "Confederation Day appears to have been generally well-observed throughout the Dominion. But in Nova Scotia, in the strongholds of anti-Unionism, the day passed over without jubilation. This is, of course, no more than we might have predicted, for weeks ago, Mr. Howe and the anti-Confederate journals recommended that the day be devoted to fastings and humiliation.... At least one Quebec Rouge — a Mr. Laberge, as Mayor of Dorchester, withheld his sanction and authority for the holding of a celebration.... He believed Confederation to be a public misfortune. Mr. Howe said he would drive a coach and pair through the Act of Confederation."

Some mutterings were heard from *The*

> John A. at the time of Confederation: "We are all mere petty provincial politicians at present; perhaps by and by some of us will rise to the level of national statesmen."

> The Big Seven, as the leaders of Confederation were called, were Macdonald, Galt, Brown, Cartier, McGee, Tupper and Tilley.

*Patriot* of July 20, 1867: "With a salary of $50,000.00 for the Governor-General and thirteen Cabinet Ministers at $8,000.00 apiece and eleven other Ministers for Upper and Lower Canada, the expenses of the Executive, under the new system will be more than doubled in the Provinces. Is this the way that a Reform Government would have commenced the work of constructing the new fabric? Most certainly not. And for this alone, if for nothing else, the Coalition must be condemned at the polls.

"Three of the ministers are to assist Mr. Galt in manipulating the finances of the Dominion. Galt, alone, was too much for the Canada of the past. Can the Canada of today support Galt and *three more* heaven-born financiers? Doubtful, very!

"We notice that divers attempts at a national anthem for the Dominion are being made. Would it not be as well to wait until we are a nation before we have a national anthem? In the meantime the ringing old strains of 'God Save the Queen' will satisfy all loyal hearts,

although we have Secretaries of State and a Minister of War of our own."

One of the songs written to celebrate Confederation was "Our Dominion."
*Thank God the glorious work is done
And long though we have waited,
Our country's life has now begun
With union consummated.
No longer we will parted be
By mountain, lake or river,
But in one band, joined heart and hand,
We're Canada forever.*

*Chorus    Then raise your voices, swell the song,
            And let it echo loud and long.
            We all to Canada belong,
            God bless our young dominion.*

*We have not left the old land dear
By which we've long been cherished,
Nor lost the flag we all revere
For which our sons have perished.
That red cross still and ever will
Float o'er each hill and valley,
And come the foe, no matter who,
We'll round its bright folds rally.*

*Chorus    Then raise your voices, swell the song,
            And let it echo loud and long,
            We all to Canada belong,
            God bless our young dominion.*

*Canadians let it be our aim
To win renown and glory,
And prove that we deserve a name
In future song and story.
And thus may we, like Britain be
With power and wealth beside us,
And in our might defend the right
With God above to guide us.*

*Chorus    Then while with heart and voice
            we sing,
            And thro' the land our anthems ring,
            May God his choicest blessings bring
            On this our young dominion.*

But there were anti-Confederation songs too, such as the one sung in Prince Edward Island, in 1873:

*There is a band within this land
    who live in pomp and pride;
To fill their store they rob the poor;
    In pleasure will they ride.*

*With dishes fine their tables shine;
    they move in princely style.
Those are the knaves that made us slaves
    And sold Prince Edward Isle.*

Although Sir John A. returned from London victorious and triumphant, he carried on in his customary, rather modest manner. He enjoyed the honours that came his way, both for his wife and his family, yet on the whole he took them rather lightly. Hailed as "l'homme de la Conférence," a designation that he well merited, he went about setting in motion the wheels of Canada's first Parliament, which opened on November 7, 1867.

As Lady Macdonald's influence was felt at diplomatic functions, the Prime Minister's friends and Cabinet associates were convinced that he had indeed made a good choice. From long habit, stemming from his childhood, this loving man had a deep need to be closely involved with a family of his own, and responded readily to her warmth and charm. She was not without social experience, and presided easily and naturally over their "at homes" and other public engagements. She was an intellectual woman, with the gift of expression, and her articles began to appear in *Murray's Magazine*, of London, *The Ladies' Home Journal* and *Pall Mall*. John A. relaxed gratefully in the pleasant cheerful home atmosphere he had so long been denied. With her care and understanding, the heavy drinking of his youth and mid-years was moderated.

Queen's

July 1, 1867. The Proclamation announcing Confederation is read in Market Square, Kingston.

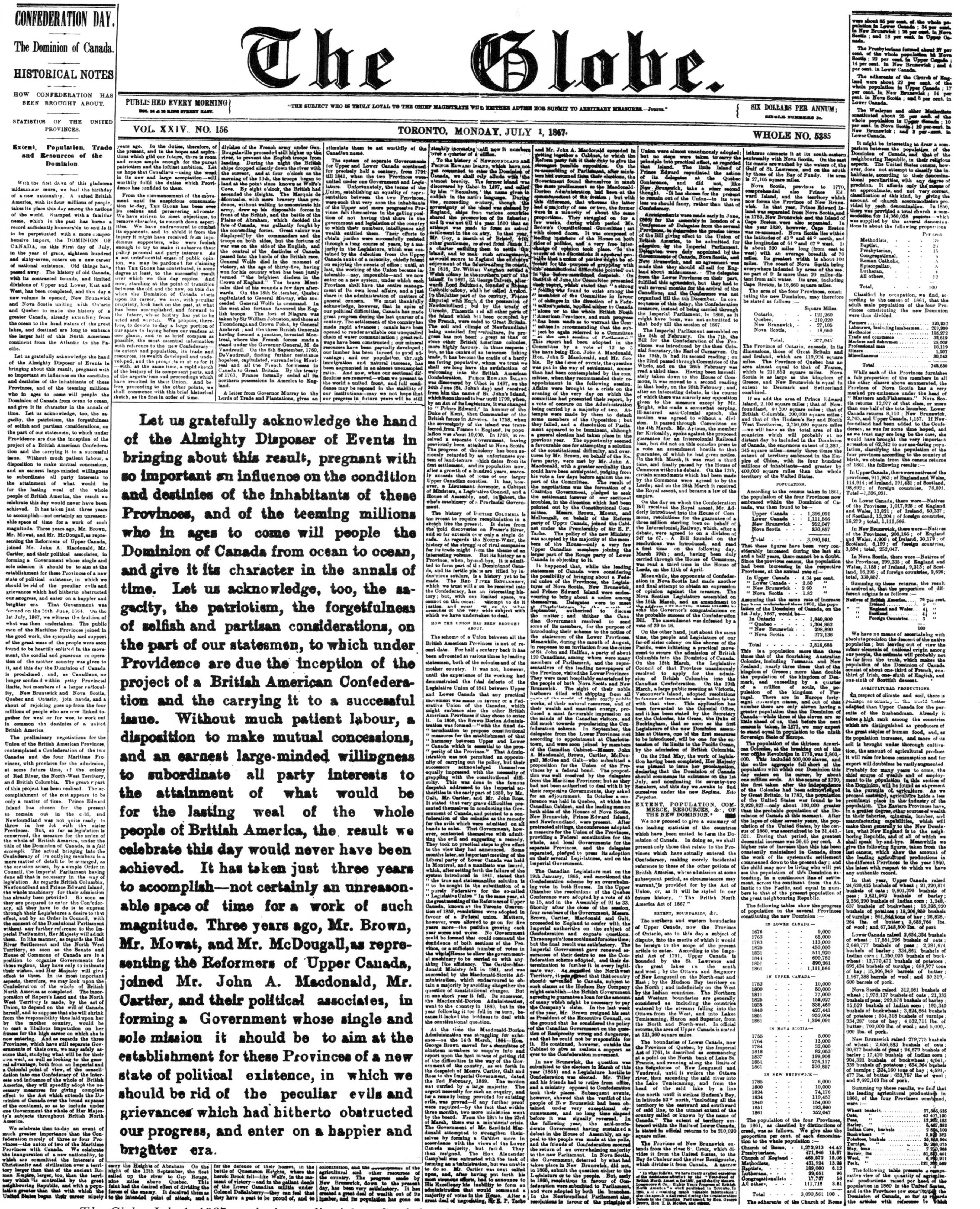

# The Globe.

PUBLISHED EVERY MORNING

"THE SUBJECT WHO IS TRULY LOYAL TO THE CHIEF MAGISTRATE WILL NEITHER ADVISE NOR SUBMIT TO ARBITRARY MEASURES.—JUNIUS."

SIX DOLLARS PER ANNUM

VOL. XXIV. NO. 156.        TORONTO, MONDAY, JULY 1, 1867.        WHOLE NO. 5385.

## CONFEDERATION DAY.

The Dominion of Canada.

### HISTORICAL NOTES

HOW CONFEDERATION HAS BEEN BROUGHT ABOUT.

STATISTICS OF THE UNITED PROVINCES.

Extent, Population, Trade and Resources of the Dominion

Let us gratefully acknowledge the hand of the Almighty Disposer of Events in bringing about this result, pregnant with so important an influence on the condition and destinies of the inhabitants of these Provinces, and of the teeming millions who in ages to come will people the Dominion of Canada from ocean to ocean, and give it its character in the annals of time. Let us acknowledge, too, the sagacity, the patriotism, the forgetfulness of selfish and partisan considerations, on the part of our statesmen, to which under Providence are due the inception of the project of a British American Confederation and the carrying it to a successful issue. Without much patient labour, a disposition to make mutual concessions, and an earnest large-minded willingness to subordinate all party interests to the attainment of what would be for the lasting weal of the whole people of British America, the result we celebrate this day would never have been achieved. It has taken just three years to accomplish—not certainly an unreasonable space of time for a work of such magnitude. Three years ago, Mr. Brown, Mr. Mowat, and Mr. McDougall, as representing the Reformers of Upper Canada, joined Mr. John A. Macdonald, Mr. Cartier, and their political associates, in forming a Government whose single and sole mission it should be to aim at the establishment for these Provinces of a new state of political existence, in which we should be rid of the peculiar evils and grievances which had hitherto obstructed our progress, and enter on a happier and brighter era.

*The Globe*, July 1, 1867 — the long editorial on Confederation was written by George Brown who sat up most of the night to do it.

79

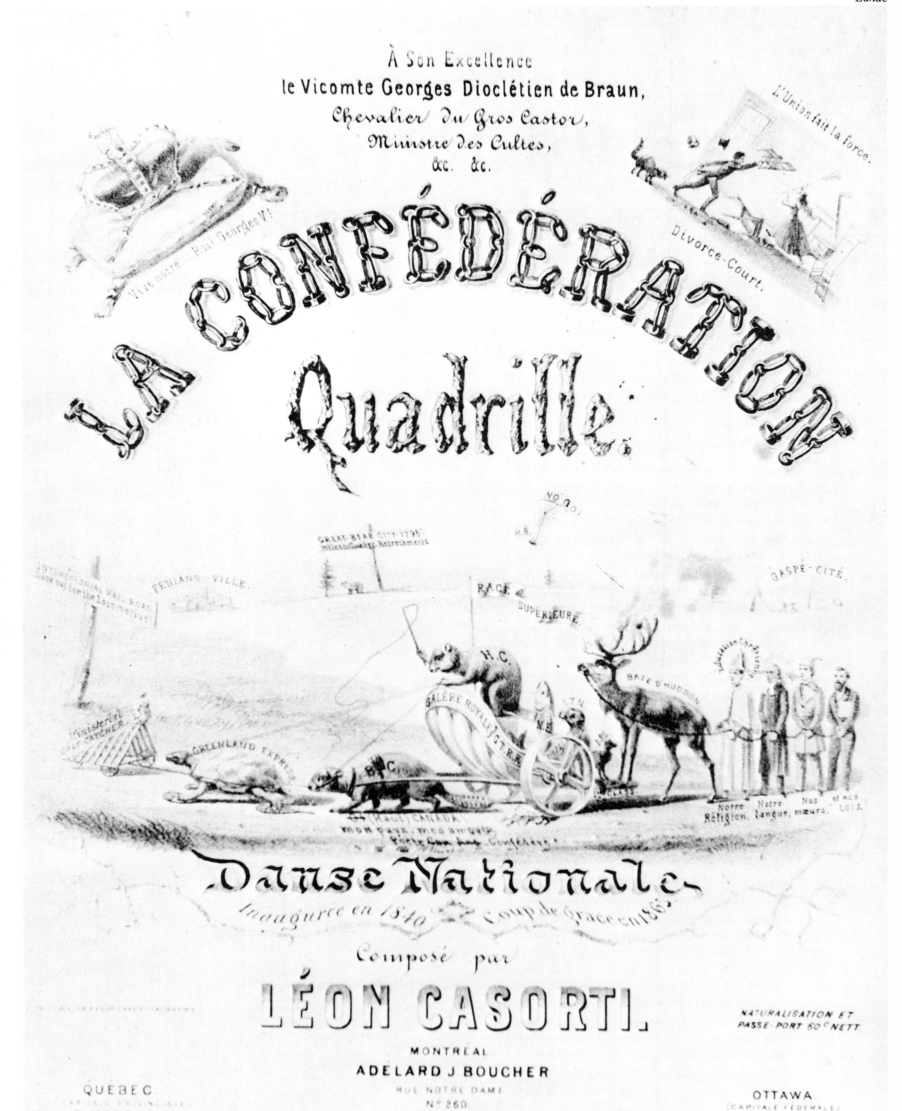

Anti-Confederation sheet music design in which the artist shows Quebec's religion, language, customs and laws chained to the royal chariot being driven by Upper Canada. In the right-hand corner is a "Divorce Court." This "Danse Nationale" was "inaugurée en 1840," presumably with the Act of Union, and the "coup de grâce" given in 1865.

# Original painting destroyed by fire

## "Fathers" repainted in 1964; Their papers in Saskatchewan

The large painting of the Fathers of Confederation which hangs in the Railway Committee Room in the Parliament Buildings in Ottawa is actually the second painting made of the gathering.

Robert Harris of Prince Edward Island did the original canvas. Among the difficulties which plagued him was a fire which had destroyed the old Parliament Building in Quebec, where the parliamentarians had gathered in 1864. This called for a partial reconstruction of the background. Fire continued to distress the artist. In 1916 the picture was destroyed in the flames which demolished the Parliament Building in Ottawa where it was displayed.

Harris, who was approaching seventy, felt unequal to accept another commission to replace his painting. He did, however, touch up an initial charcoal sketch, or "cartoon," and he turned this over to the Government.

In 1964 Toronto artist Rex Woods was commissioned to reproduce Harris's original painting. It was presented as a centennial gift to the nation by the Confederation Life Insurance Company and now hangs in the Railway Committee Room. On an adjoining wall is Harris's original charcoal study.

### Confederation Papers in Saskatchewan

Parliamentarians, archivists and antiquarians were recently surprised to learn that the original papers of Confederation are in the small town of Wilcox, Saskatchewan. They are in the keeping of their owner, Father Athol Murray, founder and President of Notre Dame College of Canada, a small coeducational university and high school about twenty-eight miles southeast of Regina.

These priceless documents, carrying the signatures of John A. Macdonald and George Etienne Cartier, came to Father Murray through his uncle, Sir Hugh John Macdonald, son of John A. and a former premier of Manitoba. The actual British North America Act of 1867 is based on these resolutions which were signed in Quebec in 1864. The papers are shown on the table in the famous portrait of the Fathers of Confederation.

The large conference table around which the delegates sat while drafting the 1864 act in Quebec is now in the Legislative Library at Regina, Saskatchewan. A plaque on the table explains how it got there: "At this table sat the Fathers of Confederation during the Conference in Quebec in 1864, which having been adjourned from Charlottetown in the same year, opened on October tenth, and led to the drafting of the British North America Act. After the close of the Conference the table was transferred to Ottawa, and for a time used in the Privy Council Chamber. Later it was sent with other furniture to Battleford, at that time the seat of Government for the North-West Territories, a position which the town occupied during the years 1878-1881 when the Honourable David Laird was Lieutenant-Governor. When Regina was made the capital, the table was sent there, and became the House table of the Assembly, remaining such up to the time when the present Legislative and Executive Building was opened up in 1912."

*Harris's charcoal sketch*  PAC

*Woods at work*

*The painting as it is now*  Confederation Life Association

81

# Are you Canadian or Tuponian?

### CONFEDERATION!

#### THE MUCH FATHERED YOUNGSTER

Canadians today consider John A. Macdonald as *the* Father of Confederation, but in 1867 several others laid claim to the title, among them George Brown, Sir Francis Hincks and William McDougall — all shown in this Bengough cartoon.

---

## Here's a convenient list of 36 "Fathers of Confederation"

Who were the Fathers of Confederation? How many of them were there? The number of delegates to the Confederation Conferences has been reported as thirty-three, thirty-four, thirty-six and thirty-seven. The confusion may have occurred because there were three conferences: in Charlottetown in 1864, in Quebec in 1864 and in London, England, in 1866. The correct number is thirty-six.

Of the thirty-six Fathers of Confederation, twenty were lawyers, three were doctors, nine were businessmen, three were editors (others were writers too) and only one was a military man (although many had served in the army at one time). All were politicians; some were statesmen. At least two — John A. and Thomas D'Arcy McGee — were notorious for their heavy drinking, a failing shared by Joseph Howe, the anti-Confederationist.

The Fathers of Confederation averaged forty-five years of age. Four were in their thirties.

The list of the thirty-six men follows. *C* denotes the Charlottetown Conference, *Q* the Quebec and *L* the London.

*Canada*

| | | | |
|---|---|---|---|
| John A. Macdonald | C | Q | L |
| George E. Cartier | C | Q | L |
| Alexander T. Galt | C | Q | L |
| William McDougall | C | Q | L |
| Hector L. Langevin | C | Q | L |
| George Brown | C | Q | |
| Thomas D'Arcy McGee | C | Q | |
| Alexander Campbell | C | Q | |
| Sir Etienne P. Taché | | Q | |
| Oliver Mowat | | Q | |
| J. C. Chapais | | Q | |
| James Cockburn | | Q | |
| W. P. Howland | | | L |

*Nova Scotia*

| | | | |
|---|---|---|---|
| Charles Tupper | C | Q | L |
| William A. Henry | C | Q | L |
| Jonathan McCully | C | Q | L |
| Adams G. Archibald | C | Q | L |
| Robert B. Dickey | | Q | |
| J. W. Ritchie | | | L |

*New Brunswick*

| | | | |
|---|---|---|---|
| Samuel Leonard Tilley | C | Q | L |
| J. M. Johnson | C | Q | L |
| William H. Steeves | C | Q | |
| E. B. Chandler | C | Q | |
| John Hamilton Gray | C | Q | |
| Peter Mitchell | | Q | L |
| Charles Fisher | | Q | L |
| R. D. Wilmot | | | L |

*Prince Edward Island*

| | | |
|---|---|---|
| John Hamilton Gray | C | Q |
| Edward Palmer | C | Q |
| William H. Pope | C | Q |
| A. A. Macdonald | C | Q |
| George Coles | C | Q |
| T. H. Haviland | | Q |
| Edward Whelan | | Q |

*Newfoundland*

| | | |
|---|---|---|
| F. B. T. Carter | | Q |
| Ambrose She. | | Q |

> Joseph Howe denounced Confederation as "the botheration scheme."

---

### Albona, Mesopolagia, Vesperia — or Canada?

With all the talk about Confederation, there was much discussion of what the "new" country should be named. On November 5, 1864, *The Globe* ran an editorial entitled "The Name": "As most parents know, it is a very difficult thing to find a name for 'Baby'.... After the fashion by which men in uncivilized societies distinguish personages from one another, we should become inundated with Messieurs Rednobs, Bowlegs, Squinteyes, Pugnose and Curlywigs; or with Misses Blueeyes, Blackhairs, Angelshapes and Pearlyteeths.... But their trouble was nothing to that which the people of British North America feel, now that we have got to find a name for our country.... We think there are very few Canadians who would want to exchange their names for any of these. Let us look to ... our mother country. Her official title is that of 'The United Kingdom of Great Britain and Ireland.' But who thinks of calling anyone born in the old land a 'United Kingdomer'? ... Just as surely as the other colonies allay themselves with us, their people will be called 'Canadians.' ... They will all go by the name of Canadians; and we have yet to learn that they have any objection to it."

*The Globe* received many suggestions from its readers for the name of the new country. Among them were: British Esfiga (from the first letters of English, Scottish, French, Irish, German and Aboriginal), Britannica, Borelia, Cabotia, Victoralia, Ursalia, Tuponia, Niagarentia, Albertania, Canadia, Mesopolagia, Albona, West Britannia, Champlainia, Transylvania, Transatlantica, Alexandrina, Canadensia, Vesperia and Albinora. Thomas D'Arcy McGee is said to have commented, "How would you like to wake up some fine morning and learn that you were not a Canadian but a Tuponian?"

Even outside Canada the opening of the first Parliament of the new Dominion was considered an event, as this illustration published in *Harper's Weekly,* November 30, 1867, shows. Viscount Monck, the Governor-General, is seen reading the Speech from the Throne, composed, it is generally accepted, by Sir John A. Macdonald.

# First Canadian Parliament meets

## Throne Speech, written by Sir John A., promises uniform laws, an intercolonial railway and western territorial extension

There were no brilliant fireworks to mark the inauguration of the first Parliament of Canada on November 7, 1867. There was too much work to be done. Sir John A. kept in the background. Instead of making an opening address, he saw to it that others made the speeches — oftimes too long and too dull. His was the master touch that smoothed out difficulties, and set up an orderly government. He may have made resolutions; generally he left the debates to others.

One of the earliest bills set the sessional salary of Members of Parliament at $600.00 a year, comfortably above the six dollar a day average wage, for an approximately ninety-day period. In addition they drew sixpence or ten cents a mile for travel, including lodging and meals en route. Both British and U.S. currencies were in common use.

The absence of members from the House cost them a $5.00 per day deduction. There was lengthy discussion about these amounts, particularly from those farthest away from Ottawa. Some wanted to be able to put in expense accounts, but the Prime Minister countered humorously: "The accounts would be contested, and it might afterwards be thrown in the face of a member on the hustings by an opposing candidate that he had travelled more like a prince than a representative of homespun peo-

> "The Government are merely trustees for the public." — Sir John A.

ple in the backwoods. Members, also, would be looking at what the others had charged before they would make their declaration" (laughter).

It was decided that there would be no bar or service of liquor in the House, including the Speaker's chambers. There was to be provision for dinner to be served and to give a series of "receptions and social reunions to smoothe down the asperities of political life."

From the very beginning, there was discussion about settling the West, for Americans were saying, "If you do not go there, we will squat you out." The "Fenian scare" also came in for study. There was a joke or two about John Sandfield Macdonald, member for Cornwall, who had expected that city to be made the capital of Canada and had, it was said, been buying up old chairs and tables to use in the assemblies.

### Speech from the Throne

There was no Hansard Report and for several years no printed records of the first parliamentary sessions. Fortunately, newspapers of the day carried fairly complete reports. The *Toronto Leader* of November 8, 1867, the day after the first session, printed the Speech from the Throne, which was read by the Governor-General Viscount Monck. It was generally accepted that it had been composed by Sir John A. Macdonald. Viscount Monck spoke as follows:

"Honourable Gentlemen of the Senate, Gentlemen of the House of Commons. In addressing for the first time the parliamentary representatives of the Dominion of Canada, I desire to give expression to my own deep feeling of gratification that it has been my high privilege to occupy an official position which has made it my duty to assist at every step taken in the creation of the great Confederation.

"With the design of effecting these objects, measures will be laid before you for the amendment and assimilation of the laws now existing in the several provinces relating to currency, customs, excise, and revenue generally; for the adoption of a uniform postal system; for the proper management and maintenance of public works and the properties of the Dominion; for the adoption of a well-considered scheme of militia organization and defence; for the proper administration of Indian affairs; for the introduction of uniform laws respecting patents of invention and discovery; the naturalization of aliens and the assimilation of the criminal laws relating to bankruptcy and insolvency.

"A measure will also be submitted to you for the performance of the duty imposed upon Canada under the terms of the Union Act of immediately constructing the Intercolonial Railway. This great work will add a practical and physical connection to the legislative bond which now unites the provinces comprising the Dominion; and the liberality with which the guarantee for the cost of its construction was given by the Imperial Parliament is a new proof of the hearty interest felt by the British people in your prosperity.

"Your consideration will also be invited to the important subject of western territorial extension, and your attention will be called to the best means for the protection and development of our fisheries and marine interests.

"You will also be asked to consider measures defining the privilege of Parliament and for the establishment of uniform laws relating to elections and the trial of contested elections."

It would appear that Sir John A. and his Cabinet had their work cut out!

Former Prime Minister Lester B. Pearson on Sir John A. Macdonald: "He was a skilled practitioner of the art of politics. I wish I had some of his skill."

Ottawa — the capital of the new Confederation — was to be John A.'s home until his death. This engraving of the Parliamentary Buildings was the title page for Grant's *Picturesque Canada*.

# PART FOUR  1867-1873

*The day has been stamped with the world's great seal, it is graven
I think with the word "disappointment."* Lady Macdonald's diary

# A great Premier's wife
# "He likes me near him"

## Lady Macdonald's diary gives intimate life with John A.

PAC

*Just as valuable as the large accumulation of the Macdonald Papers is the edifying diary which Lady Macdonald (Sir John A.'s second wife) started as a bride and kept for sixteen years. A woman of intelligence with a bright style, she gives penetrating insight into her husband and his times. (The diary is owned by Mrs. D. F. Pepler of St. Catharines, Ontario, who generously permitted its use for this album.)*

*The pages of Lady Macdonald's journal start traditionally enough.*

My beautiful new Diary Book! I am ever so pleased with it... and the lock too! My diaries as Miss Bernard did not need such precautions... what I might write didn't matter. Now, I am a great Premier's wife and Lady Macdonald, and "Cabinet secrets and mysteries" might slip off unwittingly. My husband's new title is just five days old, so... I may be excused for some little bumptiousness.

July 5, 1867 All this new constitution has been framed in my husband's brain.... Thank God he has been very successful in this pet scheme of Confederation of all the British North America Provinces — and all Canada is singing his praises. He is a *powerful* and *popular* man today — and withal the humblest, least assuming, most gently judging of all mankind.... Life was only "half" then.... I have found something worth living for — living in — my husband's heart and love.... My husband devoted himself to "patience" his well beloved game, absorbed, leaning on the large green table in my dressing-room. He says it rests his mind, and changes the current of his thoughts, more than anything else.

### Laughing Like a Schoolboy

July 6, 1867 He likes me near him. He is so equable and so good-natured, that being with him is always refreshing. I tell him that his good heart and amiable temper are the great secrets of his success. He is so thoroughly patient and gentle in spirit. It is quite remarkable in so hard worked, so busy and so thoughtful a man. He can throw off a weight of business in a

PAC

"All this new Constitution has been framed in my husband's brain ... Thank God he has been very successful in this pet scheme of Confederation ... all Canada is singing his praises" — one of the first entries in Lady Macdonald's diary, July 1867.

wonderfully short space of time; oftentimes he comes in with a very moody brow, tired and oppressed, his voice weak, his step slow, and ten minutes after he is making clever jokes, and laughing like any schoolboy with his hands in his pockets and his head thrown back.

*The diary entries give us a sharp picture of the times.*

July 14, 1867 Brown is frantic. John is tired and looking pale. Exciting political talk, John in great spirits.

November 17, 1867 I am so thankful our Sundays are quiet, that is as a rule. I made it

for months a subject of very earnest prayer that my husband might prevent Sunday visitors... on any but very pressing matters.... Now, we have such happy rest after our morning service, and all the servants go to church. John, especially, needs rest during this session time.

November 21, 1867 John sadly overworked.

*Lady Macdonald soon had to handle requests for political favours:*

December 1, 1867 A sad scene today. It is extremely painful being asked to beg John to interfere in getting places for my friends —

*(continued)*

Wednesday
September 23rd

Pouring rain, early & very chilly indeed.
The weather cleared at noon, and was afterward,
very pleasant. So happy a day — I am truly
grateful for all the Sunshine my Father gives.
Visitors & Jessie to luncheon — long chat afterwards.
Reading "Cruise alone" by McGregor.

Thursday.
September 24th

Chilly & cloudy rather. Remained in my dressing
room till noon, as I felt languid & headachy.
The Collingwood Schriebers to lunch — No council —
John only a short time at the Dept. Hughy & I
called for & came home with him — Saw Mrs Tilley.
Finished 1st vol of "Jeave" & began reading by
myself "Massacre of St Bartholomew by Vehians
White". Again a happy tranquil day —.
And my "New Hope" so bright. while so strange —
Can it be that some day I shall have the
Sweet happiness of being a Mother? It seems
so wonderful yet so beautiful — I can hardly
express what a new life it has seemed to give me
that a new life — I often think what an
Unsatisfactory existence women must lead
who, passing Girlhood, & having no particular
Vocation never realizing the joys of wife & mother &
spend their lives in trying to fill the void
which nature has decreed they should
experience —

"Again a happy tranquil day — and my 'New Hope' so bright while so strange! Can it be that some day I shall have the sweet happiness of being a mother? It seems so wonderful and yet so beautiful — I can hardly express what a new life it has given me." Mary Theodora Margaret was born less than five months later, on February 8, 1869.

87

## "He is the most unselfish heart, the very dearest and kindest, with much self restraint"

especially those I love and value. He is so just that I know it is distressing to him to be asked for what he does not think it right to give...and yet I cannot refuse to do all in my power legitimately for my good old friends — who in days gone by and under different circumstances, were so good to me.... From my seat in the Senators' gallery, I watch my husband with infinite pride. He is so evidently ruler of them all, yet he manages with infinite tact, grace and skill. It is charming to hear him adjust little differences by a few words, setting the wrong right and always turning aside any shaft too keen.

*Sir John A. was often seen to turn to the gallery, taking vitality from his wife's encouraging nod. It was her habit to call for him, and they walked home when the weather was fine. Otherwise she met him in a summer carriage or winter cabriole, with fur robes, to drive back to the "Quadrilateral" as their ugly but cozy house was lovingly nicknamed. There, over a midnight snack, he forgot the difficult hours in the House, his ailments and his vexing creditors, and relaxed as he was pampered and loved.*

*Lady Macdonald probably practiced self-censorship in her diary, as she wrote:*

Of course, one keeps a diary with some vague consciousness... at some time some person will read some part.... Living as I do with men who are now making history of their new country, I am always afraid of putting anything into these pages... I may find out ought not to have been written.... I fear my impressions and remarks may be erroneous and lead me to false conclusions.

*Hoping for a child herself, and not able to foresee the tragedy that birth would bring, she meanwhile mothered her stepson, Hugh John, with tenderness and solicitude. Her dedication to self-discipline is reminiscent of Queen Victoria's.*

January 8, 1868 Hughie arrived from Toronto. So glad to see the dear old boy. I love him if only for his likeness to my husband. A happy chatting evening at home.

January 7 and 8 As for Sir John, the doctor tells me he is working himself terribly. He is so precious to us all that we are perhaps oversolicitous, but his constant attention to close business seems to overlap. I have brought it before my Heavenly Father in my prayers, and I know all will be well.... I am trying to disentangle my life, and make my thoughts arrange themselves. In reading I have given up novels...

*John L. Russell*

all those which are frivolous.... And then I have given up wine — that is for example's sake! And because I think it is necessary. I dislike all games of cards but "Patience," which we read "Albert the Good" was fond of. I hope to be able to take a right stand about Balls and to set my face against theatricals.

### My Darling's Birthday And He Is 53

January 11, 1868 Dined at Rideau Hall. How strange it still is to be taken in by the Governor... first lady there. I try hard that these things should not be a temptation or occasion of failing to me. My darling's birthday, and he is 53.... No one could guess him as much as that.... He is so bright and active. May God bless this year to him and to me!... Sir John wore his Star for the first time tonight. I was so proud of him and of it and he looked so well with the broad red riband on his coat. Surely he deserves it for he has faithfully served both Queen and Country.

February 7, 1868 All the Ministers in town and Sir John preoccupied and busy. I feel distressed about his health and overwork. Dr. Grant spoke to me about it again today, and I feel fidgety and nervous in consequence.

February 25, 1868 John's headaches grieve me much.

February 26, 1868 As for his knowledge, there seems to be no end of it. Where he found leisure to collect so much general information, during years of political life, surprises me.

March 26, 1868 John better.... Talk at dinner and after very bright and chatty. Politics, of course, but not too much. Sandfield says he likes politically inclined women. I do, in great moderation, but too much, or anything approaching too much, is out of most women's sphere. If a woman gives too much attention to politics, I think she becomes so violent a partisan and is apt to ride her hobby to death and then a softening influence is needed — which we ought to try and spread. I do trust I may be enabled to give something of a higher tendency to the thought of the set among whom I live. It seems almost presumptuous to say so, and yet my Heavenly Father who "seeth not as man seeth" uses the least worthy instrument.

March 28, 1868 There is not much time for reading. Indeed, I miss it and self-recollection. One needs this in a busy life — one needs time for quiet thinking and self-communing. I pray that in all my days of gladness, I may nightly think of its Giver.

Sunday, March 29 (5th in Lent, 1868) These blessed quiet Sundays. What a lull. They come sweetly on one's very soul.... My Heavenly Father, who has changed my husband's life in so many ways, has also put it into his heart to deny himself on Sunday, and so idle gossip and business, and hurry and all the week's bustle is kept from my house. I am so thankful. It may seem a small thing but it is really a great one and an unspeakably happier home.

April 19, 1868 (First Sunday after Easter) ...John was well pleased at my being able to speak French all dinner time to Dr. Beaubien.... This has been a quiet happy day. Indeed, our Sundays are delightful, when I think of what they might have been... I do like the servants to have a rest and I like to mark my own exceeding reverence for the Holy Day.

### The Most Unselfish Heart

April 28, 1868 Sunday.... John was a dear and good about going to church. He said he was weary and would not, but when I looked ever so little sad, he got up at once and dressed in a hurry. He is the most unselfish heart, the very dearest and kindest with much self restraint.... Another quiet Sunday, prayed for this morning.

May 1, 1868 John was in his bed until 12 p.m. I was so scheming that I would not tell

The home of the Governor-General in Ottawa. "Dined at Rideau Hall," wrote Lady Macdonald. "How strange it is to be taken in by the Governor... first lady there. I try hard that these things should not be a temptation or occasion of failing to me."

him what o'clock it was, and when he rose he said I had been wicked! But then he said it, as he always does, so gently. . . .

May 10, 1868  Sunday. . . . The late hours at the House are so trying. Sir John and Hewitt have not been home more than once before two o'clock . . . and indeed, sometimes they are out until three or four. . . . I believe my "at home" was a success, but neither John or Hewitt could be here which laid a heavy burden of entertaining on me . . . not far from ninety guests. . . . Nothing can be greater than the glad content of my heart and life in these days. . . . I see His Hand every day . . . in my husband's political success, in his large majorities, his brilliant powers, his proud position, his increasing health.

August 27, 1868  Ten days in Halifax staying with the Governor — such a pleasant kindly host. Feted everywhere. I liked it all — the prominent part I had to play, the pretty dresses to wear, the compliments to listen to! ! ! Then a voyage home by the Gulf in a special Government steamer, a day at P.E.I., and two at dear old Quebec. How many memories the old town on the cliff brought back to us.

August 31, 1868  I was much struck in reading of the morals among the statesmen of George Third's reign. . . . I trust and believe our age purer and I pray a blessing on our public men.

September 1, 1868  I am absurdly sleepy. Last night, the wind blew like angry guns and a porch door at the back flapped and creaked until one o'clock and, almost crazy with impatience and sleepiness . . . I prayed my husband to get up and shut it. When he did so, I thought what a selfish wretch I was! . . . What a restless life politicians lead . . . wheels within wheels. And yet what a noble thing to be important and useful and not only to live because you can't help it. John, Mama and I eat our mock-turtle soup, mutton and apple pudding alone.

September 3, 1868  Called for, and walked home with my darling.

September 19, 1868  These divided nationalities must be wonderfully difficult to legislate for the French seem always wanting everything — and they get everything the English population say in Quebec. They have a sturdy outspoken little leader, the Baronet, Sir George, the fairest of men. He always seems to me full of life and pleasant chattiness but extremely egotistical. He must be clever and powerful, but somehow I don't think he is a favourite. I mean in Public Life. Still his honesty must be respected and a certain plainness that is akin to strength — to that strength, I mean that moral strength which satisfies the people even when qualities which please are wanting. . . . Hughie is here, our good steady-going dear old Hugh. One cannot help respecting and loving him. John is both fond and proud of him, but the boy has been brought up necessarily much away from his father, who was always in the Seat of Government. Hugh's home was with his aunt.

### Macdonalds to Have Child

*A year and a half after their marriage, her diary told of a promised fulfillment.*

September 24, 1868  Again a happy tranquil day — and my "New Hope" so bright while so strange! Can it be that some day I shall have the sweet happiness of being a MOTHER? It seems so wonderful and yet so beautiful. I can hardly express what a new life it has given me. . . . Since John told me to read very few novels, I am losing my taste for very light books.

November 8, Sunday  My husband went off to church so well and cheerful — alone. I have been and am still unwell. Yesterday, I was extremely complaining and suffered much. A prayer for Help refreshed me at once.

January 1, 1869  I think Sir John only paid three or four visits and then came home, so cheery, the darling — and so full of fun. After a sort of dinner off the end of the luncheon table, I was glad to be on the sofa and doze till bedtime.

January 6, Wednesday  My darling came home at five o'clock and took me to walk. I can lean on no arm like his!

January 10, Sunday  First after Epiphany There seems every probability of Nova Scotia's opposition to Union being softened and alloyed — if not subdued, although this may seem a matter with which I have nothing to do, it has often been a source of anxiety to me.

January 27, 1869  I feel gloriously proud and thankful at His having "won" in N.S. Hardly a year ago one of the leading men from there who is not timid and who advocated Union told me . . . that, "the Country" meaning N.S. was in a state of complete rebellion, and that it needed but one false or nasty move to kindle a flame there that might lead to very important and very disastrous consequences. No less than a calling out of Troops. And now the Prime Mover in the repeal cause, the most influential of all the public men in the Province, is in Ottawa "negotiating." Strange phase of affairs indeed. . . . Mr. Howe was with me today, calling, full of fun and in excellent case.

February 2, 1869, Tuesday  It is so good of my darling not to have gone to the Governor's party in Montreal. They all pressed him to go, and I know he would have enjoyed it. I even begged him to go, but I did not press it. Just now he is most necessary to me, for he is such a loving tender caretaker and nurse, and I am often poorly.

February 4, 1869  The sculptor is progressing with Sir John's bust. It promises pretty favourably. John, sitting to the sculptor, is very cheery over the nob on his nose.

*(continued)*

---

May. 1st 1869.
Saturday.

The day has been stamped with the world's Great Seal, — it is graven, I think, with the word "disappointment." Perhaps yesterday was one of the saddest times in my life — let it pass — let it die — only teach me — Heavenly Father, to see the lesson it was destined to teach, and while I learn it, to do so cheerfully —

Busy as usual on Saturday's — drove early — went to market — & came home for visitors. The Chancellor, Speaker, and many members came — with his Cousin, & some ladies. Old Rotts had to leave me suddenly, and Baby will miss her sorely —

At 7.30 — we sat down 12 to dinner — 3 selves, Mrs Bayard, Mr & Mrs Bolton — Mr Lewin,

The heartbreaking entry in Lady Macdonald's diary — May 1, 1869. She had just found out that her daughter would never be normal. "Only teach me, Heavenly Father," she writes, "to see the lesson it was destined to teach, and while I learn it, to do so cheerfully."

# "The saddest day of my life... I have suffered keenly"

## The Macdonalds learn Mary is hydrocephalic

*Mary Theodora Margaret was born on February 8, 1869. Did Sir John A., with his quick, perceptive mind and his long experience with his first wife's invalidism, become aware at once of her sickly condition? Hoping against hope for a cure, did he try to keep the terrible truth from his wife, who had been so overjoyed at becoming a mother? They consulted the most renowned physicians hoping to heal the child's ailments, but the day came when the parents had to face the fact that their Mary had an incurable birth defect. She was afflicted with hydrocephalus, or water on the brain, which enlarged her head enormously and made her a lifelong invalid. Disciplined professional that he was, Sir John A. kept the dreadful knowledge from the Canadian people as long as possible.*

**The Silence in Lady Macdonald's Diary**

*The diary, which Lady Macdonald had started with happiness and optimism at the time of her marriage, was kept very sketchily after the birth of the delicate child. Lady Macdonald does not mention her daughter until April 1, almost two months after her birth.*

April 1, 1869   She is lying asleep in her blankets, my very own darling, my little daughter, the sweet gift from Heaven, my Mary, a dark-eyed soft thing, my child. What words can tell how my heart swells with love and pride as I look at her. God gave her to me to cherish and she is truly dear.... How little I thought when last I wrote on these pages, that before another sun rose I should have been face to face with death, and yet so it was. Not only my life, but my Baby's was in danger.... The strength and encouragement given me... it almost seemed as if a presence stood by my bed.... My baby was born ... on February 8 at fifteen past three. Her first cry seemed to bring me back to life ... and a wild exultant joy ... I had been ill for so many hours, twenty-four.

April 11, second Sunday after Easter   Nine long weeks have passed since I was able to go to church. This morning, I was again permitted to go to kneel by my darling's side. Ah me! What a cold dull frame I was in all through the service. What a cold dull frame I am in still! ... Baby is such a pet and treasure — so good and fat and getting dimpled. How grateful I am that she was spared to me.

Sunday, April 25, 1869   Half Ottawa sees Baby and I linger in the nursery and talk to Mama and lounge after John.... Mr. Howe is elected and is coming up.... The members have mustered strong and the House is in excellent temper. Sir John's government has now such a large majority. I hope and believe it will make good use of its power and that all clouds which darken it may pass away.... My baby is sweet and bright and well. My dear little child. I have read nothing today. My heart has been cold and dull, my frame weak. I seem to be waiting for something. Perhaps it is for light!

*And then the terrible news:*

May 1, 1869   The day has been stamped with the world's great seal, it is graven I think with the word "disappointment." Perhaps yesterday was one of the saddest times in my life. Let it pass. Let it die.... Only teach me, Heavenly Father, to see the lesson it was destined to teach, and while I learn, to do so cheerfully.

*Then a longer silence before the time of reconciliation to the truth about little Mary.*

November 24, 1869   What has changed me since last year? ... Wonderfully little — and yet wonderfully much. Outwardly all is nearly the same, except that my darling child's smile brightens my home but in my heart I feel that much is wholly different. I ought to be wiser, for I have suffered keenly in mind.

December 1, 1869   My husband is reading "Phineas Finn" by a blazing coal fire.... Baby is sleeping in her little iron cot, and the servants are gossiping by coal-oil light in the kitchen hall.... Baby was out three times today, though it was cold, she seemed to enjoy the little change and was well wrapped up. I am so thankful that she is strong again today and has not cried at all.... Last night, dear baby was so wakeful, that I had no real rest. It is wearing.

*Lady Macdonald now wrote but seldom in her diary. The following pieces tell a little more of the Macdonalds' heartbreak for their daughter's condition — a condition of which they spoke only to their closest friends.*

January 1, 1870   The New Year began for me as I knelt in Church at St. Albans.... I thought of the joy and sorrow, the pleasure and pain I had known there, even in less than three years.

March 23, 1870   My precious child has been ailing today. The least sign of illness in her distresses me more than I can tell. She has been so mercifully spared to me that in spite of her delicacy, I trust she may be stronger soon.

April 1, 1870   I took my darling out early in the fresh, fine air, trying hard to get some colour into her cheeks and strength to her limbs. She lies, in spite of her thirteen and one half months still on the pillow of her little carriage, smiling when she sees me, and cooing softly to herself.

January 1, 1871   During the eight long months very much has passed. I really never wrote a word.... I had charge of darling baby all the afternoon and she fretted for her nurse, and I felt, as I always do, how wrong this state of things really is, when a child loves so much more dearly a stranger than its own mother.... And yet, what can be done? I am by no means fashionable, and go out seldom, yet ... so many occupations keep me from the nursery.

January 2, 1871   What a bustling day! All the fires blazing and crackling; all the house in its best order; all the servants important and in a hurry, and I, in my best black velveteen gown, receiving New Year visitors. The house was thronged from noon till dinner-time with men of all ages, sorts and sizes. Some 130 in all. Some merely shook hands and bowed, exchanged a few commonplaces about the weather; but the larger part lunched at a continually replenished table in the dining-room and wished me and mine all happiness for the New Year between mouthfuls of hot oyster soup or sips of sherry. Sir John spoiled everything by having ordered a Council. I had set my heart on having him with me, and lo! he went away before one single caller had rung the bell. I never enjoy anything much at which he does not assist and his pleasant easy manners make all go on well. He only came in at dinner-time, all covered with snow.... I must go to bed ... and by eight-thirty tomorrow I must be ready to pour tea. N.B. I do this untidily, being like most women who dream of stars and love, scribbling — anything but neat over my tea tray.

January 3, 1871   Fretting about baby being cross and flushed.

January 4   Baby has been ailing all day. And I think this American Fishery Question bothers Sir John. I suppose it is a ticklish business, as Brother Sam may show fright. I wonder Sir John can stand against all this work and worry.... Before I go to sleep, I think out a story ... "Wasted" ... I told my husband of it.... He wanted to know if the title would apply to the reader's time!

Tuesday, January 9   Sir John has gone to the Masonic Lodge.

March 16, 1872   Chapel St. Ottawa. Fourteen months since I last wrote in these pages, and almost all things continue the same.

*There came a day when Lady Macdonald's diary disclosed another cry from the heart.*

March 11, 1875   Many bitter tears.... My mother, my mother, gone from me. Can you see your desolate child now?

**The Diary Ends**

*Why did Lady Macdonald cease to keep up her diary? Could she no longer turn to the little book to relieve her pent-up emotions? Was she disturbed by the setbacks in Sir John A.'s career? Was she further distressed that he had left his abstemious ways and taken again to heavy drinking? The closing notation is a meagre description of the New Year's service at St. Albans Church and a very brief mention of the annual New Year's Day reception.*

January 1, 1883   Stadacona Hall, Ottawa. Midnight service at St. Albans unusually impressive. Large attendance and full choir. At home 1:30 a.m. and up at eight. Received large party. Also 200 callers and luncheon all day. Evening mild and pleasant.

*With this entry, Lady Macdonald's diary came to an end.*

In June 1869, when little Mary was four months old, Lady Macdonald posed her for this picture. She would write the following spring: "She lies, in spite of her thirteen and one half months, still on the pillow of her little carriage, smiling when she sees me, and cooing softly to herself." Mary lived sixty-four years, never able to walk or to look after her affairs.

*Thos. D'arcy McGee*

### Life of D'Arcy McGee

Like John A., Thomas D'Arcy McGee was an immigrant; he came to Canada from Ireland. A gifted orator and a masterful politician, he was one of the so-called Big Seven of the Fathers of Confederation.

Frederick Driscoll's *Sketch of the Canadian Ministry,* published in 1866, says that D'Arcy

McGee "is Minister of Agriculture (with a fine *field* for his labours). Mr. McGee is one of the most intelligent men of the Cabinet, and has won the repute of being a fluent and witty speaker. This is his best quality, it may be said, though he has some legislative talent also. He can go to much trouble to collect statistics, and is a careful writer on a serious subject. If Mr.

McGee is light and witty sometimes, he can, in the House, be serious and official-like, as becomes a legislator.... If we look back at the political course of Mr. McGee (as one must do in order to write a sketch of him) we cannot help seeing that it is a little irregular; and it is to be hoped by his friends that the rest of it will not be marked by any more deviations."

# A great fear came on me to see John throw up the window

## "Is anything the matter?"

### The answer came up fearfully clear and hard: "McGee is murdered!"

*Thomas D'Arcy McGee was assassinated on April 7, 1868. Lady Macdonald's diary gives an acute and sensitive report of the manner in which D'Arcy McGee was killed. (For some reason, she refers to him throughout as Wm. McGee.)*

### Sad and Fearful Tragedy

Easter Sunday, April 12, ten p.m. As I was writing so peacefully . . . in my quiet room, a sad and fearful tragedy was being enacted a short distance off. . . . This is how it was that dreadful night at half past two o'clock on the Tuesday morning. Tuesday, the 7th, my husband came home from a late sitting. It had made me a little uneasy his being away so long. To begin with I knew he would feel tired and then a sort of dread came upon me as I looked out into the cold, still, bright moonlight, that something might happen to him at that hour coming home alone. This feeling however remarkable then is one that has often distressed me when Parliamentary business has kept Sir John out late — or rather early — as was the case this bad morning.

About two fifteen a.m., I felt so restless that even my Bible reading failed to calm me and I went to Mama's room and lay down on her bed. We were talking in subdued tones and she was scolding me for sitting up, when I heard the carriage wheels and flew down to open the door for my husband.

We were so cosy after that, he coming in cheery with news of the debate, and sitting by my dressing room fire with his supper that as I knelt to say a few words of prayer before I went to bed I could not help stopping to think a moment over my many, many blessings, and to wonder at my peaceful happy life — its shadows gone. I was almost half asleep when I was roused by a low rapid knocking at the door. In an instant a great fear came on me . . . to see John throw up the window. . . . "Is there anything the matter?" The answer came up fearfully clear and hard. . . .

### McGee Is Murdered
### Shot through the Head

"McGee is murdered — lying in the street — shot through the head." The words fell like a blow of a bar of iron across my head — it was too dreadful. . . . A sad, sad hurried day followed. My husband and brother went down to the spot immediately, and did not return until five. I sat trembling with fear, and horror until they

came home, for we could not tell how many more assassins might be lurking in the grey-lit streets. . . . We felt the shot was fired by a Fenian. When John came home, he was much agitated for him whose self-command is so wonderful. He had found our poor friend's body lying in his blood, dead at the door of his lodgings, shot from behind by a cowardly assassin's hand, as he was in the act of turning his latchkey to let himself into the house.

The bullet had passed into the lower part of the back of the head and had come through his mouth carrying away two or three of his teeth as the shot was fired. The landlady . . . opening the door on the inside . . . heard the shot and saw the pistol flash. Her life was saved by a miracle, the ball lodged in the door she was holding. She ran in, gave the alarm and in a few moments the dead man was surrounded by his friends. Poor Wm. McGee — he has died nobly — a martyr . . . a sacrifice to his loyalty and flag. . . . He has been threatened often before, and now suspicion more than points to a young Fenian ruffian as the murderer. (He is apprehended and is now in jail.)

All Tuesday was so hurried — news coming and going, hurried steps and visits, gloomy faces, whispered words. John had made all the arrangements . . . and all were on the alert for the finding of the base coward who had done the foul deed. The day dragged on. John's face was white with fatigue, sleeplessness and regret, yet he never gave in . . . nor was other than cheerful to me and kind. . . . That that man, who had only three days before been in our home, sitting at our table — should be lifeless and made lifeless in so frightful a manner.

April 15   To the House where John "got through" the pension to Mr. McGee's poor family. . . . Round the wretched man, Whelan, testimony thickens and the general impression is strongly that he is guilty.

Monday, April 20   To the House for John. . . . He came home at two. How good it is of Hewitt to go down with and come up with Sir John . . . for that dreadful shadow of the murder is on every man's mind. The evidence goes on steadily accumulating — and new parties become implicated. Examination is generally within closed doors; only some part in the papers.

April 24   Examination of witnesses goes on. Not a man swears that he saw the murder committed. . . . Great talk about Fenians. Lord Monck came in after service to tell John that the Duke of Edinburgh had been fired on one day in Sydney, Australia. The feeling here is very intense about Wm. McGee's murder. Buckley, the livery stable-keeper, who has been almost a coachman of ours, is supposed to be deeply implicated. I shudder as I think how entirely my husband, Chief Crown Law Officer, has been exposed by driving with him.

May 1, Friday, 1868   As the session draws

near its end, the bustling becomes tenfold. Last night, my husband went to the House as usual at seven thirty and did not return until four thirty this morning. They were on the "Tariff" and so there was much speaking. However all went well. In everything a special Providence watches over us.

Sunday, May 10   The late hours in the House are trying. Sir John and Hewitt have not been home more than once before two o'clock . . . and indeed, sometimes they are out until three or four.

June 21   It is Sunday and Hughie is here. . . . We had a Fenian scare this month and the general opinion seemed that a raid would certainly take place. I saw John anxious and all on the alert . . . telegrams . . . manifold consultations. However the U.S. Govt. interfered about some arms; and learning, as they must have done, that Canada was preparing itself, seems to have determined the Fenians.

September 19   Whelan was convicted of Wm. McGee's assassination.

### Informs Widow

Immediately after the murder it fell to Sir John A. to inform D'Arcy McGee's widow. In *The Assassination of D'Arcy McGee,* Montreal lawyer and author T.P. Slattery writes, "The means he chose were rapid and delicate. He immediately sent a telegram to Father Patrick Dowd, the pastor of St. Patrick's in Montreal. In turn, Father Dowd asked two Grey Nuns to accompany him and they went directly to the McGee home on St. Catherine Street. Joseph H. Daley, McGee's close friend, the general agent of the Grand Trunk, was also informed and went to the McGee home. There, all met at the door.

"It was shortly after four o'clock the morning of the assassination when Father Dowd broke the news to the widow. It was related that Mrs. McGee collapsed in grief; then her friends and prayers helped her to regain some calmness."

### Scene in House

Slattery describes the scene in the House of Commons on the day following the murder: "When Speaker Cockburn took the chair, a hush fell over the crowded House of Commons. It was ten minutes past three that same Tuesday afternoon, and a thousand people were crammed into the galleries. A shaft of silver light streamed downward through a cluster of small dark pillars to fall on a pier of greyish marble across the

*(continued)*

> Joseph Howe on D'Arcy McGee: "Whatever be his errors, he is a man of genius — an elegant writer, an eloquent speaker, and a pleasant fellow over a bottle of wine."

> D'Arcy McGee said in 1862: "A Canadian nationality, not French Canadian, nor British Canadian, nor Irish Canadian — patriotism rejects the prefix — is what we should look forward to."

silent Chamber as the Prime Minister, Sir John A. Macdonald, rose to speak. He looked weary and pale and under heavy strain. After two brief hours of sleep he had returned to his office at seven o'clock that morning, and had been working steadily since, issuing a series of orders in an effort to cope with the emergency.

"His opening words were low. He faltered and seemed to have difficulty in going on as he spoke of 'pain amounting to anguish.' The spectators could hardly hear him when he continued: 'He who was with us last night, no, this morning, is no more. If ever a soldier fell in the front of the fight, it was D'Arcy McGee. He deserves well of Canada. His hand was open to everyone. His heart was made for friendship. And his enmities were written in water.'"

John A. did not attend the funeral of his close friend and colleague. Did his ministers urge him to stay away as a security measure? As his wife indicated in her diary, there was such a climate of fear that John A.'s brother-in-law, Hewitt Bernard, accompanied him to and from sessions in the House. Or was John A. so overcome by the tragedy that he drank so much that he was unable to attend the funeral? (Several years later, shattered by the death of his close friend Cartier, John A. took solace in drink. However on this occasion he managed to pull himself together in time to attend the funeral.)

### Whelan Hanged

Whelan was hanged at Ottawa on February 11, 1869. The next day, Sir John A. wrote to James O'Reilly, the Crown Prosecutor at Whelan's trial:

*Private*
My dear O'Reilly,

You will see by the papers that Whelan said nothing on the scaffold. He left a short paper stating that neither Doyle nor Buckley participated in the murder, which he signed before O'Gara and Lees. In conversation with them he freely admitted his presence at the murder, [as] he did to Goodwin, and on several occasions to the Sheriff and Governor of the gaol, but he always denied that he fired the shot. I am satisfied that he did fire the shot, and that that fact is the reason that he did not offer to turn Queen's evidence. I attach no importance to the written statement. It has evidently been dictated

---

### Mass arrests

"Sir John A. Macdonald, immediately upon receiving the news of D'Arcy McGee's murder, telegraphed to all the stations on the Grand Trunk Railway, and to the Mayors on the Ottawa and St. Lawrence, to arrest all suspicious looking persons." — *Daily News,* Montreal, April 14, 1868

---

by some superstitious feeling that as he had taken away one life, he would make amends by endeavouring to save two. The body was to have been given up to Mrs. Whelan, but information having arrived that there was going to be a great Fenian demonstration over the corpse at Montreal on its arrival, which would inevitably lead to bloodshed, it has, I believe, been buried within the precincts of the prison, the ground being blessed and Christian funeral given, attended by the clergyman who was with him at the last. This was the arrangement last night when I went to bed, and I presume it was carried out this morning.

Thanks for your congratulations.

Yours faithfully,
John A. Macdonald

P.S. to the effect that priest having declined to attend, body was buried without rites of Church.

### Who Killed D'Arcy McGee?

Slattery spent years examining the notes of the judge who presided at Whelan's trial, the documents at the coroner's inquest and newspaper accounts of the proceedings. In his book *They Got to Find Mee Guilty Yet* he suggests that there was no legal evidence that Whelan was a Fenian or an agent of the Fenians, and that his execution, the last public hanging in Canada, might have been a gross miscarriage of justice. Slattery ends his book with the words, "Who killed D'Arcy McGee under the full moon of Canada's April sky is still a mystery."

---

# WHO WERE THE FENIANS? WHAT DID THEY WANT?

## Raids from U.S. by Irish patriots to embarrass England backfire and help bring about Confederation

In the last days of the Confederation debates, John A., who was in London, received this letter from D'Arcy McGee:

Ottawa, Dec. 19, 1866
My dear Macdonald,

...As to the Fenians, we still continue to receive the average number of "startling rumours" but no one seems to put much faith in them. It may be that we are in danger of running into the extreme opposite to credibility, and when you write Campbell, you might give him a fillip on that score. Inertia is all very well in its way, but it may be carried too far....

Yours very truly,
T.D. McGee

Some months later D'Arcy McGee again wrote to John A. concerning the Fenians:

July 11, 1867, Montreal
To Ottawa
My dear Macdonald,

...I did not go to Toronto, and I am glad I did not. The Grit-Fenian clique in that vicinity would not have asked better than to offer me personal affronts, and as these things are epi-

*PAC*

Even when the raiders did not actually enter Canada, there were several scares, such as this one near St. Albans, Vermont, in 1869.

demic, the whole tone of my election tour would be spoiled at the start. Every man I can reach,

will be reached by my appeal, which I took care they should all have before assembling. I have not yet seen any news from Toronto, but I sincerely think no harm has been done....

Yours very truly,
Thomas D'Arcy McGee

*A Historical Atlas of Canada* describes the Fenians: "The Fenian Brotherhood, organized in Ireland and among Irish Americans to win Ireland's independence from Britain, took advantage of the general restlessness in the United States and hostility towards Britain following the American Civil War to make several raids on Canada. A half-hearted attempt on New Brunswick's Campobello Island was followed by a much more serious effort under John O'Neill who led 1,500 Fenians across the Niagara River on May 31, 1866, and won a victory over a Canadian force at Ridgeway before withdrawing. Simultaneously there was some plundering on the border east of Lake Champlain and a minor raid was repulsed near Huntingdon. Despite many alarms, the only other major raid was in May 1870 when a force *(continued)*

James Street, Hamilton, Ontario, as the people gather to hear news of the Fenian invasion and to find out whether their town is threatened by the raids which took place from May 31 to June 2,1866. The drawing, which appeared in *Harper's Weekly,* was based on a photograph taken by a local resident.

A convention of Fenians in Cincinnati in 1865 determined on invasion of Canada. Fenian "troops" were made up largely of Irish-American veterans of the Civil War. The *Harper's Weekly* drawing shows the skirmish on June 2 between the invading Fenians and the Canadians who were trying to drive them back. That the raiders could get so far and do so much damage before resistance could be organized made Canadians realize just how vulnerable they were and how much they needed Confederation for mutual protection.

Four years later, the Canadians were much better prepared, and the Fenians never got as far or did so much damage as they had in 1866. *The Canadian Illustrated News* published this drawing of an engagement at Cook's Corners, in the spring of 1870.

The Fenians are stampeded through Trout River Village into retreat in 1870. An attempt to enter Manitoba the following year was broken up by U.S. troops.

## John A. turns the raids to his own advantage

raised by O'Neill was met by resolute Canadians at Eccles Hill and driven back across the border. An attempt on Manitoba in 1871 was broken up by American troops."

### Fenians in Flight

The following account by a reporter of the *Hamilton Weekly Times*, Hamilton West, of June 7, 1866, describes the flight of the Fenians on Saturday, June 2, and Sunday morning, June 3: "We hired a Jehu to drive us up the village of New Germany where we heard Col. Peacocke was, on his way to Fort Erie. The road was lined with vehicles of all sorts and men and boys on horseback and on foot, many of them carrying guns that they had picked up on or around the battlefield of Ridgeway. The road is good as far as Chippewa, but beyond that is very rough . . . a perfect muddle of clay in spring or fall. . . ."

John A. managed to turn the raid to his advantage. He argued that a united Canada would better be able to resist such invasions. Thus the Fenians provided yet another reason for Confederation.

The New York papers were faintly condemnatory of the Fenian raid, criticizing the movement more as a light military blunder than as an outrage upon the obligations of two nations at peace. "A further prosecution of the scheme of Canadian invasion is generally discouraged, as utterly hopeless of success, both from the embarrassment which the American Government will place upon the movement and the ample preparation to resist the incursion from the Canadian side."

If the American newspapers were not too outraged at this raid on a friendly neighbour, perhaps it was because only two years before a band of Confederate soldiers had used Canada as a base from which to raid Vermont. Pope, Sir John A.'s secretary, gives this account of "a band of Confederate soldiers, twenty-five, or so, in number, headed by one Bennet H. Young, a lieutenant in the Southern army. The plot was organized in Chicago, from which point the main body of the marauders proceeded direct to their destination through the United States, Young and three others going by way of Canada. On the 19th October, 1864, they met in St. Albans, where they plundered three banks, attempted to fire the town, and escaped to Montreal. They were arrested with a view to their extradition under the Ashburton Treaty, but discharged by 'Judge' Coursol on technical grounds. They were immediately re-arrested and tried before the Superior Court at Montreal, but again set at liberty, the Court holding that they were belligerents and, as such, not subject to extradition. Subsequently fresh arrests were made, and the *venue* changed from Montreal to Toronto, but with no substantial results, and the latest prosecutions came to nothing."

On June 28, 1866, Sir John A. wrote to Lieutenant-General Sir John Michel, commander of Her Majesty's Forces in Canada: "I yesterday received a confidential note from Lord Monck informing me that you and he had applied to England for reinforcements, which I was very

*(continued)*

### Fenian Marching Song

*Many battles have been won*
*Along with the boys in blue,*
*And we'll go and capture Canada,*
*For we've nothing else to do.*

Whether or not the U.S. Government was only half-hearted in its attempts to curb the Fenians, it is certain that a large number of Americans considered the attacks ridiculous to the point of comic opera. The great nineteenth-century American cartoonist Thomas Nast pictures the raiders as grandiose fools. (Nast is the cartoonist who drew the donkey and elephant as symbols of the Democratic and Republican parties.)

The number of Fenians who crossed from the United States into Canada in the spring of 1866 is not known. Estimates range from 800 to 1500. The Fenians did succeed in capturing Fort Erie and winning a battle at Ridgeway — where ten Canadians were killed and thirty wounded — before they were forced to retreat to Buffalo. There U.S. troops arrested 700 of the invaders.

# D'Arcy McGee: "Fenians are political leprosy"

glad to learn.... We can inform you where the most comfortable and suitable barrack accommodation can be found. As we are in a state of semi-war, I suppose you will allow the soldiers to be packed closer than they would be in a time of complete peace, and in regularly constructed barracks. We have a very good barrack here fitted for a wing of a regiment, and with a little squeezing it would hold 400 men. We could easily provide quarters for a battalion, and I presume you would think this an eligible place. The men cannot readily desert, and the railway can carry them to the front in two and a half hours, in case of Prescott or Fort Wellington being threatened."

## Denounces Fenians — "Political Leprosy"

Though D'Arcy McGee had been involved in the independence movement in Ireland — indeed he was wanted by the British police there for his activities — he was not in sympathy with the Fenian movement. In 1865 he had denounced the Fenians in a speech to the St. Patrick's Society of Montreal: "There is another subject which more immediately concerns ourselves in Montreal and in Canada, which has lately occupied a good deal of the attention of the press — I allude to the alleged spread of a seditious Irish society, originating at New York, and which has chosen to go behind the long Christian record of their ancestors to find in Pagan darkness and blindness the appropriate name of Fenians. (laughter) ... I would say to the Catholics of Upper Canada, in each locality, if there is any, the least proof that this foreign disease has seized on any, the least among you, establish at once, for your own sake, for the country's sake, a *cordon sanitaire* around your people; establish a committee which will purge your ranks of this political leprosy; weed out and cast off those rotten members, who, without a single governmental grievance to complain of in Canada, would yet weaken and divide us in these days of danger and anxiety.

A Canadian cartoon of June 1870 showing skepticism that the U.S. Government was seriously interested in arresting John O'Neill, the Fenian leader. O'Neill's men have just been pushed back across the border by Canadian troops. O'Neill apparently took no part in the fighting but watched the skirmish from the safety of a farmhouse on the U.S. side of the border. The implication is that the U.S. marshall is really protecting O'Neill rather than arresting him.

(cheers) Instead of sympathy for the punishment they are drawing upon themselves, there ought to be a general indignation at the perils such wretches would, if permitted to exist among us, draw upon the whole community, politically and religiously. How would any Catholic who hears me like to see the parish Church a stable, and St. Patrick's a barrack? How would our workingmen like to see our docks desolate, our canals closed, our new buildings arrested, ruin in our streets, and famine shivering among the ruins? And this is what these wretched conspirators, if they had the power, would bring to pass, as surely as fire produces ashes from wood, or cold produces ice from water. (cheers) I repeat here deliberately that I do not believe in the existence of any such organization in Lower Canada, certainly not in Montreal; but that there are, or have been, emissaries from the United States among us, for the purpose of establishing it, has been so often and so confidently stated, that what I have said on the general subject will, I hope, not be considered untimely or uncalled for." (hear, hear)

### Fenian Threat Continues

Sir John continued to worry about the Fenians. In April 1870 he wrote to the Earl of Carnarvon: "The withdrawal of the troops from Canada is, I think with you, a most unwise and short-sighted proceeding. At this moment we are in daily expectation of a formidable Fenian invasion, unrepressed by the United States Government, and connived at by their subordinate officials. And we are at the same time called upon to send a military force to restore order in Rupert's Land. Her Majesty's Government have been kept fully informed of the constant threats from the Fenian body for the last five years, and they have been especially forewarned of the preparations for the present expected attack. And yet this is the time that they choose to withdraw every soldier from us, and we are left to be the unaided victims of Irish discontent and American hostility, caused entirely by our being a portion of the Empire. We must, however, bear it as best we may, and we intend, with God's blessing, to keep our country, if we can, for the Queen against all comers."

## Uncle Sam and His Boys
### or, What Will He Do With Them?

*Uncle Sam he sot a'-thinkin'*
*And a-wonderin' what to do*
*With them thar naughty boys of his,*
*They call the Fenian crew.*
*"Now here's a go," said Samuel,*
*"And what a botheration,*
*These Fenian critturs get about*
*To fight a neighbouring nation.*
*When o'er the border line they flocked,*
*With all my heart I j'ined*
*In wishing 'death or victory'*
*Would leave nary one behind.*
*But they fled like darned cowards*
*Before the Canuck bands*
*And here I am, with all the crew*
*Again upon my hands!*
*Now something must be done at once*
*To save our reputation —*
*To squelch those Fenian scamps right eout*
*Would glorify our nation.*
*But then the critters all have votes,*
*So handy at elections.*
*And they're kinder good for threatening*
*John Bull and his connections.*
*Waal, neow, I don't exactly see,*
*This tarnal thing's a muddle"* —
*He took his jack-knife, turned his quid,*
*And whistled Yankee-doodle!*

From *The Canadian Illustrated News*, 1870

THE BRITISH HIGH COMMISSIONERS, 1871
Standing, left to right: Lord Tenterden, Sir John A. Macdonald, Montague Bernard. Seated, left to right: Sir Stafford Northcote, Earl de Grey and Ripon, Sir Edward Thornton

# John A. goes to Washington

Macdonald felt the United States should pay compensation for the damages suffered by Canada because of the Fenian raids. The opportunity to press that claim came to him when he accepted an appointment to serve on the British High Commission (above) that went to Washington in February 1871 to settle the U.S.-British differences which had existed since the American Civil War. (Britain had financed the building of ships for the Confederates, and these ships sank a number of Union ships, including the *Alabama*. The victorious North expected Britain to pay damages. The quarrel had dragged on, but suddenly with the outbreak of the Franco-Prussian War in Europe, England was anxious for U.S. friendship.)

Even as he agreed to serve on the British Commission, Macdonald had misgivings. He knew the Americans would want long-standing disputes with Canada also cleared to their advantage and that Britain was not likely to support Canada. But he also believed that a Canadian should be present and so he went to Washington.

In *The Old Chieftain* historian Donald Creighton gives a fascinating detailed account of just how increasingly heartbreaking the next two

and a half months were for Macdonald. He had to buck the contempt U.S. officialdom felt for Canada. Speaking before Congress, President Grant referred to Canada as "this semi-independent and irresponsible agent." Several well-known annexationists were on the U.S. delegation. The U.S. dismissed Canadian claims for Fenian raid compensation because it was not on the agenda. (The British had omitted it.) England agreed to all U.S. requests at Canada's expense: territorial claims off Vancouver Island, free navigation of the St. Lawrence and — what

On May 3, 1872, John A. spoke in the House of Commons about the Washington Treaty: "When someone writes my biography — if I am ever thought worthy of having such an interesting document prepared — and when, as a matter of history, the questions connected with this Treaty are upheld, it will be found that, upon this, as well as upon every other point, I did all I could to protect the rights and claims of the Dominion."

would remain ever afterwards a source of Canada-U.S. friction — fishery rights in Canadian waters.

But Macdonald fought hard, as indicated in the report sent home by British delegation head Lord de Grey: "I have had to carry on quite as difficult a negotiation with Macdonald as with the United States Commissioners." The British finally agreed to guarantee a Canadian loan of £2,500,000 for railways, in compensation for the Fenian losses.

Macdonald considered the Treaty of Washington dreadful from all Canadian points of view and agreed to sign it only as a member of the "British" delegation, warning that it might not be accepted by the Canadian Parliament. Today however historians regard this as the first step in independent Canadian diplomacy. The Treaty of Washington — according to Morton in *The Kingdom of Canada* — was "the greatest diplomatic check the United States had accepted since its foundation" for "it had agreed to share the continent with a self-governing Canada, a country as free, as well organized and as stable as itself." The United States gave up all serious belief in the possibility of annexing Canada.

THE "DARWINIAN" THEORY EXEMPLIFIED

"WHAT WERE WE OR OUR GENERATION
THAT WE SHOULD GET SIC EXALTATION" BURNS

The origins of the species Mackenzie and species Macdonald are whimsically examined in this *Canadian Illustrated News* cartoon. PAC

# THE CARICATURISTS' DELIGHT

*Lumpy nose, frizzy hair—
John A. has the face
they love to draw;
he enjoys their cartoons*

With his large lumpy nose, his frizzy hair and his thin arms and legs, Sir John A. was a caricaturist's delight. He was drawn by most of the cartoonists of the time and his picture often appeared in *Grip* and *The Canadian Illustrated News*.

*Grip*

Macdonald was frequently pictured as a mischievous schoolboy. PAC

THE MIDDAY GUN AT OTTAWA.

E. Jump is one of the few artists to capture the humour of Macdonald.

A pot-bellied John A. throws in the sponge.

A SILHOUETTE BY GAS-LIGHT, OTTAWA, APRIL 20.

Another *Canadian Illustrated News* cartoon featuring John A.

"WE IN CANADA SEEM TO HAVE LOST ALL IDEA OF JUSTICE, HONOR AND INTEGRITY."—THE MAIL, 26TH SEPTEMBER.

John A. and his opponent Alexander Mackenzie — a dour Scotsman whom the cartoonists also loved to draw.

A JOB ON HAND FOR THE NEW "TURNER

John A. was often featured on the cover of *Grip*.

**CERTIFICAT.**

Nous, soussignés, déclarons et certifions que cette photographie est la vraie copie du portrait de Louis " David " Riel, dont l'original est la propriété d'Abraham Guay.

(*Signé*) { Veuve Julie Riel.       Joseph Riel.       Alexandre Riel.
{ Veuve Marguerite Riel.   Octavie Lavallée.   Henriette Poitras.

Daté à St. Vital, 12 janvier 1886.

Je certifie par la présente que le portrait de Louis Riel qui m'a été montré par M. Guay est une ressemblance parfaite.

(*Signé*) John Lee.

Montréal, 24 février 1886.

Enregistré, conformément à l'acte du Parlement du Canada, en l'année 1886, par Abraham Guay, au bureau du Ministre de l'Agriculture

LOUIS RIEL

The fiery Métis leader is one of the most fascinating and controversial figures in Canadian history. During the 1880s he was regarded by many as a demented fanatic, but now he is honoured as the founder of Manitoba.

**THE SCIENCE OF CHEEK**
or Riel's next move
Although a fugitive, Riel was elected by the Métis to represent them in Parliament. He did not dare to take his seat, but he did appear in Ottawa without being apprehended.

# Riel: Macdonald's worst blunder?

## Stormy rebel splits English and French

The Macdonald administration made a tragic blunder in its handling of Louis Riel, the fiery Métis leader. Riel is one of the most controversial characters in Canadian history. Was he a mad traitor or a loyal hero? Was he a mystic or a madman? Certainly he was deeply religious, and not by nature a fighter — he appeared at one battle unarmed, holding high a crucifix. He was serious, passionate, intense, dynamic and idealistic. It is doubtful whether Sir John A. and his Government ever really understood Riel or the nature of his grievances.

Louis Riel was born on October 22, 1844, near "the forks" — where the waters of the Red and Assiniboine rivers meet. This was in the area called Rupert's Land, which was owned by the Hudson's Bay Company. In the heart of Rupert's Land, there was a small colony called the Colony of Assiniboia or the Red River Colony. It was made up of a few Indians, of the descendants of explorers and trappers and of retired Hudson's Bay employees. These were Louis Riel's people. About three-quarters of the colonists had some Indian blood. Those

> "The French half-breeds at Red River are pertinaciously resolved to keep the North West a buffalo reserve forever."
> — Sir John A. Macdonald, 1869

who spoke French as their mother tongue were called Bois-Brûlés or Métis.

After Confederation, the new Dominion of Canada began investigating the possibility of annexing Rupert's Land. The Métis were not opposed to joining Canada — but they wanted to do so on their own terms, maintaining their traditional way of life. They formed a national council to protect their interests. Although he was only twenty-five years old, Riel became secretary of the council; he was fluently bilingual, having had some education in the East.

In December 1869 the Canadian Party (made up mainly of recent arrivals from the East) attempted to seize power in the colony. Riel and his Métis followers captured about forty

(continued)

Assisted
by Macpherson,

No doubt RIEL
had Something to do
with it

The snail Policy
was the cause

DEP'T. OF INTERIOR

REFORM
PARTY

REBELLION

GRIEVANCES

Pot-a-Pie!
yum! yum!

the REFORM PARTY
brought it about.

J.W.Bengough

"Who is responsible?" for the Riel Rebellion asks J. W. Bengough in this cartoon which appeared as a double-page spread in the *Illustrated War News*. Macdonald — called "Old Tomorrow" because of his habit of postponing unpleasant decisions — has "let the pot boil over." Louis Riel (upper left

corner) "no doubt had something to do with it." Other culprits include Blake (lower left), Mackenzie (lower right), the CPR, the Fenians, land-grabbing schemes and so on. *The Illustrated War News* was published by the Grip publishing company and solely concerned with the North West Rebellion.

members of the Canadian Party and imprisoned them. Riel then declared a Provisional Government with himself at its head. This Government began negotiations with Ottawa concerning the peaceful annexation of the Red River Colony.

### Scott Shot by Firing Squad

In February 1870 the Canadian Party prisoners were released — after having promised not to interfere with Riel's Government. However, Thomas Scott, one of the leaders of the Party, did not keep his promise. He immediately began organizing support to overturn the Provisional Government. He was arrested, tried and convicted. The next day he was shot by a firing squad.

In May the Canadian Parliament passed the Manitoba Act — creating the province of Manitoba. But in the East there were hard feelings against the "murder" of Thomas Scott. The issue became a racial and religious one; prejudice clouded reason. The people clamoured for the arrest of Riel. Sir John A. did not commit himself.

When the new Lieutenant-Governor went to Manitoba, he was of course accompanied by troops. Rumour reached Manitoba ahead of them that the troops would arrest Riel for the "murder" of Scott. Riel and some of his followers slipped across the border.

### Riel a Fugitive

Riel lived as a fugitive for the next fifteen years. Twice he was elected by his Métis to represent them in Ottawa, but he was unable to take his seat. (However, while there was a warrant out for his arrest he did appear brazenly in Ottawa without being apprehended.)

In 1885 he heard that the Métis feared that the Government was threatening their traditional way of life. Calling himself "David" Riel, after the biblical David, he returned to Canada and attempted to organize a rebellion.

In one way, this rebellion worked in Sir John A.'s favour. It hastened construction of the Canadian Pacific Railway. The Government knew it had to have speedier military transportation, and voted the funds necessary to complete the railway. Troops were rushed to Manitoba to put down Riel's rebellion, arriving in the unprecedented short time of nine days.

TOO LATE!

Old Tomorrow has waited too long to investigate the grievances of the Métis and Indians in the North West Territories. Louis Riel has come back from exile to lead them in rebellion.

Riel was captured and put on trial. Feeling still ran high. The *Toronto News* ranted, "Strangle Riel with the French flag! That is the only use that rag can have in this country." Riel was condemned to hang, but, as one juror said fifty years later, "We tried Riel for treason, and he was hanged for the murder of Scott." Sir Wilfrid Laurier wrote, "It cannot be said that Riel was hanged on account of his opinions. It is equally true that he was not executed for anything connected with the late rebellion. He was hanged for Scott's murder: that is the simple truth of it."

There was pressure on Sir John A. to pardon Riel; there was as much pressure from the opposite side. Sir John A. has been quoted as saying, "He shall hang though every dog in Quebec bark in his favour."

### "Nothing to Give But My Heart"

And so Riel was hanged. Before his execution at the Mounted Police Barracks at Regina, Riel volunteered to his priest, "I swear . . . before God, shooting Thomas Scott was not a crime. It was a political necessity. I commanded the shooting, believing it necessary to save the lives of hundreds." To a guard, who asked for a souvenir, the doomed man said, "I have nothing but my heart, and I gave it long ago to my country."

Professor George F. G. Stanley wrote, "Few characters in Canadian history have aroused such depth and bitterness of feeling as that of the Métis chieftain, Louis 'David' Riel. The mere mention of his name bares those latent religious and racial animosities which seem to lie so close to the surface of Canadian politics. Despite the fact that he identified himself, not with the French Canadians of Quebec, but with the mixed-blood population of the western plains, Louis Riel became, for a few years, the symbol of the national aspirations of French Canada and the storm centre of political Orangeism. French-speaking Canadians elevated him to the pedestal of martyrdom;

Lower Fort Garry, Manitoba — a Notman photograph

# WITNESS EXTRA

MONTREAL, SATURDAY, MAY 16TH, 1885.

# RIEL CAUGHT

## Near Batoche. He begs not to be shot.

## Indian loss, 105 killed in engagement with Col. Otter. Middleton's official report on the Battle of Batoche. Death of another volunteer. Heavy rebel losses.

*(From Our Special Correspondent.)*

**HIS CAPTORS.**

CLARKE'S CROSSING, May 15.—I have just made a trip from Gardupe's Crossing, 58 miles, since four p.m. Riel has been captured, having been found in the road a little south of Batoche, in company with three men. Hourie and Armstrong brought him in on foot, leaving their horses in the bush and walking quietly. Few knew who he was when he was brought into camp, though the sentries, his captors, made right for General Middleton's tent, where they delivered their charge safely. Riel appeared unconcerned, but begged not to be shot.

**ANOTHER DEATH.**

Sergeant-Major Watson, of the 90th Winnipeg Battalion, wounded at Batoche, died at Saskatoon to-day.

**THE "NORTHCOTE."**

The "Northcote" returned from Saskatoon at seven o'clock this evening, and proceeds to Batoche in the morning.

**THE WOUNDED.**

Code is very low. Lethbridge is unchanged.

**SHOT BY A COMRADE.**

Aiken, of the Midland Battalion here, was shot in the leg this evening by a comrade fooling with a revolver. It is a slight wound.

*(Press Despatch.)*

**POUNDMAKER'S LOSS.**

WINNIPEG, May 15.—Archbishop Tache has received word from a priest with Poundmaker's Indians, through Lepine, just arrived from the West, that there are one hundred and five graves of Indians as the result of the recent attack of Col. Otter, and many more were wounded. The conflict was terribly severe and fairly astounded the Indians.

The following appeared in our Extra Edition of last evening :

**THE REBELS GREAT LOSS.**

WINNIPEG, May 15.—Capt. Bedson telegraphs that the rebel loss was 51 killed and 173 wounded. The march to Prince Albert was begun yesterday. The Montreal Garrison Artillery is not expected to arrive till Monday or Tuesday next.

**OTTER CRITICIZED.**

Lord Melgund leaves to-night for Ottawa, to confer with the Government. He says Gen. Middleton considers Col. Otter acted injudiciously in attacking Poundmaker and Gen. Middleton knew nothing about it. Gen. Middleton will not take all the troops to Battleford, but merely a flying column, probably not much more than an escort for himself. He thinks enough troops should be sent into the Indian country to overhaul the redskins, who will then be told that if they give up their leaders and retire to their reserves there will be no more trouble. He thinks this may avoid a collision. He speaks highly of the bravery of the troops, saying he never saw braver men. The delay at Fish Creek was occasioned by the want of supplies. He does not think they will capture Riel. Prince Albert Battleford and Edmonton will be garrisoned, Batoche is a point of no importance. Middleton will probably take Boulton's scouts with him to Battleford. The half-breed uprising is regarded as over. Keppen's remains are being sent home for interment.

**GEN. MIDDLETON'S REPORT.**

OTTAWA, May 15.—In the House to-day before the orders of the day were called Mr. Caron said : I desire to read to the House a more lengthy report of the battle of Batoche which I have received from General Middleton, which will be of interest. It is as follows :

FROM BATOCHE, N.W.T., May 12.

*To Hon. A. P. Caron :—*

Since my last evening despatch to you I have ascertained some particulars of our victory, which was most complete. I have myself counted twelve half-breeds on the field and we have four wounded half-breeds in hospital and two Sioux among the wounded half-breeds is one Ambroise Jobain, a councillor, and Joseph Deborme. As far as I can ascertain Riel and Gabriel Dumont left as soon as they saw us getting well in, but I cannot ascertain for certain which side of the river they are, but think it must be this side. The extraordinary skill displayed in making rifle pits at the exact proper points and the number of them is very remarkable, and had we advanced rashly or heedlessly, I believe we might have been destroyed. As I told you I reconnoitered to my right front with all my mounted men yesterday morning with a view to the withdrawal of as many of their men as possible

from my left attack, which was the key of the position, and on my return to camp I forced on my left, and then advanced the whole line with a cheer and a dash worthy of the soldiers of any army. The effect was remarkable. The enemy in front of our left was forced back from pit to pit and those in the strongest pit facing the east found them turned and our men behind them. Then commenced sauve qui peut and they fled leaving blankets, coats, hats, boots, trousers and even guns in their pits. The conduct of the troops was beyond praise, the Midland and Tenth Regiments vying with each other well supported by the 90th and flanked by the mounted portion of the troops. The artillery and Gatling also assisted in the attack with good effect. When all behaved so well it might appear invidious to mention particular names. Still there are always some who by good luck are brought prominently before the eyes of the commanding officer, and these names I shall submit to you later on.

My staff gave me every assistance and were most energetic and zealous. The medical arrangement under Brigade Surgeon Orton was as usual most excellent and efficiently carried out. I have to regret the death of three officers as well as two soldiers, they died nobly and well. I found no want of ammunition among the enemy or food, in spite of what has been said to the contrary, and we found large quantities of powder and shot. Nearly the whole of the rebels' families were left, and are encamped close to the river bank. They were terribly frightened, but I have reassured them and protected them. There is a report that Gabriel Dumont is killed, but I do not believe it though it is likely that he is wounded. One of the killed has been recognised as Donald Ross, one of the Council.

Yesterday evening, just as the action was finished, the "Northcote" and the "Marquis" steamers arrived up, the latter having twenty-five police on board. It appears that the "Northcote" had a hard time of it as the rebels fired at it very heavily, and though it was well fortified, the rebels managed to wound two men slightly. The "Northcote" got on a shoal for a short time, but managed to keep the enemy off and to get off themselves. Finding that, owing to the barges alongside, they could not go up the stream again, they decided to run down to the Hudson's Bay crossing to get rid of them, and return. At the crossing they found the other steamer and came up together. This morning I sent out a letter, addressed to Riel, as follows :—

BATOCHE, May 11.—Mr Riel, I am ready to receive you and your council, and to protect you until your case has been decided upon by the Dominion Government.

(Signed)	FRED MIDDLETON.

Major-General commanding North-West Forces.

I cannot, of course, be sure, but I am inclined to think the complete smash of the rebels will have pretty well broken the back of the rebellion, at any rate will, I trust have dispelled the idea that half-breeds and Indians can withstand the attack of resolute whites, properly led, and will tend to remove the uncomfortable scare that seems to have entered into the minds of so many in the North-West as regards the prowess and powers of fighting of the Indians and half-breeds. There is not a sign of the enemy on either side of the river for miles.

(Signed)	FRED MIDDLETON.

It is almost impossible to find an unbiased contemporary account of Riel's Rebellion, capture, trial and execution. The newspaper accounts of Riel's trial pushed the story of the completion of the CPR off the front pages. It was probably because of the trial and the controversy and ill-feelings that it generated that no ceremony was observed at the driving of the last spike.

# THE VACANT CHAIR.
### A *RIEL* BOND OF UNION.

One thing that Macdonald and Mackenzie agree on — that Riel is a murderer and outlaw and ought to hang. Though Riel was tried for his part in the Rebellion, jurors admitted that they condemned him for the "murder" of Scott.

English-speaking Canadians damned him as a rebel. . . . Sir John A. found himself between the upper and nether millstone of racial and religious conflict. For promising an amnesty he was denounced in Ontario; for neglecting to proclaim it he was denounced in Quebec. . . . There may have been excuses for Sir John A. Macdonald in 1869; there could be none in 1885. For the problem which faced the Prime Minister was the same one which had faced him earlier; the problem of conflicting cultures, of reconciling a small primitive population with a new complex civilization. But Sir John had other things on his mind — he was building the Canadian Pacific Railway — and the Min-

istry of the Interior, Sir John's own ministry, starved the Indian services and failed to allay the fears and suspicions of the Métis that they would lose their rights as the original holders of the soil."

When the working men of Lower Canada presented Sir John A. with a suit of clothes in a Scots Highland pattern, he said, "I am not a bit too proud to accept it. I have a right to a new coat . . . for I never turned one."

*Grip*

The Riel issue split the English, who wanted to see him hang, and the French, who urged John A. to pardon him. John A.'s handling of Riel and the Métis is one of the blackest marks in his career.

Marching song of the volunteers who were sent to fight the Riel Rebels in the NWT in 1885:

> *The volunteers are all fine boys*
> *And full of lots of fun,*
> *But it's mighty little pay they get*
> *For carrying a gun.*
> *The government has grown so lean*
> *And the CPR so fat,*
> *Our extra pay we did not get —*
> *You can bet your boots on that!*

### Riel's Diary Found

In April 1969 the Canadian Government paid $16,000.00 at an auction sale for Louis Riel's own account of the 1870 Rebellion, assuring that what is perhaps the greatest manuscript in western Canadian history would remain in our country. Two years later, another extraordinary document, the original Louis Riel Diary of the North West Rebellion of 1885 was bought at auction by Gene Rhéaume, a former M. P. for the North West Territories, and like Riel a Métis. Mr. Rhéaume (whose grandfather served in Riel's Provisional Government) bid $26,500.00 to keep this treasured item in Canada. The diary is entirely in French, in red and black ink, on forty-eight ruled pages of thirteen inches by eighteen inches. It had been preserved in a red velvet bag. Soon after the Rebellion of 1885 it was lost, to be found again only in 1970. Riel's handwriting is clear, although the pages are loose, soiled and tattered. The torn sheets tell us that God spoke to Riel in both English and French, guiding him in the bitter conflicts. It is not generally known that when he fled from Canada, Riel became an American citizen in Fort Benton in 1883. The diary says: "O l'invitation du secours américain est une invitation dangereuse. Prenez garde aux aventuriers des Etats-Unis. Car je vous assure qu'ils sont à craindre; ils n'ont ni moeurs, ni foi, ni coeur. Ce sont des chiens sales; des chacals immondes; des loups ravisseurs; des tigres furieux." ("Oh the offer of American help is a dangerous invitation. Beware of the adventurers from the United States. For I assure you they are to be feared: they have neither morals, nor faith, nor heart. They are dirty dogs, foul jackals, ravishing wolves and furious tigers.")

The diary finishes: "O mon Dieu! Assistez-moi, dirigez-moi, fort charitablement afin que je place bien nos gens et que je les surveille bien, sans m'exposer inutilement, sans craindre pusillammement . . . afin que nous venions à bout de toutes nos bonnes entreprises et afin que nous ayons le bonheur d'accomplir à tout égard votre sainte volonté." ("Oh my God! Assist me, direct me, most kindly that I may station well our people and that I may look after them well, without needlessly exposing myself, without fear of cowardice . . . so that we may realize all our good works and so that we may have the joy of accomplishing in every way your holy will.")

### Founder of Manitoba

For almost a century, Riel was thought of as a demented fanatic. But at its centennial in 1970 Manitoba unveiled a monument to him, crediting him with bringing the province into Confederation 100 years before. The monument is inscribed with Riel's own words: "Yes, I have done my duty. During my life I have aimed at practical results. I hope that after my death my spirit will bring practical results. All that I have done and risked, and to which I have exposed myself, rested certainly on the conviction that I was called upon to do something for my country. . . . I know that through the grace of God I am the founder of Manitoba."

Louis Riel and other Métis and Indian leaders, drawn for the *Illustrated War News*. Riel was not a fighter by nature. He appeared at one battle holding only a crucifix, with no weapons at all.

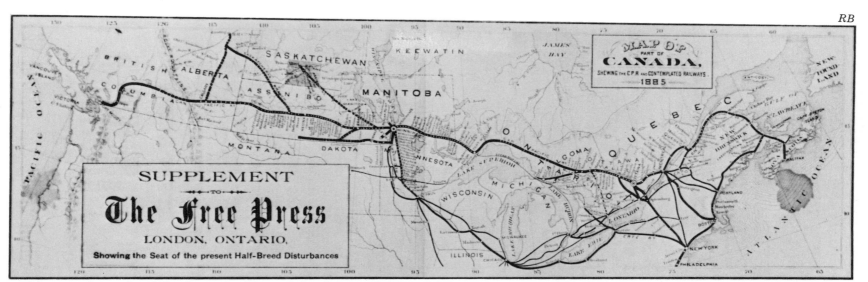

This map, drawn in 1885, shows the "Seat of the Present Half-Breed Disturbance." The CPR and contemplated railways are also indicated.

Louis Riel is captured by two scouts on May 15, 1885. He appears to be unarmed.

Riel, imprisoned at the Mounted Police Barracks at Regina, takes his daily constitutional.

# What was the colour of John A.'s ties?

PAC

PAC          PAC

## Best-dressed man or Canadian dandy? Reporters intrigued, tailor's name secret

If there had been a best-dressed list in Sir John A.'s day, he probably would have been on it. Although he often bought clothes in Britain — boots in London, Highland gear in Edinburgh — he also patronized Canadian shops. Gibb and Company, Merchant Tailors and Gentlemen's Haberdashers of Montreal, sent him this bill in 1869:

| | | |
|---|---|---:|
| *June 21, 1867* | Pair superfine striped Angola Trowsers | $10.00 |
| | Pair ditto | 9.50 |
| *June 25, 1867* | Superfine fancy striped Angola Quilting vest | 6.00 |
| | ditto | 5.00 |
| *June 11, 1868* | Superfine Berlin Angola Mor. Coat lined in silk | 23.00 |
| | Silk sleeve linings | 2.00 |
| | 2 fine white drill vests | 11.00 |
| | 2 pairs fancy Angola trowsers | 19.00 |
| | 1 dozen pairs half hose | 4.80 |
| | 2 fancy "Prince Teck" scarfs | 2.50 |
| *July 27, 1868* | 2 fancy white drill vests | 10.00 |
| | 1 linen collar | .25 |
| *July 28, 1868* | 1 dozen collars | 3.00 |
| | 3 fancy silk ties | 1.88 |
| | 2 black silk ties | 1.00 |
| *December 28* | Superfine Olive Berlin Angola Mor. Coat | 24.00 |
| | Silk serge Sleeve linings | 2.00 |
| | Superfine Olive Berlin Angola Vest | 6.00 |
| *(undated)* | 1 dozen white ties | 3.00 |
| | 1 dozen white shirts | 33.00 |
| | 1 pr. braces | 1.00 |
| | 1 fancy stick | 1.00 |

### Bright Red London Ties

Sir John A. liked ties — particularly red ties. According to an American magazine published in 1889: "There is one peculiarity of his dress which he seldom varies. He has a penchant for bright red London ties, and, except when in evening dress, rarely wears any other hue. Several people have endeavoured to discover the secret of Sir John's London tie-maker, but in vain; the genius remains an interesting incognito." An Ottawa newspaper described Sir John A. at the opening of Parliament in 1891: "The Old Chief . . . was dressed in a frock-coat, with light trousers, with the traditional red necktie, and a 'stovepipe hat' of the latest London style."

But Sir John A. didn't *always* wear red neckties. During his last campaign he sported a blue one. "Lately," he explained to a correspondent of the *Toronto World*, "I have seen so many Grits wearing red ties that I bought this blue one I am wearing now." As old accounts and photos show Sir John A. wore black ties and white ties, ties with polka dots, ties with stripes, ties of every shape and size.

# British Columbia joins the Dominion
# Is promised a railway in 10 years

## *1871 — a good year following a very bad one*

### John A. nearly died; P.E.I. vacation restored health

The Toronto workingmen present a testimonial to Lady Macdonald. She seldom spoke in public, preferring "to leave the speechmaking to my husband who, I am proud to think, makes very good ones."

John A. welcomes the representatives from British Columbia. A few years later he would lose his Kingston seat and himself be elected from the Pacific province.

In May 1870 Sir John A. almost died. According to Biggar, someone passing by Sir John A.'s office "heard a noise, and going into his office, there Sir John was found alone, lying on the floor and writhing in agony.... He was tenderly raised and laid on a sofa. Medical aid was summoned and the worst fears were confirmed. The Premier was dying!... The immediate cause of his sickness was the passing of a gallstone of unusual size. The agony caused by it had thrown him into convulsions. The stone would not come away, and his nervous force was exhausted by the pain. His utter prostration left the muscles relaxed, and this relaxation let the stone pass away. And so in a sense he had passed through death, for it was only through a collapse as in death that relief could have come."

The crisis passed, but for some weeks he was too ill to be moved from his office.

Letters of concern and sympathy poured in from all over the country. These two letters to Sir John A.'s friend and brother-in-law, Hewitt Bernard, came from political opponents:

Montreal, May 15, 1870
My dear Mr. Bernard,

I rejoice most sincerely to learn from your telegrams and Lady Macdonald's that Sir John continues to make satisfactory progress towards convalescence.

Although it has been my lot as a public man to be in constant opposition to him and the Party he has led with signal skill and ability, I have always entertained the highest admiration for his talents, and in spite of momentary estrangements resulting from the interchange of hard blows in debate, I have ever cherished the warmest personal regard for him. On every ground therefore, both public and private, do I fervently hope that his life will be spared and his health and strength restored.

With kind regards to Lady Macdonald and to Sir John himself, if his strength admits of such communications,

Believe me

Faithfully yours,
L. H. Holton

---

### Canada First —
### The Country Above Party

Motto, 1868-1875, of Conservative Party.

---

Toronto, June 2, 1870
My dear Bernard,

I have been watching anxiously the news of Sir John, but thought I would not add to your troubles by a line, even of sympathy.

I cannot help writing however today on learning the very satisfactory news that you have been able to move the sufferer to Cockburn's and that he has borne it so well. I trust this is a real march of recovery and that he will now rally without harm.

With every good wish believe me,

Faithfully,
Edward Blake

When Sir John A. became strong enough to travel he went to Prince Edward Island and there spent two months recuperating. He continued to receive letters from concerned friends.

Rosemount, Tuesday, Sept. 1870
My dear Sir John,

You can't think how pleased I was with get-

In 1872, Goldwin Smith, author and journalist, said, "In this country what is there for Conservatives to conserve or for Reformers to reform?"

ting your letter, for I know how much better you must have been to be able to write it. I can assure you, you would be very flattered if you could hear how universal is the joy at your recovery. It is almost worth being ill, to have so much anxiety so universally exhibited. Not only therefore, must you get well for the sake of your own more especial belongings, but for the sake of Canada, who with almost one voice declares you to be necessary to the future of the
*(continued)*

---

### Pearls of Wisdom

Recovering from a critical illness in 1870, Sir John A. was allowed half an oyster at dinner. Although he begged for more, the doctor refused him saying, "Remember Sir John, the hopes of Canada depend on you." "Strange," replied the Prime Minister, "that the hopes of Canada should depend on half an oyster."

---

A view of Victoria, British Columbia, taken from Indian Hill in 1871.

*Notman*

The British Columbia Legislative Council, taken in 1871, the year they joined the Dominion.

Dominion. The Party here are particularly happy at your recovery. Colonel Elphinstone quite gave a sigh of relief when he heard how you are progressing.... I hope I shall continue to hear that you are getting stronger and stronger....

If you have not read "Red as a Rose is She," and "My Enemy's Daughter," you will find them very pleasant.

Please understand I am *very grateful* to you for writing to me. I know it must have been a great exertion to you, but I appreciate it.

Give my love to Lady Macdonald. How glad she must be to see her care rewarded. I gave you up for a day or two when Doctor Grant came and told me how little hope he could give us. Please God I shall live to hear you make another speech. Sir John sends you his kindest regards and hopes it will not be very long before he sees you.

Yours most sincerely,
Adelaide Young

My dear Sir John,

I was very sorry at not having an opportunity of paying my respects to you when here the other day, and of offering my most sincere wishes that you might long enjoy the good health to which, to the great delight of the whole country, you have been restored. It was

### Sir John A. Scores a Point

During a lively debate, a Member of Parliament complained that "I have the floor. The Honourable Gentleman has made a statement in a menacing manner, pointing his finger at me, and I call upon him to explain the meaning of it." Sir John A. answered calmly, "All I can say is, if I pointed my finger at the Honourable Gentleman, I take my finger back."

PAC

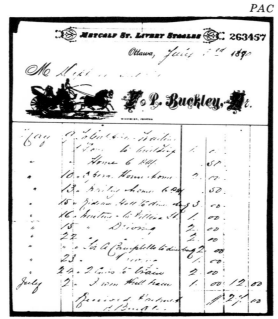

Patrick Buckley not only drove John A. in his cab, he also often gave the Prime Minister advice.

most gratifying to me as a Canadian to see the kindly interest shown by your many friends in London during the most critical period of your illness. The enquiries at Rose's office were incessant and not very usual in that somewhat selfish city....

With my most respectful regards to Lady Macdonald,

Believe me,

Yours very truly,
Geo. Stephen

Although Sir John A. recovered his health, the year 1870 was a troubled one that left him low in spirit. The political problems of Riel and the Red River Rebellions, added to his private distress at his daughter's malady and his constant financial worries, kept him in a wretched state. His friends were alarmed, fearing that he would give in to his weakness — and they were not surprised when he took solace in drink. About this time Sir Stafford Northcote sent a message to Disraeli, which referred in part to Sir John A.: "His habit is to retire to bed, to exclude everybody and to drink bottle after bottle of port. All the papers are sent to him and he reads them, but he is conscious of his inability to do any business and he does none."

### Preposterous Proposition

However, by 1871 Sir John A. had recovered his strength and spirit to the extent that he became involved in a bold, determined dream that many held to be an act of insane recklessness, one of the most foolish things that could be imagined, a preposterous proposition.

It took the promise of a railway to link the Maritime Provinces with Quebec and Ontario,

### Just Dessert

Complaining about the length of the session of 1870 the Honourable John Sandfield Macdonald hoped they could get through the bill of fare by May. The Honourable Alexander Mackenzie deplored the toughness and indigestibility of the items on the menu. Sir John A. said that the Honourable Gentlemen stuck their teeth in too far. The Government only wanted to get its dessert.

Sir John A. on the civil service: "Every government selected for the civil service their own friends, and no one could object to it."

In 1870 Sir John A. wrote to the Earl of Carnarvon: "In our new country public men are much harder worked and are obliged to attend more details than they are in England."

to coax the Atlantic citizens to join Confederation in 1867. But there were more difficult days ahead — it was necessary to bring into Confederation the rest of British North America, from as far west as the Pacific Ocean, a mighty task of organization and government.

## A Promise to British Columbia

On July 20, 1871, British Columbia became the fifth province of the Union. The *Daily British Colonist*, Victoria, B.C., wrote: "Today British Columbia and Canada joined hands and hearts across the Rocky Mountains, and John Bull, the younger, stands with one foot on the Atlantic and the other on the Pacific — with his back to the North Pole and his face looking southward — how far we will not venture to predict." To lure the most westerly province into Confederation, Sir John A. had promised British Columbia a great railroad across the entire country — to the Pacific — within ten years. The cost was estimated at one hundred million dollars.

Thus, only a few years after Confederation, young Canada — with a population of less than four million people — was committed to build

CONSTRUCTIVENESS

the world's longest and costliest railway, across largely unexplored country: a formidable undertaking. But there is magic and excitement in great plans!

Sir John A. declared, "Until this great work is completed, our Dominion is little more than a 'geographical expression'. . . . The railway once finished, we become one great united country with a large interprovincial trade and common interest."

## John A., Workingman

When Sir John A., now fully recovered in body and spirit, spoke to the Toronto Trades Assembly in 1872 he said, "I ought to have a special interest in this subject, because I am a workingman myself. I work more than nine hours a day, and I think I am a practical mechanic. If you look at the Confederation Act, in the framing of which I had some hand, you will admit that I am a pretty good joiner, and as for Cabinet making, I have had much experience."

The speech that he gave to the workingmen was well received. "Gentlemen, I ask you to move your boots pretty lively between now and the twentieth of June. (laughter and applause) I have no fear of the result if you will work. Do not sleep, do not be too confident. I have said again and again that the two most uncertain things in the world are an election and a horserace. (laughter) Don't let the Opposition horse beat the good old N. P. nag by a nose. (applause) You must show your tail to the hindermost horse. Indeed you must win the race. (continued cheering) You must remember, though, that you are fighting the purists, and with them there is such a thing as money being used. 'Oh, purists never use money!' you say; but you surely cannot forget that one of the best supporters of the Grit Party — H. H. Cook — a very good fellow — confessed to having spent in his own election as much as $28,000.00."

A voice from the audience: "And there was Walker."

Sir John A. replied, "Yes, the gentleman who wrote, 'Come along, John, let's put down bribery and corruption: I've lots of money'."

## NWMP Founded

When Sir John A. established the North West Mounted Police in August 1873 he made two significant decisions about the organization. First of all, he decreed that the 300 cavalrymen were to be issued crimson coats like the British army, for the "Great White Mother Queen Victoria" was loved by the Indians and respected because she had never broken her word to them. And second, although the original name suggested was Mounted Rifles, Sir John A. crossed out the word *rifles* and wrote in the word *police*.

Sir John A. wrote that the North West Mounted Police should be "a purely civil, not a military, body with as little gold lace, fuss and feathers as possible. Not a crack cavalry regiment but an efficient police force for the rough and ready — particularly ready — enforcement of law and justice." The NWMP motto *Maintiens le droit* was first used in 1875.

This order-in-council established a Mounted Police Force for the North West.

*RCMP*

John A. suggested that the NWMP have "as little gold lace, fuss and feathers as possible."

# John A. shattered by Cartier's death

## *"But for him Confederation would not have carried, Cartier was bold as a lion."*

In 1867 Queen Victoria created John A. a Knight Commander of the Bath in recognition of his devotion and intelligent leadership. This signal honour elevated his wife, who became Lady Macdonald before their honeymoon was over.

Sir John A. expected that honours of this sort would follow Confederation. However he was surprised to learn that while he was made a KCB, his colleagues were made Commanders of the Bath, a lesser honour which carried no title. If Sir John A. had had a say in the matter, he would not have set himself above his colleagues. The decision was made by Lord Monck, with the approval of Queen Victoria. George Etienne Cartier — John A.'s chief lieutenant — and Alexander Tilloch Galt, both feeling slighted and offended, refused the honours. Charles Tupper, Samuel Leonard Tilley, William McDougall and William P. Howland accepted them.

### Wrong Done to Cartier

Sir John A. set out at once to right the wrong done — particularly to George Etienne Cartier. The French Canadian had given Macdonald his unwavering support through all the pre-Confederation battles, although he suffered much abuse from anti-Confederation French Canadians. Cartier — legend has it that he was descended from the explorer — was fiery, energetic and impetuous. He was a sensitive poet as well, and his song "O Canada, mon pays, mes amours" almost became the national anthem.

Sir John A. intervened in Cartier's behalf, and some time later, Cartier was given a baronetcy — an honour higher even than Sir John A.'s. Lady Macdonald wrote in her diary: "Yesterday Sir John announced Cartier's baronetcy. The House applauded. He is now Sir George. He has been, and is, a useful man, and an honest one which is saying a good deal. It often strikes me that the politicians, Sir John's contemporaries, five, six and eight years ago, who as the popular phrase goes, tried 'to feather their nests' have struck pretty much oblivion, while he and Cartier still rule and reign and are respected. The analogy to Radway's Ready Relief in the above is unintentional."

SIR GEORGE ETIENNE CARTIER    *PAC*

Thus, in spite of the grave blunder in protocol, a breach in the new Confederation was avoided, and Sir George continued to give Sir John A. solid political support.

Sir John A. valued Cartier as a friend as well as a political ally. Once when Cartier was visiting the Macdonalds' home, John A. thought that his friend seemed depressed. To cheer him up, he said, "Come on, George, sing some of your crazy French songs for us!"

### Cartier Dies in England

On May 20, 1873, very bad news came from England. Sir George Etienne Cartier, after a valiant struggle to retain his health, had died in London of Bright's disease. When he heard of Cartier's death, Lord Dufferin wrote to Sir John A., "I can quite understand how very deeply you must be affected by the news of poor Cartier's death. Having fought so many tough battles side by side, and having had so many opportunities of appreciating his courage, energy, and loyal friendship, the sudden disappearance of such a colleague cannot fail to create a great and almost irremediable gap in your political surroundings."

### Sir John A. Shattered

The loss of this beloved friend and colleague, who had stood by him in so many political battles, left Sir John A. in a shattered state. He was already depressed by political and personal troubles, and this new grief was more than he could take. Lord Dufferin wrote about Sir John A. to the Earl of Kimberly: "As a consequence [of Cartier's death] for this last few days, he has broken through his usual abstemious habits, and been compelled to resort to more stimulants than suit his peculiar temperament. It is really tragical to see so superior a man subject to such a purely physical infirmity against which he struggles with desperate courage, until fairly prostrated and broken down."

In 1885, after unveiling a statue of Cartier in Ottawa, Sir John A. said of him: "Cartier was bold as a lion. He was just the man I wanted. But for him Confederation would not have carried."

---

### O Canada! mon pays! mes amours!

*Comme le dit un vieil adage:*
*Rien n'est si beau que son pays;*
*Et de le chanter, c'est l'usage;*
*Le mien je chante à mes amis.*
*L'étranger voit avec un œil d'envie*
*Du Saint-Laurent le majestueux cours;*
*A son aspect le Canadien s'écrie:*
*O Canada! mon pays! mes amours!*
*Mon pays, mon pays, mes amours!*

The funeral procession of Sir George Etienne Cartier passes Place d'Armes and moves along St. James Street. Somewhere among the chief mourners following the coffin is Sir John A., barely able to walk. He was so shattered by the news of Cartier's death that he resorted "to more stimulants than suit his peculiar temperament" and could only with difficulty be roused from his Montreal hotel room to attend the funeral.

Cartier's body lies in state aboard the *Druid*. He died of Bright's disease in London where he had gone to consult a doctor.

Montreal Harbour as the *Druid* arrives bearing Cartier's body home for burial in the new Dominion he helped to create.

117

# John A. Macdonald's contemporaries described him as:

adaptable
adroit
all-comprehending
amiable
astonishing
audacious
autocratic

bad-tempered
bankrupt
bawdy
blithe
boisterous
brilliant

cantankerous
clear-headed
clever
cogent
companionable
conciliatory
contemptuous
cosmopolitan
courageous
courteous
crotchety
cunning

debauched
debonair
deceitful
dedicated
defiant
diligent
disreputable
distinguished
droll
drunk

fierce
flippant
foppish
frustrated
fun loving

gaudy
genial
gentle

homely

incisive
indefatigable
inflexible
ingenious
insincere

jaded
jaunty
jolly
judicious

kind

laconic
lonely
loyal

melancholic

painstaking
passionate
pawky
peculiar
perceptive
persevering
persuasive
philosophical
polite
pragmatic
profound
prophetic

quaint
quick-tempered

resourceful

sagacious
sardonic
saturnine
sedentary
sensitive
shrewd
sickly
sly
solitary
sparkling
spindly
spirited
steady
strong-willed
stubborn
studious

thoughtful
tough

undeviating
ugly
urbane

vain
vigorous
vindictive

warm
wary
wily
witty
wretched

# PART FIVE    1873-1878

*These hands are clean. (Send me another $10,000.00.)* J. W. Bengough, quoting John A.

WHITHER ARE WE DRIFTING?

One of the most famous Bengough cartoons on the Pacific Scandal. Parliament was prorogued in August 1873 when the cartoon appeared, but the scandal was gaining momentum in newspapers across Canada.

# THE PACIFIC SCANDAL ALMOST RUINS JOHN A.

## *Pleads he sought best interests of Canada*

### *Famous five-hour speech impresses but does not convince*

The Canadian Pacific Railway, one of Sir John A.'s greatest dreams, almost ruined him.

In Sir John A.'s time Ottawa was a crude lumbering town. Corruption was rife and politics were unprincipled; there were three major scandals in the second half of the century. But even for those times Sir John A.'s actions were "a deal too rough" as Bruce Hutchison wrote.

Overtired, desperately in need of campaign funds for the coming election and grief-stricken about the incurable illness of his three-year-old daughter, the Prime Minister lost himself in a prolonged and heavy drinking bout, which may have clouded his usually clear judgement.

Sir John A. was nearly ruined not because he was worse than those about him, but because he was caught redhanded accepting more than $350,000.00 for his 1872 election campaign fund from the Montreal financier and shipping magnate, Sir Hugh Allan, in return for promising him that "the power of the Government will be exercised" in making him president of Canada's first railway.

At the time of the divulgence of Sir John A.'s misdemeanours, there was more astonishment at his unbelievable carelessness than at his morals.

### "I Must Have Another Ten Thousand"

What tripped up Sir John A. was this telegramme to J. C. C. Abbott. He was the legal adviser to Sir Hugh Allan, who had been granted a charter for construction of the Canadian Pacific Railway: "Immediate. Private. I must have another ten thousand. Will be the last time of calling. Do not fail me. Answer today."

One thing was clear: it was not personal pecuniary advantage that embroiled Sir John A. in this deal, but the urgent need for election funds and for uniting farflung British Columbia with the rest of Canada. He wrote his friend Sir John Rose, Minister of Finance, on March 5, 1872: "I am as you may fancy exceedingly desirous of carrying the elections again; not from any personal object, because I am weary of the whole thing; but Confederation is only yet in the gristle, and it will require five more years before it hardens into bone."

The "payoff" money to his entreating wire came at once. With the additional election funds the Tories were returned to power, but with a minority government.

Ottawa was then, as now, a rumour mill. Hearsay gossip began to circulate. Premonitions of disaster were broadcast. A general air of

### A Devilish Reply

A Member of the Opposition once related to the House of Commons a long list of Sir John A.'s misdeeds. When he sat down, Sir John A. rose and said with a grin, "Aren't I the old devil, though?"

---

## THE STORY

OF

## THE PACIFIC SCANDAL!

### A TEN-COLUMN BROADSHEET,

CONTAINING

### A Synopsis of the Facts of the Whole Case.

### NOW READY AND FOR SALE.

### TWO CENTS PER COPY, $1.25 PER 100 COPIES, $10 PER 1,000 COPIES.

Send in orders immediately to

## THE GLOBE PRINTING CO.

## THE PACIFIC SCANDAL

IN PAMPHLET FORM,

### 64 PAGES OCTAVO,

## THREE SPEECHES

OF

### THE HON. EDWARD BLAKE, Q.C., M.P.,

ON

## THE PACIFIC SCANDAL

NOW READY AND FOR SALE,

### Ten Cents per Copy; Five Dollars per 100; Forty-five Dollars per 1,000

---

Orders must be sent in immediately to

## THE GLOBE PRINTING CO.

---

tension prevailed. Yet Sir John A., though uneasy and troubled, was still unaware of the bombshell that was about to fall and well-nigh destroy him.

On April 2, 1872, Lucius Seth Huntingdon, a little-known Liberal M.P., to the utter astonishment of the Prime Minister told the House of Commons that Sir Hugh Allan had bought the Pacific contract with election donations. Trapped, fearful, and with no way of knowing how much evidence was in the hands of the Opposition, Sir John A. went on drinking. Burgundy, claret, port and brandy — in large quantities — were his escape. In this terrible situation, he cut a poor figure. For weeks he kept what his accusing opponents called a "studious silence." Finally, when goaded into a reply, he assumed an air of injured innocence and said, "Neither by thought, word, deed or action has the Government done anything of which it can be ashamed. From the conception of the idea to the placing of the charter in the hands of the Pacific Railway Company, we were actuated and moved by a desire to promote the best interests of this Dominion."

### Clerk Steals Incriminating Telegramme

Scarcely had he made this speech when the bottom fell out from under him. The Liberals produced the incriminating telegramme which a young clerk had extracted from the files of financier Allan's attorney and sold for $5,000.00. Shock followed shock. Both sides played rough. Both sides played to win. Almost at once the damaging wire made front page news in *The Globe* in Toronto, the *Montreal Herald,* and *L'Evénement,* of Quebec.

Professor Donald Creighton, the distinguished historian and twentieth-century biographer of Sir John A., could not condone the action. In *The Old Chieftain* he wrote, "His crime was the crime of accepting campaign funds from the very man with whom he was negotiating a contract of major importance in the national interest."

### John A. Drunk and Exhausted Speaks for Five Hours

Sir John A. could foresee the dire results of the Pacific Scandal, as more and more of his fellow Conservatives deserted him. With defeat inevitable, he made a last valiant stand and addressed the House for five hours — an unforgettable declamation for he was completely fatigued and extremely drunk. The Parliamentary Debates of November 3, 1873, report the speech: "I say this Government has been treated with foul wrongs. (cheers) I say this Government has been treated as no government has ever

*(continued)*

### Charter-Sellers

Liberals' term for those who continued to support Sir John A. after the Pacific Scandal.

121

**THE BEAUTIES OF A ROYAL COMMISSION**

"When shall we three meet again?"

A week after he published his "Whither are we drifting?" cartoon attacking Macdonald's claim of innocence in the Pacific Scandal,
Bengough dramatized what he thought of the Royal Commission Sir John A. had appointed to inquire into the charges.

*PAC*

been treated before. It has been met with an opposition the likes of which no government in any civilized country was ever met. (loud cheers) I say we have been opposed not with fair weapons… but opposed in a manner which will throw shame on Honourable Gentlemen opposite. (renewed cheers)

"I have fought the battle of Confederation, the battle of Union, the battle of the Dominion of Canada. I throw myself upon this House, I throw myself upon this country, I throw myself upon posterity, and I know that, notwithstanding the many failings of my life, I shall have the voice of this country and this House rallying around me. (cheers) And, sirs, if I am mistaken in that, I can confidently appeal to a higher court — to the court of my own conscience and to the court of posterity. (cheers) I leave it with this House with every confidence. I am equal to either fortune. I can see past the decision of this House, either for or against me, but whether

### Tory Characters

Mr. Mackenzie (discussing a new bill): "If that is considered an improvement, it is certainly one of a Tory character." Sir John A.: "Certainly, a satisfac-TORY character."

it be for or against me, I know — and it is no vain boast for me to say so — for even my enemies will admit that I am no boaster — that there does not exist in Canada a man who has given more of his time, more of his heart, more of his wealth, or more of his intellect and power, such as they may be, for the good of this Dominion of Canada." (loud and prolonged cheers)

### Speech Impresses Lady Dufferin

Lady Dufferin, wife of the Governor-General of Canada, was present in the House with her guest, Lord Rosebery, a future Prime Minister of England. She wrote in her book *My Canadian Journal, 1872-1878:* "At ¼ to 9 Sir John rose, and spoke for five hours, making a very fine speech, full of power, lively and forcible to the end. He did not fail in the slightest degree while speaking, but when he sat down he was completely exhausted, and his voice was quite gone."

Lord Dufferin wrote to Sir John A. the next day: "Lady Dufferin came home at 3 o'clock in the morning brimful of your speech. Her Excellency was pleased to keep me awake from 3 to 5, repeating it with appropriate action, and told me that nothing could have been more wonderful than your effort. Round the breakfast table at Rideau this morning there was a continuous chorus of admiration from all my English friends. I hope you are not the worse

for the strain of the last few days must have tried you terribly."

On the same day, Lady Dufferin wrote to Lady Macdonald: "I hope Sir John is well this morning after his great exertions. We have all been talking with the greatest admiration of his splendid speech. It grows upon one as one thinks over its various points, and we all feel that it was great good fortune for us to have been present at it."

Not everyone was as impressed with Sir John A.'s speech as Lady Dufferin, however.

When accused of dishonesty, Sir John A. replied, "I have never denied being a thief, because I was never charged with being one." To another scathing taunt he murmured, "We are all miserable sinners."

*(continued)*

### Hot Money

Sir Hugh Allan was known for his love of money and sharp business practice. When Lady Macdonald asked for a contribution for her church work, he hedged about giving what she wanted. She laughed and said, "You know, you can't take all that money with you when you die." "No," quipped Sir John A. "It would soon melt if he did."

# BLACKWASH AND WHITEWASH.

*PAC*

A month later, in September 1873, Bengough was still attacking the Royal Commission investigating the scandal for attempting to "whitewash" Macdonald. In Canadian history, parties in power have often been charged with setting up Royal Commissions to whitewash their actions — or to "blackwash" those of their opponents.

## The Unspecific Scandal

*An Original, Poetical, Grittical, and likely to be
Historical Extravaganza performed by her
Majesty's Servants at the Great Dominion
Theatre, Ottawa*
(Edited from *The Canadian Illustrated News*
of January 3, 1874)

### Act I

Scene I. A newspaper office. In the middle
a cauldron boiling. Thunder and lightning.
Enter three Editors as Wizards. They circle
round the cauldron, throwing in scraps of paper.

*1st Wizard:*  Round about the cauldron go,
In our facts and fictions throw,
Money by Sir Hugh subscribed,
Names of members foully bribed,
Information basely got,
Boil thou first in the charméd pot.

*2nd Wizard:*  Conversations misreported,
Suppositions much distorted.
For a charm of powerful trouble,
In our cauldron boil and bubble.

*3rd Wizard:*  All these matters mix and mangle,
To form a great Pacific Scandal.

*All:*  Double, double, cauldron bubble,
Bring the Premier lots of trouble.

*(Enter Alexander, the chief Wizard.)*
*Alex.:*  Oh! Well done. I commend your pains,
And everyone shall share i' the gains.

*2nd Wizard:*  By the pricking of my thumbs
A wicked Premier this way comes.

*(Enter John A.)*
*John A.:*  Hallo! my friends, what is your little
game? What is't you do?

*All:*  A deed without a name!

*John A.:*  "No name," well that's a very
clever story,
But Collins used that title long
before ye;
I fancy too, I could suggest a better,
Suppose you call your work "The
Purloined Letter."

'Twould be a taking title, and
'tis known
You're great at taking what is not
your own.

*Alex.:*  Excuse me if upon your speech I
break in,
You'll find ere long we're great at
undertaking.
And we expect the country soon will call
Us to perform your Party's funeral.

Scene II. Anywhere in Ontario. A number of
Grits collected together.

*Enter Alexander, who addresses them after the
manner of Brutus over the body of Caesar.*
Grits, followers and office seekers, lend me
your ears.
From all that I can see it now appears
As if the day which we so long have waited
Has come at last as we anticipated.
And now with hopes of power I'm so elated
I feel quite overcome and dizzy-pated!
This cry with which we've made the country
ring,
I mean "corruption," has proved just the thing.
'Tis true the means we've used are rather base.
But that don't matter when the end is place.
At any rate we've gone too far to stop
And have at last caught John A. on the hop;
And you as members of the hop-position
Must try to make the most of the position.
But wait a moment, I'll not keep you long,
Before you go I'd like to sing a song.

*Sings*  "Grits Wha Hae"
Grits wha hae wi' George Brown bled,
Grits wham Blake has aften led,
Welcome to the downy bed,
Of the Ministry.
Now's the day and now's the hour
Sees the front o' battle lour
Sees the fall of John A.'s power
And office sweet for me.

Scene III. The Premier's Office in Ottawa.

*Song by the Premier*  "Prorogation"
*Tune* — "I want money"

Prorogation, prorogation,
That's the dodge for the situation;
It will cause the Grits vexation
And save ourselves much botheration.
Blake will make a fierce oration
And hold me up to detestation.
I rather dread an appeal to the nation
In its present state of fermentation
So upon consideration
I'd better go in for prorogation!

### Act II
Scene I. The House of Commons.

*Chorus of Oppositionists*
Prorogation, prorogation
Has caused us all great consternation;
'Tis of our rights an usurpation
And fills us all with indignation.
We will send a deputation
To present our protestation
And make a strong representation
Against this shameful prorogation.

Scene II. Senate Chamber.

*Governor-General*
For very near an hour you've kept me waiting
While in the other chamber you've been prating;
To keep me here from such suspense a sufferin' —
As though I were a duffer, not a Dufferin —
Is a proceeding which has caused me pain,
And I expect 'twill not occur again.

*Song by his Excellency* — "Cock-a-doodle-do"
A few remarks I'd like to make
Before I leave you now,
And just express my sentiments
About this precious row;
The House is in an uproar
And you make a great a do
But after all it's nothing more
Than Cock-a-doodle-do!
Sir John the matter has explained
And very glibly too;
But I fancy much of what he says
Is Cock-a-doodle-do.

*Chorus of Senators*
Cock-a-doodle-do, cock-a-doodle-do!

Sir John A. is shown here with the Governor-General, Lord Dufferin, at the opening of Parliament on March 22, 1873. By this time John A. knew the threat of the scandal hanging over him although it would not break fully until ten days later when Lucius Seth Huntingdon, member for Shefford, Quebec, would claim that the CPR was financed with U.S. capital and that the Conservatives had been advanced election funds in return for the construction contract. Lady Dufferin, shown in the picture on the right, was very impressed with John A.'s speech in his own defense.

### Ye Ballad of Lyttel John A.

*Wearye it is in the Commons house
Where men talke loud and longe,
And Grits abuse ye Mynisteres
With wordés hot and stronge.*

*Syr John he satte in ye Commons house
All wearye with ye rout.
And he almost wished ye Grits were in
And ye Mynisteres were out.*

*And he syghed and sayd, Oh, woe is me
That ever they brought me here,
I had rather keepe a beere saloone
Than be a Premieere.*

*For oh, 'tis harde to list each night
To Mackenzie's speeches longe,
But worse to sitte and be abused
By Blake and Dorion.*

*In Ottawa towne it is ill to byde
Amonge ye dirte and duste,
I wis that men would never there dwelle
Onlye thatte they muste.*

From *The Canadian Illustrated News*

Sir Hugh Allan had been promised the CPR presidency and had contributed heavily to John A.'s election funds. Allan had been raising money and making promises, many of them unknown to Macdonald, in the name of the Canadian Cabinet.

### An Angel Who Knows All the Angles

*Everybody has a favourite story about Sir John A., who was noted for his witty, apt retorts. This is the one that the Right Honourable John G. Diefenbaker likes to tell:* Sir John A. was at a meeting which was very noisy, and those who preceded him as platform speakers were literally howled down. When Sir John A. was introduced, the uproar was deafening.

Suddenly amidst the noise, an enormous man at the back of the hall stood up and said in a loud voice, "Let us listen to Sir John! We have a reputation in this town of granting speakers a good hearing." He commanded attention and there was silence. Sir John A. thanked the man for his help. The big voice boomed out, "Just because I did what I did doesn't mean I would vote for you. I wouldn't vote for you if you were the Angel Gabriel."

Sir John replied, "You're so right; you wouldn't be in my constituency."

At the Governor-General's Christmas party in 1873, feuds were briefly forgotten, according to this cartoon of Macdonald and the new Liberal Prime Minister, Alexander Mackenzie, dancing together. Macdonald had been forced to resign on November 5, two days after his famous five-hour defense. Dufferin, one of the most handsome, charming and meddlesome of Canada's Governor-Generals, liked Macdonald and considered him "by far the ablest public man in Canada." He tried to get John A. to "admit the imprudence and indiscretion of his dealings with Allan" and "obtain an acquittal at the hands of Parliament."

On December 6, 1873, Sir John A. is pictured as Aeneas, consoling his ousted fellow Conservatives after they were forced to turn the Government over to the Liberals.

Sir John A. is no longer Prime Minister; his party holds only forty-five seats out of 206 in the House of Commons. But the new Prime Minister, Alexander Mackenzie, is warned that the "naughty schoolboy" — holding the "First Book of Politics" — has been re-elected to the House and will no doubt continue to misbehave. Mackenzie, reading *The Globe* and keeping the "History of the Pacific Scandal" handy, wonders what he should do. Cartoonist Bengough adds his own whimsical comment with Mackenzie's map of the CPR on the wall.

# Macdonald defeated!

## *Globe predicts his total eclipse*

## People turn away in "terror and shame"

After a strenuous but futile election campaign, in which Sir John A. further drained his debilitated body into a collapse, he and his Government were thrown out of power — from 1873 until 1878. They had been left with only forty-five members out of a House of 206.

### Doomed to Disgrace

The November 12, 1873, issue of *The Globe* gloated: "It can hardly be doubted that his role as a Canadian politician is played out, and that his career . . . has come to a close in the midst of disgrace. . . . [His] gifts have been poisoned by a cynical view of human nature, which has led him to appeal to the least worthy side of human character. His great facility in managing men applied only to a certain class of men and broke down when brought face to face with rectitude of character and elevation of sentiment. No one could surpass him in power over men of the baser sort. . . . His resolve to approach every man through his special foible or ambition placed the selfish and the vain within his reach; in pandering to low tastes

and mean aspirations . . . he paid the heavy price of dignity and truth. . . . The most striking lesson of his career is not the success which attends mere adroitness and recklessness regarding principle, but the sure Nemesis which dogs the steps of the statesman whose only guide is selfish ambition. [Macdonald] is doomed to see his name cease to be any longer a power from ocean to ocean and his sun, as an official personage, go down in shame."

Many people were sure that this was a permanent eclipse, but they did not take into account Sir John A.'s resilience and recuperative powers. With courage and resourcefulness, he rebuilt his Party on the National Policy of

> Sir John A. has been quoted as saying, "Given a Government with a big surplus, a big majority, and a weak Opposition, you could debauch a committee of archangels."

> "My sins of omission and commission I do not deny; but I trust that it may be said of me in the ultimate issue, 'Much is forgiven because he loved much,' for I have loved my country with a passionate love."
> — Sir John A. Macdonald

High Protection.

The attitude of the representatives of the Queen to Sir John A.'s defeat is shown in these letters between the Earl of Dufferin, Governor-General of Canada from April 1872 until October 1878, and the Earl of Carnarvon, who held the office of Secretary of State for the Colonies from February 1874 until January 1878.

Dufferin to Carnarvon
Ottawa, March 18, 1874
Private. . . . Since the new election, I have not seen Sir John, as for the last three or four weeks, he has been laid up with a bad cold, caught during his canvassing, but I expect him to call upon me soon. It would be premature to forecast the future, but I should be sorry to think that his public career is over. His health is very precarious, otherwise he would be sure to come to the front, as he is certainly the best statesman in Canada, though too prone to maintain his power by expedients condemned by the moral standard of modern politicians. . . .

### A Most Unfortunate Scrape

Macdonald unfortunately got himself into a most unfortunate scrape, which no Government either could or ought to have survived, but his position at the moment is a very uncomfortable one. His Party is for the moment entirely broken up. . . . I pressed him very strongly at the time not to defend an indefensible position or to drag his Party through the dirt, but to obtain an acquittal at the hands of Parliament in regard to the graver charges, with which he has been assailed, namely, those of personal corruption, and of trafficking away

> Sir William Osler on Sir John A.: "With a strong and daring personality, he had all the qualities for success in public life — calmness and clear judgement in victory, resolution and hopefulness in defeat."

the interests of Canada to foreign stockjobbers and to admit the imprudence and indiscretion of his communications and dealings with Allan. Though this course would not have saved him, he would have stood better with the Country than he does at present.

The whole business vexed and annoyed me more than I can say. It cut me to the heart, that a career so creditable to himself, and so serviceable to his Country as that of Macdonald's should be ended in such humiliation — moreover the means by which his opponents effected his overthrow were in many respects disgraceful and implied criminal conduct on the part of some members of the Confederacy; but though I had no sympathy with the Opposition in the matter, I was very much moved by the terror and shame manifested by the people at large, when the possibility first dawned upon them of their most trusted statesman having been guilty of misconduct.

Carnarvon to Dufferin
June 17, 1874
Private. . . . I knew Macdonald well formerly and would fain hope that though guilty of grave political error he is individually pure of all money taint.

The Rebellion Losses Bill of 1849 — to compensate those in Lower Canada who had suffered during the Rebellions of 1837 and 1838 — failed to define what claims were legitimate. The possibility that Rebels might receive recompense enraged Protestant Tories. Rioting in Montreal led to the burning of the Parliament Buildings.

# Parliament Buildings go to blazes

Punch in Canada

THE MAN WOT FIRED THE PARLIAMENT HOUSE!

The cartoon shows Lafontaine, who was head of the Government when the Rebellion Losses Bill became law. The strong opposition to this bill in Montreal culminated in riots which lasted eight days.

## Montreal's burn in 1849 Quebec City's in 1864 and Ottawa's in 1916

Canadian Parliamentary Buildings have burned three times: in Montreal in 1849, in Quebec City in 1864 and in Ottawa in 1916. Only the first fire was the result of violence.

The year 1849 was one of political turmoil centering around the Rebellion Losses Bill. Lord Elgin (Governor-General of British North America from 1847 until 1854) — unaware of the mood of the people — had supported the bill. When he left the Parliament Buildings in Montreal on April 25, 1849, the day the bill became law, he was pelted with brickbats, rotten eggs and stones. (In fact, Lord Elgin was so unpopular that his name was struck off the membership of the St. Andrew's Society.)

In the evening a frenzied mob on Champ de Mars shouted "To the Parliament Buildings!" There the cry of "Fire!" was soon heard and in a few minutes the buildings (on what is now Youville Square) were ablaze. The only things that were saved were the seven-foot silver gilt mace and the portrait of Queen Victoria, which was carried out of the burning building by Sanford Fleming, later to be one of Canada's "grand old men."

According to Biggar, John A. was in Montreal at the time but he "took no part in the riots. He had protested in the debate against passing the bill, and had warned the Government that they were drawing down grave dangers, not alone upon their own heads, but upon the peace of the province; and to kill time and tire out the

Robert Harris's historic painting of the Fathers of Confederation was destroyed in the 1916 fire in Ottawa's Parliament Buildings.

ministry, he kept the floor through the night, reading thirty of William Lyon Mackenzie's letters. But he took no part in the riot."

Because of the fire, says Biggar, "the city was punished by the removal forever of the seat of Government."

The Parliamentary Buildings in Quebec City

suffered a fire in 1864 — the very year that John A. and other Fathers of Confederation had met there for the Quebec Conference.

When the Parliament Buildings in Ottawa burned down on February 3, 1916, it took ten years and 12 million dollars to rebuild them. The Parliamentary Library was saved from complete

destruction only because it was detached from the main building. A quick-witted attendant closed the fire doors, preserving the half-million books. Water seeping into the beautiful old floors caused a permanent squeak. It was in this fire that the historic painting by Robert Harris of the Fathers of Confederation was destroyed.

# Canadian cities have very fiery history

## *Quebec suffers many fires, called City of Doom*

Quebec was not the only city to be ravaged by fire. Among the many major fires in Canadian history: Fredericton in 1825; Saint John, N.B., in 1837 and 1877; St. John's, Nfld., in 1846; Toronto in 1849; Vancouver in 1886.

Quebec suffered another serious fire in 1876. *The Canadian Illustrated News* published a picture of the fire, along with this editorial: "Must Quebec be called the City of Doom? It is certainly the most unfortunate city on this continent, being periodically destroyed by fire . . . It is inconceivable that so large a city as Quebec should not have proper appliances for combating this terrible element. The water for the city is obtained from Lorette, a distance of ten miles, through a single eighteen-inch main, and the supply has to be divided, one portion of the city being furnished with it in the morning, and the other in the afternoon." A story in the same issue describes the scene of the tragedy: "The sight of the unfortunate inhabitants flying from their dwellings, each one bearing away some portion of his chattels, was not one easily to be forgotten. It was like an army flying before an approaching foe. Carts, carriages, caleches, even sleighs, were in requisition, hurrying away from the approaching flames with loads of household goods piled on in any shape just as they were torn from the houses. A large portion of these were first sent to friends' houses, only to be taken up again and hurried farther off. People could be seen bending under loads that at other times they could scarcely lift — old women carrying beds on their backs and bearing them bravely away; boys carrying off poultry or a favourite dog and pups; others, birds and flowers. Whatever way you turned, the streets seemed full of people flying as it were for their lives, but loaded like horses."

If Macdonald and his Conservatives had to go out of power, the timing (if not the reason) could not have been better chosen. A great world depression started in 1873 and the new Liberal Government of Alexander Mackenzie was hit by the decline of trade and industry and falling national revenues, at the very time they were advocating free trade. Richard John Cartwright (1835-1912) left the Conservative Party in 1873 to become Alexander Mackenzie's finance minister. He was known as the "Blue Ruin" and the "Knight of the Rueful Countenance" because of his gloomy predictions. Here he is suggesting that high tariffs mean empty pockets, while John A. shakes his fist in opposition.

# John A. sits it out in "Loyal Opposition"

## Great Depression of 1873 hits country
## John A. blames free trade and waits

Sir John A.'s sixtieth birthday was not a happy one. He was out of power politically. His affairs were in a turbulent state. The gruelling and ineffectual struggle — and Cartier's death — in 1873 had left him depressed and exhausted. He still had not recovered. It seemed almost as though he drew strength from his power while in the Prime Minister's seat. Out of office he was not at his best. Again his weakness overcame him: he became a two-bottle man, retreating with his favourite brandy. There were rumours of his death from prostration. The news spread that he was a suicide. Leading newspapers had his obituary notice brought up-to-date, ready to go at any time. In *Canadian Magazine* W.F. Maclean wrote: "If ever there was a man in low water it was Sir John as I saw him one day in the winter of 1875, coming out of the House in

130

Alexander Mackenzie (1822-1892) became Prime Minister when the Pacific Scandal forced John A. out of office. Mackenzie lacked the flair and imagination to keep the country moving forward. Upright and scrupulously honest, he could not believe when he lost the 1878 election that the people had rejected him for that proven rogue, John A. Macdonald.

Edward Blake (1833-1912) was Mackenzie's chief lieutenant and a brilliant lawyer. It was said of him that "There are scores of earnest and able young men who would range themselves under Mr. Blake's leadership, were it not that they are repelled by a manner as devoid of warmth as is a flake of December snow, and as devoid of magnetism as is a loaf of unleavened bread."

the bitter air, dressed in a Red River sash and coat and the old historic mink-skin cap, tottering down the hill to the eastern gateway alone, others passing him with a wide sweep."

Even so, Sir John A. was still a force to be reckoned with. He may not have been in the centre of the stage — but he was prominent in the background!

### "Old Brown Stuff"

That same year, in an effective homespun yet sarcastic speech on the subject of free trade and industry, Sir John A. attacked his opponents George Brown, the Ontario leader; Alexander Mackenzie, the federal leader; and Edward Blake, M.P. for South Bruce. The House of Commons debate read: "Everyone knows what the lawyers term the principle of 'selling by sample.' The administration goes to the country and asks, 'Will you buy this article? Here is an excellent article and one of the strongest claims of this cloth to the good housewife is that there is a strong fibre in it, coming all the way from South Bruce.' And when the people of this country, believing this to be a good kind of cloth that would stand sun and wind and anything else, found that fibre drawn from it immediately after purchasing, it seemed, as if the Honourable Member from South Bruce would observe, that the Government had been guilty

---

### Understanding Sitting Bull

A Member of Parliament one day inquired if the Government would be asked to pay the expenses incurred in relation to the crossing of the Canadian frontier by Sitting Bull, the Indian chief. The Honourable Alexander Mackenzie, then Prime Minister, replied, "It is not the intention to make any representation on the subject."

Sir John A. interrupted with, "I do not see how a Sitting Bull can cross the frontier."

Mr. Mackenzie: "Not unless he rises."

Sir John A.: "Then he is not a Sitting Bull."

---

of selling under false pretences, and the people would say, 'Here we have pawned off upon us the old Brown stuff!'"

Sir John A. still received the occasional dunning letter. This one, taken care of in a few days, read:

Sir, I would not send this account at this time but I have a large note to retire on the first of December and I am very short of funds. Times is so dull, and it is a renewed note. By letting me have the above a/c you will much oblige
Yours truly
A. Sutherland

In the House of Commons on March 10, 1876, Sir John A. offered boldly "a thorough reorganization of the tariff . . . which ought to be constructed in such a manner, that it would, while producing sufficient revenue for the current expenses of the country, also afford a stimulus and protection to home industry, entice capital to the country, and keep our artisans at home at the employment which must arise under the fostering legislation." Once again the cry went abroad — and at this time at the dictation of the Conservative chief — "Canada for the Canadians!"

In April 1876 Sir John A. lost his "sincerest friend" with the death of his sister Margaret. More than ever he felt his years, and asked that his party find a younger leader. *(continued)*

---

### Sir John A. Slept Here

The Right Hon. John G. Diefenbaker, P.C., Q.C., M.P., F.R.S.C., LLD., D.C.L., Lit. D., D.S.L., Canada's thirteenth prime minister, has always been closely identified with Sir John A. These two prime ministers shared the profession of law, Conservative political affiliations and strong Scottish ancestral roots.

The unpretentious but charming yellow clapboard home of the Diefenbakers in Rockcliffe Park, Ottawa, houses the largest collection of Macdonald memorabilia in Canada. Among other Macdonald mementoes are the first prime minister's office desk complete with secret drawers, inkwells, canes, documents, letters, and books, a needlepoint chair, a small mantelpiece clock, a blue sofa, fireplace irons, umbrellas with carved handles, wall plates, drawings, cartoons and photographs, and a touching item — a tiny chair, with a Valentine decoration carved out of the back, which was used by the Macdonalds' invalid daughter.

Mr. Diefenbaker sleeps in a large four-poster bed — made in the 1870s — which Macdonald used. It was given to Mr. Diefenbaker by Mrs. Claire Moyer. The bed has heavy turnings on the posts which are not identical, as one would expect, but vary in size. The maker (whose name is unknown) used three different kinds of Canadian wood in its construction — birch for the bedposts, oak for the rails and pine for the panels. Since Sir John A. was under six feet tall and Mr. Diefenbaker is over six feet, Mrs. Diefenbaker had thirteen inches put into the side pieces of the bed to make it more comfortable. (No doubt she also added a good mattress.)

Of their fascinating collection of Macdonald memorabilia Mrs. Diefenbaker says, "It's valuable to us for the historic association and not for the financial value . . . A house with nothing like this would be dull." Mr. Diefenbaker explains that most of his acquisitions were gifts from people who donated pieces inherited from relatives who bought them when the furnishings of Earnscliffe were auctioned off after Sir John A.'s death. It is his intention to bequeath these historic items to the Public Archives of Canada and to the University of Saskatchewan.

---

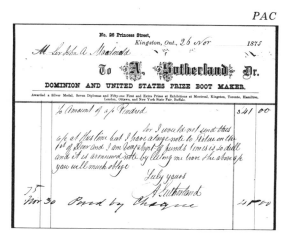

"Times is so dull" explains John A.'s bootmaker as he appeals for a bill to be paid. Payment was made within four days.

Prime Minister Mackenzie says good-bye to his Loyal Opposition. The Liberal Government of 1878 brought in voting by ballot, established a Supreme Court and curbed the power of the Governor-General. (Mackenzie had rebutted Dufferin with: "Canada is not a Crown Colony.")

### Politicians Gather for a Spell

*Spelling matches were very popular in the 1800s. Not only school children, but leading citizens and prominent politicians participated in public orthographical contests, in crowded halls with important dignitaries acting as referees. Newspapers gave these events wide coverage. The following appeared in a June 1875 issue of* Grip: A number of prominent politicians convened for the fashionable amusement of a spelling match . . . The contestants were divided according to their political proclivities. To universal surprise, three parties appeared, with three gentlemen representing a "Canada First" party . . . The rest of the contestants were led by Sir John A. Macdonald and the Hon. George Brown.

The first word given out was *canvas*, which dispersed all three "Canada First" men whose early retirement was greeted with cries of derision. Dr. Tupper got hopelessly confused with *intercolonial*; the Premier [presumably of Ontario] came to grief with a new way of spelling *prohibition*. Mr. McKellar made an extraordinary mess out of *agriculture*. Sir Francis Hincks, who had come down especially for the occasion, was completely bewildered by *currency*. The competition finally narrowed down to the leaders of the two great parties, who had spelled every word in safety . . . Amid breathless silence, Sir John A. frankly confessed that he had never heard of the word *purity* and declined to attempt it. "P-A-R-I-T-Y!" shouted Mr. Brown. On being informed that he was wrong he left the room in a passion.

"When a man has done me an evil turn once," said Sir John A., "I don't like to give him the opportunity to do so twice."

Sir John A. never held a grudge; he said, "A public man should have no resentments."

In 1876, while Sir John A. was in the Opposition, *Grip* maintained that "the Government postage stamps are like Sir John A. The more they're licked, the less they'll stay in the corner."

Sir Richard Cartwright said of John A.: "I will say this for that old scoundrel John A. Macdonald, that if he once gave you his word, you could rely on it."

During discussion of a bill relating to crime and punishment, Mr. Blake commented, "The Honourable Gentleman has not yet convinced me. I am open to conviction." Sir John A. quickly answered, "A good many persons will be open to conviction under this bill."

Once when Sir John A. was a Member of the Opposition he twitted the Prime Minister about rumoured Cabinet changes. "I hope my honourable friend, the head of the Government, was not disturbed at his Sunday devotions by the necessity of making several changes in the Cabinet," said Sir John A.
Suspecting nothing, Mackenzie replied sharply, "I was at church as usual."
Quickly Sir John A. answered, "The Honourable Gentleman went to church as usual and I have no doubt he paid great attention to the sermon, especially if the sermon impressed upon him the necessity of 'resignation'."

### Great Love of Family

In spite of his many tribulations, and indeed he had more than enough problems on his mind, Sir John A. never deviated from his concern for his family, as these letters demonstrate:

Toronto, April 26, 1876
My dear Louisa,
Little Mary has a bad cold, but Agnes as usual. She was very much touched at Margaret's remembrance of her and will prize the bowl doubly. . . . I don't think it can be good for you to be left alone from day to day in that big old house. You will be continually reminded of the loss of your dearest Margaret. I think you should look out for some nice companion. . . . See to this.

Agnes is up at our new house watching the progress of painters and carpenters. We hope to have the house ready by the 10th of May. . . .
Love from,
John A.M.

Toronto, August 14, 1876
My dear Louisa,
I don't know whether the professor told you that John Creighton has awarded you eleven hundred dollars for your four acres. If he has not, do not allude to the subject with him. If he speaks to you on the subject, say that he can pay you at his own convenience. He has written to me that he agrees to the award.

Agnes and Baboo [his pet name for his daughter who was then seven and a half] are at Cobourg and are to remain until the 24th. If it continues hot here, then would it inconvenience you if Baboo and her maid should pay you a visit for a little while? Let me know candidly how that would be.
Love to Maria and Joanna,
Yours always,
John A.

Toronto, November 17, 1877
My dear Louisa,
I have here duly received the cheque for $500. I had intended to have applied your money on the additional stock that had been bought in your name, but instead of doing so, I paid it up in another way. This will make you so much the richer when I kick the bucket. Now you see I have a thousand dollars of yours which I will invest for you as I find an opportunity of doing. Meanwhile I will pay you seven per cent for the money as it is worth that to me. As the first payment from Dr. Williamson of $500 was paid 11th Nov. 1876, I owe you one year's interest which amounts to $35. I send you a cheque for that amount which is your own money to be spent as you please. . . . You will receive the money from the investment and not from me.
Love,
John A.M.

COMBAT-IVENESS

# Hugh John follows father into politics

## Overcomes tragedy-ridden childhood
## To become Premier of Manitoba

Hugh John Macdonald was the second son born to Sir John A. and Isabella Macdonald. Sir John A.'s nephew, Macpherson, says: "... a second baby boy made his appearance, and from this event, there grew another pleasant fiction which was that, from the hour of his arrival, this small atom of humanity was aware of the recurrence of birthdays, Christmas Day, and other important events, and was graciously pleased to testify his approval of the conduct of his youthful friends by presents of books, balls, fishing rods and various other articles dear to the hearts of young boys. About the time that this wonderful possessor of supernatural powers had grown to such mature age as to be able to inform the world that his name was 'Hugh John Jin,' I was sent away to a boarding school at Cornwall."

Sir John A. showed his concern about Hugh in the following letters, the first written when the boy was six, the second when he was seven.

Toronto, Jan. 26, 1856
My dearest Mother,

Isabella has been very very ill.... She was so low one day that the doctor sent for me to my office, thinking that she was dying. She has rallied wonderfully again.

I send Hugh every day to Mrs. — to keep him out of the way and not interfere with Janet who was constantly employed in looking after Isabella. Hugh is very well and in good spirits. He is quite a favourite at the houses which he visits.... There are growing people, well brought up so that he has the advantage of good companionship. He and I play "Beggar-My-Neighbour" every evening and you can't fancy how delighted he is when he beats me. He knows the value of the cards as well as I do, and looks after his own interests sharply.

Believe me, my dear mother,
Your affectionate son, John

Toronto, March 1857
My dear Louisa,

Hugh is quite well, and now that the weather is getting warmer, we can allow him to play in the open air. Poor little fellow, he was confined to the house all winter as the doctor thought it would not do for him to go out, when he was obliged to take a hot bath daily. He takes a two-hour lesson every day and is a wonderful arithmetician.... I think of going off early for a trip as soon as the House rises. I will leave Isa and Hugh somewhere at the seaside. Give my love to Mama.

Yours affectionately,
John

After his mother died, Hugh John lived with his aunts and grandmother. When he was ten

*PAC*

Hugh John Macdonald was born in Kingston in 1850, a year and a half after the death of the Macdonalds' first child. His mother was sick throughout his infancy and died when he was seven. He attended the University of Toronto, became a lawyer in 1872 and a Q.C. in 1890. He was elected to the House of Commons in 1891, became Prime Minister of Manitoba in 1900 and was knighted in 1912.

"Dalnavert" — the Winnipeg home Hugh John Macdonald built in 1885 and lived in until his death in 1929. It is now a museum.

years old, in 1860, John A. wrote to his sister Louisa, with whom the lad was living in Kingston: "If Hugh wants the Shetland pony, let him have it ... but he must ride every day. When it rains, let him wear the waterproof I sent him, but he must ride daily. I suppose you got the increased allowance ... for the household. I will send $100.00 to be divided between you and Moll, and on July '61 the other $100.00." A letter written to the same sister a year later said, "Tell Hugh that I am extremely pleased at his report. I am quite proud of it and have shown it to all my friends."

### Father and Son Estranged

Hugh John became a lawyer. He joined his father's firm, but left it at the age of twenty-five when Sir John A. disagreed with him about his choice of a bride. Although Sir John A.'s first wife had been older than he, and his mother older than his father, Sir John A. disapproved when Hugh John became engaged to an older widow. Hugh John wrote:

My dear Father,

I had better go out ... and start on the bottom in the beginning of 1876.... Wherever I may pitch my tent ... I will always hold myself in readiness to advance your interests in any way in my power, for although I think you are acting in an unnecessarily harsh manner towards me respecting my engagement, I have no doubt ... from your standpoint you are justified.... I can certainly never forget the ... kindnesses done to and favours conferred upon me in times past.

Your obstinate and affectionate son,
Hugh J. Macdonald

Happily they resolved their differences and Hugh often visited his father, accompanied by his wife and children. Sir John A. was a very warm and loving grandfather.

Hugh John followed his father into politics, serving in Parliament and becoming Prime Minister of Manitoba in 1900. He was made a Knight Bachelor in 1913. Hugh John looked like his father. Once, so the story goes, he was walking down the street in Winnipeg when a little boy saw him and shouted, "Mother, there goes that bad man!"

"What bad man, dear?" the mother asked.

"That bad man," replied the boy. "That one in *Grip.*"

Hugh John also had his father's charm and wit, and is the subject of many anecdotes. He delighted in "red beef" and not even his own chef could get the steaks rare enough. Sir Hugh John was constantly telling him, "I want them no more cooked than chasing a cow through a red-hot kitchen."

Another story is attributed to both Nellie McClung and Janey Canuck. When Hugh John had to have a leg amputated, he received a wire from one of these famous ladies that read: "What's a leg, anyway?"

### Father Visits Son
### Thanks to CPR

Hugh John Macdonald resided in a beautiful house at 61 Carlton Street in Winnipeg. He built it in 1885 and named it "Dalnavert," after the home of his maternal grandfather in Scotland, living in it until his death in 1929. Sir Hugh John hosted his famous father in this house only once — in July 1886, after the CPR was completed. The house was purchased by the Manitoba Historical Society and opened as a museum in 1974 to coincide with the centennial celebrations of the city of Winnipeg.

# LITTLE DOWNY;

OR,

## THE HISTORY

OF

# A FIELD-MOUSE.

———

## A MORAL TALE.

———

EMBELLISHED

WITH TWELVE COLORED ENGRAVINGS.

LONDON:
*Printed for*
DEAN AND MUNDAY THREADNEEDLE-STREET.
1822.

*Little Downy* is a moral tale that John A. might have read as a schoolboy, as it was published in 1822. Its author was later to immigrate (or, as they preferred to call it, "emigrate," stressing the homeland left rather than the new land arrived in) to Canada and write several books about her experiences as a homesteader, including *The Backwoods of Canada* and *The Female Emigrant's Guide*. She was Catharine Parr Traill, sister of another important nineteenth-century Canadian writer, Susanna Strickland Moodie.

# "John told me to read it"
## *Lady Macdonald is guided by husband's taste in books*

Lady Macdonald's literary horizons were broadened by her husband. In her diary she listed the books, stories and magazines which she read as well as some of Sir John A.'s reading material. She often let herself be guided by his approval or interests: "trying and absurd, puerile. John says some stories are bad"; "I am interested in lives of statesmen because of my husband's tastes and career." The books were primarily biographies, geographies and fiction.

"The Anxious Inquirer After Salvation Today" by Angus James;
"The Old Helmet" by Mrs. Wetherell;
"Life of the Last Duchess of Gordon";

### "John Did Not Approve of for Me"

Deson's "New America" (which John read but did not approve of for me);
"Citoyenne Jacqueline" about the French Revolution (in French);
"By the Trent" a Prize Temperance story;
"The Last Chronicle of Barset" (good but tedious);
"Jesuits in America" by Parkman (read with Mama);
"Le Blocus" by Chatrian (interesting enough);

"Homme du Peuple";
Pall Mall magazines;
"Life of Mrs. Elizabeth Fry" by her daughter Mrs. Cresswell (most interesting);
"Northwest Passage by Land" by Lord Milton and Dr. Cheadle (really charming);
"Forney's Letters from Europe" (Forney is a fierce Republican owner-editor of two or three Northern newspapers. I agree that England is a delicious country for the rich, but I should hate to be poor there. And the middle class toady and fawn. Every ninth man in England is a pauper or nearly so);
"Life of Wilberforce" 5 vols. by his sons (his aims were high indeed. I like the lofty spirit in which he worked. This style of reading is so satisfactory);
"The Huguenots" by Smiles (read this with Mama. The final chapters disappoint me);
"Travels in Abyssinia" by Rev. Henry Sterne, the missionary;
"Batavia" by Henri Conscience, in French;
"Life of Trust" by Muller (a remarkable book);
"Polynesia" by Pritchard;
"Joanne of Arc" by Paris;
"Life of Mrs. Hannah More" (perhaps disappointing);

"Cometh Up as a Flower" (decidedly objectionable. I accepted to read and am sorry);
"Paul the Pope and Paul the Friar" by Trollope (read with Mama);
"The Silent Hour" essays by well-known divines for Sunday reading;
"Froude's Essays on The Times of Erasmus and Luther";
"The Judge Advocate General" by Larpent;
"Home Life in the Holy Land" by Mrs. Finn (pleasant, readable);
"Sir Philip Francis" (in biographies, what dislike one sometimes feels for the hero);

### "Pure as the Sound of Silver Bells"

"Le Récit d'une Soeur" by Mme Augustus Craner (a lofty style yet tender. Pure as the sound of silver bells. Disappointed by the commencement but charmed with its purity of tone);
"Life of Mrs. Schimmel-Pennick" (excellent religious biography);
"Duran's Monarchs" (read to Mama);
"The Analogy of Religion Natural and Revealed to the Scheme of Nature" by Bishop Joseph Butler (John says this is the most difficult book in the English language);

"Really charming" was Agnes Macdonald's comment on this book, *The Northwest Passage by Land,* published in London in 1865. Viscount Milton, an Englishman, and Dr. Cheadle, his physician, travelled across the Northwest to the Pacific Coast in 1862-1863, and this book — subtitled *Being the narrative of an expedition from the Atlantic to the Pacific, undertaken with the view of exploring a route across the continent to British Columbia through British territory by one of the northern passes in the Rocky Mountains* — is an account of their journey.

"Journal in the Highlands" (a spirit of content and happy tenderness through its pages);

"Memoirs of the Court of George 3" by Jesse (to Mama, light and amusing);

Diaries and correspondence of the Hon. Geo. Rose (very political);

"Life of Pitt" by Stanhope (John told me to read it);

### "Sneering, Prejudiced"

"English Note Book" by Nathaniel Hawthorne (so sneering, so prejudiced in style);

"Contes" by Alfred de Musset in French (trying and absurd, puerile, John says some stories are bad);

"Monks of the West" by Moulalemverts (like the devotional style);

"Life of Bishop Mackenzie" by Dean Goodwin of Ely (tells of mission work in Natal and Central Africa);

A Critique in Blackwood's on "Le Récit d'une Soeur" (a good review);

### Slick Logic

An oil painting of each Speaker in the Canadian Parliament is hung on his retirement in one of the lobbies or reading rooms. According to custom, each selects his artist. But when Sir David MacPherson, Speaker of the Senate, had his portrait painted by an Englishman, there was criticism because a Canadian had not been commissioned.

Expressing surprise that any man of culture would object to a gentleman choosing his favourite painter, Sir John A. said that the incident made him think of Sam Slick (in Justice T. C. Haliburton's *The Sayings and Doings of Sam Slick of Slickville*) who said, "In Italy I saw old smoked, dried up pictures that cost five or six thousand dollars. Why, I can get new ones painted on my clocks, with new paints and new gildings, at five dollars a head."

*PAC*

John A. really had no right to use this coat of arms which he "borrowed" to use as a bookplate. Note the similarity of motto to that of Canada: *Ad mare usque ad mare.*

*PAC*

The present Macdonald crest, which John A.'s great-grandson petitioned for in 1969.

"Helena's Household";

Article on Disraeli in Blackwood's;

"Lost and Saved" a novel (hearty fit of crying, went to bed unhappy);

"A Churchman's Guide to Faith and Piety" (liked very much for some things);

"Adam and the Adamite" by McCausland;

"Cruise Alone" by McGregor;

"Massacre of St. Bartholomew" by Vivian White;

"The Scaboard Parish" (à Sunday story — charming);

"Dombey and Son" by Charles Dickens;

Essays on Pitt and Fox;

"Life of the Rev. Henry Vern Elliott" a Rector

*(continued)*

### Booked Solid

Sir John A. was forever buying books. He bought them for himself; he bought them for friends. He bought them in Britain, in Montreal, in Ottawa. His interests were wide, as his receipts from booksellers show. From Dawson Brothers, Montreal, he bought: Volume 15 of *Punch; Cavendish on Whist; Hadje Babi; London People;* and Tenant's *Ceylon.* His library contained such books as *On Corns, Bunions &c., and the Management of the Feet; Modern Cavalry: Its Organization, Armament and Employment in War; The Peerage of Scotland; Decline and Fall of the Roman Empire; The Works of Lord Byron; The Law of Hotel Life; The History of Scottish Song; The Philosophy of Eating; General Todleben's Defence of Sabastopol; A Treatise on Gout, Rheumatism, and the allied Affections.*

William Lyon Phelps, of Yale University, once wrote in *Scribner's Magazine* that the most unfortunate thing that could happen to a poet was to be born in Canada.

of a Brighton chapel;

"Cruise of the Galatea";

Article on Jean-Baptiste Colbert;

"Historical Characters" by Sir Henry Bulwer (I am interested in lives of statesmen because of my husband's tastes and career);

"Talleyrand" by Sir Henry Bulwer (most interesting);

"Prince Alfred's Cruise" (a dreadful waving of flags);

"Martin Chuzzlewitt" by Charles Dickens;

"Cobbett's Life, the Contentious Man" by Sir Henry Bulwer;

Canning's Life;

"Our New Way Round the World" by Mr. Coffin, a Yankee (gave me the only information about China that I ever possessed);

"The Draytons and Davenants" story of the Civil War by the author of "Schonberg Gotha Family."

### Sir John A.'s Library

Sir John A. was a man of erudition and scholarship, a bookish man, catholic in his interests. Wherever he was he bought books, as receipts from Montreal, Ottawa, Toronto and Great Britain show. He was always sure to know about a new book, a recent magazine article, the popular play.

Worn with cares, he sat far into the night reading to his sick, painracked first wife, or to himself while she dozed. Books brought him some solace. His memory was prodigious and he was able to quote whole passages when the occasion demanded a special statement.

After his death, many of his books were sold by Public Auction at Earnscliffe, Ottawa. A catalogue may be found in the Lande Collection of the Rare Book Department, McLennan Library, McGill University, Montreal.

The catalogue lists 1678 volumes with the largest quantity in the departments of biography (411 books); French, English and foreign literature (330); history (276); religion and religious history (171); geography and travels

---

## The Enchanted Traveller

*We travelled empty-handed*
*With hearts all fear above,*
*For we ate the bread of friendship,*
*We drank the wine of love . . .*
*We looked on life and nature*
*With the eager eyes of youth*
*And all we asked or cared for*
*Was beauty, joy and truth.*
*We found no other wisdom,*
*We learned no other way,*
*Than the gladness of the morning*
*The glory of the day.*

Bliss Carman

---

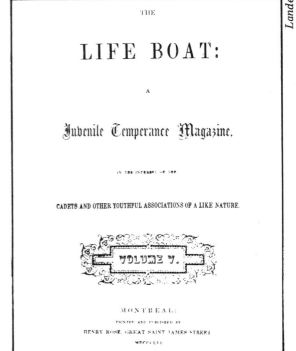

This juvenile temperance magazine published in Montreal in the 1850s is typical of the uplift emphasis of Victorian children's books.

---

One of the many bookstore bills found in the Macdonald Papers in the Public Archives of Canada. This bill from a Montreal bookstore covers the first six months of 1861. John A.'s political interests are reflected by May's *Constitutional History of England* and Stanhope's *Life of Pitt* and nineteenth-century heavyweight biographers Carlyle and Macauley.

---

"Nothing improves a man's manners like an election." (Justice T. C. Haliburton, in *The Clockmaker, or The Sayings and Doings of Sam Slick of Slickville*)

"It is, I believe, not an uncommon mode with Americans when they talk to amuse rather than convince." (Sam Slick)

"You may change the constitution for ever, but you cannot change man." (Sam Slick)

"What a pity that marryin' spoils courtin'." (Sam Slick)

"Popularity lasts but a day; respect will descend as a heritage to your children." (Sam Slick)

"Whenever you make an impression on a man, stop; your reasonin' and details may ruin you." (Sam Slick)

"It's no use to make fences unless the land is cultivated." (Sam Slick)

"Wherever there is authority, there is a natural inclination to disobedience." (Sam Slick)

"Politics is like a good thick homemade soup. Arter ye stir, the rich stuff settles down for the fellers as know how to wait." (Sam Slick)

Charles G. D. Roberts said, "I have lived for poetry, but I have lived by prose."

(142). The number of law books — constitutional law and constitutional history, colonial and provincial law, common and international law, military law and state trials — was small. Most of Sir John A.'s law library went to his son, Sir Hugh John Macdonald, who practiced law, first in Toronto and, after 1882, in Winnipeg.

Sir John A.'s interests were incredibly wide ranging. The catalogue listed books and magazines in the following categories: agriculture and horticulture; almanacs and annuals; architecture and the conservative arts; Greek and Latin classics; colonial handbooks; education; encyclopedias; transactions and proceedings; engineering and public works; finance and statistics; fine arts; heraldry and genealogy; French and other foreign magazines; medical science; military and naval science; music; natural history; philology; literary history and biography; political economy; political and social science and legislation; sports and games.

Sir John A. subscribed to many magazines. At least sixteen were listed in the catalogue.

### Composed in Canada

With special agents looking out for literature that would interest him, Sir John A. kept in touch with what was being composed in Canada. His lifetime was a very fruitful period for Canadian writers, as the following very limited list of authors indicates:

Frederick George Scott, poet;

John Wilson Bengough, cartoonist and poet and founder of the humorous Toronto weekly *Grip* which satirized political events;

Edward William Thomson, author;

Charles Mair, poet;

Pauline Johnson (Tekahionwake) the Mohawk Indian princess poet;

Judge Emily Murphy (Janey Canuck) author;

The sisters Mrs. Susanna Strickland Moodie and Mrs. Catharine Parr Traill, who wrote books about their pioneer experiences;

Mrs. Anna Brownell Jameson, another author who wrote of the life of the early settler;

Theodore Harding Rand, poet;

Bliss Carman, poet;

Charles Heavysege, poet;

Sir Charles George Douglas Roberts, poet;

James Evans, the missionary who devised the system of syllabic characters still in use among the Cree Indians;

Judge Thomas Chandler Haliburton, author of "The Sayings and Doings of Samuel Slick of Slickville";

William Kirby, author of "The Golden Dog."

Louis Honoré Fréchette (1839-1908) poet, lawyer, editor and politician, was the first Canadian to be honoured by the French Academy. His poem "Liberty" was translated from *Songs of French Canada* by Charles G.D. Roberts.

### Liberty

*A child, I set the thirsting of my mouth*
*To the gold chalices of loves that craze.*
*Surely, alas! I have found therein*
*but drouth,*
*Surely has sorrow darkened o'er my days.*
*While worldlings chase each other madly round*
*Their giddy track of frivolous gaiety,*
*Dreamer, my dream earth's utmost longings*
*bound:*
*One love alone is mine, my love is Liberty.*

Joseph Howe, anti-Confederationist, journalist and orator, said, "Poetry was the maiden I love, but politics was the harridan I married."

*Scenes in America* was published in England in 1821 and it is possible that John A. might have known it as a child. Exquisite engravings such as these decorate the book.

A blizzard in Winnipeg

Notre Dame from St. Urbain Street, Montreal

Quebec from the Old City Wall

Wharves at Quebec City

McGill Street, Montreal

King Street, Toronto

# Confederation took 82 years

## John A. always hoped Newfoundland would join

Main Street of Winnipeg, 1887, a Notman photograph.

The west end of Calgary. This Notman photograph was taken in 1887, before Alberta became a province of Canada.

*CIN*

The visit of a Governor-General was *the* social event of the year in many towns. The stylish and dashing Dufferin was a particularly popular attraction. Here — in Manitoba — he is being welcomed to Rockwood.

140

> **Dates of Admission or Creation of the Other Provinces**
> *Manitoba    May 12, 1870*
> *British Columbia    July 20, 1871*
> *Prince Edward Island    July 1, 1873*
> *Alberta    September 1, 1905*
> *Saskatchewan    September 1, 1905*
> *Newfoundland    April 1, 1949*

### "Indignation" Meeting in Charlottetown

Although Prince Edward Island was the site of the first Confederation Conference, the Island declined to join the new Dominion. Six years later, they were still reluctant. The people were suspicious that the Government planned to annex the Island to Canada — without the consent of the voters or even the legislature. Protest meetings were held all over the Island; the mayor of Charlottetown called an "indignation" meeting.

However, not all the Islanders were opposed to joining Canada, and Prince Edward Island became a province on July 1, 1873. Lord Dufferin, the Governor-General, wrote to Sir John A.: "I found the Island in a high state of jubilation and quite under the impression that it is the Dominion that has been annexed to Prince Edward Island."

### Festivities in Saskatchewan

Alberta and Saskatchewan were created in 1905 out of the Northwest Territories. Among the festivities that marked Saskatchewan's entry into the Dominion on September 1, was a game of "pushball." The game was described by the *Regina Leader* as "an impossible pastime. At the conclusion of the Royal North West Mounted Police musical ride, six riders removed their tunics, and took part, three to a side. The ball, an immense inflated sphere of leather, from England, was propelled by the horses' knees. One of the horses struck the ball with its shoe . . . causing it to collapse and the game to finish prematurely."

The Marquis of Lorne, Governor-General of Canada 1878-1883, wrote these lines for his wife, Princess Louise Caroline Alberta, after a visit to the West, when they named the province.

### Alberta

*In token of the love which thou hast shown*
*For this wide land of freedom, I have named*
*A province vast, and for its beauty famed*
*By thy dear name to be hereafter known.*

### Bitter Opposition in Newfoundland

John A. expected to see Newfoundland in the Dominion. In December 1867 he was negotiating with the Governor of Newfoundland concerning the terms under which the island might join Canada. John A. wrote to the Governor on December 27 of that year, discussing such things as the public debt, fishing rights, the militia and so on.

Although John A. had failed to get Newfoundland into Confederation in 1867, he still had hopes in 1884 that the island would eventually become a Canadian province. "We expect someday to get Newfoundland into the Dominion," he wrote. "I think the final adjustment

## DOMINION DAY.

SOMETHING FOR THE FATHER OF CONFEDERATION TO THINK OVER.

SIR JOHN.—"MY DEARS, I CONGRATULATE YOU ON THE TWELFTH ANNIVERSARY OF YOUR GLORIOUS VICTORY. WHAT CAN I DO TO ADD TO YOUR HAPPINESS?"
MADEMOISELLE QUEBEC (VIGOROUSLY).—"MIND YOUR OWN FEDERAL BUSINESS, AND PERMIT US TO MANAGE OUR LOCAL AFFAIRS TO SUIT OURSELVES, ACCORDING TO THE TERMS OF UNION,—*THAT'S* WHAT YOU CAN DO, SIR!"

The Father of Confederation and his children, July 1, 1879. By this time British Columbia, Manitoba and Prince Edward Island had joined Quebec, Ontario, Nova Scotia and New Brunswick in the Dominion. But it wasn't always a happy family. There was a strong anti-Confederation movement in Nova Scotia. British Columbia threatened to leave the Dominion because the railway wasn't being built fast enough. In this cartoon Quebec is telling John A. to mind his own federal business and keep out of provincial affairs.   *PAC*

of our coat of arms can stand over until then." But another sixty-five years passed before Newfoundland joined Canada.

Many Newfoundlanders were strongly opposed to Confederation, as this poem shows:

*Men, hurrah for our own native Isle,*
*Newfoundland—*
*Not a stranger shall hold one inch of her strand;*
*Her face turns to Britain, her back to the Gulf,*
*Come near at your peril, Canadian Wolf!*

*Cheap tea and molasses they say they will give,*
*All taxes taken off that the poor man may live—*
*Cheap nails and cheap lumber,*
*our coffins to make,*
*And homespun to mend our old clothes*
*when they break.*

*If they take off all taxes, how then will they meet*
*The heavy expenses on Army and fleet?*
*Just give them the chance to get into the scrape,*
*They'll show you the trick with pen,*
*ink and red tape.*

*Would you barter the right*
*that your fathers have won?*
*No! let them descend from father to son.*
*For a few thousand dollars Canadian gold*
*Don't let it be said that our birthright was sold.*

### Newfoundland Joins Dominion
### Many in Mourning

Newfoundland became a province of Canada on April 1, 1949. (However, the occasion is commemorated at the end of March, to avoid April Fool's day.)

Some Newfoundlanders still wear black armbands on April 1.

This editorial appeared in *The Daily News*, St. John's, March 31, 1949:

#### End of An Era

"There are occasions in the history of a people when sentiments of such deep rooted and high emotional content are involved that nothing short of the genius of a Winston Churchill can translate them into appropriate and adequate words. This day which is to see the extinguishing of Newfoundland as a national entity is one of those occasions. A light goes out that can never be relit. A new road must be taken along which those who go may never return. An indefinable something dies in the hearts of men and women and can never be brought back to life....

"Through all the vicissitudes of the centuries,

in spite of repression and retardation, in spite of the neglect of politicians in London and the shocks and buffetings of nature, in spite of bitter reverses and cruel sufferings, this Newfoundland of ours has held its individuality intact and its spirit proud.

"An era ends but whether we grieve or rejoice we must keep uppermost in our minds the love of our country to which all grievances must be subordinated. The Newfoundland that bred in us the strong and burning sentiments of deep-rooted nationalism will cease to exist at midnight but we cannot afford, as we enter the new era in association with Canada, to waste our time or our talents on vain regrets. There is work to be done. There is a country's security yet to be built. There is a better Newfoundland yet to be made. Let us never forget a great and glorious past, a past that for all its vicissitudes bears in its annals the imprints of great and patriotic men who strove devotedly for progress and let us make of our memories an inspiration to succeed and an incentive to toil in unity and good will with our fellow citizens for the building of a happy and prosperous future. It will be a noble venture and, please God, given unity of thought and deed, given good will and honest purpose, it will succeed."

141

# The cities of the Confederation

Sealers leaving for the ice — St. John's, Newfoundland, around the time of Confederation

Saint John, New Brunswick, as it looked before the fire of 1877

Halifax, Nova Scotia, around the time of Confederation — a Notman photograph

# Some of Lady Macdonald's favourite recipes

PAC

## Figs and treacle as a laxative, Opium porridge for the puppy

"I am a laborious housekeeper and still awkward at it," wrote Lady Agnes Macdonald on December 3, 1867. She had been married less than a year.

Like many of the women of her time she kept a "Household Treasury." She inscribed in its title page "Agnes Macdonald, Earnscliffe, Ottawa, July 18." (The year is indistinct.) The book contains carefully handwritten recipes of what were probably Sir John A.'s favourite dishes. A few are given here.

### Stock

4 or 5 lbs. middle cut shin of beef. 1 onion. 1 head celery. Small piece turnip. 1 carrot. ½ dozen cloves. 1 teaspoonful white, ditto black, pepper. Place in saucepan veg. cut in small pieces. Pour over it cold water, one pint to each 1 lb. beef. Cover. Allow this to come quickly to boiling point. Skim carefully at once. (It can never be skimmed properly later.) Throw in seasoning. Allow to boil slowly for 5 hrs. It must simmer after first heat has been applied. The first heat opens pores and lets juices out.

### Wyndham Cutlets

4 or 5 mutton cutlets from back rib
1 lb. potatoes
1 carrot
1 turnip
½ teaspoonful pepper and salt
2½ gills cold water
2 egg yolks
½ tablespoonful mushrooms, ditto catsup

Place in frying pan. Sprinkle pepper and salt and pour over them ½ gill cold water [4 gills = 1 pint]. Now place saucepan on fire, allow water to boil. Then add thin slices carrots and turnips. Allow to simmer 20 mins. During this time I turn the cutlets once. While this boils slowly I place into a saucepan of boiling water carrots. Boil this 20 mins. also. Pass through a coarse loose sieve — 1 lb. boiled potatoes. Put in fresh saucepan yolks of 2 eggs. Put saucepan on fire and stir together potatoes and yolks over fire, until yolks get bound. Flour a bowl very slightly, take spoonful of potatoes, roll very slightly with flour, then flatten with a knife. Place cutlet in potato, and roll round all this on board. Slightly flour a little baking tin, place cutlet upon it, and brush over with little egg or milk as quickly as possible. While cutlets are browning, I make brown sauce as per page 108.

### Brown Sauce for Wyndham Cutlets (à la red hot shovel)

Catsup and Worcester sauce put into water which has boiled cutlets. In this — one ounce butter. While butter melts, stir into it one ounce of dried flour. Then add by degrees a gill of cold water. Stir until boils. Then I add a little pepper and salt, the catsup and Worcester sauce. Cook for 2 minutes. Pour over vegetables in centre. Brown cutlets 5 minutes. If oven not hot enough, red hot shovel held over them.

### As A Laxative

Mrs. Williamson's receipt for M. ¼ lb. figs, 1 oz. henna leaves, ½ pint treacle. Chop the figs finely and rub the leaves together to a powder. Mix thoroughly with the treacle. A large tablespoonful morning and evening is the ordinary dose for an Adult. For a child, less than half this quantity.

Lady Macdonald, 1871

*An opium recipe for the dog, courtesy of Lady Ritchie, wife of Sir William Johnstone Ritchie, Chief Justice of Canada in 1879.*

### For Distemper

2 grains tartar emetic
3 grains opium
Make into 2 pills, one to be given at night in a bowl of warm gruel. Keep the dog confined in a warm place.

### Fried Fish

Bone and skin haddock. Place on sheet of paper, 1 tablespoon of flour. Then place on a plate yolk of an egg beaten. On another sheet of

PAC

A page from Lady Macdonald's household treasury in her own handwriting, giving her recipe for oat water, her fig and treacle laxative and her opium gruel remedy for distemper.

paper 2 or 3 tablespoonful of bread crumbs (very stale bread). Add little pepper and salt. Strain crumbs through coarse sieve. Take fish up with fork, dip into flour. (Unless fish is thoroughly dry, it will be heavy.) Dip into beaten egg, place on sheet of paper with crumbs, shake about paper, lift with fork. Half fill saucepan with lard or rendered fat of mutton. Wait until smoke rises, put fish in and allow five minutes. (Water boils at 212°, lard takes 500°) Keep fish until smoke proves lard hot enough, then dip. If lard is hot a piece of bread will burn and crisp. Put fish on paper to soak out grease. Then serve.

### Unfermented Wine

Express the juice from the grapes and take a pound of sugar to a gallon of juice, bring to a boil. Heat the bottles by placing them in warm water. Leave them in till it boils. After skimming the juice, pour as quickly as possible into the bottles. Cork tightly and seal with beeswax and rosin. Will not keep long after opening. This has kept 4 months.

### Yeast — Mrs. Tilley's Receipt

To a handful of hops, add 8 potatoes. Boil altogether. Strain but do not mash the potatoes. Add a breakfast cup of flour, with a pint of cold water to the hops spread on the ingredients. Boil altogether after the flour is in a few minutes. When cold, stir in a cup of brown sugar and raise it.

### Brown Bread

1 quart milk
2 teaspoonful soda
1 cup molasses
2 cups Indian meal
Strain 3 hours, then put into the stove oven 1 hour and brown.

# John A. buys corn plasters, tonics

## *Macdonalds' daily life in household accounts*

## A corset for 28s 6d
## $11.90 spent on brandy
## One dollar at church

Account books give us an intimate picture of what life was like in the Macdonald household in the 1870s. The prices are sometimes in British and sometimes in Canadian currency. Some entries are itemized as follows:

| | |
|---|---|
| Church, L. M. | 2 shillings |
| Repairs, umbrella | 1 shilling |
| Repairs, parasol | 6 shillings |
| 6 prs. gloves | 18 shillings |
| smelling bottle | 10 pence |
| library books | 6 pence |
| theatre tickets | £1/2/6 |
| corn plasters | 6 pence |
| cab hire | 2 pounds |
| toothbrush | 6 pence |
| Lady Macdonald | 7 pounds |
| gloves | 10 shillings |
| share woman | 25 cents |
| cord | 9½ pence |
| blotting paper | 3 pence |
| lamp glass | 1s. 4d. |
| washing, 3 days | £2/2/5 |
| horse | £5 7s. |
| 1640 lbs Hay | $8.66 |
| coal oil | £1/4/0 |
| Cab hire | 2 pounds |
| man's wages | 6 dollars |
| 2 dozen bread | $3.40 |
| kitchen maid, wages in full | $6 |
| tickets for opera | $3 |
| man with cow | 25 cents |
| at church | one dollar |
| cab for visits | one dollar |
| at church | fifty cents |
| bottle ink | 2s. 5d. |
| Wine | £1 6s. |
| telegramme | 1s. 3d. |
| postage | 6 pence |
| oysters | 50 cents |
| radishes | 50 cents |
| ducks | three dollars |
| oatmeal | one dollar |
| load of wood | $2.25 |
| 1 dozen brandy | $11.90 |
| 1 pane glass | 45 cents |

There were bills from several chemists — in Montreal, Ottawa, Toronto and Quebec.

Medical Hall, Kenneth Campbell and Co., 23 Great St. James Street Montreal, July 1866

| | |
|---|---|
| Pomade | .63 |
| Cologne | .50 |
| Sponge | 3.00 |

W. H. Massey, 28 Sparks Street, Ottawa, July 2, 1869

| | |
|---|---|
| English peppermints | .30 |
| Violet powder | .12½ |
| Liniment | .40 |

E. Hooper and Co., King Street West, Toronto December 14, 1870

| | |
|---|---|
| Elixir of Bark, 3 bottles | $3.00 |

### INTERCOLONIAL RAILWAY.

**1873.    Summer Arrangement.    1873.**

On and after MONDAY, 26th inst., a Passenger and Mail Train will leave Halifax daily, at 7:40 a.m., and be due in St. John at 8:30 p.m. A Passenger and Mail Train will also leave St. John daily, at 8:00 a.m., and be due in Halifax at 8:50 p.m.

*Trains will connect*

At Painsec with trains to and from Shediac and intermediate stations.

At Truro with trains to and from Pictou and intermediate stations.

At Windsor Junction with the trains of the Windsor and Annapolis Railway.

At St. John with the Consolidated European and North American Railway for Bangor, Danville Junction, Montreal, Quebec, Portland, Boston, also with the International Steamers to and from Eastport, Portland, and Boston.

**LEWIS CARVELL,**
*General Superintendent*

Railway Offices,
MONCTON, N.B., May 1873.           7-2-tf

### COAL AND WOOD.

**CONGER COAL COMPANY.**

Main Office - 6 King Street East.

John P. Featherston, 44 Rideau Street, Ottawa

| | |
|---|---|
| Vichy Salts | .25 |
| Pears Shampooing Soap | .35 |
| ½ dozen Vichy water | .65 |

From Mrs. Adley Bourne, Wedding Trousseau and Indian Outfits, and Swanbill Corsets (registered) 37 Piccadilly, Opposite St. James Church, London, Prices Regulated for ready money.   July 19, 1879

| | |
|---|---|
| 1 corset | 28 shillings and 6 pence |

G. M. Holbrook, Elgin and Sparks Streets, Ottawa, Merchant tailor and importer of British and Foreign Manufactures, sent a bill for:

| | |
|---|---|
| Repairing frock coat | $1.00 |
| repairs to vest | .25 |
| Lining o'coat | $4.00 |
| altering coat | .50 |
| repairing pants | .50 |
| repairing o'coat | $1.50 |
| new sleeves in coat | $2.00 |

John Leighton, Bootmaker, sent a receipted bill on November 10, 1869, for "elasticizing 3 pairs of boots at 60 cents a pair."

Mrs. Marsh, Ladies Trousseaux and Indian

Outfits, Osborne House, 189a Sloane Street, London SW, submitted a statement for "1 silk gown for Lady Macdonald six pounds six shillings" in August 1879.

From Satchell Bros., Ottawa, Butchers to His Excellency, the Governor-General of Canada, came an account in 1879 that covered a little over a week:

| | |
|---|---|
| Leg mutton 6 lbs 4 oz | .78 |
| Rib 16, 4 | 2.04 |
| side | 2.50 |
| sweetbreads | 2.00 |
| 2 ox tails | .40 |
| Rib 18, 2 | 2.31 |
| Rib 9, 2 | 1.19 |
| sausages 3 | .38 |
| veal 14 | 1.75 |
| rib beef 16, 4 | 2.04 |
| lamb | 1.50 |
| mint | .10 |
| butter | 1.25 |
| lamb | 1.50 |
| sweetbreads | .75 |
| rib 14 | 1.75 |
| kidneys | .13 |

These provisions were ordered in 1867:

| | |
|---|---|
| leg mutton | .48 |
| kidneys | .04 |
| lamb | .30 |
| roast, 10 lbs. | .63 |
| fish | .13 |
| 12 lbs corned beef | .60 |
| chops, 3 lbs | 1.10 |
| kidneys | .07½ |
| steak 3½ lbs | .33 |
| 2 salt tongues | .50 |
| shank, beef | .29 |
| suet, 5 lbs | 1.10½ |

In 1871 there was an order for three dozen peaches at seventy-five cents, melons at one dollar and "green peases" for forty cents. In 1874 Lady Macdonald bought asparagus for forty cents, radishes and onions for thirty cents and three cabbages for seventy-five cents.

A statement (including several "hair cutts") from John Curtis, hairdresser, 57 Rideau Street, Ottawa, tells of the personal habits of the Macdonalds.

| | | |
|---|---|---|
| November 1868 | Lady Macdonald's hair | $1.00 |
| December 1868 | Sir John, attendance | $1.00 |
| March 1869 | Cutting hair | .25 |
| May 1870 | 2 bottles hair wash | 1.00 |
| | hair cutt, shave, shampoo | .75 |
| July | 4 shaves | .40 |
| October | 2 shaves and hair cutt | .40 |
| November | 2 shaves and hair cutt | .40 |
| November 1871 | bay rum | .40 |
| March 1872 | French pomade | .50 |

And still more bills from pharmacists:

A. Christie, 87 Sparks Street Ottawa 1876

| | |
|---|---|
| Drops | .25 |
| 1 package boudoir paper | .40 |
| pot ointment | .20 |
| linseed | .10 |
| toothbrush | .25 |

July 1879

| | |
|---|---|
| mixture | .75 |
| 2 boxes, hairpins | .34 |
| elixirs | .75 |
| bottle Allen's Balsam | .50 |
| cod liver oil | .50 |
| beef, iron and wine tonic | 1.00 |

E. Hooper and Co., Toronto   December 1882

| | |
|---|---|
| hair brush | $1.25 |
| comb | .50 |
| toothbrush | .25 |
| barley sugar | .40 |
| mixture | .85 |
| mixture | 1.00 |

John Roberts, Chemist, 76 Rideau Street, Ottawa

| | | |
|---|---|---|
| June 7, 1889 | Bottle Maltine plain | $1.00 |
| | 2 bottles tincture of myrrh | .50 |
| June 14 | lavender water | .75 |
| | pills per Dr. H. P. W. | .40 |
| June 20 | Bay rum | .50 |
| | pills per Dr. H. P. W. | .40 |
| June 28 | pills per Dr. H. P. W. double quantity | .65 |
| August 23 | pills | .35 |

A MECHANIC'S HOME

UNDER THE NATIONAL POLICY

NO WORK, NO MONEY.

UNDER A FREE TRADE OR REVENUE TARIFF.

Posters like this were very pointedly related to the economic depression that hit Canada in 1873 and forced many Canadians in search of work to leave for the United States. The depression was not, of course, the fault of Mackenzie's Liberal Government, but Macdonald was able to suggest — effectively, as it turned out — that the way out of the depression was through his National Policy.

Uncle Sam is very displeased with Macdonald's speech favouring tariffs. John A. started arguing for protective tariffs — to prevent the U.S. from dumping cheap goods across the Canadian border — in 1876.

# John A. points way to prosperity

## Suggests a "National Policy" to cure Canada's economic ills

An American selling "Yankee Notions" is trying to sneak across the border without going through customs. But John A. is on guard.

### A National Policy for Canada

*Sir John A.'s National Policy Resolution, moved in the House of Commons, March 12, 1878:*

That it be resolved that this house is of the opinion that the welfare of Canada requires the adoption of a national policy, which, by a judicious readjustment of the tariff, will benefit and foster the agricultural, the mining, the manufacturing and other interests of the Dominion; that such a policy will retain in Canada thousands of our fellow-countrymen now obliged to expatriate themselves in search of the employment denied them at home, will restore prosperity to our struggling industries now so sadly depressed, will prevent Canada from being made a sacrifice market, will encourage and develop an active inter-provincial trade, and moving (as it ought to do) in the direction of a reciprocity of tariffs with our neighbours, so far as the varied interests of Canada may demand, will greatly tend to procure for this country, eventually, a reciprocity of trade.

In a debate on National Policy, Sir John A. said, "Those who cared to be protected at all wanted all the protection they could get. They were like the man who said of whisky that 'a little too much is just enough.'"

Sir Charles Tupper on national policy: "I say what Canada wants is a national policy — a policy that shall be in the interests of Canada, apart from the principles of free trade, apart from the principles of protection."

John A. was pictured as being against not only cheap U.S. goods but also cheap British goods — which would compete with goods of Canadian manufacture. Although openly he always presented himself as pro-British, he could maintain considerable independence in private negotiations.

One reason that John A.'s National Policy caught on was that it was so "visible": so easily pictorialized in cartoons like this one where John A. is trying to lure Cartwright into the Dominion Dry Goods Association — through a door marked N.P. — and away from American House which offers "Imported Goods at a discount."

John A. is shown courting John Bull. He believed that to strengthen the national economy, not only was protectionism needed, but diplomatic and financial support must be secured in Britain, particularly to help build the national railroad and to foster industrialization. He would also ask England to help direct immigrants to the lands the railways would open. He was an effective suitor!

Sir John A. talked of "National Policy" repeatedly, until it became the political slogan for 1878. It called for protection for everyone —
manufacturer (and, by implication, worker) and farmer. But he did not call a tariff a tariff; instead he argued for "reciprocity of tariffs"
and promised to "make the tall chimneys smoke."

# Enjoying Canadian cities in winter

## *John A. asked to pose for William Notman's famous "Curling in Canada"*

The Canadian Government commissioned this photograph for the Paris World's Fair of 1878. Photography had not yet developed to the extent that crowd scenes could be taken. Notman invited prominent Canadians to sit for the picture. For the next few months they drifted into his studio and he placed them in appropriate poses and photographed them at various distances from the camera. The individual photographs were pasted onto a sheet and the background — Mount Royal and the Montreal skyline — was sketched in. The collage was then photographed. In the middle foreground of the picture are Lord and Lady Dufferin. John A. is seated in the background to the left of centre.

The invitation from pioneer photographer William Notman to pose for
"Curling in Canada"

"New Brunswick Fashionables, Fredericton, January 1834" — Canadian winter scenes have always delighted artists and photographers.

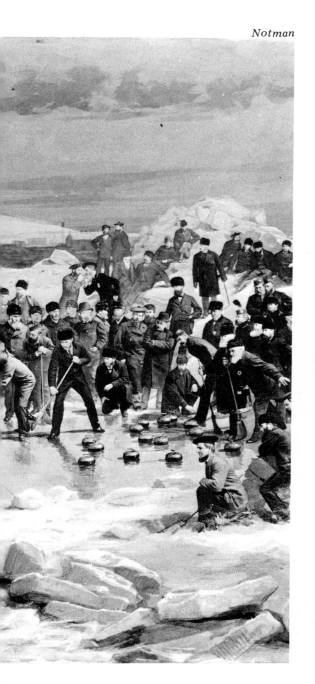

"Cul de Sac Street in Winter, Quebec, Lower Canada, 1830" — a watercolour by
James Pattison Cockburn

151

**THE ONLY SATISFYING PICNIC, AFTER ALL!**

John A. was onto a good thing with the political picnic — just the thing, in fact, to win the election of 1878, for him and the Conservatives.

# MACDONALD PICNICS HIS WAY TO POWER

## Parties for votes = votes for the Party

The first political picnic was held at Uxbridge on Dominion Day in 1876. It was followed by hundreds more, all over the country. Sir John A. and the Conservatives sponsored many of these open-air get-togethers.

### Devil Tempts with Picnics

In 1878 an opponent attacked the political picnics saying that Sir John A. "was not a man, that was the Devil...who went around the country holding picnics and tempting the people."

But the people enjoyed the picnics. Families and friends from various areas, long separated, arranged to meet for a good long talk fest. In all their finery, they came by train, wagon, buggy, democrat, buckboard, oxcart, dogcart, carriage, stagecoach, steamboat, canoe, raft, ferryboat, on horseback or on foot, laden with hampers of wonderful food and drink.

The women prepared enormous amounts of delectable provisions, which were eaten in between the excitement of campaign speeches, band music (featuring the new hit song "Our Dominion" and popular tunes like the "Welcome Galop" and the "Loyal Opposition

Galop"), picnic-site parades, fireworks, singsongs, feats of strength like tug-of-war and weight lifting, horseshoe pitching and the like.

The hosts and organizers sometimes provided a spectacle like a balloonist, or circus performers that left young and old agape. Decorations included Conservative streamers and banners that proclaimed:

*A National Policy for Canada*
*Canada for the Canadians*
*No Compromise — Reciprocity or Protection*
*Good Times Coming*
*See the Conquering Hero Comes*
*A Thousand Welcomes*

### Tipsy Cake and Shoo-fly Pie

Triumphal arches festooned with canvas drapery promising "Welcome" and "Victory" led the way to long tables laden with succulent turkeys, chickens and geese, roast ducks with

---

### The Campaign of Picnics

The election of 1878, in which Sir John A. and the Conservatives returned to power.

---

wild rice stuffing, garnished tongues, aspic hams, huge roasts, pigeon pastries, giblet pies, sausage smoked in maple syrup, roasted pig tails and black pudding. There were pickled peaches and pears, sweet mustard pickles, an old settler's "secret" pepper relish, piccalilli and all sorts of breads — a pumpkin loaf served with slathers of freshly churned butter, corn and blueberry muffins, hoe and ash cakes and still hot biscuits. Desserts included cakes such as tipsy, pound, cheese and Huronia maple layer; charlotte russe, flummery and varieties of pies — shoo-fly, honey rhubarb and mince. Suet pudding with dried plums competed with Indian pudding, *schnitz und knepp* and raised doughnuts. Huge bowls of strawberries, blackberries and currants disappeared along with toppings of thick rich cream. For those who could handle more there were Northern Spy, Royal Russets and Canadian Nonesuch apples, homemade candy kisses and cheeses in great variety. There was a constant refilling of great pitchers of iced lemonade, berry cordials, cider, domestic champagne and dandelion wine.

Mrs. M. C. Sheed, of Toronto, tells how Sir John A. received an ovation at a political picnic near Trenton.

"Grandpa was born and raised on a farm just north of Trenton, Ontario. In his boyhood days, the River was a very important waterway, and no doubt that was why a meeting place had been set aside on its banks. It was just a cleared, grassy spot, with a rough platform built at one end, which was open to the wind and weather.

"This was the place where the politicians who wished to be elected came and spoke to the crowds with varying success, and this was where my grandfather was taken by his father to hear the contenders of an election, one of whom was Sir John.

"The great day came, sunny and warm, and the place was jammed with people who came in every type of conveyance imaginable. The first to speak was Sir John's opponent and he talked to the people about the current problems and what *he* intended to do about them if elected. Suddenly there was a loud splintering sound and the poor man was seen floundering helplessly on the floor of the platform with one leg down through a gaping hole. The weather-worn boards had given way. Immediately farmers near the platform jumped up on it and helped him to his feet. One farmer produced a hammer and nails, and a board was hastily nailed over the hole.

"The flustered politician then finished his speech and was roundly applauded.

"Now it was Sir John's turn. Slowly he mounted the steps and cautiously he walked over the entire platform, testing the boards with an outstretched foot before committing his full weight to that particular spot. Satisfied that the boards would hold, he then turned to the waiting audience and said in a

"A platform one could stand on"

loud, clear, ringing voice: 'Ladies and gentlemen: When *I* take a stand it *never* fails!'

"The applause was instant and tremendous.

"When the tumult finally died down, Sir John A. went on with his speech, but Grandpa said that he needn't have spoken another word. He had that audience in the palm of his hand."

On September 26, 1876, Sir John A. was presented with an address from Norfolk County, which said in part: "It is not because you are deemed faultless that this large Assembly has met to do you honour, it is because Conservatives believe that if you erred in the administration . . . your errors were of judgement and not of intention, and they have ever been proud of you because your slanderers . . . numerous and malignant, have never succeeded in connecting your name with any act by which the interest or honour of your country was sacrificed; or with having used your position to enrich or aggrandize yourself or your friends by dishonourable means. The ovations you receive . . . that you still possess the fullest confidence of Conservatives — and, we believe, of a vast majority of

the Canadian people — and are omens that you are soon to be restored to power which was wrested from you by dishonest means and by oft-repeated charges of wrongdoing, which were unsustained by evidence and which were false, but which for a time so blinded the electors to your real worth and to the true merits of the case that your party was defeated at the polls. Conservatives believe that your restoration to power will be a blessing to your country."

### Reviled, Calumniated and Abused

Sir John A. replied: "If I have for thirty years been in public life; if I have for nearly twenty years been a member of the Govern-

ment; and if, during the greater part of that period, I have been the most reviled, calumniated, and abused man in Canada, I have my compensations here. No man is more conscious than I am of my faults. Looking back at my history and at the history of Canada, I freely admit that, guided by the light of experience, there are many things in my political career that I now could wish had been otherwise. There are acts of omission and commission which I regret; but your testimony, and the testimony of my own conscience, alike show that, as you believe, and as I know, whether I was right or wrong in any political act at the time, I was acting according to the best of my judgement for the interest of our common country. I want no more impartial jury than you. I want no other verdict than from your hands and from men like you in this Dominion."

The Conservatives were exhilarated by the picnics. Was this their way back to power? They encouraged further open-air gatherings for followers who came from Colborne, Belleville, Port Hope, Cobourg, Guelph, Norfolk, Fergus, St. Catharines, Milton, Woodstock and Ingersoll.

John A. was a master politician. He could gauge the mood of a crowd and speak accordingly.

# The many faces of John A. delight artists

*John Wilson Bengough captures PM's spirit in Grip magazine*

While Sir John A. was in power, his picture appeared in *The Canadian Illustrated News* at least once a month, if not oftener. Readers of *Grip* were also very familiar with his likeness. He was portrayed as an old woman, Sherlock Holmes, the conductor of a symphony orchestra, a Beefeater, a ship's captain, a doctor, a king, a shoemaker, a fisherman, a naughty schoolboy, Ulysses, an Indian chief, a hotel bellboy, an actor playing Shakespeare, a unicorn, a circus performer, a policeman, Aeneas, a judge, a magician, a fox, a chef, a barber, a flying insect, Sinbad, a mailman — and sometimes even a politician!

**Most Famous Caricaturist**

John Wilson Bengough, who drew so many political caricatures of Sir John A. Macdonald and who captured the spirit of the Prime Minister so well, was a poet and political writer as well as a cartoonist. Born in Toronto, Canada West, in 1851 he founded *Grip*, a Toronto humorous weekly, when he was twenty-two and immediately attained success for his satirical sketches. In 1892, the year after Sir John A.'s death, he severed his connection with *Grip* and was successively cartoonist for *The Montreal Star* and the Toronto *Globe*. He was a strong advocate of prohibition and free trade, and very popular as a humourous lecturer. Sir John A. must have enjoyed Bengough's cartoons. He said, "There is one Canadian artist who draws me with power and graphic skill.... My friend Bengough possesses ... artistic skill and perfect accuracy in portraying my countenance."

## O, OUR PROPHETIC SOUL!
### (See last week's Cartoon.)

JOHN A.—"I DON'T KNOW, BUT IT SEEMS TO ME THIS PICTURE OF YOURS, MY PROPHETIC FRIEND, NEEDS A LITTLE 'RE-ADJUSTMENT,' DON'T IT, HEY?"

A self-portrait by artist Bengough, called to task by Sir John A. The previous week, Bengough had drawn for the cover of *Grip* — being held here by Macdonald — a cartoon predicting a Liberal victory in the election of 1878. Now the newly elected Tory Prime Minister has stopped by to ask the artist to "re-adjust" the picture. Typical of the charming detail in many Bengough cartoons is the bird on top of the easel who promises to "retire from the prophecy business after this."

## John A. laughed loudest and enjoyed them most

In a debate in the House a Member of Parliament said of a bill that if the principle was bad when carried to extremes, it must always be bad. Dryly Sir John A. observed: "Yes, it is always bad to shave your head in order to cut your hair."

**FLY-TIME!**
The pesky flies trying to eat off John A. as he eats out of the public crib include the Orange Vote, the French Vote, the Franchise Act and politicians Mulock, McCarthy, Devlin and others.

THE COMING ATTRACTION

Here Bengough shows his remarkable inventiveness and artistry as he presents "tragedian John A. Macdonald" in assorted Shakespearean roles, "supported by a powerful company from the provinces," while his defeated opponents look on in dismay.

## Canadian Illustrated News Also finds John A. fun

In a series on "The Classical Gallery of Canadian Heroes" John A. is pictured as "The Many-Counselled Ulysses."

METING OUT THE DOLE
John A. as the farmer's wife, feeding the Civil Service "poultry."

Sir John A. leads the Grand Ministerial Overture at the Parliamentary Opera House.

WE CAN'T UNDO THE LOCK, SIR JOAN IS ON GUARD.

PROSPERITY

FACTORY
MARKET
BANK

N P LOCK

HAND IT OVER THE FENCE?

PUBLISHED BY THE INDUSTRIAL LEAGUE, FREDERIC NICHOLLS, HON. SEC.

Toronto Lith. Co.

PAC

Grip

J.W.Bengough

Following Sir John A.'s death, a despairing Bengough tries to think of something to say about his successor (Sir John Abbott) but the fun seems to have gone out of it all. Shortly thereafter, Bengough left *Grip* to work for *The Montreal Star* and later *The Globe* in Toronto.

# HOMESTEAD RIGHTS.

All persons interested in obtaining Homestead Grants will please give attention to the following clause of the "Act respecting the Public Lands of the Dominion," and govern themselves accordingly:

## HOMESTEAD RIGHTS, OR FREE GRANT LANDS.

33. Any person who is the head of a family, or has attained the age of twenty-one years, shall be entitled to be entered for one quarter section or a less quantity of unappropriated Dominion Lands, for the purpose of securing a Homestead Right in respect thereof. (Form A.)

*1.* Provided that the limitation of quantity in this clause shall not prevent the granting of a Wood Lot to the same person under the provisions hereinafter made with respect to Timber in surveyed Townships.

*2.* When two or more persons have settled on and seek to obtain a title to the same land, the Homestead Right shall be in him who made the first settlement.

*3.* Provided, that in cases where both parties may have made valuable improvements, the Secretary of State may order a division of such land, in legal sub-divisions, in such manner as may preserve to the said parties, as far as practicable, their several improvements; and further, may direct that what the land of each of such parties, as so divided, may be deficient of a quarter section, shall be severally made up to them in legal sub-divisions from unoccupied quarter sections adjoining.

*4.* Questions as to the Homestead Right arising between different settlers shall be investigated by the Local Agent of the Division in which the land is situated, whose report and recommendation, together with the evidence taken, shall be referred to the Secretary of State for decision.

*5.* Every person claiming a Homestead Right from actual settlement must file his application for such claim, describing the land settled, with the Local Agent within whose District such land may be, within *thirty days* next after the date of such settlement, if in surveyed lands; but if in unsurveyed lands, the claimant must file such application within three months after such land shall have been surveyed; and in either case proof of settlement and improvement shall be made to the Local Agent at the time of filing such application.

*6.* Persons owning and occupying Dominion Lands may be entered for other land lying contiguous to their lands; but the whole extent of land, including that previously owned and occupied, must not exceed one hundred and sixty acres, and must be in legal sub-divisions.

*7.* A person applying for leave to be entered for lands with a view of securing a Homestead Right therein, shall make affidavit before the Local Agent (Form B.), that he is over twenty-one years of age, that he has not previously obtained a Homestead under the provisions of this Act, that to the best of his knowledge and belief there is no person residing on the land in question or entitled to enter the same as a Homestead, and that the application is made for his exclusive use and benefit and for the purpose of actual settlement.

*8.* Upon making this Affidavit and filing it with the Local Agent [and on payment to him of an office fee of *ten dollars*—for which he shall receive a receipt from the Agent]—he shall be permitted to enter the land specified in the application.

*9.* In entries of contiguous lands, the Settler must describe in his Affidavit the tract he owns and is settled upon as his original farm. Actual residence on the contiguous land entered is not required, but *bona fide* improvement and cultivation of it must be thereafter shewn for the period required by the provisions of this Act.

*10.* No Patent shall be granted for the land until the expiration of *three years* from the time of entering into possession of it except as hereinafter provided.

*11.* At the expiration of *three years* the Settler or his widow, her heirs or devisees—or if the Settler leaves no widow, his heirs or devisees—upon proof to the satisfaction of the Local Agent that he or his widow, or his or her representatives as aforesaid, or some of them, have resided upon or cultivated the land for the three years next after the filing of the Affidavit for entry, the Settler or such claimant shall be entitled to a Patent for the land: provided such claimant is then a subject of Her Majesty by birth or naturalization.

*12.* When both parents die without having devised the land, and leaving a child or children under age, it shall be lawful for the Executors (if any) of the last surviving parent, or the Guardian or Guardians of such child or children, with the approval of a Judge of a Superior Court of the Province or Territory in which the lands lie, to sell the lands for the benefit of the infant or infants, but for no other purpose; and the purchaser in such case shall acquire the Homestead Right by such purchase, and on carrying out the unperformed conditions of such right, shall receive a Patent for the land [upon payment of the office fees.]

*13.* The title to lands shall remain in the Crown until the issue of the Patent therefor; and such lands shall not be liable to be taken in execution before the issue of the Patent.

*14.* In case it is proved to the satisfaction of the Local Agent that the Settler has voluntarily relinquished his claim, or has been absent from the land entered by him for more than *six months* in any one year, then the right to such land shall be forfeited; and the Settler so relinquishing or abandoning his claim shall not be permitted to make more than a second entry.

*15.* Any person who has availed himself of the foregoing provisions may, before the expiration of the three years, obtain a Patent for the land entered upon by him, including the wood lot, if any, forming an addition to the grant thereof, as hereinafter provided, on paying the Government price thereof at the date of entry, and making proof of settlement and cultivation for not less than twelve months from the date of entry.

*16.* Proof of actual settlement and cultivation shall be made by Affidavit of the claimant before the Local Agent, corroborated on oath by two credible witnesses.

*17.* All Assignments and Transfers of Homestead Rights before the issue of the Patent shall be null and void, but shall be deemed evidence of abandonment of the Right; and the person so assigning or transferring shall not be permitted to make a second entry.

*18.* The above provisions relating to Homesteads shall only apply to Agricultural Lands and shall not be held to apply to lands set apart as Timber Lands, or to those lands on which coal or minerals are at the time of entry known to exist.

G. McMICKEN, *Agent Dominion Lands.*

MANITOBAN PRINT.

The building of the CPR opened the West for settlement. The railroad carried the settlers by the thousands to their homesteads on the prairies.

# PART SIX 1878 - 1890

*Canada is a hard country to govern.* One of John A.'s favourite sayings

## WHAT THE CHIEFTAIN HEARD.

"WHEN I WAS IN THE EASTERN TOWNSHIPS, I HEARD THE CRY ECHOING FROM ROCK TO ROCK, ACROSS THE BOSOMS OF THOSE BEAUTIFUL LAKES, AND OVER THE EMERALD FIELD,—'COME TO OUR RESCUE, JOHN A., OR WE ARE LOST.'"

In this clever cartoon drawn in 1877, Bengough scoffed at John A.'s florid speech on how everyone wanted him back in power. But Bengough had to admit his mistake the next year when the voters showed that they *did* want Macdonald back.

The return of Macdonald to power in 1878 (after the disgrace of the Pacific Scandal of 1873) was compared to Napoleon's return from Elba. But the country's desire to have him back was unmistakable. His Conservatives won in every province except New Brunswick, giving him a seventy-seat majority in the House.

# 1878 — Tories sweep into power

*Victory for John A.'s N.P. He loses Kingston seat, is given one in B.C.*

While out of power from 1873 until 1878, Sir John A. was in great demand as a masterly attorney and solicitor. Again and again he spoke of leaving politics, but he was never quite able to make the break. Not for a moment did he cease to study and guide his politician confreres.

It was the "National Policy" of high protection for Canadian industries that carried Sir John A. and the Conservatives back into leadership. In the National Policy of protecting Canadian manufacturing with tariffs, many saw excellent prospects for the development of Canadian industry.

The idea of a national fiscal policy that would make Canadians masters of their economic affairs had been bruited about since 1870 but did not meet with acceptance and was dropped. Now American industrialists, well protected in their own markets, were cut-rating Canadian products, bringing on a crisis of depression. Macdonald's philosophy was anti-

*(continued)*

John A. had lost his seat in Kingston and was given a "safe" seat in Victoria, B.C. — starting what would almost become a tradition for Canadian Prime Ministers.

Another pictorial reference to Kingston rejecting John A. and Victoria picking him up. Party leaders often lose their seats even though their party is returned to power because — it is alleged — they are so busy campaigning across the country that they haven't the time to campaign adequately in their own constituencies.

---

### Unrestricted Reciprocity

Free trade with the USA, advocated by the Liberals, especially Cartwright in 1887, and a chief plank in their platform of 1891.

---

Sir John A. was often quoted as saying, "Give me better wood and I will make a better Cabinet."

---

# New Governor-General welcomed by Sir John A. and poet James Gay

Yankee: "We will not be trampled upon and ridden over, as we have been in the past, by the capitalists of a foreign country." His expression "A fair day's wage for a fair day's work" became widespread and popular. In Britain, however, Canada's protective tariff was in ill favour. British financiers were somewhat skeptical of investments in Canada.

### Governor-General Arriving — Sir John A. "Unwell"

Back in office in 1878, Sir John A. had not yet recovered his abstemious habits. There was some concern that he would not be able to do the honours when Lord Dufferin, the Governor-General, left on the expiration of his term of office. Would he be able to greet the new Governor-General the Marquis of Lorne, and his wife, the Princess Louise, a daughter of Queen Victoria?

According to a famous anecdote about him, Sir John A. was completely drunk, even when the Governor-General's ship was docking at Halifax. When an aide came in to tell the besotted Prime Minister that he had very little time to get himself ready for the reception, Sir John A. stood up — rather unsteadily — pointed his finger at the aide, and growled, "Vamoose from this ranch!"

---

### THE DIVORCE REVOKED

After a five-year separation, Miss Canada agrees to take John A. back — but she warns him that he must behave himself this time.

---

Sir John A. (replying to the Liberal M.P., Mr. Blake): "I quite agree with the Honourable Member that we should go through these notices of motion. There has not been an opportunity of working them out — of cleaning the stable as it were."

Mr. Blake: "I do not think the stable is on this side of the House."

Sir John A.: "Perhaps not. I am quite willing to admit on this side that we are a stable government."

At the very last moment Sir John A. pulled himself together, as he had so often done in the past, and very much the complete gentleman of the world, did all that was expected of him in the way of deference to the Queen's representatives.

The Marquis of Lorne and Princess Louise were also welcomed by James Gay — Canada's self-appointed Poet Laureate — in his poem for the occasion:

## Welcome to Our Dominion

*In Halifax are just arrived the Marquis and his wife,*
*Their passage was a stormy one, it almost cost their life.*
*Thanks be to the powers that rule both sea and land,*
*The happy pair are welcome both to our Canadian land.*
*When they arrive in Ottawa to inhabit their new home,*
*I hope they will feel as happy there as the one they left at home.*
*It's easy to leave one's native home with their handsome cot,*
*Still the land of your birth can never be forgot.*
*Our kind-hearted Queen will feel sad for a while*
*For the loss of her dear Louise, her sweet and loving child;*
*The kindest of mothers, of this we are sure:*
*Her children, though many, they all her adore.*
*They have left their dear homes, their hills, and their heather,*
*In Ottawa for a time will live happy together.*
*In our beloved Queen there is no selfish pride,*
*I hope she will often hear from her daughter and her husband by her side.*
*As they are both landed safe let us rejoice and sing,*
*In our dominion of Canada, long life to our Queen.*
*I hope our bonny Scotch will not be nigh-sighted,*
*As our Governor took his English wife we should be more united;*
*Leave off party feelings as it's not becoming man,*
*And live as brothers ought to live on our Canadian land;*
*Live together without malice or strife,*
*Like our Governor and his beloved wife.*

---

### The Yeahs and the Nays

When a Member of Parliament disagreed with him, Sir John A. said, "I have not the slightest objection to the Honourable Member retaining his opinion — if he will only give us his vote."

### A Measure Worth Weighting For

A Member of Parliament commented, "I see that J. A. Wilkinson draws a salary as Inspector of Weights and Measures, but when an election is going he spends his time on that."

Sir John A. quickly replied, "He is in favour of good measures."

"Only a Mohammed can come back to Mecca; only a Napoleon can return from Elba . . . and only a Macdonald could come back to Ottawa after what occurred in 1873."

### Who Was James Gay?

Like Sir John A., Gay was an immigrant. He was born in the village of Bratton, Devonshire, England, on March 24, 1810. In 1834, he emigrated to Canada and arrived in Guelph that summer. He published at least two books of poetry: *Canada's Poet* and *Poems by James Gay*.

He called himself "Poet Laureate of Canada"

**CANADA'S POET.**

— the title was not official. Gay dedicated his book *Canada's Poet* to Alfred, Lord Tennyson. He wrote the following letter to Tennyson; there is no record of what — or whether — Tennyson replied.

To Dr. C. L. Alfred Tennyson
Poet Laureate of England, Baron, &c., &c.

Dear Sir,

Now Longfellow is gone there are only two of us left. There ought to be no rivalry between us two.

"A poet's mind is clear and bright,
No room for hatred, malice or spite."

To my brother poet I affectionately dedicate these original verses, not before printed. Other verses from my pen, when so inspired, have been numerously printed in Canadian and American papers:

"Giving a few outlines of my fellow-man,
As nigh as I can see or understand."

Almost the first poetry I can remember is the beautiful line —

"Satan finds some mischief
still for idle hands to do;"

and similar sentiments likewise occur in my own poems —

"Up, up with your flag, let it
wave where it will: A natural
born poet his mind can't keep still."

I do not know whether a Baron or a Poet Laureate gets any wages in England. In Canada there is no pay.

"Ambition is a great thing, of this I must say;
This has been proved by the poet James Gay;
He feels like Lord Beaconsfield,
and best left alone;
Respects every man and yet cares for none."

It is a solemn thing to reflect that I am the link connecting two great countries.

I hope when I am gone another may raise up.

I believe you have one boy, dear Sir, and I read in the papers the other day as he had been play-acting somewheres. I once exhibited a two-headed colt myself at several fairs, ten cents admission, and know something about play-acting and the like.

DON'T YOU LET HIM.

I hope to be in England sometime during the present year, if spared, and shall not fail to call round, if not too far from my lodging for a man nigh upon seventy-four, which, dear Sir, is the age of

Yours alway,
James Gay
(this day)

Poet Laureate of Canda,
and Master of all Poets.
Royal City of Guelph, Ontario.

ONE SHILLING]

RB

*Canada's :: Poet*

*yours alway*
*James Gay*

*"Poet Laureate of Canada & Master of All Poets this day."*

*Then you can Publish These Poems and send Them Through England And no mistake you will Find they will sell like Hot cakes.*

No description could possibly explain the uniqueness of self-appointed poet laureate James Gay's talent. Only a reading of his poetry can give a clue. An additional example will be found in "Liquor common as water," the section of this book on nineteenth-century Canada's drinking habits.

# A MASTER POLITICIAN

PAC

## Get to know a crowd, Court the ambivalent, "Burn this letter"

Long before the term "public relations" came into our conversations, Sir John A., albeit unconsciously, had shown himself to be a master of this art. Many stories have been told of the great impression the Chief made during his campaigns of the eighties. He would visit a schoolhouse in the rural areas, be introduced to twenty or thirty farmers and chat with them for half an hour. Then he would call each one by name as he shook hands before continuing on to the next meeting. Not one of these farmers could ever do enough for Sir John A. thereafter. They never forgot that they had shaken hands with the Prime Minister.

In his biography of Sir John A., W. Stewart Wallace writes: "In his genius for remembering people, and in attaching them to him, Sir John had greatly the advantage of the Liberal leaders. Alexander Mackenzie, the Prime Minister, was a man of the strictest integrity and sense of duty; but he had in his makeup a strong admixture of that 'dourness' which is one of the characteristics of the Lowland Scot. The story is told that, in the seventies, a Canadian journalist who had at one time been a parliamentary correspondent, but who had been for a number of years in the United States, returned to Ottawa on a visit. He went up to the Parliament Buildings, and one of the first persons he encountered was Mackenzie. Going up to him, he held out his hand, and said: 'How do you do, Mr. Mackenzie? I wonder if you remember me'

"Mackenzie looked at him with a cold eye, and replied, 'No, I do not. And let me tell you this, young man: I'm too old to be taken in by any confidence tricks.'

"A few minutes later the expatriated journalist ran into Macdonald. Rather abashed by the rebuff which he had received from Mackenzie, he was diffident about calling himself to the recollection of Macdonald, but the latter caught sight of him out of the corner of his eye, and, recognizing a familiar face, immediately came over and shook hands with him, saying at the same time, 'Now don't tell me your name. I'll have it in a minute. Smith —John Smith—of the *Detroit Free Press*. How are you, John? I'm glad to see you again.'"

Sir John A. had an intuitive understanding of people — individuals and crowds. Once while travelling down the Saint John River from Fredericton to Saint John his steamer stopped at sev-

THE AID OF A GLASS!
"Ah! you're right, Sir John; looking through *this* medium I do see factory chimneys in every town and village in the country."
*(John A. was good at making people see things his way!)*

eral towns where crowds had gathered to see the Prime Minister. Before the first stop, a companion asked Sir John A. if he planned to make a speech. "I can't tell until I see the crowd," the Prime Minister answered. As the

steamer came into the wharf, Sir John A. studied the crowd. "I am going to make a speech," he decided. He delivered a short and witty speech which was very well received.

As the steamer approached the next town, Sir John A. was asked if he planned to speak there also. Again he replied that he would have to see the crowd first. When the boat was made fast, Sir John A. announced, "I'm going ashore." He immediately went onto the wharf where he chatted with small groups of people, kissed babies, knelt down and told jokes to children and shook hands with as many people as could reach him. When the steamer was on her way again, Sir John A.'s companion asked, "Why did you speak to the first crowd, and go ashore here?" "Why," said Sir John, "they were mostly men at the first stop, and mostly women and children here."

### Notes and Votes

Tirelessly, Sir John A. kept in touch with everybody. He was the first to send out little notes, handwritten of course, of congratulations, encouragement, praise or friendly advice, often humourous in tone. To the receiver — a newly appointed clerk, deputy, toll or hotel keeper — the note had great importance and, as Sir John A. knew, would influence the elections.

---

### It's All Greek to Him

When Lord Dufferin, then Governor-General of Canada, delivered an address in Greek at McGill University, Sir John A. told the newspaper reporters that His Lordship had spoken in the purest ancient Greek, without a single mistake in pronunciation. Overhearing the comment, Sir Hector Langevin said to John A., "I wasn't aware you knew so much about Greek." "I don't," said Sir John A. "But I know a little about politics."

PAC

UNITED AND HARMONIOUS!
How Sir John A. was accused of arousing "spontaneous" enthusiasm in his Party.

Politicians like George Brown, statesman and editor of *The Globe,* were austere, domineering and autocratic. But Sir John A. was witty and kind to friend and opponent alike. He never held a grudge. He had a way of walking up to a stranger and saying, "How do you do? I'm glad to see you here. Shake hands. I'm John A."

A pragmatist, Sir John A. used to keep long lists of voters. He spoke jokingly of these lists, but he knew how important they were. The blue-pencilled men were dependable supporters; the red-ticked were determined opponents. The ones he spent the most time courting and flattering were those of the third group — the ambivalent voters.

Sir John A. was able to disagree charmingly and had learned early that a politician has no room in his makeup for revenge. He was warm and cordial to Members of the Opposition. An often repeated anecdote tells of the time that Liberal David Thompson returned to the House after being absent for a whole session due to illness. Members of his own Party greeted him coolly or ignored him completely. Then Sir John A. came along, grasped Thompson's hand warmly and said, "Davy, old man, I'm glad to see you back. Hope you'll be well again soon and live many a long day to vote against me — as you always have done!"

Sir John A. loved his people, and most of them loved him in spite of his weaknesses. In *Canadian Magazine* W. F. Maclean wrote: "Sir John had a wonderful influence over many men. They would go through fire and water to serve him, did serve him, and got some of them little or no reward. But they served him because they loved him, and because with all his great powers they saw in him their own frailties. He abounded in the right kind of charity. And speaking of the love his old friends and followers had for him, Mr Pope dwells on the 'old guard' and the old loyalty to the chief. So it was, but there were dark days also, when even those who afterwards enrolled themselves in the guard passed by on the other side.... But Sir John's real 'old guard' were not the men who stood with

PAC

**THE CAUSE OF THE CHAPLEAU-LANGEVIN FIGHT.**

In this cartoon Sir John A. was blamed for encouraging the feud between Chapleau and Langevin as a political manoeuvre.

him at Ottawa, but the greater old guard who stood and fought for him in every township year after year, and to whom a call by name or a nod of the head was all the recompense they got and yet the recompense they most prized."

The "wheels within wheels" of politics are revealed in these letters which Sir John A. wrote to Isaac Buchanan, who sat in the Legislative Assembly of Canada from 1841 until 1844 for Toronto and was returned in 1857 and 1861 for Hamilton. These communications are evidence of the way that Sir John A. kept in close touch with his colleagues.

Quebec June 6, 1861
*Confidential*
My dear Buchanan,

I really *do* hope and trust you will not work up the Municipality matter as a test question at the polls. It will defeat me — defeat all your friends and do the Municipalities no good. Come in as strong as you can and do carry the question if you can, but do not ask us to lose *every constituency* in Lower Canada by a premature and useless inquiry of the question.

I ask it of your friendship to come out and to avoid the question. I think I have a claim on you after last session. You may of course state to the Hamiltonians that you ask for re-election for *the purpose* of carrying the question if you can.

Remember the Southern Road and the delicate handling it requires.

In great haste,
Faithfully yours,
John A. Macdonald

Quebec Oct. 16, 1864
*Confidential*
My dear Buchanan,

We are very busily engaged in conference and things go on satisfactorily but slowly...many interests and prejudices.... My great aim is to approach as nearly to a Legislative Union as is practicable.... I fear that our discussions may be so protracted as to force them...to abandon the idea of going Westward.... All our interests are Northern and must continue to be so. We can't help the South.... Sir Etienne Taché is the chairman of our conference... he will, I fancy, be unable to take up Militia matters till the Conference adjourns. Then he will doubtless take up the case of your battalion. I am quite sure that he will endeavour to carry out your views as much as possible. He is a very intelligent man and can understand.... I think we will be able in the United Parliament (if we have one) to secure a sufficiently protective tariff....

Believe me, I am,
My dear Buchanan,
John A. Macdonald

**Cloak and Dagger Politics**

Sir John A. was a master of maneuvering and manipulating — and probably enjoyed it! In 1871 he wrote to a colleague: "I want you to make arrangements with the friendly newspapers...to hold back, if possible, any expression of opinion on the treaty when it is promulgated, until *The Globe* commits itself against the treaty. I want to endeavour so to manage it, as to let *The Globe* write under the impression that I have assented to the treaty. Brown will then pitch into the treaty and into me for sacrificing the interests of Canada. He will afterwards find out, when it is too late, that he is on the same side as myself, and will not be able to retract. My chief object in doing this is that, if Brown finds that I am opposed to the treaty, he will try to find reasons for supporting it. He may take up the loyalty cry, and state that it is the bounden duty of Canada to sacrifice something for the sake of insuring peace to the Empire. This course would give him a strong influential position with the Home Government, which might react prejudicially on our Party. The French might, if they found that the Grits were strong in England, continue the coquetting is, therefore, of very considerable consequence that Brown and *The Globe* should be committed irretrievably against the treaty.... I need not say that this is for yourself alone, except in so far, of course, as it may be necessary to get our colleagues to deal with the newspapers influenced by them.... I think you had better not discuss the matter at all with our Quebec colleagues."

A letter written in 1884 ends with "Burn this letter when read. You need not say to L. that I have written you."

John A.'s speeches were usually short, witty and effective.

# "The P.M. is the image of Dizzy" Same wit, grace, audacity

## Resemblance between John A. and Disraeli intrigues British

PAC

In 1879, when he was sixty-four, Sir John A. was sworn to the Privy Council in England. *The Illustrated London News* of August 23, 1879, gives this account:

"The Queen held a Council on Thursday week, at which were present the Duke of Richmond and Gordon, the Lord Chancellor, the Duke of Northumberland, and the Right Hon. R. A. Cross. Sir John Macdonald, Prime Minister of Canada, was introduced and sworn in as a member of the Privy Council. Previously to the Council the Minister to the United States of America was introduced, and presented his letters of recall. The Minister for Siam, his Excellency Phya Bhaskaawonge, was then introduced, and presented his credentials, and H. R. H. Prisidang Choomsui of Siam, Chan Sarabhay, and Nai Tuan Surawongse were presented to Her Majesty. The Hon. Edmund John Monson was also introduced and kissed

---

### A Close Shave for Sir John A.

An apprentice barber in Toronto held Sir John A.'s nose in order to scrape his upper lip. Sir John A. quipped, "You're the only one who can lead me by the nose and you have your hands full."

---

hands on his appointment as Minister Resident at Montevideo. Princess Beatrice was present with her Majesty during the audiences. The Duke of Richmond and Gordon, the Lord Chancellor, the Right Hon. R. A. Cross and the Right Hon. Sir John Macdonald had audiences of the Queen. At the Council Parliament was prorogued from the 15th inst. to Nov. 1 and the Convocations of the Provinces of Canterbury and York were prorogued to Nov. 3."

Sir John A. always felt in his element on British soil. Like Lady Macdonald, he enjoyed the sophisticated circles of good company and good talk, the concerts and theatres.

### The Disraeli of Canada

It was inevitable that Sir John A. should be measured against Disraeli, Lord Beaconsfield, the British Prime Minister. In 1879 the *London World* said, "The amazing similarity in appearance between the two prime ministers, Sir John A. Macdonald, of Canada, and Disraeli, Lord Beaconsfield, of England, caused much comment on both sides of the Atlantic. Sir John A. Macdonald, the Canadian Prime Minister, is likely to create a good deal of sensation, for reasons

### Hiving the Grits

Sir John A.'s phrase, April 1882, to describe redistribution of Ontario seats and an alteration of boundaries to the disadvantage of the Liberals (called "gerrymandering" in the United States). "The Grits complain that they are all hived together," he joked. "It seems that they do not like the association. They do not like each other's company. They like to associate with Conservative gentlemen."

SIR JOHN A. MACDONALD

other than those connected with his mission. If Sir John, having observed our Premier's dress, were to possess himself of a costume of the same make, and were to walk into the House of Lords, none would think of stopping him.

"Consciously or unconsciously, Sir John assists nature with a few touches of art. He wears his hair precisely as Lord Beaconsfield wears his, or rather as the Premier wore his when he was eight years younger. His face is closely shaven, and the whole shape, colour and expression are phenomenally like Lord Beaconsfield. Nor is the similitude confined to physical features. Sir John Macdonald has many of the social and political qualities of Lord Beaconsfield. He is witty and graceful in conversation, epigrammatic in Parliament and audacious in politics."

### "The Image of Dizzy"

Five years before, Lady Dufferin had written in *My Canadian Journal:* "The P.M. is the image of Dizzy." When Sir John A. received his honourary degree at Oxford the students shouted out, "Dizzy, Dizzy!"

In *Reminiscences Political and Personal* Nicholas Flood Davin compares the two leaders as politicians: "Sir John A. Macdonald is a

BENJAMIN DISRAELI, LORD BEACONSFIELD

PAC

type of politician which has never failed to delight the English people — the man who, like Palmerston, can work hard, do strong things, hold his purpose, never lose sight for a moment of the honour and welfare of his country, and yet crack his joke and have his laugh, full of courage and good spirits and kindly fun.... Sir John Macdonald in the English House of Commons would have been equal in my opinion, to Mr. Disraeli in finesse in the art of forming combinations and managing men. He could never have equalled him in invective, or in epigram, or in force as an orator. Sir John Macdonald brings up his artillery with more ease. He is always human, even in his attacks. Lord Beaconsfield, as Mr. Disraeli, in the House of Commons, approached his opponent like some serpentine monster, coiled himself ruthlessly round him, fascinated with his gaze and struck out with venomed fang. But Sir John is probably the better debater of the two.... Lord Beaconsfield has the charm which is inseparable from genius but it may well be doubted if his power of conciliating men and fixing their affections surpasses that of the Prime Minister of the Dominion. I am sure that in sober strong sense the balance is in favour of the Canadian statesman. There is nothing viewy about Sir John Macdonald. Though a man of imagination, reason is lord every time."

When Sir John A. visited Britain after Disraeli's death, he created quite a stir at a reception where a woman fainted, thinking he was Disraeli restored to life.

Sir John A.'s strong and craggy appearance never went unnoticed. Another remarkable likeness existed between him and the Ojibway Indian Chief John Prince, or Ah-yan-dwa-wah (The Thunderbolt), from Manitoba, who visited Ottawa in 1889 to protest against the depletion of Lake Winnipeg by American fishermen. Biggar writes, "In Toronto, many not personally acquainted with the P. M. mistook the Chief for Sir John A. Macdonald. Ah-yan-dwa-wah was six feet tall and arrow straight. Like the P. M. he had bushy gray hair, a strongly outlined nose, a pursed-up mouth and eyes that twinkled shrewdly. In addition he wagged his head, and walked very much like John A., who was commonly called 'the old chief' or the 'chieftain.' Mr. Robertson, of the *Toronto* (continued)

(continued)

### You Must Bee Fair

At the formal opening of the Toronto Industrial Exhibition in 1886, Sir John A. listened attentively to an explanation of the apiary department: how the foundation was made from wax, with the bases of the cells implanted; how this labour was saved the bees, enabling them to spend more time gathering honey. Sir John A. admonished the president of the fair, "You promised us that nothing immoral would be permitted at this fair."

"That is so," answered the president.

"Well," said Sir John A., "you permit an exhibition of stolen property; the receivers are allowed to aid and abet the thieves; and you show a systematically arranged plan of defrauding the little thief out of his hard-earned labours."

# Old Chieftain given Indian name — "Our Brother-in-Law"

*Telegram,* asked the Ojibway chief how he was related to Sir John A. and was answered, 'I suppose he is my brother.' Asked if he might win the affections of Lady Macdonald, the old chief replied, 'No, I have too much respect for my sister-in-law.' "

Sir John A., who as Prime Minister was Superintendent-General of Indian Affairs, was given an Indian name by Crowfoot, Chief of the Blackfoot Indians. He called Sir John A. "Kis-ta-mo-ni-mon" — or "Our Brother-in-Law."

### "Old Tomorrow"

As controller of the North West Mounted Police, Sir John A. kept postponing appointments with men who wished to discuss police affairs and the half-breed rebellion by saying, "Come back tomorrow." This inspired Chief Crowfoot and Chief Poundmaker to give Sir John A. another Indian name — "Ap-e-naq-wis" meaning "Old Tomorrow." Sir John A.

took it all good-naturedly. At one time there was talk that he would be elevated to the peerage, an honour that did not come to him. When a friend asked what title he would take, he replied with a grin, "Lord Tomorrow."

Once, when one of his ministers tried to resign, Sir John A. said, "You would do me a great favour by holding your resignation until Wednesday." The Minister agreed. A colleague later asked Sir John A., "Why Wednesday?"

"Because," the Prime Minister replied, "it is not today."

---

Sir John A. often repeated the story about the Conservative farmer's wife who solemnly affirmed that her hens laid more eggs, larger eggs, fresher eggs and more to the dozen after the Conservative administration was voted in.

---

*The traitor's hand is at thy throat,*
*Ontario! Ontario!*
*Then kill the tyrant with thy vote,*
*Ontario! Ontario!*
A Liberal Party song by John W. Bengough, the famous cartoonist, to the tune of "Maryland, My Maryland," sung in the 1882 election. Edward Blake said the song would cost him the Quebec vote as it referred to French Canadians.

### Embarrassing Moments

At a social gathering in Washington, Sir John A. fell into conversation with a senator's wife. When he told her that he was from Canada she said, "You've got a very smart man over there, John A. Macdonald."

"Yes, ma'am, he is."

"But they say he is a regular rascal."

"Yes ma'am, a perfect rascal."

"But why do they keep such a man in power?"

"Well, you see, they can't get along without him."

Just then the Senator arrived and said to his wife, "My dear, let me introduce the Honourable John A. Macdonald."

John A. immediately put the lady at her ease by saying, "Now, don't apologize. All that you have been saying is perfectly true, and it is well known at home."

---

George M. Grant, principal of Queen's University, said in 1884: "The idolatry of the heathen is not greater than the idolatry of party politics today."

---

Sir John A. on Cabinet ministers: "If I had my way they should all be highly respectable parties whom I could send to the penitentiary if I liked."

*PAC*

The House in session, Prime Minister Macdonald standing to the Governor-General's right.

# CROWFOOT, THE CHIEF OF THE BLACKFEET

Blackfoot Chief Crowfoot gave John A. the Indian name "Ap-e-naq-wis" — "Old Tomorrow." When the CPR was built through Blackfoot lands, Chief Crowfoot persuaded his people not to oppose the railroad. Van Horne gave Crowfoot a lifetime pass on the railroad, as a reward for his peace-keeping efforts. This picture of the Chief and his family appeared in the *Illustrated War News* at the time of the Riel Rebellion. Although his son urged him to join Riel, Crowfoot took no part in the fighting.

*PAC*

The austerely self-righteous and humourless George Brown had opposed efforts of his printers to form a union at *The Globe*. In March 1880 an employee — who had been dismissed, allegedly for drunkenness — broke into his office and shot him. He never recovered from the wound, dying about six weeks later.

# John A. loses his greatest enemy

*George Brown shot by an employee; he dies six weeks later*

George Brown drawn as St. George slaying the dragon of slander: in 1874 he won a legal decision against a Conservative paper that had libeled him.

*CIN*

The funeral of George Brown was one of the largest ever to take place in Toronto. The procession is shown gathering at his residence. Newspapers ran columns of tributes to his journalistic and political achievements and included excerpts from sermons on his moral rectitude, which were delivered throughout the city.

In March 1880, Sir John A. was shocked to hear that Brown had been wounded by a would-be assassin, a printer who had been dismissed from *The Globe* for drunkenness. Brown died about six weeks later. Wallace describes Brown and contrasts his personality with John A.'s: "George Brown is one of the most amazing figures in Canadian history. A man of magnificent stature (he stood six feet four in his stockinged feet), he began to make his mark almost immediately after he came to Canada in 1843. He was one of the greatest journalists Canada has ever known; and he built up for his paper, *The Globe,* a position such as has never been occupied by any other Canadian newspaper. For many years *The Globe* was familiarly known as 'the Scotchman's Bible'.... He was intensely ambitious, without a trace of humour, and full of moral fervour. On the platform, the full tide of his vehement rhetoric carried all before it; and few men cared to brave the avalanche of his invective.

"Between John A. Macdonald and George Brown there was a striking contrast. Though both were Scots, Macdonald's antecedents were Highland and Jacobite, whereas Brown's were Lowland and Cameronian. Macdonald made no such pretensions to moral superiority as Brown did; but his actions were more in accord with his professions than Brown's always were. It is perhaps too much to say that George Brown was a hypocrite; but he had the happy faculty of convincing himself that he was always right, no matter what course his ambition led him to adopt."

No two men could have been more dissimilar in manner, thought or character than Sir John A. and George Brown. They made it a point never to be together and never to speak to one another. Their differences were to a degree set aside during the framing of the coalition government and the Confederation, which caused them to spend many hours together at home, on the boat taking them to England and in London. It is even reported that they attented a performance of the opera *Lucretia Borgia* together in London in 1865. Yet the minute their political duties allowed, they ignored one another. *The Life and Speeches of Hon. George Brown* written in 1881 by his friend Alexander Mackenzie (Prime Minister of Canada 1873-1878) says: "When he [Brown] left the coalition government he resumed his former relations of non-intercourse with Mr. John A. Macdonald, though doubtless prepared at any time to accept in its right spirit any expression of regret for so unjustifiable an accusation as had been made. That expression never was uttered. It is known that Mr. Macdonald promised when the coalition government was formed to make a public retraction of the false charges he had brought against Mr. Brown.... This promise he failed to fulfill, thereby lowering his own position and justifying Mr. Brown in refusing any social recognition of him."

*The Globe* attacked Macdonald violently and often — for his politics, for his policies, for his drunkenness. In a fairly typical editorial *The Globe* once wrote: "Mr. Macdonald is a kind of political ogre who demands a virgin reputation every year at least, to satisfy his needs, and casts aside his victim when every shred of popularity and character has disappeared."

After Brown's death, his widow, Anne, returned to Edinburgh. Some years later she was vacationing in Oban, a resort town on the west coast of Scotland, when (according to Careless's biography of Brown) the widow of another noted Canadian appeared — Baroness Macdonald. The two old ladies stared stiffly ahead and ignored each other as their carriages passed.

GEORGE BROWN 1818-1880      *PAC*

Brown, owner and editor of *The Globe,* helped to found the Liberal Party and was one of the Big Seven Fathers of Confederation. He and Macdonald were a study in contrasts; the only thing they agreed on was Confederation. Their feud went back to 1851, when John A. had accused Brown — whose political ambitions were showing — of improper political manoeuvering and refused to apologize. Few individuals ever dared cross Brown, but Macdonald seemed to welcome the fight and — except for their alliance in the Great Coalition and during the Confederation Conferences — Brown was the frequent butt of Macdonald jokes, while John A. was vilified with regularity in *The Globe.*

# Ottawa from 1867 to 1891 The Macdonalds' Home

## Stadacona Hall and Earnscliffe
### Two lovely houses still stand

From 1877 until 1883 Sir John A. and Lady Macdonald lived in Stadacona Hall, in Sandy Hill, Ottawa. In 1883 they moved to Earnscliffe.

Stadacona Hall was built in 1871 for John A. Cameron, a successful lumber merchant with a penchant for gracious living and the means to indulge his fancies. The next resident, Mrs. Joseph-Edouard Cauchon, named it Stadacona Hall. Stadacona was the Indian name for Quebec, and the Macdonalds were happy to retain it as the name of their home.

Architects and historians compare this stone structure with the finest of the vintage homes across Canada, delighting in the woodwork, cornices, fireplaces and pillars as well as the ornamental plasterwork. A wide staircase, which has an unusual "nested" newel cage or post at the bottom, fretwork design on the stringer and a polished hardwood handrail, takes one from the main hall up to the square centre hall on the second floor.

The present dining room and kitchen were once occupied as offices by Sir John A. and his private secretary, Sir Joseph Pope (who later became Under-Secretary of State for Canada, from 1896 until 1909, and Under-Secretary for External Affairs, 1909-1926).

Sandy Hill residents used to stroll by the house, hoping for a glimpse of the peacocks strutting on the lawn, or of Lady Macdonald walking in the grounds and sometimes working in the garden.

Earnscliffe, the stately grey stone residence on the south bank of the Ottawa River, has been described as a "heavenly house with a lot of character, rather like a rambling nineteenth century English vicarage." Perhaps that was why the Macdonalds, with their love of England's fine homes, were so pleased with it.

### Sir John A. Names House

The house was built between 1855 and 1857 by John MacKinnon. Its most famous tenant — Sir John A. — was the one who named it.

"Eaglescliffe" was first suggested, but the Prime Minister preferred the old English word "earn" for eagle and adopted that name.

Sir John A. bought the property in 1883 for $10,040.00 and lived in it until his death in 1891, devising structural changes, enlarging the grounds and building the stables. Earnscliffe was Lady Macdonald's pride and joy.

After Sir John A.'s death, Lady Macdonald moved out, leasing the residence to three generals in succession before selling it for $15,000.00 to Mrs. Ella B. Harriss in 1900. Mrs. Harriss and her husband, Dr. Charles Harriss, a distinguished musician, lived their lives out there.

The beautiful historic home with its lofty foyer and spacious rooms has since become the residence of British High Commissioners in Canada, maintaining the Macdonalds' close connection with the Mother Country. A bust of Sir John A. stands in an alcove in the vestibule. Items dating from his occupancy can be seen in other rooms.

*(continued)*

Stadacona Hall in Sandy Hill, Ottawa. The Macdonalds moved into this house in 1877, from "Quadrilateral" where they had lived since their marriage in 1867.                PAC

Earnscliffe as it looked before the Macdonalds moved in. It had been built between 1855 and 1857 and was bought and named by Sir John A. in 1883. Lady Macdonald kept her own chickens ("so that John can have fresh eggs every day") and even a cow. *PAC*

A favourite corner of Sir John A.'s — the terrace at Earnscliffe overlooking the Ottawa River. The wheelchair is Mary's. This photograph was first published in *The Dominion Illustrated News* at the time of Macdonald's death. *PAC*

# New capital given nickname: Westminster in the Wilderness

Ottawa's Parliament Buildings seen from Major's Hill across the river — an engraving published in 1882. These buildings were destroyed by fire in 1916. It took twelve years to rebuild them.

### Ottawa

*(From our Special Comical, Cynical Correspondent)*

Ottawa is composed of the Parliament Buildings and the Russell House.

In the daytime the Government employes spend their time in the former place, and the greater part of the night in the latter.

The most interesting part of Ottawa is that burnt down.

The people are very peculiar, and, as a result, many of the customs of the place are peculiar. For instance, if you want a coal-oil lamp, you must go to a drug store, or should your watch need repairing it must be taken to a tinsmith's.

It is very similar to Montreal, in the respect that every one knows more about his neighbour's business than he does of his own.

Whenever a fire takes place, you may rest assured that somebody has a large note soon falling due in one of the banks.

There is so much water surrounding the city that the people drink very little of it. Water, they consider, and very rightly too, should be devoted to manufacturing purposes.

Owing to the active existence of several Temperance Societies, which are considered competent to throw any quantity of cold water on things, there are no tanks or hydrants in the city. The water is brought to the fire-engines in barrels or tubs placed on carts.

The steady progress of Ottawa may be instanced by the fact that the richest men in the city have returned their incomes as reaching the extraordinary figure of $800 per annum. Accordingly, there is great difficulty in telling what a poor man lives on.

The principal amusement of the people at present seems to be that of publishing newspapers. There will be no less than four new ones appear on the same day at an early date.

There are few tavern-keepers who have soda water in the morning, thus proving that very little else can be drunk the night before, or perhaps the people stay up to an early hour to drink it.

So great sticklers are the people for the liberty of the subject, that the idea of confining even the brute creation will not for a moment be tolerated. They are therefore allowed to roam at large. If you find a cow in possession of the sidewalk in the main street, you must go round the beast. It is easily done.

The City Hall is a building not to be equalled by any in Montreal. As an instance of economy of municipal funds, it is highly creditable to the people. It is a small clap-board building, surrounded by a gallery. The side nearest the city is painted white. As nobody ever sees the other sides, it would be a waste to paint them.

From *Grinchuckle*, December 30, 1869

The Parliament Buildings in Ottawa (right above) at the time Sir John A. occupied the office of Prime Minister. The engraving shows the post office with Dufferin and Rapper's bridges.

CIN

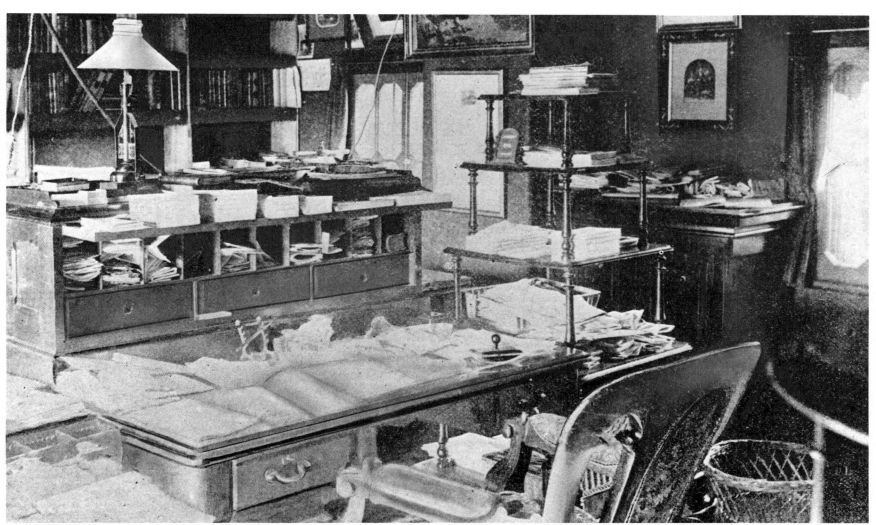

Sir John A.'s study at Earnscliffe. The photograph — showing his vacant chair — was published at the time of his death. It was one of the first half-tone photographs to appear in a Canadian newspaper.

RB

# Years bring new cares, new honours

## "If John A.'s stomach holds out, the Opposition will stay out"

Critical illnesses bothered Sir John A. He was greatly distressed by stomach trouble and agonizing gallstone attacks. When he spoke of retiring, Sir Charles Tupper answered, "Nonsense, you will bury most of us yet."

### Sir John A.'s Day

The Prime Minister was temperate in diet. Although 5 feet 11 inches tall, he never weighed more than 190 pounds. He rose at eight a.m. and after a cup of tea or coffee worked until eleven a.m. Then came breakfast, generally with visitors, workers and political associates. He had a light dinner at six or seven and a small snack at ten or eleven. He slept only five or six hours.

He wrote to his brother-in-law Professor Williamson: "I saw in the Scientific American... a cure for corns. As I am troubled with these things, I shall be obliged by your copying it out for me." And again, "Pardon me for stealing your hat. I owe you a new one. Get one from Clark Wright or anywhere else and charge it to me. Kindly send me the Bismuth prescription." The prescription was sent from Kingston: "Stomach powder — 1 oz. rhubarb, 1 oz. bicarbonate of soda, ½ oz. bismuth. Take as much as would lie on a sixpence, one-quarter hour before food."

Behind Sir John A., if not forgotten, were the shattering party upsets of 1872. In addition to the constant duties of his leadership, ahead were three more cruel election contests — 1881, 1886 and 1891. He was to endure many more shocks and vicissitudes. His colleagues thought him indestructible, and he pushed himself mercilessly, demanding the impossible of his overworked, feeble frame. A cry began to be heard

### Millions for Corruption, but not a Cent for Nova Scotia

Nova Scotia Liberal Party anti-Confederation slogan, 1886.

British Columbia, unhappy about how slowly the promised transcontinental railway is being built, threatens to leave the Dominion. John A. is supplicating her to stay.

**Toronto Yacht Club.**

TORONTO, 11th June, 1888.

DEAR SIR,

I beg to advise you that acting under instructions issued by the Committee, the names of those in arrear will be *posted in the Club Room* on Saturday, 23rd instant.

You are indebted to the Club to the amount of $ 5 — (as per memo. below) which kindly remit before 23rd instant to Mr. Jeffery Foot, the Assistant Secy.-Treas., who will be found at the Club-House between 10 a.m. and 6 p.m.

Yours truly,

W. H. PARSONS,
*Hon. Sec.-Treas.*

MEMO.

Subscription, . . . . . $ 5 —
Yacht Locker, —
Dressing Room Locker,
Smoking " "
Boat Rack,

Total . $ 5 —

No man is a hero to his yacht club accountant. Even the grand old man of Canadian politics could be threatened with the ignominy of his name being posted in the club room for not paying his dues on time.

that grew into a legend: "You'll never die, John A.!" Perhaps he came to believe it himself. Why had he not resigned and gone into private life? Was he never to have the well-earned rest for which his weary body cried out? Appropriately, one of Sir John A.'s favourite hymns was "Rest."

*My feet are wearied and my hands are tired,*
*My soul oppressed*
*And I desire, what I have long desired*
*Rest — only rest.*
*The burden of my days is hard to bear,*
*But God knows best;*
*And I have prayed*
*but vain has been my prayer*
*For rest — sweet rest.*
*'Tis hard to plant in spring and never reap*
*The autumn yield;*
*'Tis hard to till and when 'tis tilled to weep*
*O'er fruitless Field.*
*And so I cry a weak and human cry*
*So heart-oppressed:*
*And so I sigh a weak and human sigh,*
*For rest — for rest.*

Stretching ahead were looming clouds of worry — the financial difficulties of the Canadian Pacific Railway, the Riel Insurrection, the problems of the North West Territories, the Reciprocity Treaty affair, the Jesuit Controversy, the Rebellion of the Provinces, the Trade and Fisheries Treaty. Perhaps he should have left office in 1881, for he was then at his zenith.

Lady Macdonald, with heroic spirit and understanding sympathy, did all she could to keep their homelife — what there was of it — relaxed and serene. But they fretted about their daughter constantly. The prognosis of her condition was discouraging.

Honours came to Sir John A. copiously — both at home and abroad. In England Mr. Gladstone created him a member of the "Grand Cross of the Bath," with the investiture taking place with great pomp at Windsor Castle.

In Toronto on December 18, 1884, there was a demonstration honouring him for his forty years of service in Parliament. The *Toronto Mail* reported his speech: "This is not only a great and glorious incident, but... a very solemn one. I look back through my forty

## A Slippery Customer

As honourary patron of the Oshkosh Toboggan Club of Ottawa, Sir John A. was asked to open the new slide. Before the old chieftain seated himself on a toboggan to shoot down the slide at thirty miles an hour across the frozen Rideau River, he said, "Some might wonder why I am here, as I am evidently going downhill fast enough. My opponents, however, would consider it appropriate enough, because they have always considered me a slippery customer."

years of public life.... I bear in mind how few remain of those who with me entered full of hope, life, and the earnestness of youth.... I come back to you nearly as good as new.... I was much amused, when in England, to read, 'If John A.'s stomach holds out, then we [the Opposition] will stay out.' (continued laughter) You will be glad to know that there are strong indications that they will stay out." (Hear, hear!)

In 1886 Sir John A. went to England again, to receive a degree from Cambridge University. He spent some time in London and enjoyed himself thoroughly. Throwing off parliamentary pressures, he accepted invitations to dinner parties, concerts and theatre performances. To usher in the new year, he went to see *Aladdin*, the annual pantomime at the Drury Lane Theatre. *The Illustrated London News* of January 2, 1886, gave the pantomime rave reviews: "Costliness, magnificence, and daring in spectacular arrangement are the distinguishing features of the Drury-Lane stage 'annual.' . . . The properties are more elaborate than have ever been seen on the holiday stage before; the dresses, in their richness of colour and design, would astonish an Eastern potentate; procession follows procession, each more dazzling than the last; the eye is almost fatigued with the contemplation of all the splendour."

In Britain and in the United States, as well as in the Dominion, friend and opponent alike admitted that it was the faith of Sir John A. that built the Canadian Pacific Railway. He said, "Canada's teeming millions will remember it was the Conservative Party that gave this country its great railroad." He continued unconquerable at the polls. However, his stamina was gone. Ever increasing physical distress and frequent periods when he was confined to his bed made him doubt whether he would ever ride on the now completed railway. The first transcontinental train left Montreal for the Pacific on June 28, 1886, without the Prime Minister aboard.

### "Darned Old Fellow"

The Prime Minister enjoyed his birthdays — he liked getting cards and letters of congratulations. He wrote this prompt thank-you letter to a friend, Minnie Macdonnell, the day after his seventy-third birthday:

My dear Minnie,

Many thanks for your kind congratulations on my birthday. Ain't I getting to be a darned old fellow.... Thank you very much for the handsome pair of socks you sent me. I shall wear them with great pride.

Always my dear Minnie,
Sincerely yours,
John A. Macdonald

On his seventy-fourth birthday, Sir John A., as ever bowed down with duties and cares, wrote to his brother-in-law, Professor Williamson, that he was "in fairly good health for my age, but I cannot expect to last very long as my work increases faster than my years."

There was talk of his being raised to the

*(continued)*

The House of Commons in session, 1879.      *PAC*

A thirty-three pound bill for a one week stay in the Westminster Palace Hotel in London, 1880. An interesting feature of the bill is that it lists each kind of liquor individually. John A.'s taste seemed to run to champagne, chablis, sherry and brandy.

### Rare 'un to Go

Once while riding to Markham Township Fair, Sir John A. met an Irishman on an old horse. When Sir John A. commented on the nag, the man said, "Faith, he's like yourself, Sir, a bit the worse for wear." Sir John A.'s reply was, "Yes, he's like myself — a rum 'un to look at, but a rare 'un to go."

peerage. Those close to him knew that he would never accept the honour, that he thought it ridiculous for a man without a fortune. The Manufacturer's Life Insurance Company certainly hoped that their newly elected president would be honoured, as they indicated in a letter written to him in 1888: "It is not, we venture to hope, beyond the bounds of probability that Her Most Gracious Majesty whom you have so faithfully served may at no distant day confer on you even greater favours than those you now wear, and should the result be your promotion to a position nearer the Throne, we would all feel that the honours have been well deserved and gallantly won." According to Biggar, Sir John A. was offered a peerage but refused it.

There was further talk that he would be appointed the British Minister at Washington. He turned a deaf ear to that honour as well. Actually the truth of the matter was that he had work to do — he felt that he was needed. Five more years to complete the grand design of Canada, he thought. It was in his nature and political wisdom to look ahead.

### Cheerful, Defiant Old Lion

In 1889 *The Dominion Illustrated* printed an article about Sir John A.: "When he shakes his

*The October 20, 1888, issue of* The Dominion Illustrated *reprinted this paragraph from a Syracuse, New York, paper:*

Miss Hulda Baker, the elocutionist, arrived home from Thousand Island Park last evening. Miss Baker is the fair Syracusan who made herself famous at Kingston, Ont., by accosting Sir John Macdonald, and assuring him that in case he came to the United States he would be heartily received. Miss Baker gives this account of the incident:

"I am much mortified at being heralded over the country, and had no thought of anything only saying in as private a way as I could what I did, after having my patriotism aroused by the Premier and his suite (especially the Premier) saying such hard things of the United States. I had a position on the grandstand where I could hear all that was being said. When they had finished speaking and were about to leave, the Premier happened to turn, and pass me, and, quick as thought, I extended my hand and bowing and smiling said to him: 'Excuse me, sir, but I am a loyal American, and we open our doors wide to you and you shall come in and dwell peacefully with us if you will.' Amid great applause he laughingly replied, as he shook my hand: 'Of course you would let such a good-looking old fellow as I in?' To which I replied: 'Certainly, and I will stand in the door.' Then more laughter and applause, and Sir John immediately offered himself as my escort and introduced me all round, and, in the company of the Premier and his suite, I was escorted through the buildings and into outside attractions. When it was time for me to take the boat for Thousand Island Park he very gallantly placed me in a carriage and I was gone."

A toast to the Old Chieftain — in a *Canadian Illustrated News* drawing of a Conservative Party banquet in 1879. Sir John A. had jokes and anecdotes for all occasions and was always a popular speaker at such affairs.

*PAC*

head in a laughing passage-of-arms, his long hair sways to and fro upon his shoulders, like the mane of an old lion, in cheerful defiance. And he is an old lion — the 'Grand Old Man' of the Dominion, and one of perhaps half a dozen of the world's greatest personalities of today. The most striking feature of his face, into which a stranger could not take the merest glimpse without becoming immediately impressed with the fact that he was in the presence of a great man, are his eyes, which are as keen and as full of vitality and observation as those of a stripling of twenty. In his place in the House nothing escapes him, and he sits through the debates until the small hours with unflagging interest and an endurance really remarkable. He is tall

and erect, and bears himself with something of military alertness. In his dress he is most scrupulous. He generally wears a black diagonal morning coat and vest, and a collar of the Gladstone shape. Sometimes, however, he appears in tailless and jaunty Bohemian velvet coat."

In the summer of 1890 Sir John A. was given an almost royal reception in the Provincial Building at Charlottetown, Prince Edward Island. There was a moment of great excitement when Joe Louie, chief of the province's Micmac Indians, spontaneously elbowed his way to the Prime Minister, extending his brawny hand for a shake. Sir John A. grasped it immediately, and the crowd cheered as the two old silver-haired chieftains shook hands vigourously.

Part of John A.'s expense account during his trip to London in 1880. At Batts Hotel he rented a "sitting room for Ministers when in England."

### Ask the Papers!

In the early months of 1890 there were rumours that an election would soon be held. Sir John A. wasn't talking. When an aide asked him the date of the election, Sir John A. smiled, "Well, I cannot say, as I haven't seen the morning papers yet. They settle all these things for us, you know."

---

### A Timely Remark

Sir John A. and Principal Grant of Queen's University, Kingston, approached a wealthy man who had already contributed handsomely to the endowment fund, and asked him for a further subscription. "No, no," he said. "What I have already given is for all time."

Sir John A. laid his hand on his knee and asked winningly — and successfully, "Won't you give as much more for eternity?"

### Fair Enough!

At the Kingston Provincial Fair of 1888, Sir John A. and others were taken to see a "sideshow" consisting of the performances of some Viennese lady acrobats. One of the Members of Parliament asked haughtily, "Is this the kind of introduction you give us to an agricultural fair?"

"Why of course," said Sir John A. "We should see the calves first."

---

### Vanity

Then there was Patrick Buckley, the faded, wizened, bristly old cabman, who drove Sir John A. for thirty-eight years. When Sir John A. was out of power, the faithful old man insisted on driving him about without accepting a cent. Of him, Patrick said, "I never heard him say a cross word, nor speak in temper. Do you remember his grey suit? One time I was driving him to some important people and he wore another suit. 'Sir John,' I said. 'Why don't you put on your grey suit. You look better in it.' 'Do I?' he said . . . and went home and changed."

RB

# Can CPR be built in 10 years? No, five!

## Pledge made to B.C. fulfilled

### Sir John A. lives to see his dream realized

The miracle had started . . . and indeed it was a miracle. In 1880 the world's longest and most expensive railway was begun. After many financial setbacks, this year saw the formation of a new Canadian Pacific Railway Company with George Stephen, Donald Smith and James Hill promising to lay 2900 miles of track in ten years or less. The best terms Sir John A. could get were "25 million cash and 25 million acres."

There were incredible hardships. In addition to financial difficulties, there were other dreadful obstacles — the terrain, the weather and the trouble with the Indians, who protested the invasion of their land by the Iron Monster. Night after night, angry Indians tore up the tracks laid during the day. (Later, however, Chief Crowfoot of the Blackfoot Indians helped to keep the peace between his people and the whites.) Recklessly determined men drove locomotives over swaying trestles above wild waters, or watched in despair as muskeg areas swallowed whole sections of newly finished track together

### CPR — Can't Pay Rent

*Mr. Tilley, will you stop*
*Your puffing and blowing,*
*And tell us which way*
*The railroad is going?*
[From a Fredericton newspaper, 1865]

Public concern about the railroads did not diminish in the years that followed. Nicknames — affectionate or not so affectionate — were given to most of the lines. The Canadian Pacific Railway was known as *Can't Pay Rent, Can't Promise Returns, Chinese Pacific* (referring to the Oriental labour used in its construction), the *Great Octopus* and the *Sleepy R.*

The Canadian National Railway was called *Certainly No Rush* and *Collects No Revenue.*

The Grand Trunk Railway was known as the *Big Suitcase*, the *Big Valise* and the *Leaky Roof* (from the stencilling on many box cars) and the Grand Trunk Pacific as *Get There Perhaps.*

The Alberta Great Waterways became known as *Almighty God Wonders* as well as *And God Willing.*

The Edmonton, Dunvegan and British Columbia (Northern Alberta Railways) had many names — *Eat, Drink and Be Cheerful, Endless Ditches and Big Curves, Enormously Dangerous and Badly Constructed* and *Eternally Damned and Badly Constructed.*

The Toronto, Hamilton, and Buffalo line was nicknamed *To Hell and Back, Tramp, Hobo and Bum* and *Tried Hard and Busted.*

Passengers on the White Pass and Yukon Railway were told to *Wait Patiently and You'll Ride.*

Grip

In this caricature of William Cornelius Van Horne, the builder of the CPR, cartoonist Bengough pictorializes his famous quote: "I eat all I can, I drink all I can, I smoke all I can and I don't give a damn for anything."

with locomotives. The granite pre-Cambrian shield required heavy blasting; the mountain ridges were assaulted with several tons of dynamite each day for long months. Each task was backbreaking. There were few reliable maps. Surveying in this "great lone land," where no man had yet travelled the whole route, was a herculean undertaking.

### Van Horne's Promise

In 1885 Louis Riel's men attacked a group of North West Mounted Police and killed ten of them. William Cornelius Van Horne, who was in charge of the construction of the railway, promised Sir John A. that he would move

*(continued)*

182

# *The most famous photograph in Canadian history*

The most famous photograph in Canadian history commemorates the completion — after overcoming seemingly insurmountable obstacles — of the Canadian Pacific Railway. On November 7, 1885, Donald Smith — later Lord Strathcona — prepares to drive in the last spike, not a golden spike but one of plain iron ore.

A few of the 10,000 men who actually built the railway to the Pacific stage their own last spike photo. More than 10,000 labourers, made up of Americans and Canadians — including Indians — and Europeans and Chinese, worked on the railway.

Bedecked with flowers like a winning race horse, this CPR locomotive — the first passenger train to reach Vancouver from the East — is heralding Queen Victoria's forthcoming Golden Jubilee, celebrated in 1887, the fiftieth year of her reign.

*PAC*

troops to the scene in less than two weeks. At the time of the Métis uprising in 1869, it had taken sixty-nine days to move troops to the Red River area. However Van Horne was as good as his word, indeed even better: the troops were on the military parade ground at Qu'Appelle in nine days.

With Van Horne's indomitable will, driving, driving, driving, 10,000 men and 1700 teams of horses laid several miles of track each day, even with snow on the ground. That first year 417 miles of track were operating.

Optimistically Sir John A. now believed that the railway would be finished in five years instead of ten. Earlier he had said, "I shall not be present [to ride on the railroad]. I am an old man, but I shall perchance look down from the realms above on a multitude of younger men — a prosperous, populous and thriving generation — a nation of Canadians who will see the completion of this road." But this year he felt that "I now have some chance, if I remain as strong, please God, as I now am, of travelling over it in person before I am quite an angel."

### From Halifax to Vancouver Under the British Flag

As he was pressing forward with the construction of the Canadian Pacific Railway, delayed for almost a decade because of the Pacific Scandal, Sir John A. spoke in the House of Commons on January 17, 1881, as follows: "The pledges made to British Columbia and the pledges made in reference to the future of this Dominion will be carried out. . . . I am proud to say that if our scheme is carried out, the steamer landing at Halifax will discharge its freight and emigrants upon a British railway, which will go through Quebec and through Ontario to the far west on British territory under the British flag, under Canadian laws, and without any chance of either the immigrant being deluded or seduced away from his allegiance or his proposed residence in Canada, or the traffic coming from England or from Asia being subjected to the possible prohibition or offensive restrictive taxation or customs regulations of a foreign power."

All through the summer of 1885, the laying of steel for the Canadian Pacific Railway went on steadily, triumphing over the handicaps of the territory. Now the great work was finished. On November 7, 1885, in less than five years instead of the expected ten, the last span was fitted into place, at Craigellachie, British Columbia. The papers said: "No golden spike for Donald A. Smith! He considered the plain iron ore that Roadmaster F.A. Brothers fitted into place as a better augury for long service and prosperity. . . . Donald Smith was a little excited. . . . He struck the spike sideways instead of driving it home. The Roadmaster . . . set another in its place. . . . The hammer was raised. *The last spike had been driven!*"

(continued)

---

### No Yankee Dictation!
A cry raised, 1872, by opponents of American control of the Canadian Pacific Railway Company.

---

### Loco-motive
The citizens of Winnipeg were astounded on the morning of October 9, 1877, to hear the shriek of a whistle from the *Countess of Dufferin,* locomotive on the first transcontinental train of the Canadian Pacific Railway. Named for the wife of Lord Dufferin, Governor-General of Canada 1872-1878, the locomotive had a specially built Baldwin engine. However, the *Countess of Dufferin* had to be floated down the river on a barge bedecked with flags, banners and bunting, because the railroad tracks were not yet finished. But in spite of the fact that there was no railway, the entire populace cheered and marvelled at the locomotive.

---

### Horse Sense
Out West where almost everybody in the 1800s was a character, Fred Stimson of the Bar U ranch was giant size. Not only did he tell a good story, he was colourful copy and provided material for endless discussion. People were always saying, "Didja hear what Fred Stimson said?" Once he was called upon to testify in court about some horses that had been killed on the railroad tracks. Said Fred: "Any horse that can't outrun a CPR train is no good anyway and deserves to be killed."

## STATUE

ERECTED BY MR. GRIP IN COMMEMORATION OF THE FIRST THROUGH TRAIN ON THE CANADA PACIFIC RAILWAY.

Cartoonist Bengough's proposed statue. Looking on is Liberal Edward Blake, who predicted that the CPR would become "two streaks of rust across the wilderness." He is also reported to have said that "it will never pay for its axle grease."

# Carrying settlers to the new frontiers

*John L. Russell*

A rare glimpse into the interior of a sleeping car on the CPR carrying new settlers to homesteads across the Dominion is provided by artist Melton Prior, who drew the sketch in 1888.

The last spike would not be driven for another three years after this engraving was published in *Picturesque Canada* (1882). But already the image of a transcontinental train crossing the Western wheat fields seemed to symbolize the future of Canada.

## No Ceremony Was Observed

*The Gazette,* Montreal, November 9, 1885, gave this account of the "completion of the national highway": "The last rail of the Canadian Pacific railway was laid yesterday morning at Craigellachie, in the Eagle Pass of the Gold Mountains, British Columbia, Hon. Donald A. Smith driving the last spike. No ceremony of any kind was observed, the decision of the Directors not to signalize the event in any noteworthy manner being fully carried out."

## Twenty-four miles per hour

The newspaper also contained congratulatory telegrammes which Sir John A. received. A telegramme from a W.D. Smith said, "I congratulate you most heartily on the completion of the transcontinental railway on Canadian soil. May it prove a permanent bond of union between the eastern and western portions of this great Dominion." Van Horne wired the Prime Minister: "Thanks to your far-seeing policy and unwavering support the Canadian Pacific railway is completed. The last rail was laid this (Saturday) morning at 9.22 o'clock." Sandford Fleming's telegramme read: "The first through train from Montreal to Vancouver is within twenty-four hours of the Pacific Coast. The last spike was driven this morning by Hon. Donald A. Smith at Craigellachie in the Eagle Pass, 340 miles from Port Moody. On reaching the coast our running time from Montreal, including ordinary stoppages, will be exactly five days, averaging twenty-four miles per hour. Before long passenger trains may run over the railway from Montreal to Vancouver in four days, and it will be possible to travel specially from Liverpool to the Pacific Coast by the transcontinental line in ten days. We are greatly pleased with the work done. It is impossible to realize the enormous physical and other difficulties which have been overcome with such marvelous rapidity and with results so satisfactory."

## Russian Immigrants Help Build CPR

Historians have told us of the extraordinary contribution of thousands of Chinese labourers during the construction of the Canadian Pacific Railway. Few people know that Russian Jewish immigrants also helped in the building of the railway.

Rabbi Arthur Chiel, who served the Rosh Pina Congregation in Winnipeg, writes, "In June of 1882 over 300 Russian Jewish immigrants who had fled czarist pogroms arrived in Winnipeg . . . About 150 were assigned to work with the Canadian Pacific Railway, which was in 1882 laying its tracks through the central and western regions of Canada. The Jewish newcomers joined labour gangs working their way as far west as Medicine Hat, a stretch of some 600 miles from Winnipeg. They lived in their railway cars, sleeping in the upper section, and eating in the dining room below.

"Working under the supervision of a Jewish foreman (Kaufman, by name) who spoke English and Yiddish, the group was provided with kosher food. The gang was allowed to hold its own worship services. With funds raised among themselves they were able to purchase a Torah and to carry the Holy Scroll with them into the wilderness to the end of the track."

Except that they were allowed to observe their Sabbath from Friday sundown to Saturday sunset, they suffered the same privations as other workers, labouring in ditches, hewing rocks, etc. Many saved their wages and were talked into buying building lots in the new town sites along the railway line. They lost their hard-come-by stakes when the boom for such lots collapsed.

This track-repair gang is surrounded by the mountains that had presented some of the most difficult surveying and excavating during the building of the line.

## Spiking the Drinks

The last spike, which was driven on November 7, 1885, has been commemorated with the Last Spike cocktail, made as follows: To 4 oz. of champagne (or sparkling white wine) add: ⅓ oz. of curaçao, ⅔ oz. of cognac, dash of orange bitters, a slice of fresh orange. Stir gently and briefly. This may also be served as a Last Spike cooler by adding an equal quantity of soda water to the cocktail.

The publishing of Pierre Berton's *The Last Spike* was celebrated by the serving of this cocktail.

*The Globe,* Toronto, wrote in 1870: "With the construction of the railway, the country will be populated by Englishmen; without it by Americans."

It was said in 1890 that "Canada is a country with coal fields at both ends and the railways in between."

Once the Canadian Pacific Railway was chartered, construction went ahead very rapidly. The pressures on the survey crews and the gangs of labourers were terrific, but we are told they kept their sense of humour — at least some of the time. In *Steel of Empire* Gibbon reports this verse found written on a bleached animal skull:

> *Long have I roamed these dreary plains,*
> *I've used up horses, men and brains;*
> *And oft from virtue's path I've strayed*
> *To find a fifty-two foot grade.*
> *But now, thank God! I'll take a rest,*
> *Content I've done my level best.*
> *To this green earth I'll say farewell*
> *And run a railway line through hell.*

Reminiscing in their old age — and they had much to talk about — are Donald Smith (now Lord Strathcona) and Father Lacombe, who was one of the first missionaries in the North West and spent his life in the service of the Indians and Métis. It was he who persuaded Chief Crowfoot not to oppose the railroad.

Lady Macdonald started a new fad when she insisted on riding the cowcatcher through Kicking Horse Pass. Here another group — photographed in the Selkirk Mountains by Notman around 1889 — is shown emulating the First Lady by riding on the front of the train. Lady Macdonald had even coaxed the Prime Minister to join her briefly in spite of his protestations that the idea was "rather ridiculous and most dangerous."

# HE GETS TO RIDE IT!

## *"The darling dream of his heart — a railway from ocean to ocean"*

Sir John A. and Lady Macdonald did make the glorious journey on the world's greatest railroad in July 1886, nine months after the driving of the last spike. They left Ottawa on July 13, almost secretly, in a special car, "The Jamaica" — so named as a compliment to the First Lady who had lived in the West Indies as a girl. Van Horne turned his genius for organization to many details that made the Macdonalds' special "railway home" comfortable during the hot summer days and nights. Little did he know that Lady Macdonald would desert the luxurious quarters for the cowcatcher of the engine!

An officer of the Mounted Police was with the small party of the Prime Minister, his devoted secretary Joseph Pope, Lady Macdonald and her travelling companion. The great adventure unfolded, thrilling them with wonder, Sir John A.'s dream come true. Each area they traversed charmed and delighted them, but it was the breath-taking beauty of the West that challenged Lady Macdonald's spirit. Determined as she was charming, and perhaps a little restless with the confinement of the railway carriage, she decided that the view would be better if she sat on the cowcatcher. The Prime Minister pronounced the idea "rather ridiculous and most dangerous." Nor was the engineer pleased. To appease them somewhat, Lady Macdonald allowed herself to be tied on securely and to be protected by a carriage cover. Then, pulling on an English felt hat to keep wind and cinders from her hair, she was all set to enjoy the "scoop" westwards from Calgary.

Lady Macdonald took such pleasure in her intimate view of Kicking Horse Pass and the valleys of the Columbia and Fraser Rivers that she persuaded Sir John A. to join her in this most unorthodox mode of travel. This he did — but briefly. She, however, kept her position through tunnels, at fifty miles an hour, enjoying the spray from springs.

Sir John A. had been elected in British Columbia when he lost his Kingston seat. However he had never visited the western province or met his constituents until now.

On the long trip across the country, the little party was honoured and feted by celebrities and working people. They were greeted by the intelligent and loyal Chief Crowfoot of the Blackfoot Indians and by North Axe, Red Crow, One Spot and Three Bulls — who were all treated with honour and deference. With dignified protocol, solemn words were spoken and carefully chosen gifts were exchanged. Some time before, Van Horne had presented Chief Crowfoot with a lifetime pass on the Canadian Pacific rail lines, in recognition of his help in preserving peace between his people and the builders of the railroad.

Rest and relaxation had been arranged for the Prime Minister and his entourage. They were refreshed by a fortnight's stay at a pleasant hotel in Victoria and were offered hospitality at many other points of scenic beauty. Sir John A. was delighted with it all. He loved people — and the elections were not too far ahead.

On August 30, after fifty marvellous days, "The Jamaica" returned to Ottawa. What with zigzag sidetrips on branch lines and many stopovers, the exhilarating expedition had clocked 6000 miles.

Lady Macdonald wrote an account of the trip for *Murray's Magazine,* London, England, to which she was a frequent contributor. When the

> When a Regina citizen asked Sir John A. his opinion of the "prospect," Sir John A. replied: "If you had a lit-tle more wood, and a lit-tle more water, and here and there a hill, I think the prospect would be improved."

article was published in 1887 it caused much comment on both sides of the Atlantic. Excerpts follow:

"Before we reach Port Arthur, where business begins, I must introduce some of our travelling party. Our 'Chief' — who among many other offices holds that of Superintendent-General of Indian Affairs — I shall sometimes call by the translation of an Indian name given him by Crowfoot, Chief of the Blackfeet, *Kis-ta-mo-ni-mon,* or 'Our Brother-in-law.'

### The Darling Dream of His Heart

"First then comes 'Our Brother-in-law,' a very well-known personage in Canada, who is taking this special trip for a 'special' purpose. He has come to see the realization of the darling dream of his heart — a railway from ocean to ocean, the development of many million acres of magnificent country, and the birth of a new nation. During seventeen years, in and out of Parliament, he had battled for these changes, through discouragement, obloquy, and reverse, and with a strong patience all his own had bided his time until as years went on, men, resolute like himself, had arisen to take the aid his Government were determined to offer for the development of this vast territory by the completion of this railway. During the forty years and in the various capacities he had tried, in his poor way, faithfully to serve Queen and country, no happier hours had come to him, I think, than these, as he sits thoughtfully in 'The Jamaica' looking on the varied scenes through which we pass. . . .

"The Chief, seated on a low chair on the rear platform of the car, with a rug over his knees and a magazine in his hand, looked very comfortable and content. Hearing my request [to ride on the cowcatcher] after a moment's thought he pronounced the idea 'rather ridiculous,' then remembered it was dangerous as well, and finally asked if I was sure I could hold on. Before the words were well out of his lips, and taking permission for granted by the question, I was again standing by the cowcatcher, admiring the position of the candle-box, and anxiously asking to be helped on.

"Before I take my seat, let me try briefly, to describe the 'cowcatcher.' Of course everyone knows that the bufferbeam is that narrow, heavy iron platform, with the sides scooped out, as it were, on the very forefront of the engine over which the headlight glares, and in the corner of which a little flag is generally placed. In English engines, I believe, the buffers proper project from the front of this beam. In Canadian engines another sort of attachment is arranged, immediately below the beam, by which the engine can draw trains backwards as well as forwards. The beam is about eight feet across at the widest part, and about three feet deep. The description of a cowcatcher is less easy. To begin with, it is misnamed, for it catches no cows at all. Sometimes, I understand, it throws up on the bufferbeam whatever maimed or mangled animal it has struck, but in most cases it clears the line by shoving forward, or tossing aside, any removable obstruction. It is best described as a sort of barred iron beak, about six feet long, projecting close over the track in a V shape, and attached to the bufferbeam by very strong bolts. It is sometimes sheathed with thin iron plates in winter, and acts then as a small snow-plough.

### "This Is Lovely, Quite Lovely"

"Behold me now, enthroned on the candle-box, with a soft felt hat well over my eyes, and a linen carriage-cover tucked round me from waist to foot. Mr. E.— had seated himself on the other side of the headlight. He had succumbed to the inevitable, ceased further expostulation, disclaimed all responsibility, and, like the jewel of a Superintendent he was, had decided on sharing my peril! I turn to him, peeping round the headlight with my best smile. 'This is *lovely*,' I triumphantly announce, seeing that a word of comfort is necessary, '*quite lovely*; I shall travel on this cowcatcher from summit to sea'."

When the town of Port Arthur seized a CPR train for taxes in 1889, railway president Van Horne moved the company offices and warehouses to Fort William. "For this," he said, "the grass shall grow in the streets of Port Arthur."

Harold Lockwood

In spite of the 6000 miles that Sir John A. travelled in his 1886 journey across Canada to visit his constituents in Victoria (where he was elected after losing his Kingston seat) and the hundreds of shorter trips, this is the only picture known to exist of him on a train. Here he is seen with Lady Macdonald on the platform of their private car, "The Jamaica." Such informal outdoor pictures were still difficult to take in the newly developed art of photography.

### The Chief on the Cowcatcher Everyone Horrified

[At Palliser]: "The Chief and his friends walked up to the cowcatcher to make a morning call. I felt a little 'superior' and was rather condescending. Somewhat flushed with excitement but still anxious to be polite, I asked 'would the Chief step up and take a drive?' To the horror of the bystanders he carelessly consented, and in another moment had taken the place of Mr. E.—, the latter seating himself at our feet on the bufferbeam. There was a general consternation among our little groups of friends and the few inhabitants of Palliser — the Chief 'rushing through the flats of the Columbia on a cowcatcher.' . . . Everyone was horrified. It is a comfort to the other occupant of the buffer to find someone else wilful, and as we steamed away towards Donald, at the eastern base of the Selkirks, I felt not so bad after all!"

*Grip*

### VAN BREAKS THE TRANS-CONTINENTAL RECORD.

William Cornelius Van Horne, builder of the CPR, is drawn by the irrepressible Bengough as a jockey, breaking the transcontinental speed record of 1891: Vancouver to Montreal at thirty-one miles per hour. The comparison between trains and horses was frequent.

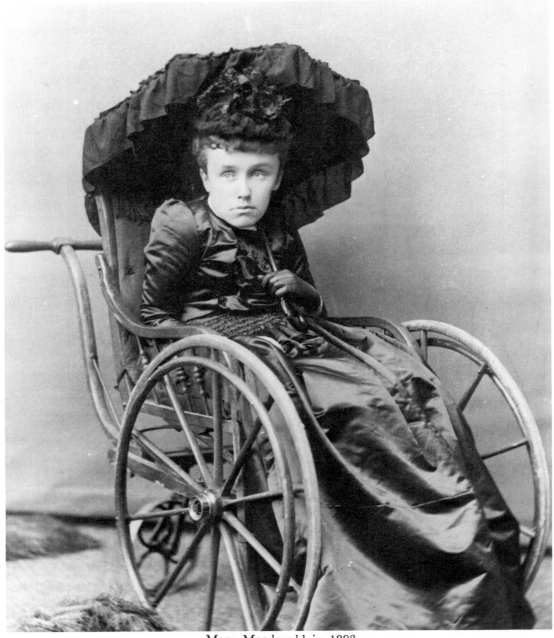

Mary Macdonald in 1893

# Mary Theodora Margaret Macdonald

## "Mary is a great source of anxiety"

### Sir John A. surrounds his afflicted "Baboo" with unfailing tenderness

"Mary is a great source of anxiety," wrote Sir John A. to his brother-in-law, Professor Williamson. The only child of Sir John A. and Lady Macdonald suffered from hydrocephalus — an incurable birth defect.

Sir John A. had a great love for all children and they were drawn to him. Each time he left his daughter's bedside, he was sick at heart. He was deeply attached to the child and with infinite tenderness attempted to arrange her life and surroundings as though she were an average growing girl. Contriving many simple ruses, he was aided by close friends in such little deceptions. John A. found time to read to her, to share jokes, to write letters to her when she was away. He personally shopped for toys, picture books and trinkets, and often pretended that Baboo (as he called her) was the one helping and comforting him.

**Father Like a "Cropped Donkey"**

The little girl was four-and-a-half years old and away with her grandmother when her father wrote to her:

My dearest Mary,

You must know that your kind Mamma and I are very anxious to see you and Granny again. We have put a new carpet in your room and got everything ready for you.

The garden looks lovely just now. It is full of beautiful flowers and I hope you will see them before they are withered.

There are some fine melons in the garden. You must pick them for dinner, and feed the chickens with the rind. You remember that Mamma cut my hair and made me look like a cropped donkey. It has grown quite long again. When you come home, you must not pull it too hard.

I intend to have some new stories for you when you come in the morning into Papa's bed and cuddle him up.

Give my love to dear good Grandmamma and give her a kiss from me. Give my love to Sarah too. And so good-bye my pet and come home soon to your

Loving Papa,
John A.

At the age of eight and a half, Mary dictated this letter:

My dear Father,

. . . I have a little dog that my Uncle gave me. Dear Father, when are you coming back? . . . The house seems so dull and lonely without you, and I miss my evening stories very much. . . .

Your affectionate Baboo and daughter,
Mary Macdonald

Oh! What a scrimmage I've made, I forgot to say anything about my old hen. Sarah is very well and as chirpy as ever. That's all.

Was Mary mentally retarded as well as physically handicapped? In his will, Sir John A. appointed his wife as guardian of Mary, saying that his daughter "will probably be throughout life incapable of managing her own affairs." Although hydrocephalus is generally accompanied by retardation, there is some evidence to indicate that Mary might not have been severely retarded. In 1941, Annie Bethune McDougald wrote in the Montreal *Gazette:* "I recall many

*(continued)*

190

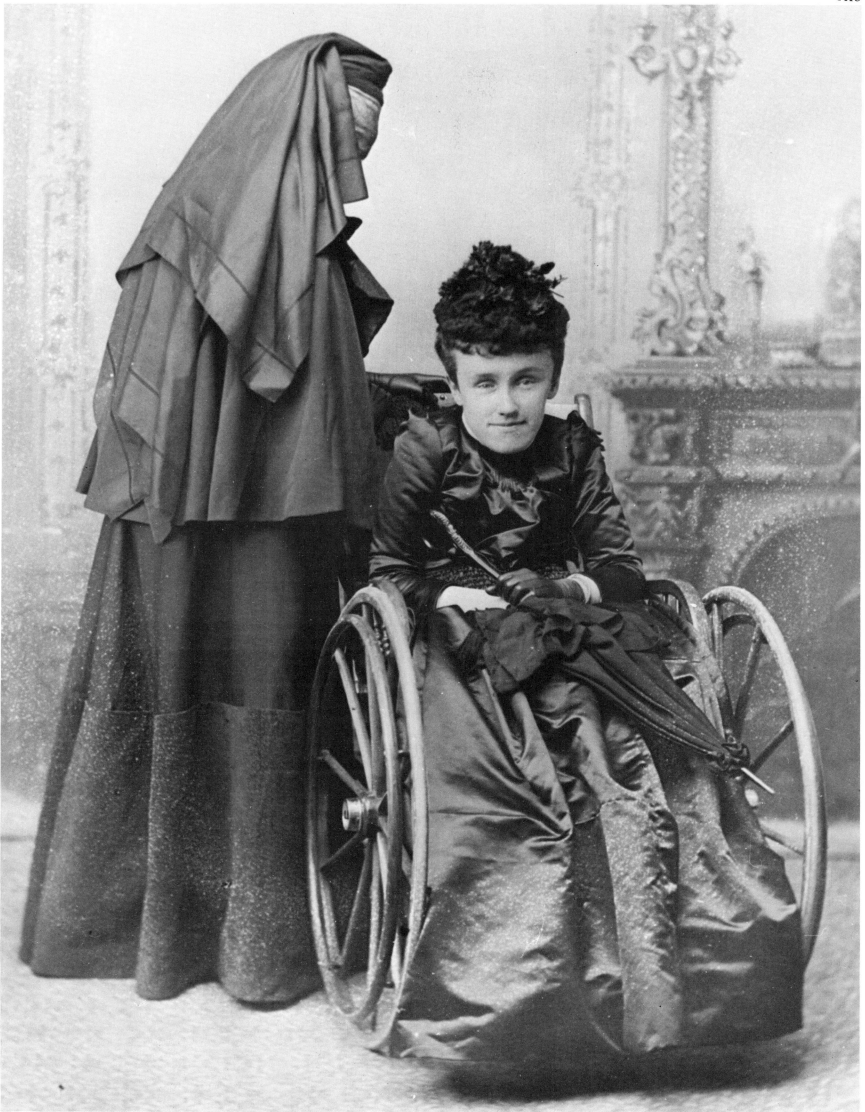

This poignantly beautiful photograph shows Baroness Macdonald in widow's weeds standing behind Mary's wheelchair. "I am just going out with Mary to see if we can get a photo of her," Baroness Macdonald wrote on May 23, 1893 — two years after Sir John A.'s death — to her brother-in-law, Professor Williamson (Sir John A.'s sister's husband). "If it should turn out well, I will send you one, dear friend, ever kind and true to me, one who when *he* was gone, did not fail me as did others." Whether this particular photograph was intended to hide the mother's face, or whether it was taken accidentally and its dramatic beauty recognized later, we are not told. It is the only picture we have of Mary Macdonald smiling.

191

happy days at 'Stadacona Hall' that winter, playing with 'Little Mary,' as we then called Sir John's afflicted child ... and Sir John often romping and playing with us. Little Mary, who sat all the time in a little carriage, though defective in body, was mentally bright and alert and a pleasant companion."

Lady Macdonald kept her daughter well dressed. Here is a list of apparel bought for her in 1881 from Harris and Tom's, Costumiers and Milliners, Cavendish Square, London. Lady Macdonald and her mother also bought their clothes here.

For Miss Mary
| | |
|---|---|
| 1 Blue Cloth Hat | £1/1/– |
| 1 Blue Cloth Frock | £3/13/6 |
| 1 Green satin Frock, mantle and muff | £11/–/– |
| 1 doll's outfit | £3/10/– |
| 1 black silk jacket and bonnet | £4/11/– |
| (for her nurse) | |

Sir John A. just couldn't do enough for his Mary. This note accompanied his gift on her fourteenth birthday: "To my darling Mary on her birthday and with a sincere wish that I may be able to give her many birthday presents hereafter."

### Father's Touching Concern

Biggar gives this account of the father's touching concern: "Not very long ago Mary had a girls' party. When the young people were preparing to leave, he persuaded them to stay a little longer, as she was fond of seeing them dance. When they resumed the dance, he leaned over his child's chair and said, 'You see, Mary, they want a little more of your society — and a little dancing by the way.' "

When Mary was fifteen Sir John A. wrote in a letter to a friend, "Mary is beginning to stand. We hope to see her walk yet."

This bill for treatment during the years 1874-1883 came from Dr. Alex Martin, dentist, Ottawa.

| | |
|---|---|
| December 12, 1874 | |
|    Extraction of child's teeth | $2.00 |
| May 11, 1875 | |
|    Extraction of child's teeth | $2.00 |
| April 10, 1876 | |
|    Extraction for Lady Macdonald | $1.50 |
| December 13, 1881 | |
|    Professional services for daughter | $3.50 |
| July 4, 1882 | |
|    Professional services for daughter | $2.50 |
| June 27, 1883 | |
|    Professional services for daughter | $1.00 |

In 1887 Lady Macdonald wrote to her sister-in-law, Louisa: "I teach Mary what my mother tried to teach me, that she must do or have done, what is best for others, and not grumble. She has perfect faith in our plans for her."

Lady Macdonald wrote to Professor Williamson, her brother-in-law, to thank him for a Christmas gift.

My dear Professor,

Mary and I were equally delighted with your very pretty and useful Xmas gift to her. She wore it at dinner on Xmas day and looked so sweet in the soft colours. It is just what I like for her, as we are obliged to dress her very warmly and to put on an outer wrap in very cold weather.... She caught a severe cold and I am now a prisoner in her room to keep her quiet lying down, wrapped up warmly. She coughs badly.... She was imprudent in going to church on Xmas day but she was in such spirits over her presents and so anxious to go that I had not the heart to say "no."

---

### Hydrocephalus

Medical opinion on the effects of hydrocephalus varies. A leading textbook on pediatrics says: "The results of surgical treatment are not brilliant. Without operation, perhaps two thirds of all children with hydrocephalus of whatever cause will die at an early age. With operation, about two thirds of the children will survive, and the status of many of them will be improved. Of survivors, perhaps two fifths will have intelligence quotients below 70; about three fourths, below 90. Less than 5 percent achieve an intelligence quotient of 110 or better. Even the most optimistic authorities do not claim that more than 15 to 20 percent of treated patients will be normally competitive, both physically and intellectually. Even the physically sound person of dull or borderline intelligence faces many problems. The hydrocephalic is often additionally burdened by ... seizures, poor vision and squints, and many more problems."

---

He returned from his long fatiguing trip looking lovely (as Aunt Maria would say) and does not seem a bit the worse for labours that might easily have laid up a younger man. Now he is deep in Councils and in his office but nothing seems to be too much for his endurance.... My cows and two fowls are very satisfactory.... We make ... fresh butter weekly. A great boon to Sir John who likes it. He has all the cream he wants. I have plenty of newlaid eggs now, even in the coldest weather.... It is a great interest to me. They (chickens) are all so ... glad to see me every day, early, when I take out their warm food.

> Yours affectionately,
> Agnes Macdonald

Fearing that he might predecease his wife and invalid daughter, Sir John A., never a monied man, was always troubled that they might not be provided with an adequate income. (Mary survived her father by forty-two years and her mother by thirteen.) There is a possibility that old friends and associates established a trust fund for them.

### A Comfort, Not a Burden

According to Biggar, when Mary heard that her father was dead, "she said in her peculiar slow and measured accents, 'I must try and be a comfort to mother now, instead of a burden to her.' "

After Sir John A.'s death, Lady Macdonald — now Baroness Macdonald of Earnscliffe — took

PAC

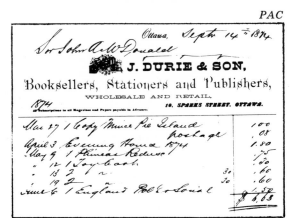

An Ottawa bookseller's bill to Sir John A. includes five toy books bought in the space of a week in 1874. Mary was then five years old.

---

her invalid daughter to England and the Continent. They spent their winters at a quiet spot in Italy. They spent the summer months at the English seaside or in London.

Letters from Sir Hugh John Macdonald to his stepmother show that he inherited his father's concern for Mary. Professor Williamson also continued in his family solicitude for Baroness Macdonald and Mary, and his sister-in-law often wrote to him from Europe. (In 1893 Mary was twenty-four years old.)

Batt's Hotel, Dover St., London
July 11, 1893
My dear old Friend,

We had a very good voyage over.... Mary enjoyed it extremely (rather too much) at first, for she coaxed us into letting her sit up an evening on the ... deck and caught a cold which kept her in her room for the last 3 days. However, she soon recovered without a doctor. I have a man to push her chair ... and she goes out daily and sees no end of interesting things ... and is very happy and I think much improved. Today, she has spent at the aquarium.... She goes to the park constantly to watch the gay throng of carriages, horsemen, and pedestrians which throng that very fashionable rendez-vous from 4 to 7:30 daily.

### Courageous Little Woman

December 24, 1893
Grand Hôtel des Anglais
San Remo, Italy
My dear Professor,

We left at Dover, crossed to Calais. A gale had blown for 18 hours previous and was blowing furiously when we left. You can imagine what a crossing it was! ... Mary ... was desperately ill, though the voyage lasted only one hour and a half. Mary really frightened me, but she is such a courageous little woman, that as the stewardess said, she was "an example." ... This place is capital for Mary. She can be out all day and is delighted with it already. I have engaged a man and chair for her daily use. We can have them all day, or at any time, and the man will always be at our disposal like a servant. It is not so expensive a place as I expected, though, of course, one has to be careful and watchful. The journey was expensive with all the comforts necessary for Mary, but I managed it all pretty well.

Villa Degli Olivi
San Remo, Italy
Jan. 9, 1895
My dear Professor,

Our little party, Kathleen Peacock, darling Mary and myself, have been cheered and brightened by two visitors of late.... We lead a very quiet and regular life, taking lots of exercise daily, living much in the open air, so good for Mary and the rest of us.

I wish you could see Mary in her bath chair drawn by a small donkey. She sits up so straight holding the reins while the donkey-man walks at the head and we walk by her side. In this way we go everywhere so easily, and the roads are dry, hard and so excellent that we have not been obliged to omit our little excursions once all winter from want of good walking, and only two or three times from weather.

> Yours very affectionately,
> Macdonald of Earnscliffe

Love to all Kingston friends.

When in Britain, Baroness Macdonald and her daughter lived at the Ladies' Empire Club, 69 Grosvenor Square, London, and at 47 Grand

*To my darling daughter Mary on her birthday and with a sincere wish that I may be able to give her many birthday presents hereafter*

*John A Macdonald*

*February 8th 1883*

A birthday note from Sir John A. to Mary on her fourteenth birthday. Was the wish "that I may be able to give her many birthday presents hereafter" a subconscious prayer for her or for himself? He was then sixty-eight.

Parade, Eastbourne, on the south coast of England.

### Mary in England

Jane Coward attended the Baroness for nineteen years and after her death in 1920 cared for Mary. Her mother gone, Mary lived for some years in Brighton. She later moved to 19 St. Aubyns, Hove, Sussex; her name appeared on the voters' lists until 1933, when she died.

The St. Aubyns building development was begun sometime before July 1863. The property passed through many hands over the years, being used, among other things, as a gentlemen's preparatory school, a ladies' school and a medical and surgical nursing home. Numbers 17 and 19 were used as a block of flats from 1918 to 1923 under the name of St. Aubyns Court. Number 19 was taken over by a couple called Charles and Sarah Clarke in 1924, who remained there until 1933, after which the house was again used as flats.

During Mary's years in the building, old records show the tenants as being two separate households, with Mary, Jane Coward (and later her husband) in the upper part of the house.

A cable from the Royal Trust Company, Ottawa, to the Bank of Montreal, London, shows that Mary's income was $9,000.00 a year.

Sir Hugh John Macdonald wrote the following letter concerning his stepmother's will. In it he shows his concern for his half-sister Mary.

Winnipeg, Canada
15th October 1920
Colonel C.A. Eliot
Manager, Royal Trust Company, Ottawa
My dear Colonel Eliot,

Very many thanks for your letter of the 9th inst., and for the copy of my stepmother's Will, which you enclosed in it, and which I was more than pleased to receive, as I had not before seen a copy of this document although I knew its contents pretty well, as she wrote me just after it was made telling me the provisions contained in it, and explaining that she had not named me as one of the guardians to my sister Mary because she considered it would be useless to do so as I was a resident of Canada while my sister had made up her mind to make her home in England. She also explained to me that after

talking the matter over with Mary, they had decided that Coward was to live with her, and I yesterday received a letter from Mary telling me that Coward intended to be married, but that she knew the man who was to be her husband and liked him, and that she had arranged with Coward that she was to continue living with her after her marriage. I am certain from what I have heard from both my mother and my sister that an arrangement of this sort is the best that can be made, although I regret that Coward has made up her mind to change her state, as it is of course possible that Mary and Coward's husband may not get on well together when they find themselves inmates of the same house. However, I think the only thing to do is to give the plan hit upon by Mary and Coward a fair trial, provided of course that the terms agreed upon are fair to Mary.

I am awfully pleased to know that the business is to be carried on through your office, as I now feel at ease as to Mary's interests being properly looked after and fully protected.

The horses, carriages and automobiles mentioned in the Will must have been put there. [by the solicitors] because articles of this sort are generally owned. . . . I know my mother was not the happy possessor of any of these things. . . .

With kindest regards,
I remain,
Yours very sincerely,
Hugh J. Macdonald

The Honourable Mary Macdonald sent the following letter to the Royal Trust Company

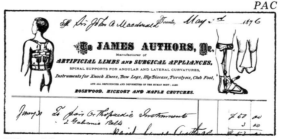

When Mary was seven, Sir John A. bought some orthopaedic equipment from a Toronto manufacturer. Throughout their daughter's childhood and youth the Macdonalds never seem to have given up hope that she would walk.

in Ottawa. It refers to a dressing bag and jewelry that Mary received from the estate of her mother: "I received your letter dated the 9th of June. I am sorry that I am not able to sign the form of receipt for the Dressing Bag delivered to me by Mr. Clarke. I am not able to write except with the typewriter. I find the inventory quite correct."

A letter, dated February 18, 1927, indicates that the Honourable Mary Macdonald wished to support the Orphan's Home of the City of Ottawa (often called The Protestant Orphan's Home). Lady Macdonald had been director of this institution for six years.

From the Bank of Montreal
47 Threadneedle Street
London EC2
18th February 1927
To The Manager
The Royal Trust Company, Ottawa
Dear Sir,

We are informed by Miss Dymond that the Hon. Mary Macdonald wishes to pay to the Protestant Orphan's Home of your City the sum of $100.00 (One hundred dollars) annually as a subscription from herself. We shall be glad therefore if you will kindly pay this annual subscription on behalf of Miss Macdonald, charging same to her account with yourselves. You will recollect that a donation of $100.00 was made by Miss Macdonald to the Home about this time last year. For your information, Miss Dymond says that since Lady Strathcona's death her daughter, Lady Congleton, has kindly undertaken co-guardianship with her.

The letters written by, about and on behalf of Mary suggest that perhaps her mental retardation was not as severe as some historians have assumed. If she sometimes acted childishly, was it because she was treated like a child? Or had the love and care that her parents surrounded her with enabled her to develop beyond what her handicap would seem to permit? It would seem that she was capable of deciding where and how to live as well as how to spend her money.

The Honourable Mary Theodora Margaret Macdonald died on January 28, 1933, in her home in Hove. She was buried in Hove Ceme-

*(continued)*

*PAC*

Mary at the age of thirty-three, taken by a photographer in Ramsgate, England. She was never able to walk or to write with a pen, but she could use a typewriter. She outlived her mother by thirteen years, dying at the age of sixty-four in Sussex.

tery on February 2. The following editorial, written by editor R.B. Farrell, appeared in the *Ottawa Journal* on February 18, 1933:

"The announcement of the death of Hon. Mary Macdonald, last surviving child of Sir John A. Macdonald and the Baroness Macdonald *at Hove, England, in her 64th year,* will bring back colourful memories to older Ottawa residents and evoke recollections of Earnscliffe in its heyday.

"Mary Theodora Margaret Macdonald was the only child born of Sir John's second marriage to Susan Bernard, daughter of the Hon. T. J. Bernard, of Jamaica. As a result of an accident she was crippled for life, but although she spent the best part of her waking hours in a wheel chair she was a woman of unusual vitality and mental energy.

"Up to a short time before her death she corresponded with old Ottawa friends, all her letters being typewritten. Devotion to the typewriter came years ago in its first vogue, and as a girl she got her practice by copying the speeches of her father, the Prime Minister.

"Mary Macdonald grew up amongst the comings, and goings, the movement and stir of a nation in its birththroes. As a child she was carried in by her nurse, the faithful Sarah Chilton, to be presented to Donald Smith, Sanford Fleming, George Stephen, Cartier, Tupper, Chapleau, Caron and a host of others.

"When old enough to understand she read both Grit and Tory papers and grew angry when Opposition scribes declared Macdonald was plunging the Dominion into bankruptcy with his madman's dream of a railway across the wilderness."

The inscription on Mary's tombstone reads as follows:

*In Loving Memory of
Mary Theodora Margaret Macdonald
Only Daughter of
Sir John Macdonald
Prime Minister of Canada
and of the Baroness Macdonald of Earnscliffe
Born February 8th 1869
Died January 28th 1933
Blessed are the pure in heart*

# PART SEVEN    1891

*I trust that it will be said of me in the ultimate issue, "Much is forgiven because he loved much," for I have loved my country with a passionate love.* Sir John A. Macdonald

# THE OLD FLAG, THE OLD POLICY, THE OLD LEADER.

PUBLISHED BY THE INDUSTRIAL LEAGUE. FREDERIC NICHOLLS, HON SEC

TORONTO LITH CO.

A flag-waving Sir John A. is carried by a farmer and worker with flourishing farms and smoking chimneys in the background. This simple poster said everything that people wanted to hear. The Liberals ("Grits") argued futilely that John A.'s National Policy against tariffs was overtaxing the farmer.

The 1891 election was the first in Canada in which posters were used extensively. Many of them were handmade and crude, like the above, but they suggested a kind of homey identification with John A. that was very effective.

# The Old Chief fights last campaign

## *Through snowstorms and freezing rain*

### "You'll never die," they cried. Did he believe it too?

Sir John A. was seventy-six — an old seventy-six. Frail, unsteady, sick, haggard and weary, he was immersed in the same sort of election campaign that he had waged in younger years. His supporters in every constituency demanded that he appear in person and speak. What was the Conservative Party thinking of to allow such a tour? Did his colleagues really believe their slogan "You'll never die, John A."?

#### "A British Subject I Was Born"

The election of 1891 was a hard-fought and memorable one. On February 7, Sir John A. issued an address giving the Conservative Party platform in detail: what his party had done, what they planned to do. He ended with these words: "As for myself, my course is clear. A British subject I was born, a British subject I will die. With my utmost effort, with my latest breath, will I oppose the 'veiled treason' which attempts by sordid means and mercenary proffers to lure our people from their allegiance. During my long public service of nearly half a century I have been true to my country and its best interests, and I appeal with equal confidence to the men who have trusted me in the past and to the young hope of the country, with whom rests its destinies in the future, to give me their united and strenuous aid in this my last effort for the unity of the Empire and the preservation of our commercial and political freedom."

The speech had great impact, inspiring posters and poetry:

#### For God and Country

*The Patriot raised his aged arm,*
 *And gazed to Heaven with reverent eye;*
*"A British subject I was born,*
 *A British subject I will die.*
*No foreign yoke shall bind my neck,*
 *No chains my free limbs shall enthral;*
*No captive's garland e'er shall deck*
 *The brow which I have bared for all.*

*Oh! favoured land, 'tis thee I love,*

(continued)

THE GRIT TOBOGGAN SLIDE, AND WHERE IT LEADS TO!

GRIT POLICY

STRICTED RECIPROCITY

But the Canadian People will come to the Aid of their Patriotic Premier on the 5th of March, and Rescue their Country from the impending Danger.

John A. is pictured single-handedly holding Canada back from the brink of disaster — i.e. U.S. annexation — in another of the home-made posters of 1891.

*To thee my choicest years I gave;*
*And grant me power from above,*
*I ne'er will see thee made a slave.*
*Free as thou art thou shalt remain*
*And stand amongst the nations — free!*
*And floating o'er thee, without stain*
*The 'Old Flag' still so dear to me.*

*No azure stars shall blind my sight,*
*No crimson bars shall float o'er me;*
*A Briton born, my British right*
*Unsullied evermore shall be.*
*And when I die, place o'er the spot,*
*Wherever I may chance to lie,*
*'A British subject he was born,*
*A British subject did he die'."*

Meanwhile, across the border, a New York paper threatened:
*Sir John, Sir John*
*Go on, go on!*
*Poor Canada, you vex it.*
*'Twill soon get tired —*
*And when you're fired*
*We'll step in and annex it.*

It became harder and harder for Sir John A. to leave the comparative comfort of his travelling headquarters, "The Jamaica," the CPR car in which he had taken his first trip over the new railway in 1886. Yet his constituents begged him to address them in person. Inevitably, although worn and near prostration, he was drawn into the thick of the fray.

**The Famous Academy of Music Speech**

Sir John A. received a grand reception in the Academy of Music in Toronto, where he was to speak. The hall was draped with banners that proclaimed:

*Hail to Our Chieftain*
*Ottawa, Not Washington, Our Capital*
*No United States Senators Need Apply*
*No Tariff Discrimination Against Britain*
*Canadian Labour for Canadians*

According to a Toronto paper, Sir John A. "wore the customary cardinal tie with cameo pin and sat easily in his big chair."

The Montreal *Gazette* of February 17 describes the scene outside the Academy of Music: "Thousands in Toronto were unable to gain admission to the Academy of Music tonight to hear Sir John Macdonald and Sir Charles Tupper. . . . Long before six o'clock the building was crowded . . . men were actually fighting to get in."

A Toronto newspaper continues: "Sir John Macdonald was greeted with a perfect uproar. The whole house rose en masse and cheered loud and long. Handkerchiefs and hats waved over the vast throng, and cheers were renewed again and again. Sir John stood smiling and looking quite happy. Finally the chorus 'For he's a jolly good fellow' was sung as it was never sung in Toronto and the old chieftain was allowed to speak. . . . Perfect quiet prevailed. Sir John said, 'The policy of the Government of which I am the leader, the aged leader — perhaps the weak and inefficient leader (shouts of NO! NO!) — but the honest and well-intentioned leader . . . (cheers and applause) I say that the policy of the Government is the same as it was in 1878.

The policy of protection that we brought before the people then has been faithfully carried out. The results of that policy need not be dwelt upon. I was here in 1874 and I have seen what Toronto is in 1891. Then our workingmen were out of employment. . . . Now I see progress and prosperity on every hand. . . . I say all this has been done by the effect and through the influence of the National Policy."

**A Bombshell from Sir John A.**

Then, according to *The Gazette* of Montreal, "Sir John threw a bombshell, which when it explodes, will scatter confusion and consternation in the Liberal ranks." Sir John A. produced a document, written by a Canadian, which "showed Americans how they could force Canada into welcoming annexation by encouraging discontent in the Maritime provinces, hampering the fisheries industry, refusing the bonding privileges to Canadian railways, and the cutting of the Canadian Pacific Railway's connections with roads on the other side of the border."

Sir John A. claimed, "I say there is a deliberate conspiracy, by force, by fraud or by both, to force Canada into the American union." The audience cried out for the name of the traitor.

"What is that I hear?" asked Sir John A. "You ask me to name him? Yes, I will name him. People know who Mr. Farrer [a Liberal and the editor of *The Globe*] is . . . Mr. Farrer, a man of great ability as I happen to know and a man of utter want of principle, as I happen to know. . . . Mr. Farrer prepared that document with his own hand."

*(continued)*

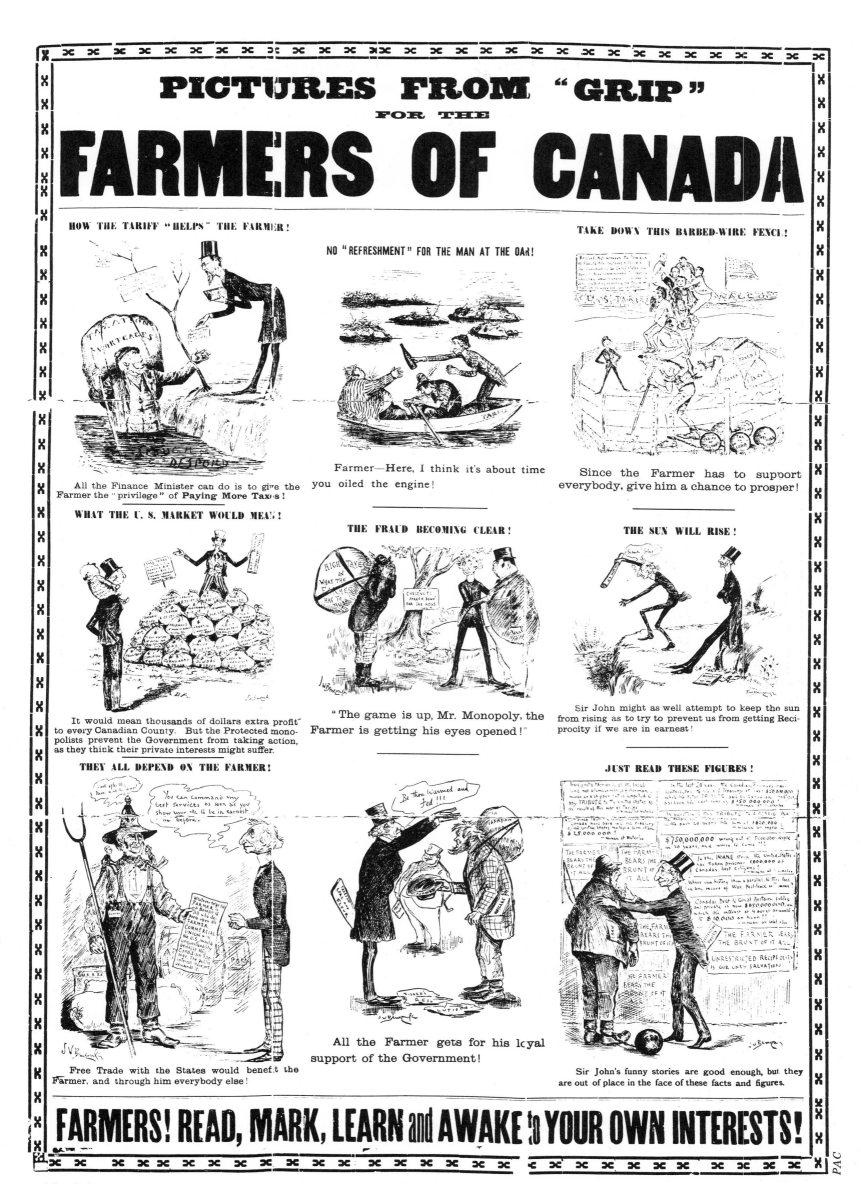

The Grits also had their posters. This one (artistically on a much higher level) was by Canada's greatest caricaturist, J. W. Bengough. In nearly every picture, John A. is presented as standing against the farmer's true interest, i.e. free trade with the U.S. John A. is shown variously as trying to keep the sun from rising, greasing the protected industrialist at the expense of the farmer and trying to divert the farmer with his funny stories. As can readily be seen by the posters of both parties, John A. himself was the issue.

The implication of this anti-Liberal, anti-free trade poster was that the Conservatives had brought about prosperity and that the Liberals would destroy it. The Liberals had the misfortune to have been in power during the terrible depression of 1873, and even though the depression was not their fault, it was indelibly connected with them in the public mind.

Another homemade poster — the result no doubt of home industry that had not suffered "distruction" — shows Liberal "Wilfred" Laurier leading the Canadian beaver right under the claws of the American eagle, while Uncle Sam welcomes his candidate.

The meeting closed with the people singing, "We will hang Ned Farrer from a sour apple tree."

*The Gazette* continued: "The production of the document caused an immense sensation, and after the meeting was over a great crowd surrounded *The Globe* building, hooting and yelling at it....

### Edward Farrer Confesses

"Edward Farrer...lamely explains that the pamphlet was prepared by him for an American gentleman at the request of the latter. He did it in a private capacity and quite openly, he

**EXALTING FARRER INTO AN ISSUE.**

John A. knew how to make the most of his opponents' mistakes, and he was able to make the indiscreet circulated opinions of Edward Farrer, editor of *The Globe,* sound like a plot to turn Canada over to the U.S. In this cartoon, Bengough tries to suggest that the Farrer issue has been blown out of all proportion.

says.... He goes on, 'I admit that I am the writer and the sole author of the brochure, and I should not hesitate under like circumstances to write another or a dozen more on that or any other subject and to state my views if they are worth anything to anybody in print or out of it, about fisheries or even about Sir John himself or his policy. This is a free country as yet.... All, or nearly all of this, took place before I had any connection with *The Globe* ... but surely a writer on a newspaper ... is entitled to private opinions and his individual liberty of action.

### Mailed Them to the States

" 'To the best of my belief only twelve copies of the pamphlet were printed, though it now seems that the thirteenth was procured by the First Minister Macdonald. Two of the twelve I mailed to the States, one was sent to England and the remainder I retained.... Not a single one was circulated in Washington or elsewhere, I can vouch for that....

### Globe Not Responsible for its Editor's Writings

" 'I deny that *The Globe* or the Liberal Party is bound by anything written, said or done by any mere writer for *The Globe* in his private hours or private capacity.' "

Now the Liberals were on the defensive.

## Conspiracy Against Canada

Although near prostration, Sir John A. campaigned as long as he could stand on his weary legs. The *Toronto Empire* reports a speech on February 18, in which he again stresses allegiance to Britain. His reference to "democracy" was typical of that period:

"There is somewhere ... a conspiracy to drive Canada into the arms of the United States....

*(continued)*

# TWO PICTURES

National Policy under Macdonald.

Unrestricted Reciprocity if Laurier and Cart- wright succeed.

The "two alternatives" theme that had worked so well for John A. and the Conservatives in earlier elections was put to work again in 1891. Laurier had become leader of the Liberals following the resignation of Edward Blake in 1887. The Liberal policy of "unrestricted reciprocity" — i.e. free trade — was dropped at their convention of 1893, leaving the way open for them to take over the Government in the 1896 election.

201

We look up to England and to English tradition for our guidance; we have everything to lose — much more than wealth, much more than money's worth — we have everything to lose in being severed from England; we have everything to gain by the benign influence of Her Majesty's Government, a free queen over a free people, but governed by principles of religion, by principles of morality, by principles of equality, which a democracy never had and never will have. (applause) ... But if it should happen that we should be absorbed in the United States the name of Canada would be literally forgotten; we should have the state of Ontario, the state of Quebec, and state of Nova Scotia, and state of New Brunswick; every one of the provinces would be a state; but where is the grand, the glorious name of Canada? ... All that I can say is that it is not with me, not by the action of my friends, or not by the action of the people of Canada, will such a disaster come upon us. I believe that this election which is a great crisis, and upon which so much depends, will show to the Americans that we prize our country as much as they do, that we would fight for our existence as much as they fought for the preservation of their independence ... that the spirit of our fathers, which fought and won battle after battle still exists in our sons; and if I thought it was otherwise I would say the sooner the grass grows over my grave the better, rather than I should see the degradation of the country which I have loved so much and which I have served so long."

Two days later Sir John A. was campaigning in London, Ontario. Although rain was pouring down in torrents, thousands of people appeared at the hall where the Premier was to speak. Fireworks and torches illuminated the way, and inside the people waved hundreds of small Union Jacks. Banners proclaimed:

*No Sympathy with Treachery or Treason
in London
This, My Last Effort, For the Unity of
the Empire
Canada's Noblest Heritage Will Not Be Sold
for a Mess of Potage
London Will Not Favour Annexation*

Exhilarated by his successful speeches, Sir John A. continued on the campaign circuit as though he were twenty years younger. Even though the weather was particularly foul, the people continued to turn out in great numbers. Sir John A. forced his poor, tired body to go everywhere in the freezing rain, the chilly gales and bitter snowstorms. Only his will kept him going.

The *Toronto World* records that he spoke from the rear platform of his train at Oakville, and, that same evening, spoke *twice* in Hamilton, to accommodate the large crowds that wanted to hear him. At every stop the red parlour of his railway car was filled with friends and campaign workers. There was never a quiet moment for rest. He was still to speak at Strathroy, Stratford, St. Mary's, Guelph, Acton, Brampton, Kingston and Napanee.

### Return to his Boyhood Home

A Toronto newspaper tells of the "Grand meeting in honour of the Old Chieftain" in Martin's Opera House in Kingston on February 24. "A windstorm blew violently.... The rain came down harder.... Later the night became very dark, so black that it was feared the inclement weather would have an effect upon the welcome to Sir John but it didn't.... As early at 6:30 crowds began to collect.... Ten minutes later the doors could not stand the test. The crossbar was pressed from its fastenings.... The crowd rushed in.... At 7 o'clock the hall was crowded, even the standing room being occupied.... Just when the applause terminated Sir John popped through the door in a pretty scene. What a shout arose! The cheering continued for some time.... Sir John hinted that he would be brief, alluding ... to the terrible strain on him during the past few weeks. He said he had returned to his old love and asked for her favours. For fifty years he had been a Member of Parliament, and for thirty-three his Party had held power and he was pleased to say that he was responsible for most of the desired public events which had transpired since 1864. He accepted the responsibility because those events had been of great benefit to the country."

The meeting cost him dear in health. "I never felt so wearied in all my life," Sir John A. told his physician, Dr. Michael Sullivan. His every bone ached to follow the doctor's advice to "go to bed and stay there." But it was deemed imperative that he speak in Napanee. He was flushed, his eyes were dull, yet he was taken in an open carriage down the main street of Napanee — where as a lad of seventeen he had been in charge of George Mackenzie's law practice. Sir John A. was at first chilled and then overheated as he stumbled into the jammed town hall. Discipline and force of habit saw him through the meeting. His secretary Joseph Pope wrote: "I did my utmost to induce the local politicians to allow him to return to his car. Nothing however would satisfy them but his presence at *another* meeting in a different part of town. The open carriage was again called.... The performance was repeated." Back in "The Jamaica" he collapsed.

### Too Ill to Be Moved

To his doctor Sir John A. said, "I am exhausted." The doctor found "a congested chest and threatened pneumonia; pain on inspiration and over the left lung and a very weak and irregular pulse." Then, and only then, was his tour cancelled. Others, including Sir Charles Tupper who had come from Britain to campaign for Sir John A., continued the electioneering. Sir John A. lay in "The Jamaica" in Kingston — too ill to be taken to his home in Ottawa.

On March 4, the day before the polls opened, the doctors thought that he was sufficiently recovered to return to Earnscliffe. Settled in his own bed, but terribly weak from the ordeal, he was brought the triumphant news that his Party had been returned to power. It cheered him to learn that he had carried Kingston by 483 votes. Newspapers all over Canada flashed the headlines "Tory Victory." Queen Victoria expressed "great gratification"; the Marquis of Lorne, Sir George Stephen and countless others sent congratulatory messages. Sir John A.'s favourite letter of congratulation was probably the one he received from his granddaughter Daisy (Hugh John's daughter):

Sault au Recollet
March 8, 1891

My dear Grandpapa,

I am writing this to congratulate you upon the result of the Elections. I am so very glad you got in. You could not tell how hard your little puss prayed for you.

With love and kisses to all, I remain,
Your loving child,
Daisy

Cover of a Conservative pamphlet giving the "facts & figures" to the electors, one of the first information-type political ads in Canada.

SIR JOHN ON HAND AGAIN!

**A CHIP OFF THE OLD BLOCK. TIME WILL TELL.**

SIR JOHN—"My dear old party, make your mind easy about the succession question. Permit me to introduce my boy, Hugh. Could anything be more like yours truly?"

THE TORY PARTY—"If the inner likeness is as striking as the outer, Sir John, he's the very man I've been looking for."

# FATHER AND SON BOTH ELECTED!

### *Kingston returns John A. Winnipeg, Hugh John Last days in House*

Continued bed rest helped Sir John A. By mid-April he began to feel stronger.

When the new sessions of Parliament opened on April 29, Sir John A. had the satisfaction of walking into the legislative chamber with his son, Hugh John. A local newspaper reported: "Just as the hands of the clock pointed to the half-hour after 12, a burst of applause from the Conservative benches greeted the veteran Premier as he entered arm in arm with his son, the new member for Winnipeg. The Old Chief . . . never looked better. His cheek was clear, his step was elastic, and everything betokened that he was in good condition for the hard work of the Session. After the Premier had exchanged greetings with his followers, who pressed forward to grasp his hand, father and son together took the oath and together affixed their autographs to the parchment, the son signing on the line below Sir John. Then more handshaking was in order."

The year before, when Hugh John had been vindicated in a timber scandal, Sir John A., deeply moved, had said, "I know my son has faults, but dishonesty is not one of them."

Although his doctor had told him that recovery from his collapse demanded a long period of constant rest, Sir John A. replied that he had

work to do. And work he did. The results in terms of his health were appalling.

It was during this session that Sir John A. was criticized in the House for his expenditures for cab fare to and from Parliament. When an expense item of $134 for such transportation was scrutinized, he replied as follows: "I am sorry the Honourable Gentleman objects to that item. I do myself . . . but my limbs are weary and weak. I cannot walk. . . . After half a century of active work, it does seem hard that I am not to be allowed to ride for business purposes. . . . In the winter I took a cab from my house to Parliament, but I economized last summer by riding in a bus instead of Buckley's cab. But the buses are too cold for my feet in winter and I get a cab now. . . . As long as I am Premier, the overburdened taxpayers will have to pay my cab hire. I think they will be quite willing."

On May 22, 1891, a colleague remarked, "Sir John A. is very well and bright again." And indeed the Prime Minister seemed more like his old self. The House of Commons debates give us the closing discussions of that session.

Mr. Patterson: "Might I ask the First Minister, did the High Commissioner tell the truth to the people of Kingston?" (Sir John A. had brought Sir Charles Tupper, then High Commissioner in England, back to Canada to speak for him at Kingston and other rallies.)

Sir John A.: "Well, Mr. Chairman, I cannot resist the seductive tones of my honourable friend and I may answer him: Sir Charles Tupper did go there at my request, and he made the speech

at my instance, and I fancy that his speech must have had a considerable influence, because in the previous election I was elected by a majority of seventeen, and after Sir Charles Tupper made his speech, I was elected by a majority that only wanted seventeen of five hundred. You see I was pretty wise in asking Sir Charles to go there and make a speech for me."

Mr. Patterson: "You would be wise if you stopped him at that point."

Sir John A.: "I will go a little further and I will say that Sir Charles Tupper came out from England to give us the advantage of his skill and influence and eloquence, at my special request."

Questioned subsequently as to Tupper's lack of influence when he spoke elsewhere, whether Sir John A. had lost his shrewdness, or Sir Charles his eloquence, Sir John A. replied, "I will tell you what he did: he lost his voice."

### "It Is Late . . . Goodnight"

When Sir Richard Cartwright asked about subsidies given roads and railways in Kingston, Sir John A. said, "You did not do much for them." They were his last words in the House of Commons. Sir John A. moved much more than usual about the House that evening among the members, and in the light of his succeeding illness, it was a memorable occasion. The adjournment came at eleven p.m. Sir John A. left the House with Sir Mackenzie Bowell and when they parted he said, "It is late, Bowell, goodnight."

Hugh John, John A.'s only surviving son, gave his father one of his last moments of glory when he was elected to Parliament from Winnipeg in 1891. Arm in arm, the two walked triumphantly into the House of Commons just a few weeks before John A. suffered the stroke that killed him. Because of his mother's chronic illness and early death, Hugh John had been brought up by John A.'s mother and sisters. He had served in the Red River Expedition of 1870 and the North West Rebellion of 1885, and was interested in a military career but instead — possibly because it was expected of him — followed his father into law and politics. Hugh John was a kind man and was known as the most loved man in Winnipeg. His later years were as tragic as his early years had been. His first wife died five years after they had married, leaving Hugh John with a small girl. His son, the only child of his second marriage, died before he was twenty-one.

INTERIOR OF HOUSE OF COMMONS.
*(Shewing Sir John's Desk and Chair Draped.)*

RB

# JUNE 6, 1891 10:15
## "Sir John A. Macdonald is dead"

*Week-long deathwatch ends at Earnscliffe*
*Ottawa bell tolls 76 times*

Sir John A. called a special Cabinet meeting for Saturday, May 23. Long discussion kept him from returning to Earnscliffe until six in the evening. Lady Macdonald, waiting at the front door, carried his bulging briefcase and guided his weary frame. He would not hear of cancelling their usual Saturday night dinner party. At the large gathering, the guests remarked on his renewed vitality — but it was his last party.

With medical help, he fought off symptoms and insisted on dealing with his ever-growing mass of correspondence. Despite a slight paralysis, from which he recovered partially, he went to his downstairs study to work with his secretary, noting two resolutions which he hoped to make in the House on the Monday. But this plan was squelched when doctors, in consultation, insisted on complete bed rest. Sir John A. was making a remarkable recovery but he insisted, "I cannot lie here with my eyes shut. It would drive me crazy."

When he finally took to bed, the Governor-General, Lord Stanley of Preston, called on him, but the Prime Minister had not the strength to greet him.

On Friday May 29, when Sir John A. had recovered enough to have a morning cup of tea, he welcomed with enthusiasm the Minister of Justice, John Thompson. The Minister was bogged down with worry about the Opposition, which was organizing to "make a rush like a lot of pirates." Thompson's unspoken question was who would succeed the Prime Minister. Sir John A. understood intuitively and said, "Thompson, some time ago I said to you, rally round Abbott, that he was your only man. I have changed my mind. He is too selfish." (Sir John Joseph Caldwell Abbott did succeed him, as a compromise nominee, and served until December 5, 1892.)

In the late afternoon Sir John A. suffered a second excrutiating stroke and fell back speechless, his entire right side paralyzed. There followed a brain hemorrhage and he lost all power of speech.

A courier was sent to inform the Premier's son at the House and the Governor-General of the now hopeless situation. Sir Hector Langevin announced the grave news to the House, which adjourned immediately.

The Queen was informed by cable. The news sped by wire to every part of Canada. The front pages of the newspapers said, "He Is Dying."

All of Ottawa was concerned and considerate. Bells were taken off the horse-drawn streetcars that passed Earnscliffe. Steamers plying the Ottawa River and tugboats towing barges and rafts of lumber ceased to blow their whistles and

*(continued)*

PAC

## SIR JOHN IS DEAD.

## The Premier's Long Struggle at an End.

## HE IS VANQUISHED BY DEATH.

## The Unequal Combat Closed on Saturday Night.

"The bright young spirit who had arduously and valiantly won a wide fame and remained in later years in the front of battle, had at last reached the brink of eternity." The Toronto *Globe,* the Liberal paper that had been John A.'s most vitriolic enemy through the years turned poetic in announcing his death.

The last person to be recognized and smiled upon by Sir John A. was his grandson, Jack, who visited Earnscliffe during the last days. Although his home was in Winnipeg, he was in Ottawa with his father, Hugh John, newly elected Member of Parliament. Never a healthy child, Jack died before he was twenty-one.

# Toronto Daily Mail.

TORONTO, MONDAY, JUNE 8, 1891.   PRICE THREE

## THE PREMIER

---

### The Old Chief's Career is Closed.

---

### THE LAST CHANGE.

---

### After Life's Fitful Fever He Sleeps Well.

---

### SKETCH OF HIS CAREER.

---

### Birth, Parentage, and Early Education.

---

### HIS EFFORTS FOR CONFEDERATION.

---

### The Pacific Scandal, His Defeat, and Return to Power.

---

### PRIVATE LIFE AND DOMESTIC RELATIONS.

---

### Honoured by the Queen and Mourned by the People of Canada.

*From Our Own Correspondent.*

OTTAWA, June 7.—The silver cord is loosed and the great leader is now no more. At fifteen minutes past ten last night Sir John Macdonald

Front page of the *Toronto Daily Mail* announced Sir John A.'s death with the words: "The silver cord is loosed and the great leader is now no more."

muffled their engines as they approached the cliff. Friends, colleagues and citizens walked by the house, not wishing to disturb the family, yet driven by a desire to be near their esteemed leader. Newspaper people watched round the clock, to dispatch the latest bulletins to a waiting nation.

One of Sir John A.'s last visitors was his six-year-old grandson, Jack. According to Biggar, "On Wednesday he came in and, meeting Lady Macdonald, said, 'I want to see grandpa.' Lady Macdonald told him he could not, but the child pleaded, and at last he was led into the room. At that moment the Premier had his eyes wide open, which had not occurred for some time, and as the lad came to the bedside and stroked his hand his countenance brightened with pleasure. While the child prattled away, Lady Macdonald, seeing the good effect on the patient, immediately sent for her daughter Mary. Jack did not know how powerless his grandfather was to answer the questions he was continually asking, but Mary did, and with a tenderness and skill that were pathetic she managed to persuade him to forego his questions. The excitement soon told on the weakened old man, however, and in a few moments, with little Jack's hand still in his, he dozed off to unconsciousness."

Medical bulletins were issued frequently, and told of the Prime Minister's steadily worsening condition.

NOW LET HIS ERRORS BE BURIED AND FORGOTTEN

A saddened Bengough drew this cover for *Grip*.

"June 4, 6 a.m. Sir John Macdonald passed the night without any change to record. He took his nourishment at the usual interval and slept a good deal. His strength remains as yesterday. Respiration 30; pulse 106, and having the same character as during the past few days."

"June 4, 12:25 p.m. Sir John Macdonald passed a very comfortable night and partook of nourishment at intervals. His cerebral symptoms are slightly improved and at the time of our consultation owing doubtless to the fact that having lived six days since attacked partial absorption has had time to take place. His heart action, however, is extremely feeble and very irregular and its failure is at the present time the chief danger."

"June 4, 6:45 p.m. Sir John Macdonald's condition throughout the day has been simply one of continuous weakness from a deficient heart action. This afternoon he exhibited an increase of consciousness lasting over two hours."

"June 4, 11 p.m. Sir John M.'s condition throughout the day was unchanged until 4 p.m. when he became slightly more conscious of his surroundings. This evening his general condition is much as it was yesterday evening at the same hour, excepting that his heart's action is weaker and still more irregular. Respiration 30; pulse 100."

The patient's right side was immobilized; he was bereft of speech; but he was still conscious and he made known his needs through a

*(continued)*

# Le Mon

PAC

XXIVᵐᵉ ANNEE—Nᵒ 246     NUMERO DOUBLE—MONTREAL LUNDI 8 JUIN 1

## SIR JOHN

**Tout pour le pays**

Samedi soir, à dix heures et quart, Sir John a succombé dans la lutte héroïque qu'il soutenait depuis huit jours contre les assauts de la mort.

Ce résultat était prévu, et c'est dans une angoisse poignante et douloureuse que le pays tout entier assistait à ce dernier combat, et attendait, avec anxiété, le dénouement du drame lugubre de Earnscliffe. Quand, il y a huit jours, le fil électrique fit connaître la situation désespérée de la santé du Premier Ministre, il y eut, dans tout le pays, comme un profond tressaillement de douleur et une éclatante explosion de respect, d'admiration et de crainte.

Si grandes et si universelles furent les sympathies pour l'illustre malade, que la mort elle-même sembla hésiter pendant quelques jours à continuer son œuvre de destruction, de deuil et de larmes.

On aurait dit que cette impitoyable moissonneuse s'était laissée toucher, et qu'elle reculait devant la douce et suave harmonie de ce beau concert de prières et de louanges qui s'élevaient de toutes parts en faveur de la victime qu'elle venait immoler.

Vendredi encore, nous espérions,—contre toute espérance,—que le ciel épargnerait au pays la terrible épreuve de l'heure présente. Mais ni les vœux ardents de la nation, ni les soins empressés de la femme admirable qui veillait au chevet du malade, ni toutes les ressources de l'art appliquées par les médecins les plus habiles, rien n'a pu retenir la flamme de la vie qui s'est éteinte tranquillement comme la lumière d'un beau jour, lorsque le soleil disparaît de l'horizon.

Mais tant que le Saint-Laurent roulera ses flots bleus vers la mer, tant que les Chaudières de l'Ottawa bouillonneront au pied des falaises de la capitale, tant que les échos de nos montagnes, unis aux échos de nos lacs et de nos rivières, répéteront les roulements de la locomotive emportée par le feu ou les cris de la vapeur, la mémoire du Père de la Patrie se perpétuera, grandissant d'âge en âge, sur cette terre du Canada qu'il a illustrée par son génie et ses œuvres étonnantes.

La preuve de son immortalité,—même ici-bas, — si nous pouvons nous exprimer

re politique, mais nous devons tous reconnaître son incomparable talent et les grands services qu'il a rendus à son pays. Prions Dieu qu'il adoucisse ses souffrances et le conduise à la récompense dans la patrie."

On nous rapporte le trait suivant si touchant de foi et de sympathie.

Le matin du jour de la "Grande Procession" du Saint Sacrement, à Montréal, deux petits enfants, l'un de sept et l'autre de dix ans, s'étaient levés de bonne heure pour pouvoir assister à la "Fête de Dieu," comme ils appelaient cette solennité.

Avant de partir, leur mère leur dit de bien prier le bon Dieu à genoux et prosternés, lorsque le Saint Sacrement passerait auprès d'eux. N'oubliez pas non plus, leur dit-elle, de demander une grâce à Dieu, car il

vail et les succès ont jeté le plus de gloire dans les plis de son drapeau. En effet,—et l'histoire impartiale ne pourra s'empêcher de le proclamer, —Sir John était avant tout de son pays.

Malgré son attachement pour la Mère-Patrie, la patrie canadienne a toujours eu la place d'honneur dans son cœur, et la première place de ses affections. Il n'avait qu'un objet en vue : la consolidation des institutions coloniales de l'Amérique Anglaise, afin d'arriver, par ce moyen, à faire du Canada un grand pays, capable de vivre par lui-même, possédant ses institutions particulières, formant, en un mot, dans cette partie du Nouveau-Monde, un peuple distinct, indépendant des puissances étrangères, et allié par le sang, l'amitié et les intérêts

dution, savoir entre autres : Sir Etienne Pascal Taché, sir George Etienne Cartier, sir Leonard Tilly, sir Charles Tupper, sir Hector Langevin, les honorables George Brown, Alexandre McKenzie, Olivier Mowat, etc.

Sir John était convaincu que des relations de commerce plus étendues entre ces colonies, contribueraient puissamment à provoquer chez leur population le désir de s'unir et d'établir entre elles un échange plus facile et plus rémunérateur de leurs productions respectives. Pour cela, il fallait des chemins de fer, il fallait améliorer notre système de navigation, construire de nouveaux canaux et améliorer ceux qui existaient déjà.

Aussi Sir John n'a pas hésité un instant à soumettre ses projets au peuple et à engager le Canada d'alors,

In Montreal *Le Monde* wrote: "In spite of his attachment for his mother country, Canada always had the place of honour in his heart and the first place in his affections. He had only one objective: the consolidation of colonial institutions of English America in order to create of Canada a great country, capable of living by itself, possessing particular institutions, forming in this part of the new world a distinct people, independent of foreign powers and allied by blood, friendship and common interests."

pressure of his left hand.

"June 5, 7 a.m. There is no change in Sir John's condition this morning and no new facts to record. He has been very somnolent all night and exhibited no restlessness whatsoever."

"June 5, 2 p.m. At our consultation today we found Sir John Macdonald altogether in a somewhat alarming state. His strength which has generally failed him during the past week shows a marked decline since yesterday. He still shows a slight flickering of consciousness. Respiration 38; pulse 120; more feeble and irregular than heretofore. His hours of life are steadily waning."

"June 5, 7 p.m. Sir John's end is fast approaching. He has been unconscious since four p.m."

At eleven in the evening of that day Sir John A.'s physician, Dr. Powell, said, "We have decided to issue no bulletin, because there is no need. The situation is unchanged. He is sinking and sinking perceptibly. There has been a gradual wasting away and the end cannot be far off. Sir John had a bad relapse about two hours ago, but since then his wonderful vital powers produced a slight, very slight, rally. . . .

There has been a slight consciousness through all his illness, and in fact I believe he will retain his slight consciousness to the end. This last rally is the last flicker in the socket. There is every sign of impending dissolution."

It was his trusted and devoted friend, Joseph Pope, who gave out the grievous news on the night of Saturday, June 6, at twenty-four minutes past ten, when he told the newspaper corps, "Gentlemen, Sir John A. Macdonald is dead. He died at a quarter past ten, quietly and peacefully." As the City Hall bell tolled seventy-six times, Dr. Powell's last bulletin was placed on the gate of Earnscliffe:

"June 6, 10:30 p.m. Sir John Macdonald died this evening at a quarter past ten o'clock."

With these sad words came the sounds of lamentation throughout the nation and empire. Bells began to toll almost at once in Ottawa. By midnight the sorrowful dirge resounded from all parts of the country where photographs of Sir John A. were swathed in sombre black and purple. Flags were at half mast upon Parliament and other public buildings and on the ships in the harbours. The death of Sir John A. marked the end of an era in Canadian history.

Capital Hill, Ottawa, on the morning of June 10, 1891, as the state funeral procession moved down the eastern walk. Some of the first news photographs to be published in half-tones in Canadian newspapers were these of Sir John A. Macdonald's funeral. They appeared in a special issue of *The Dominion Illustrated News*. Some of them were taken by amateur photographers.

# Mourners converge on Ottawa

## *Thousands come to pay their respects*
## *Memorial services throughout Canada*

### Railway he built carries John A. to final resting place

On Sunday morning, June 7, a large wide hall at Earnscliffe, his Victorian ivy-covered stone residence, was draped in purple and white, and there the body of the late Prime Minister lay in state, clothed in his uniform of an Imperial Privy Councillor and with the insignia of his orders at his side. The Governor-General, ministers and close friends filed in singly for a special farewell.

Vast crowds were converging on Ottawa by every means of transportation for the state funeral which had been decreed.

As the body lay in state in the Senate Chamber of the Parliament of Canada on Tuesday June 9, a multitude — the powerful and great, the poor and humble — filed past all day and far into the night. The representative of the Queen, Sir Casimir Gzowski, laid her tribute, a wreath of roses, upon the bier. The Queen's message read "In memory of her faithful and devoted servant."

On the next day, the state funeral procession moved through the crowded Ottawa streets to

St. Alban's Anglican Church, which Sir John A. had attended. After the service, and as the catafalque approached the railway station, a haze which had threatened the beautiful day, turned into a severe rainstorm drenching the desolate mourners.

**Macdonald of Kingston Comes Home**

Sir John A. had promised his mother to be buried at Cataraqui Cemetery in Kingston beside her, his father, his first wife, infant son

Thousands of Canadians from all walks of life came to Ottawa — by whatever means of transportation they could arrange — to file by John A.'s coffin.

and two sisters. In the Ottawa Station, his body was placed in a draped hearse on the first funeral train to go over the Canadian Pacific Railway — the railway which he had given the nation. En route to Kingston, the cortege was met at each station in respectful silence by sorrowing citizens. Again, the body lay in state on Thursday June 11, in the City Hall of Kingston, where Sir John had started out as an alderman. Many sought to ease their sense of bereavement as they walked with him on his last course to Cataraqui. Others followed in the thousands, in every sort of conveyance. "Macdonald of Kingston" had come home.

There were memorial services in hundreds of churches throughout Canada. A requiem was conducted in Westminster Abbey, London, at the request of Lord Salisbury, Mr. Gladstone and other prominent men. It was attended by personal representatives of the Queen and the Prince of Wales and by the former Prime Minister's old friend, the Marquis of Lorne. Years later, when Lord Rosebery unveiled the monument to Sir John A. in the Abbey, he said, "We will be well to remember our responsibility and not fail or flinch from it."

Sir John A. was shown still further illustrious reverence when St. Paul's Cathedral in London, known as the "Parish Church of the British Commonwealth," placed a carved bust of him in an underground crypt. At the unveiling it was said that Sir John A. "grasped the central

idea that the British Empire is the greatest secular agency for good now known to mankind." Over 150,000 Canadians visit the shrine each year.

Yet another signal honour was announced when Lady Macdonald was raised to the peerage by a grateful Empire. She was to be known as Baroness Macdonald of Earnscliffe and her daughter as the Honourable Mary.

A month after Queen Victoria's first letter of condolence to Lady Macdonald came another, written on July 2, 1891. The Queen's message is given here. (Punctuation and capitals are as she gave them; she always started the words "husband" and "wife" with capital letters.)

Dear Lady Macdonald,

Though I have not the pleasure of knowing you personally, I am desirous of writing what I have already done, my deep sympathy with you in your present deep affliction for the loss of your dear distinguished Husband. I wish also to say how truly and sincerely grateful I am for his devoted and faithful services which he tendered for so many years to his Sovereign and the Dominion.

It gives me much pleasure to mark my high senses of Sir John Macdonald's distinguished services by conferring on you a public Mark of regard for yourself as well as for him.

Your health has, I trust, not suffered from your long and anxious nursing.

Believe me, always,
Yours very sincerely,
Victoria R.

*(continued)*

The Old Chieftain lies in state in the Senate Chamber of the Houses of Parliament.

# First CPR funeral train leaves the Canadian capital

Draped with satin and flowers, the funeral train carrying John A.'s body moved slowly out of Ottawa. All the way to Kingston, crowds lined station platforms in silent homage as the train passed.

Lady Macdonald's reply to her sovereign was in a compact hand on a tiny sheet of mourning-edged paper, folded twice to fit an envelope two and one half inches long.

Dear Madam,

I have received with the deepest emotion and with feelings of warm satisfaction the kind letter of sympathy with which your Majesty has desired to honour me on the sad occasion of my great loss and crushing sorrow.

The words of gracious acknowledgement in which your Majesty is pleased to refer to my Beloved Husband's long and faithful service to your Majesty, Throne and Person are indeed the richest earthly consolation I can ever know and in gratefully receiving the high mark of favour to myself with which your Majesty has been pleased further to express this acknowledgement I beg to convey my profound sense of your Majesty's Government to me and to him whose useful and unselfish life has now in the wisdom and providence of God been brought to a peaceful close.

With every assurance of loyalty and renewed devotion to your Majesty and the Empire, I have the honour to remain always

Your Majesty's
faithful and humble servant,
A. Macdonald

This tribute from Sir John Willison in "Reminiscences" (1919) is particularly interesting because it comes from a Liberal to a Conservative: "Sir John Macdonald was rarely at fault in those whom he trusted. . . . Human as he was, he was not too susceptible to flattery. Not by adulation did men obtain his confidence and recognition. . . . He was sensitive to the predilictions of Quebec, not only because he needed the support of the French Province, but because he believed that Quebec should have coordinate authority in Confederation, and that unity of feeling was the essential condition of national stability.

"Other Canadian statesmen had great qualities which were not his in equal degree, and freedom from faults which he possessed, but in the sum of his service and in high fitness for the tasks of his time, he was greater than any of his contemporaries. . . .

"I think of . . . the universal sorrow which bound all Canadians together on June 6, 1891, when he passed out of the turmoil of the world into whatsoever God willed for him. It was no common man who so touched a nation's heart, and as time passes we see his stature more clearly and forget the way in which some things were done in gratitude for all that was achieved."

The anniversary of his death has been taken cognizance of with suitable tributes on June 6 of each year, at his graveside at Cataraqui Cemetery, Kingston. Largely due to the Kingston Historical Society, these observances have, in the past few years, become ecumenical in spirit and nonpolitical in content.

### His Life Is the History of Canada

Two days after Sir John A.'s death, Sir Wilfrid Laurier, a political opponent and yet one of his great admirers, rose in the House of Commons to say: "The place of Sir John A. Macdonald in this country was so large and so ab-
*(continued)*

---

### Sir John A. Macdonald

*Thou art not dead. The pulse in thee now stilled*
*Has with its quick'ning power a nation thrilled.*
*Thou art become a part of that new life*
*Thy genius fashioned 'mid the storm and strife*
*Of jarring factions, and the eager greed*
*And sleepless jealousies of race and creed.*
*Thou art not dead, though passed beyond*
*our ken:*
*While love of country stirs the soul of men*
*Thy presence will abide, thy spirit dwell*
*In the Canadian land it loved and served so well.*
From *The Dominion Illustrated*,
June 20, 1891

---

### In Memoriam: Sir John A. Macdonald

*Cold is the hand which grasped a people's fate,*
*At rest the master brain whose mighty ken —*
*Subtle in council, king-like in debate —*
*So dwarfed the efforts of his fellow-men.*

*And as a child who knows its first of grief,*
*Unreassuring and hopeless in its woe,*
*The nation mourns her best beloved chief,*
*Prostrate and broken neath the cruel blow.*

*He saw her birth, he led her falt'ring feet,*
*Rough hewn he found her, perfect now she*
*stands,*
*The grand creation of his life complete,*
*The envy and the peer of older lands.*
*Guard well the heritage — his great intent —*
*Be, Canada, his lasting monument.*
Frank J. Clarke, Winnipeg, 1891

---

Sir John A. was called
*The Father of Confederation*
*The Chief Architect of Confederation*
*The Father of Our Dominion*
*The Father of His Country*
*Père de la patrie*
*Sir John A. Macdonald — Cabinet Maker*
*Old Tomorrow*
*The Wizard of the North*
*Builder of Our Nation*
*Old Reynard*
*The Old Chieftain*
*The Old Chief*
*Canada's Myth Maker*

The satin-draped interior of the railway car in which John A.'s coffin travelled from Ottawa to Kingston.

The hearse leaving the City Hall, Kingston.

# *"As if one of the institutions of the land had given way"* — *Laurier*

Funeral car at Cataraqui Cemetery                                    *Fort Henry*

sorbing that it is almost impossible to conceive that the politics of this country — the fate of this country — will continue without him. His loss overwhelms us. For my part, I say, with all truth, his loss overwhelms me, and that it also overwhelms this Parliament, as if indeed one of the institutions of the land had given way. Sir John A. Macdonald now belongs to the ages, and it can be said with certainty that the career which has just been closed is one of the most remarkable careers of this century . . .

"As to his statesmanship, it is written in the history of Canada. It may be said without any exaggeration whatever, that the life of Sir John Macdonald, from the date he entered Parliament, is the history of Canada."

"Let us be English or let us be French, but let us always be loyal and above all let us be Canadians." (Sir John A. Macdonald)

### Bengough's Tribute

J. W. Bengough, who for almost twenty years had satirized Sir John A. in his cartoons, wrote these lines when the Old Chief died:

*Dead! Dead! And now before*
*The threshold of bereaved Earnscliffe stand*
*In spirit, all who dwell within our land*
*From shore to shore!*

THE EMPTY SADDLE.

*Before that black-draped gate,*
*Men, women, children mourn the Premier gone,*
*For many loved and worshipped old Sir John,*
*And none could hate.*

*And he is dead they say!*
*The words confuse and mock the general ear —*
*What! can there yet be House and Members here*
*And no John A.?*

*So long he lived and reigned*
*Like merry monarch of some olden line,*
*Whose subjects questioned not his right divine*
*But just obeyed.*

*His will's e'en faintest breath,*
*We had forgotten — 'midst affairs of State,*
*'Midst Hansard, Second Readings, and Debate,*
*Such things as Death!*

*Swift came the dread eclipse*
*Of faculty, and limb and life at last,*
*Ere to the Judge of all the earth he passed*
*With silent lips,*

*But not insensate heart!*
*He was no harsh self-righteous Pharisee —*
*The tender Christ compassioned such as he,*
*And took their part.*

*As to his Statesman-fame,*
*Let History calm his wondrous record read,*
*And write the Truth, and give him honest meed*
*Of praise or blame.*

# "Macdonald of Kingston" comes home for the last time

The City Hall in Kingston as it looked on the morning of the funeral. Again, John A.'s body lay in state to give his hometown mourners a chance to express their grief.

Fulfilling the promise he made to his mother, John A. was buried beside her, his father, his first wife, his infant son and two sisters in the cemetery at Cataraqui. Thousands of Kingstonians had walked the long route to the graveside.

This formal portrait of Sir John A. was painted by Henry Sandham.

10:15 p.m.

Saturday, 6th June,

1891.

# Leading events in the life of Sir John A. Macdonald

| Age | | Date |
|---|---|---|
| | Born in Glasgow | January 11, 1815 |
| 5 | Family immigrates to Canada | 1820 |
| 15 | Enters upon the study of Law | 1830 |
| 21 | Called to the Bar of Upper Canada | February 6, 1836 |
| 25 | Appointed a Commissioner to enquire into the losses arising out of the Rebellion of 1837-1838 | November 28, 1840 |
| 26 | Death of his father, Hugh Macdonald | September 1841 |
| 28 | Elected to Kingston Town Council | March 28, 1843 |
| 28 | Marries cousin, Isabella Clark | September 1, 1843 |
| 29 | Initiated into Order of Ancient Free and Accepted Masons of Canada | March 14, 1844 |
| 29 | Elected to Provincial Legislature | October 14, 1844 |
| 31 | Appointed Queen's Council | December 11, 1846 |
| 32 | Member of the Executive Council | May 11, 1847 |
| 32 | Receiver-General | May 21, 1847 |
| 32 | Birth of first child, John Alexander | August 2, 1847 |
| 32 | Commissioner of Crown Lands | December 8, 1847 |
| 33 | Resigns with colleagues | March 10, 1848 |
| 33 | Infant son, John Alexander, dies | September 21, 1848 |
| 35 | Second son, Hugh John, born | March 13, 1850 |
| 39 | Attorney-General of Upper Canada | September 11, 1854 |
| 42 | Prime Minister of the Province of Canada | November 26, 1857 |
| 42 | Wife Isabella dies | December 28, 1857 |
| 43 | Resigns with colleagues | July 29, 1858 |
| 43 | Postmaster-General | August 6, 1858 |
| 43 | Resigns | August 7, 1858 |
| 43 | Attorney-General of Upper Canada | August 7, 1858 |
| 47 | Resigns with colleagues | May 23, 1862 |
| 47 | Mother, Helen Shaw Macdonald, dies | October 24, 1862 |
| 49 | Attorney-General of Upper Canada | March 30, 1864 |
| 52 | Marries Susan Agnes Bernard | February 16, 1867 |
| 52 | Appointed Knight Commander of the Bath, now Sir John A. Macdonald | June 29, 1867 |
| 52 | Member of the Queen's Privy Council for Canada | July 1, 1867 |
| 52 | Prime Minister of the Dominion of Canada | July 1, 1867 |
| 52 | Minister of Justice | July 1, 1867 |
| 54 | Birth of only daughter, Mary | February 8, 1869 |
| 58 | Resigns | November 5, 1873 |
| 61 | Sister, Margaret Williamson, dies | April 1876 |
| 63 | Prime Minister of the Dominion of Canada | October 17, 1878 |
| 63 | Minister of the Interior | October 17, 1878 |
| 64 | Sworn of Her Majesty Queen Victoria's Most Honourable Privy Council | August 14, 1879 |
| 68 | President of the Queen's Privy Council for Canada | October 17, 1883 |
| 69 | Receives the Grand Cross of the Bath | November 25, 1884 |
| 73 | Sister, Louisa, dies | Autumn 1888 |
| 74 | Minister of Railways and Canals | November 28, 1889 |
| 76 | Dies | June 6, 1891 |

# Bibliography

G. Mercer Adam (1891) *Canada's Patriot Statesman,* London, McDermid.

Margaret Angus (1966) *The Old Stones of Kingston,* Toronto, University of Toronto Press.

William Henry Atherton (1914) *Montreal,* Montreal, S. J. Clarke Publishing Co.

A. G. Bailey, D. G. Creighton, C. P. Stacey, G. F. G. Stanley, W. Ullman, P. B. Waite (1967) *Confederation Readings,* Canadian Historical Society, University of Toronto Press.

J. Murray Beck (ed.) (1964) *Joseph Howe: Voice of Nova Scotia,* Toronto, McClelland and Stewart.

J. Murray Beck (1965) *Joseph Howe, Anti-Confederate,* Ottawa, Canadian Historical Association.

William Bell (1824) *Emigrants: In a series of Letters from Upper Canada,* Edinburgh, Waugh & Innes.

Pierre Berton (1965) *A Century of Photographs,* Toronto, McClelland and Stewart.

Pierre Berton (1970) *The National Dream,* Toronto, McClelland and Stewart.

Pierre Berton (1971) *The Last Spike,* Toronto, McClelland and Stewart.

E. B. Biggar (1891) *An Anecdotal Life of Sir John Macdonald,* Montreal, John Lovell and Son.

John Bland (1971) *Three Centuries of Architecture in Canada,* Montreal, Federal Publications Service.

*The Boy's Handy Book of Amusements, Sports and Games,* London, Ward, Lock.

G. Brown, E. Harman and M. Jeanneret (1967) *Canada in North America,* Copp Clark.

James Browne (1909) *The History of Scotland, Its Highlands, Regiments and Clans,* Edinburgh, Francis A. Nicholls & Co.

H. C. Burleigh (1973) *Forgotten Leaves of Local History,* Kingston, Brown and Martin.

*Canadian Anthology of Prayer* (1867).

*Canadian Antiques Collector Magazine* (various issues) Toronto.

*The Canadian Illustrated News* (various issues) Montreal.

*The Canadian Lawyer* (1914) Toronto, The Carswell Company.

Wm. Caniff (1894) *The Medical Profession in Upper Canada.*

J. M. S. Careless (1963) *Brown of the Globe: Statesman of Confederation,* Toronto, Macmillan.

Richard Cartwright (1912) *Reminiscences,* Toronto, Briggs.

William Cattermole (1831) *The Advantages of Emigration to Canada,* London, Simpkin and Marshall.

Edward Marion Chadwick (1895) *Ontarian Families,* Toronto, Rolph, Smith and Co.

Arthur Chiel (1961) *The Jews in Manitoba,* University of Toronto Press.

David B. Clark (1969) *The Nervous System — Textbook of Pediatrics,* Philadelphia, Saunders.

Gerald Clark (1965) *Canada: The Uneasy Neighbour,* Toronto, McClelland and Stewart.

J. E. Collins (1883) *The Life and Times of Sir John A. Macdonald,* Toronto, Rose Publishing Co.

Edgar A. Collard (1971) *The Story of Dominion Square,* Toronto, Longman.

Paul G. Cornell (1966) *The Great Coalition,* Canadian Historical Association.

Donald Creighton (1952) *John A. Macdonald: The Young Politician,* Toronto, Macmillan.

Donald Creighton (1955) *John A. Macdonald: The Old Chieftain,* Toronto, Macmillan.

Allen Ross Davis (1973) "Bay of Quinte Landmarks" in *Forgotten Leaves of Local History,* Kingston, Brown and Martin.

*The Dominion Illustrated News* (various issues).

Frederick Driscoll (1866) *Sketch of the Canadian Ministry,* Montreal.

Lady Dufferin (1891) *My Canadian Journal,* London.

*The Dufferin-Carnarvon Correspondence, 1874-1878* (1955), Toronto, The Champlain Society.

William "Tiger" Dunlop (1967, reprint) *Upper Canada,* Toronto, McClelland and Stewart.

Blodwen Davies (1954) *Ottawa,* Toronto, McGraw-Hill.

Gardner D. Engleheart (1860) *Journal of the Progress of H.R.H. the Prince of Wales through British North America,* London.

Wilfrid Eggleston (1961) *The Queen's Choice,* Ottawa, The Queen's Printer.

James Gay *Canada's Poet.*

J. Murray Gibbon (1938) *Canadian Mosaic,* Toronto, McClelland and Stewart.

J. Murray Gibbon (1935) *Steel of Empire,* Toronto.

*The Graphic* (various issues) London.

George Munro Grant (1882) *Picturesque Canada,* Toronto, Belden Brothers.

James Gray (1974) *The West and That Old Demon Whisky,* Toronto, Macmillan.

Ralph Greenhill (1965) *Early Photography in Canada,* Toronto, Oxford University Press.

Edwin C. Guillet (1933) *Early Life in Upper Canada,* Ontario Publishing Co.

Edwin C. Guillet (1963) *Pioneer Farmer and Backwoodsman,* Ontario Publishing Co.

Edwin C. Guillet (1967) *You'll Never Die, John A.,* Toronto, Macmillan.

W. G. Hardy (1960) *From Sea Unto Sea,* New York, Doubleday.

J. Russell Harper (1962) *Une imagerie canadienne,* National Gallery of Canada.

J. Russell Harper (1966) *Painting in Canada,* University of Toronto Press.

J. Russell Harper and Stanley Triggs (1967) *Portrait of a Period,* Montreal, McGill University Press.

J. Russell Harper (1970) *Early Painters and Engravers in Canada,* University of Toronto Press.

Adelaide Hechtlinger (1970) *The Great Patent Medicine Era; or without benefit of doctor,* New York, Grosset & Dunlap.

Christian Hesketh (1961) *Tartans,* London, Octopus Books.

E. E. Horsey (1942) *Sir John A. Macdonald and His School Days and Law Offices,* Kingston, manuscript.

J. Huston (1893) *Le répertoire national,* Montréal, J. M. Valois & Cie.

Bruce Hutchison (1943) *The Unknown Country,* Toronto, McClelland and Stewart.

Bruce Hutchison (1957) *Canada, Tomorrow's Giant,* Toronto, Longman.

Bruce Hutchison (1964) *Mr. Prime Minister,* Toronto, Longman.

*The Illustrated War News* (1885) Vol. 1, Grip Printing Co.

J. K. Johnson (ed.) (1969) *Affectionately Yours,* Toronto, Macmillan.

James Edmund Jones (1885) *Every Man His Own Lawyer.*

James Edmund Jones (1924) *Pioneer Crimes and Punishments,* Toronto, Morang.

Kathleen Jenkins (1966) *Montreal,* New York, Doubleday.

D. G. G. Kerr (1966) *Historical Atlas of Canada,* Nelson.

Alfred E. Lindesmith (1968) *Addiction and Opiates,* Chicago, Aldine.

Robina and Kathleen M. Lizars (1897) *The Humours of '37,* Toronto, Briggs.

*The London Illustrated News* (various issues) London.

The London *Times* (various issues) London.

Elizabeth Longford (1969) *Wellington — The Years of the Sword,* London, Weidenfeld and Nicholson.

Elizabeth Longford (1972) *Wellington — Pillar of State,* London, Weidenfeld and Nicholson.

T. W. L. MacDermot (1933) *The Political Ideas of John A. Mac-*

*(continued)*

# Bibliography

*donald,* Canadian Historical Review.

Agnes Macdonald (1950) *Simple Tartan Weaving,* Leicester, Dryad Press.

J. A. Macdonald (1910) *Troublous Times in Canada,* Toronto, W. S. Johnston.

Alexander Mackenzie (1882) *Life and Speeches of Hon. George Brown,* Toronto, Globe Printing Co.

Michel de Montaigne (many editions) *Essays.*

Susanna Moodie (1852) *Roughing It in the Bush,* New York, Putnam.

D. C. Masters (1958) *A Short History of Canada,* Van Nostrand.

D. C. Masters (1965) *Reciprocity, 1846-1911,* Ottawa, Canadian Historical Association.

Grant MacEwan (1958) *Fifty Mighty Men,* Saskatoon, Modern Press.

Leslie Macfarlane (1965) *The Last of the Great Picnics,* Toronto, McClelland and Stewart.

Kenneth A. MacKirdy, John. S. Moir and Yves F. Zoltvany (1967) *Changing Perspectives in Canadian History,* Dent.

J. Pennington Macpherson (1891) *Life of the Right Hon. Sir John A. Macdonald,* Saint John, N.B., Earle Publishing Co.

W. L. Morton (1963) *The Kingdom of Canada,* Toronto, McClelland and Stewart.

W. L. Morton (1965) *The West and Confederation,* Ottawa, Canadian Historical Association.

*New Brunswick Almanac* (1865).

Lena Newman (1967) *Historical Almanac of Canada,* Toronto, McClelland and Stewart.

*New Statistical Account of Scotland* (1845) Edinburgh, Blackwood.

*Nova Scotia Almanac* (1836).

Wm. Osler (1892) *The Principles and Practice of Medicine,* New York, Appleton.

George Robert Parkin (1908) *Sir John A. Macdonald,* Toronto, Morang.

Edith Paterson (1970) *Tales of Early Manitoba,* Winnipeg Free Press.

Joseph Pope (1894) *Memoirs of the Right Honourable Sir John Alexander Macdonald,* Ottawa, J. Durie and Son.

Joseph Pope (1915) *The Day of Sir John Macdonald,* Glasgow, Brook.

Joseph Pope (1921) *Correspondence of Sir John Macdonald,* Oxford University Press.

Robert Wynward Powell (1890) *The Doctor in Canada,* Montreal, Gazette Printing Co.

T. R. Preston (1840) *Three Years in Canada,* London, R. Bentley.

R. W. W. Robertson (1970) *Sir John A. Builds a Nation,* Burns and MacEachern.

John D. Robins (1946) *A Pocketful of Canada,* Toronto, Collins.

James A. Roy (1952) *Kingston — The King's Town,* Toronto, McClelland and Stewart.

Joseph Schull (1967) *The Nation Makers,* Toronto, Macmillan.

Adam Shortt and Arthur G. Doughty (1917) *Canada and Its Provinces,* Toronto, Edinburgh University Press.

Oscar Douglas Skelton (1920) *Life and Times of Sir Alexander Tilloch Galt,* Toronto, Oxford University Press.

T. P. Slattery (1968) *The Assassination of D'Arcy McGee,* New York, Doubleday.

T. P. Slattery (1972) *They Got to Find Mee Guilty Yet,* New York, Doubleday.

F. St. George Spendlove (1958) *The Face of Early Canada,* Toronto, Ryerson.

G. F. G. Stanley (1956) *Louis Riel, Patriot or Rebel,* Canadian Historical Association.

J. Douglas Stewart and Ian E. Wilson (1973) *Heritage Kingston,* Queen's University.

Donald D. Stewart (1950) *The Setts of the Scottish Tartans,* Edinburgh, Oliver & Boyd.

C. Stuart (1820) *The Emigrant's Guide to Upper Canada,* London, Longman, Hurst, Rees, Orme and Brown.

Donald Swainson (1971) *John A. Macdonald, The Man and the Politician,* Toronto, Oxford University Press.

Lewis H. Thomas (1970) *The North West Territories, 1870-1905,* Canadian Historical Association.

Walter Traill (1970, reprint) *In Rupert's Land,* Toronto, McClelland and Stewart.

Jack Tremblay *Canadian Pacific,* Fredericton, Brunswick Press.

P. B. Waite (1963) *The Charlottetown Conference,* Ottawa, Canadian Historical Association.

Andrew Wallace (1882) *A Popular Sketch of the History of Glasgow.*

W. Stewart Wallace (1926) *The Dictionary of Canadian Biography,* Toronto, Macmillan.

W. Stewart Wallace (1924) *Sir John Macdonald,* Toronto, Macmillan.

John Willison (1919) *Reminiscences Political and Personal,* Toronto, McClelland and Stewart.

Beckles Willson (1902) *The Life of Lord Strathcona,* London, Methuen.

W. M. Whitelaw (1966) *The Quebec Conference,* Ottawa, Canadian Historical Association.

*York Almanac and Provincial Calendar* (1821).

*York Almanac* (1823).

## Picture credits

| | |
|---|---|
| BC | Provincial Archives, Victoria, B.C. |
| CIN | The Canadian Illustrated News |
| DI | The Dominion Illustrated |
| Glasgow | The Library of the University of Glasgow |
| HPS | Historical Pictures Service — Chicago |
| ILN | The Illustrated London News |
| Lande | The Lande Collection in the Rare Book Department, McLennan Library, McGill University |
| Notman | The Notman Photographic Archives, McCord Museum |
| Osborne | Osborne Collection of Early Children's Books, Toronto Public Libraries |
| PAC | The Public Archives of Canada |
| Queen's | Queen's University Archives |
| RB | Rare Book Department, McLennan Library, McGill University |
| Toronto | Metropolitan Toronto Library Board |
| WN | The Illustrated War News |

# Acknowledgements

With great generosity and understanding, collectors, archivists and librarians — surely the nicest people in the world — have put before me rare historical treasures that have enriched this book.

I am particularly aware of my indebtedness to Mrs. D. F. Pepler, of St. Catharines, Ontario, and her daughter, Mrs. C. R. Sharpe of Clarkson, Ontario, for allowing me to study and make excerpts from Lady Macdonald's illuminating diary. This cherished manuscript was given to Mrs. Pepler by her late husband, Don Francis Pepler, a great nephew of Lady Macdonald.

Very special thanks go to the Rt. Hon. John G. Diefenbaker, P.C., Q.C., M.P., F.R.S.C., LLD., D.C.L., Lit. D., D.S.L., for his insight into the nature of Sir John A. Macdonald; and to Mrs. Diefenbaker, who was so kind as to take me on a personally conducted tour of the Diefenbaker Collection of Macdonald Memorabilia.

I would like to acknowledge my very great obligation to Lt. Col. Louis J. Flynn, O.B.E., E.D., and Mrs. Flynn, a most knowledgeable couple who were interested enough to show me much of the historical heritage of Kingston, Ontario.

Many individuals and institutions have helped by providing material for this book. For allowing me access to documents, letters, newspapers, magazines, title deeds, maps, illustrations, cartoons, photographs, memorabilia, furniture and other items of Canadiana, I must record my grateful appreciation to learned people in many areas.

The largest collections of material are in the Public Archives of Canada, in Ottawa; the Queen's University Archives in Kingston; and the various divisions of McGill University, Montreal: the Lawrence Lande Foundation for Canadian Historical Research, the McCord Museum, the Notman Photographic Archives, the Rare Book Department of the McLennan Library, the Osler Library, the Reference Library, the Law Library and the newspaper files. Special thanks go to the staffs of these institutions and departments.

Other pertinent material was gathered in Montreal at the Montreal Museum of Fine Arts, the Sir George Williams Library, the Château de Ramezay, La Bibliothèque de Saint Sulpice, La Bibliothèque de l'Université de Montréal, Salle Gagnon de la Bibliothèque de la Ville de Montréal, the Fraser Hickson Library, the Notre Dame de Grace Library for Boys and Girls, Westmount Public Library, the Montreal Children's Library, the George Vanier Library of Loyola College, the National Film Board and the Montreal Book Auctions Ltd.

Ottawa offered help from the Canadian Department of Transport; Canada Post; the Bank of Canada; House of Commons Debates; the Progressive Conservative Party of Canada; the National Library; the National Gallery; the National Museum of Man; the Library of Parliament; the Department of Indian Affairs and Northern Development; the Royal Canadian Mounted Police; the Department of the Secretary of State; the Office of the Prime Minister; the Royal Trust Company; the Canadian Historical Society; the University of Ottawa Archives; Canadian Historic Sites; and Hansards.

Information in Toronto was given by the Law Society of Upper Canada, Osgoode Hall; the Metropolitan Toronto Library Board and the Osborne and Baldwin Collections of the Toronto Public Library; the Royal Ontario Museum; the Canadian Antiques Collector; Eaton's of Canada Archives; the Manufacturers Life Insurance Company; the Confederation Life Association; the Royal Commission on Book Publishing, Government of Ontario, 1972; Ridpath's Ltd.; Sotheby and Co. (Canada) Ltd.; the Ministry of Education, Ontario; and the Toronto Department of Public Records and Archives.

In Kingston relevant matter was collected through the Douglas Library of Queen's University; the Kingston Historical Society; the Bellevue National Historical Park; and the *Kingston Whig-Standard*.

Other research facilities were granted by the Quebec National Archives, Government of Quebec; the Public Archives of Nova Scotia; the Minister of Colleges and Universities, Ontario; the Mills Memorial Library, McMaster University, Hamilton; the Corporation of the Hamilton Public Library; the Library Arts and Cultural Centre of Memorial University and Provincial Archives, St. John's, Newfoundland; Confederation Library, Art Gallery, Museum and Archives of Charlottetown, Prince Edward Island; the Notre Dame of Canada University, Wilcox, Saskatchewan; the University of British Columbia; Simon Fraser University, British Columbia; the Provincial Archives of British Columbia, Victoria; the University of Calgary; the University of Alberta; the Provincial Museum and Archives of Alberta and the E. Brown Collection; the Glenbow, Alberta, Institute; the Nicholls Papers; Beaverbrook Art Gallery and the Archives of Fredericton, New Brunswick; New Brunswick Museum; the Archives of St. Mary's University, Halifax, and Acadia University, Wolfville, Nova Scotia; the Manitoba Historical Society; Brandon University Archives; the Provincial Library and Archives of Manitoba; Saskatoon Archives; Brighton Public Library, Brighton, England; the University of Glasgow Library, Scotland; and the Edinburgh City Library, Scotland.

I am most appreciative of special items from: Dr. John H. Archer, Regina, Saskatchewan; Ancient Free and Accepted Masons of Canada, Grand Lodge, Hamilton; British Tourist Authority, London; Mrs. John Burnet, Montreal; James A. Bartlett, Toronto; Caledonia House, Montreal; Canadian Pacific Railway, Montreal; Mrs. A. A. Cockburn, Ottawa; Robt. C. Coates, M.P.; Borough of Brighton, England; Mrs. J. Chalin, Montreal; Mrs. M. H. Draper, Montreal; W. Chris Dougall, Willowdale, Ontario; Linda Doyle, Hove, Sussex, England; Mrs. E. Purvis Earle, Gananoque, Ontario; Craig Fraser, Waterdown, Ontario; Wayne D. Fry, Saint John, New Brunswick; Dr. L. J. Flynn, O.B.E., E.D., and Mrs. Flynn of Kingston, Ontario; Major E. R. Friel of Kingston; Hugh Alexander George Macdonald Gainsford, Winnipeg; Mrs. J. Cartwright Gordon; Mrs. Caroline Gunnarsson, Winnipeg; Mrs. E. Grant, Montreal; Haine and Son, Eastbourne, England; J. Russell Harper of Alexandria, Ontario; Mrs. Jean Hibbert, Toronto; Historical Association, London, England; Hove Cemetery and Borough, Hove, Sussex, England; Mrs. Doyle Klyn, Sidney, British Columbia; Dr. Lawrence M. Lande, Montreal; Michael Lavin, Kingston; Lt. Col. Gordon D. Leggett, Islington, Ontario; Harold Lockwood, Thunder Bay, Ontario; Lloyd's Registrar of Shipping, London, England; London Tourist Bureau, England; Mrs. Marguerite MacLauchlan, Woodstock, New Brunswick; W. Steward Martin, Q.C., Winnipeg; Norman McLeod, Lennoxville, Quebec; the Librarian at the Montreal Children's Hospital; Dr. W. Alex Newlands, Tarrytown, New York; Ocklynge Cemetery, Eastbourne, England; Robert D. Owen, Kingston; Mrs. Edith Paterson, Winnipeg; Dr. D. S. Penton, Montreal; Mrs. Eleanor Powley, Islington, Ontario; A. G. Pruden, Winnipeg; Jennifer Peles of the Rare Book Department, McLennan Library; John L. Russell Antiques, Montreal; T. P. Slattery, Q.C., Montreal; Mrs. Garnet Steacy, Gananoque, Ontario; Mrs. Roy D. Sheed, Toronto; Peter O. Scargall, Toronto; Melanie Simon, Hove, Sussex, England; Dr. Charles Sorbie, Kingston; Dr. A. Stewart, University of Maine; Mrs. Erika Solivo, Rosemere, Quebec; Donald Turcotte, Montreal; Mrs. T. A. Van Eeghen, Florida; Vickers and Benson Ltd., Edmonton; Mrs. Wm. A. Winslow, Dorval, Quebec; Howard W. Warner, C.L.J., Ottawa; Prof. T. S. Webster, Kingston; Jack Wilkie, Pointe Claire, Quebec; William P. Wolfe, Montreal; Mrs. M. Young, Montreal; Mrs. M. Zieman, Toronto.

*Lena Newman*

# Index

*Italic* numbers indicate pictures.

## *About the author*

Lena Newman loves travel, attic sales and people — not necessarily in that order. During the five years she spent working on this book she had plenty of opportunity to indulge her passion for browsing among brittle letters, aged documents and ancient photographs. Her training as a teacher and background in journalism have given her a unique approach to research. She looks for the human interest angle, the story behind the headlines, the scoop — and she finds them in old recipes, bills, diaries, letters, cartoons and advertisements. She has turned up a wealth of never-before published material that confirms her strongly held opinion that a country's trivia is as important to its history as its Constitution is. She prefers characters to generals and establishment types and glories in the fact that Canada boasts strong, unorthodox, resourceful pioneers. She draws on infinite patience when she is sleuthing on a research binge, but she can be most impatient and intolerant when people remark that Canada has no history or that Canadian history is dull. Her syndicated weekly column "Your Canada and Mine" proves them wrong. More than a million readers of the column agree with Lena Newman that Canada and Canadians have a lively, colourful and fascinating past.

**The following are quoted with permission from sources stated:**

"The Enchanted Traveller" from *Later Poems* by Bliss Carman reprinted by permission of The Canadian publishers, McClelland and Stewart Limited, Toronto.

H. C. Burleigh, *Forgotten Leaves of Local History,* published by Brown and Martin, Kingston, © 1973 by H. C. Burleigh.

Paul G. Cornell, *The Great Coalition,* published by the Canadian Historical Association.

Donald G. Creighton, *The Young Politician,* published by Macmillan of Canada, © 1952 by Donald G. Creighton.

Donald G. Creighton, *The Old Chieftain,* published by Macmillan of Canada, © 1955 by Donald G. Creighton.

Elizabeth Longford, *Wellington — The Years of the Sword,* published by Weidenfeld and Nicolson, London, England.

James A. Roy, *Kingston — The King's Town,* published by McClelland and Stewart.

T. P. Slattery, *The Assassination of D'Arcy McGee,* published by Doubleday, © 1968 by T. P. Slattery, Q.C.

G. F. G. Stanley, *Louis Riel: Patriot or Rebel,* published by the Canadian Historical Association.

Donald Swainson, *John A. Macdonald, the Man and the Politician,* published by Oxford University Press, Toronto.

W. Stewart Wallace, *Sir John Macdonald,* published by Macmillan of Canada.